1812

SLB
CHU

The law
of the sea

R. R. CHURCHILL

and

A. V. LOWE

The law
of the sea

MANCHESTER
UNIVERSITY PRESS

First published 1983, reprinted with addenda 1985
New, revised edition 1988

Manchester University Press
Oxford Road, Manchester M13 9PL, UK

Distributed exclusively in the USA and Canada
by St. Martin's Press, Inc., 175 Fifth Avenue, 10010, USA

British Library cataloguing in publication data

Churchill, R. R. (Robin Rolf)
The law of the sea.—New rev. ed.
1. Oceans. International law
I. Title   II. Lowe, A. V. (Alan Vaughan),
1952–
341.4′5

Library of Congress cataloging in publication data
Churchill, R. R. (Robin Rolf)
The law of the sea/R. R. Churchill and A. V. Lowe. — New, rev.
ed.
p. cm.
Includes bibliographies and index.
ISBN 0-7190-2634-2 (pbk.): $15.00 (U.S.: est.)
1. Maritime law.   I. Lowe, A. V. (Alan Vaughan)   II. Title.
JX4411.C48   1988
341.4′5—dc19   88-10276
ISBN 0 7190 2922 3 *hardback*
ISBN 0 7190 2634 2 *paperback*

Typeset in Hong Kong
by Best-set Typesetter Ltd

Printed and bound in Great Britain
by Biddles Ltd., Guildford and King's Lynn

CONTENTS

LIST OF TABLES

LIST OF FIGURES

PREFACE

From the preface to the first edition

Although the past ten or fifteen years have witnessed the production of an enormous amount of literature relating to the law of the sea, there appears to be no single book in English which gives an up-to-date introduction to the subject as a whole. It is this gap in the literature which the present work seeks to fill. This book therefore attempts to give an introductory survey not only of the 1982 United Nations Convention on the Law of the Sea, but also of the customary and conventional law which supplements it. In covering such a large body of law in a relatively small number of pages our discussion of many topics has had to be more concise than we would ideally have wished. To economise on space, we have been sparing with footnotes, and in particular we give references to the sources of conventions and cases only in the tables at the front of the book and not in the text itself. As a guide and, we hope, a stimulus to further reading and research, a select list of recommended books and articles in English and French appears at the end of each chapter.

Preface to the second edition

Although the first sentence of our original preface is no longer true, the aim and scope of this book remain as stated above. We have preserved the format of the first edition, apart from putting all the material on maritime boundary delimitation into a separate new chapter. Otherwise our changes have been largely confined to recording the many (but essentially minor) developments that have taken place since the first edition. As far as possible, the law is stated as at 31 August 1987.

In preparing this edition we have again had help from many people, and would particularly like to thank for information, Mr C. Dundas of the Commonwealth Secretariat; Dr B. B. Parrish, General Secretary of the International Council for the Exploration of the Sea; Mr A. D. Watts and Mr D. Anderson of the Foreign and Commonwealth Office; and for typing, Mrs Zöe Selley, UWIST. Once more, we would like to thank our friends and colleagues in Cardiff, Manchester and other universities for their willingness to discuss the issues with which this book deals, and above all, our families, for their forbearance and support.

RRC, AVL
Cardiff and Manchester
September 1987

ABBREVIATIONS

ACOPS	Advisory Committee on Pollution of the Sea, London
AD	*Annual Digest of Public International Law Cases*
AFDI	*Annuaire Français de Droit International*
AJIL	*American Journal of International Law*
ALR	*Australian Law Reports*
Art.	Article
BYIL	*British Yearbook of International Law*
Cmnd.	*Command Paper*
CSC	Geneva Convention on the Continental Shelf, 1958
CTS	*Consolidated Treaty Series*
DLR	*Dominion Law Reports*
DUSPIL	*Digest of United States Practice in International Law*
EEZ	Exclusive economic zone
EFZ	Exclusive fishing zone
ER	*English Reports*
FAO	(United Nations) Food and Agriculture Organisation
GA	(United Nations) General Assembly
GATT	General Agreement on Tariffs and Trade
HSC	Geneva Convention on the High Seas, 1958
ICJ	International Court of Justice
ICLQ	*International and Comparative Law Quarterly*
IJIL	*Indian Journal of International Law*
ILC	(United Nations) International Law Commission
ILM	*International Legal Materials*
ILO	(United Nations) International Labour Organisation
ILR	*International Law Reports*
IMCO	(United Nations) Intergovernmental Maritime Consultative Organisation
IMO	(United Nations) International Maritime Organisation
IOC	(United Nations) Intergovernmental Oceanographic Commission
JDI	*Journal du Droit International*
Jessup	P. C. Jessup, *The Law of Territorial Waters and Maritime Jurisdiction*, New York, 1927
JMLC	*Journal of Maritime Law and Commerce*
Limits in the Seas	*Limits in the Seas*, published by the Geographer, United States Department of State
LNTS	*League of Nations Treaty Series*
LOSB	UN, *Law of the Sea Bulletin*

LOSC	United Nations Convention on the Law of the Sea, 1982
LQR	*Law Quarterly Review*
MARPOL	International Convention for the Prevention of Pollution from Ships, 1973
Moore, *Digest*	J. B. Moore, *A Digest of International Law*, 8 vols, 1906
Moore, *Int. Arb.*	J. B. Moore, *History and Digest of the International Arbitrations to which the United States has been a Party*, 5 vols., 1898
National Legislation on the EEZ	UN, *The Law of the Sea. National Legislation on the Exclusive Economic Zone and the Exclusive Fishery Zone*, New York, 1986
ND	*New Directions in the Law of the Sea*, ed. R. R. Churchill *et al.*, vols I–XI, 1973–81
NYIL	*Netherlands Yearbook of International Law*
ODAS	Ocean data acquisition systems
O'Connell	D. P. O'Connell, *The International Law of the Sea*, 2 vols., Oxford, 1982, 1984
ODIL	*Ocean Development and International Law*
OJEC	*Official Journal of the European Communities*
PCIJ	Permanent Count of International Justice
Receuil des Cours	*Receuil des cours de l'Académie de droit international* (The Hague)
Rep.	Reports
Res.	Resolution
RGDIP	*Revue générale de droit international public*
RIAA	*United Nations Reports of International Arbitral Awards*
Smith	R. W. Smith, *Exclusive Economic Zone Claims: An Analysis and Primary Documents*, Dordrecht, 1986
SOLAS	Safety of Life at Sea (Conventions)
TIAS	*Treaties and other International Acts Series*
TSC	Geneva Convention on the Territorial Sea and the Contiguous Zone, 1958
UKTS	*United Kingdom Treaty Series*
UN	United Nations
UNCITRAL	United Nations Commission on International Trade Law
UNCLOS I	First United Nations Conference on the Law of the Sea, 1958
UNCLOS II	Second United Nations Conference on the Law of the Sea, 1960
UNCLOS III	Third United Nations Conference on the Law of the Sea, 1973–82
UNCTAD	United Nations Conference on Trade and Development
UNEP	United Nations Environment Programme
UN Leg. Ser.	*United Nations Legislative Series* (see p. 21 below)
UNTS	*United Nations Treaty Series*
UST	*United States Treaties and other International Agreements*
VJIL	*Virginia Journal of International Law*
Whiteman	M. M. Whiteman, *Digest of International Law*, 15 vols., 1963–74

TABLE OF CASES AND INCIDENTS

TABLE OF CONVENTIONS

The various conventions referred to in this book are listed in chronological order. In each case information is given as to the place and date of signature; the date of entry into force; the number of ratifications (in the case of multilateral conventions); and references to the source of the convention. As regards ratifications, in the case of UN and ILO conventions the information is correct as at 31 December 1986; in the case of IMO conventions as at 31 January 1987. With other conventions (unless a particular date is given) the number of ratifications has been ascertained from the UKTS (up to and including No. 36 of 1987) and/or the *Department of State Bulletin* (up to and including June 1987). To find subsequent ratifications the reader should refer to one or more of the following: UN, *Multilateral Treaties deposited with the Secretary–General* (published annually); the *Department of State Bulletin* (published monthly: the relevant parts are reproduced in *ILM*); *Treaties in Force* (published annually by the Department of State and covering those treaties to which the USA is a party); and the UKTS (four updating lists of ratifications of treaties to which the United Kingdom is a party are published each year).

CHAPTER ONE

Introduction

Scope of the book

This book is concerned with the public international law of the sea — that is to say, with the rules which bind States in their international relations concerning maritime matters. Accordingly, it does not discuss, except incidentally, the rules of private maritime law, which concern such matters as marine insurance, carriage of goods by sea and maritime liens; nor does it provide a survey of the municipal law of the United Kingdom, or of any other country, relating to the law of the sea. Furthermore, it is concerned with the laws of peace and not of war, and consequently topics such as maritime neutrality and prize law fall beyond its scope. Nonetheless, this leaves a considerable body of law within the purview of the book. Our treatment of the subject falls into two broad divisions. First, we take each of the major maritime zones recognised in international law, and explain the rules presently applicable to that zone against the background of the main stages of the historical development of those rules. Increasingly, however, the law of the sea is being developed along functional, rather than zonal, lines: for example, whereas the 1958 United Nations Conference on the Law of the Sea concentrated mainly on producing a framework of rules governing States' rights and duties in the territorial sea, continental shelf, and high seas, many of the more recent international agreements have been concerned not with particular zones but with particular uses of the seas, such as pollution, fishing (which was, in fact, also the subject of one of the conventions produced by the 1958 conference), and navigation. We have, therefore, thought it necessary in order to bring together the many rules of international law relating to the various uses of the seas, to provide separate surveys of each of the main activities carried out in the seas; these functional surveys appear in the later chapters of the book.

Although the international law of the sea is in principle limited in its application to States and other entities having international personality, it has immediate significance for individuals. Thus, for instance, individuals may be arrested in coastal waters on charges of illegal fishing, or find that their ships are denied passage through the waters of an archipelago: in both cases they are immediately involved in questions of international law, which may be discussed 'on the spot', or arise in subsequent proceedings in a municipal court, or be taken up on the international plane by their government. In the last chapter we discuss the ways in which such disputes arise and are handled, and the interrelationship between international and municipal law.

Laws, whether international or municipal, do not grow up in isolation, but mould and are moulded by the politics, economics and geography of the 'real world' to which they apply. This is particularly apparent in relation to the law of the sea. From the early seventeenth century up to the end of the nineteenth century the seas were largely subject to a *laissez-faire* regime: beyond the narrow belt of coastal seas, the high seas were open to free and unrestricted use by all. Such a regime reflected the interests of the dominant European powers of the period in promoting seaborne trade and maintaining communications with their colonies. Such a *laissez-faire* regime was also adequate for the two main uses of the sea — navigation and fishing — during this period, since ships were small and relatively few in number compared with today, and fish stocks were thought to be inexhaustible. In the twentieth century this has all changed. The traditional hegemony of the European States has been challenged both by the emergence of the two Superpowers (whose interests are nevertheless in maximising the freedom of maritime communication) and by the nationalism and demands for economic autonomy of the developing countries, most of which have become independent since the Second World War. Furthermore, the uses of the sea, as a result of developments in technology and an increasing demand for resources, have multiplied and intensified, with increased possibilities for conflict.

These changes have led to radical developments in the law. Thus, the threat of pollution from tankers — especially the generation of supertankers built to maximise efficiency on the long sea routes adopted between 1967 and 1975 when the Suez Canal was closed by the Arab–Israel conflict — has led to pressure from coastal States for tighter controls over vessels passing near their coasts. The threat of overfishing similarly has led to demands for extended coastal jurisdiction over resources adjacent to their coasts. The exploitation of the continental shelf resources, made feasible by their reduction into ownership by the coastal State, has provided yet another use of coastal waters and with it an increased possibility of conflict between different users. It is the task of the law both to accommodate these uses and to provide a framework for resolving conflicts between them.

Plainly, States have differing kinds and degrees of interests in the seas, ranging from major maritime powers such as the United States and Soviet Union, to small landlocked countries such as Bolivia and Nepal. Some

States fish exclusively off their coasts, but others have important distant-water fishing fleets; some States have broad continental shelves rich in mineral resources, but others do not. While these differences have a strong influence on the maritime policies of the States concerned, it should not be forgotten that even within States there are conflicting interests at work — the United Kingdom, for instance, is both a major shipping nation and one of the major victims of oil pollution from tanker casualties. Each nation's maritime policy represents a compromise between such divergent interests.

Early development of the subject

The development of the law of the sea is inseparable from the development of international law in general. It grew up only when the emergence of independent States made possible truly international relations, instead of the imperial relations which subsisted throughout the life of the Holy Roman Empire. This occurred, roughly speaking, from the sixteenth century onwards. Early rules were drawn partly from the canons of Roman law, which underwent a revival in Western Europe beginning in the late eleventh century, and partly from State practice, which gave rise to customary rules concerning, for example, the exchange of legations and conduct of war.

The articulation and refinement of rules appropriate to international relations underlying Roman law and custom were largely the province of jurists who, under the general intellectual influence of the Renaissance and Reformation, drew on many sources in their work. For example, the Dutchman Hugo Grotius (1583–1645), commonly regarded as the father of modern international law (which reflects rather unfairly upon his distinguished predecessors, such as the Spaniards Vitoria, 1480–1546, and Suarez, 1548–1617, and the Italian Gentilis, 1552–1608), drew on reason and the law of nature, supported by references to scripture and a wide range of classical Greek and Roman writers, for his statements of the law. State practice was, at this stage, given a subsidiary role: Grotius regarded it as generating a 'voluntary law of nations', of lesser importance than the rules of natural law.

Early treatises on the law of the sea were often written in the context of particular disputes, as were tracts on other subjects of international law. For instance, Grotius's great work *Mare Liberum*, published in 1609, was written in order to vindicate the claims of the Dutch East India Company, by whom he was employed, to trade in the Far East, despite the monopoly on trade in the area claimed by the Portuguese at that time. That book upheld the doctrine of the freedom of the seas, and was seen as threatening contemporary British claims to control the seas around Great Britain. It was met by spirited responses from writers such as the Scot Welwood in his *Abridgement of all Sea Lawes* (1613) and the Englishman Selden in his

Mare Clausum (1635). Such literary exchanges did much to clarify understanding of the issues involved in the law of the sea, and to refine the concepts upon which it was based.

The natural law tradition persisted throughout the eighteenth century, although the most influential writers, such as Wolff (1679–1754) and Vattel (1714–67), attached to customary law an importance equal to that of natural law. But natural law, as a political doctrine, was losing its influence in the course of struggles against royal absolutism, and was being steadily displaced by politicial theories based upon the notion of consensual government, such as Rousseau's 'social contract'. In international law this development found expression in the rise of the positivist school, which regarded the voluntary assumption of obligations by States, as evidenced by their practice and contained in the rules of customary and treaty law, as being of greater importance than natural law. Though the positivist approach, with its emphasis upon what States actually do rather than upon what Greeks, Romans, Prophets and common reason might have though States should do, can be traced as least as for back as the great English lawyer Richard Zouche (1590–1660), it is pre-eminently a child of the Enlightenment. It had many distinguished followers, such as Bynkershoek (1673–1743) and Martens (1756–1821), and has been over-whelmingly dominant in international law since the nineteenth century.

Although modern international law has almost wholly abandoned the intellectual basis upon which many of the early writers built, their work remains of continuing importance both because it enshrines the prevailing views of their day upon the law of the sea and because the modern law has developed, by a continuing process of modification and refinement, from those foundations.

Sources of the modern law of the sea

Since the end of the last century, international law has been seen as the product of the voluntary subscription of States to rules of law, rather than as principles of natural law binding upon States regardless of their will. This is reflected in article 38 of the Statute of the International Court of Justice, which directs the Court to apply, in deciding international disputes brought before it:

(a) international conventions, whether general or particular, establishing rules expressly recognized by the contesting States;
(b) international custom, as evidence of a general practice accepted as law;
(c) the general principles of law recognized by civilised nations;
(d) ... judicial decisions and the teachings of the most highly qualified publicists of the various nations, as subsidiary means for the determination of rules of law.

It is necessary to say a little about each of these in turn.

International conventions

Conventions, or treaties or agreements as they are often called, are the clearest expression of legal undertakings made by States. Furthermore, States are, in general, allowed to modify by treaty rights and duties attaching to them under customary law (there is an exception in the case of customary law rules of *jus cogens*, such as the rules forbidding genocide or the waging of aggressive war, but this controversial category of 'peremptory norms' allowing of no derogations has little relevance to the law of the sea). Accordingly, the existence of a treaty relating to any particular matter will usually provide a clear and conclusive statement of the rights of the States parties to it in their relations with each other. Treaties are binding only upon the States parties to them, their relations with non-party States continuing to be regulated by customary law; however, the provisions of treaties may, as we shall see, become binding upon other States if they pass into customary law. Treaties often require, in addition to signature, ratification by the parties — and, in the case of multilateral treaties, ratification by a prescribed minimum number of States — before they enter into force. They remain binding until any time limit set down in them expires or, if the parties intended to allow denunciation, they are denounced, or until the parties conclude a later treaty relating to the same subject matter. These and other rules concerning the conclusion, interpretation, termination and suspension of treaties are set out in the 1969 Vienna Convention on the Law of Treaties, which codified and in some respects added to the customary international law on the subject.

There are many treaties dealing with various aspects of the law of the sea. Some are multilateral, such as the 1958 conventions on the territorial sea, high seas and continental shelf, and the 1973 Convention on the Prevention of Pollution from Ships. Many others, dealing with matters such as access to ports, fishing rights and maritime boundary delimitations, are bilateral. Details of the main collections of treaties can be found in 'Further reading' at the end of the chapter.

Customary international law

The International Court's Statute refers to 'international custom, as evidence of a general practice accepted as law', as a source of international law. This formula is, however, in some ways misleading: it would be better phrased, 'international custom, as evidenced by a practice generally accepted as law'.

Orthodox legal theory requires proof of two elements in order to establish the existence of a rule of customary international law: first, a general and consistent practice adopted by States. This practice need not be universally adopted, and in assessing its generality special weight will be given to the practice of States most directly concerned — for example, the practice of coastal States in the case of claims to maritime zones, or of the major shipping States in claims to jurisdiction over merchant ships. The second element is the so-called *opinio juris* — the conviction that the practice is one which is either required or allowed by customary international law. This second requirement prevents such practices as the provision of red carpets for visiting heads of State and, as we shall see in chapter four, the exercise of restraint in certain cases in enforcing coastal State laws against foreign ships in passage through the territorial sea, from becoming rules of law: they remain merely 'rules' of comity or courtesy.

The combination of these two elements in the formation of customary law can be seen, for instance, in the emergence of the continental shelf as a legal concept. In 1945 President Truman claimed for the United States ownership of the resources of the sea bed adjacent to the American coast, and this was followed by similar claims by many other States. These claims, coupled with the belief that they were permissible in international law, provided the basis of a customary rule, recognising coastal States' ownership of continental shelf resources, which emerged by the late 1950s. This example has an added interest because these rights were, in 1958, set out in articles 1–3 of the Continental Shelf Convention, and in the *North Sea Continental Shelf* cases (1969) those articles were regarded by the International Court as 'reflecting, or as crystallising, received or at least emergent rules of customary international law'.[1] This illustrates the point that conventional provisions having a 'norm-creating character' — that is, provisions purporting to lay down rules of law of general applicability, rather than merely settling issues between the particular States parties on the basis of expediency — may arise from or pass into customary law, and so become binding upon States not party to the convention. There is nothing mystical about this transformation: customary law requires only practice coupled with *opinio juris*, and the practice may be prompted by and crystallise around a proposition set out in a treaty in the same way as it may do so in relation to a putative rule of law stated anywhere else. If there is a sufficiently general acceptance of treaty rules by non-Parties, coupled with the necessary *opinio juris*, or by Parties acting in a manner evidencing a belief that the treaty rules represent customary law, those rules may become binding as a matter of customary law.

Customary international law is, in principle, binding upon all States. However, the essential role of consent in the formation of customary law has two important consequences as far as this general principle is concerned. First, if a State persistently objects to an emerging rule of customary law, it will not be bound by that rule. The objection must be persistent: States will not be permitted to acquiesce in rules of law and later claim exemption from them at will. This point arose in the *Anglo–Norwegian Fisheries* case (1951), in which the United Kingdom attempted to show that State practice had established a customary rule imposing a ten-mile limit upon lines drawn across the mouth of bays where such lines served as the baselines from which the territorial sea is measured. The United Kingdom failed to prove sufficient generality in the practice of adopting a ten-mile limit to establish it as a rule of customary law, but the International Court added:

In any event the ten-mile rule would appear to be inapplicable as against Norway inasmuch as she has always opposed any attempt to apply it to the Norwegian coast.[2]

The alleged rule would not, therefore, have been 'opposable' (to use the common term) to Norway anyway. Thus, even if a general practice has generated a rule of customary law, which is in principle binding upon all States, particular States may be able to claim the status of persistent objectors, with the result that they will not be bound by the rule. Thus, for example, at least until 1980, the United States consistently refused to accept the legality of territorial sea claims in excess of three miles, and consequently it was not bound by such claims, even though the overwhelming majority of States made or recognised claims to a twelve-mile territorial sea so that customary law could be said to have admitted such wider claims. The general rule of customary law was not opposable to the United States as long as it maintained its persistent opposition.

Viewed in this light, it will be readily understood that the primary function of proof of a 'general practice accepted as law' is to create a *presumption* that all States, whether or not they have contributed to that practice, are bound by the resultant rule: they are presumed to have assented to that to which States in general have assented. In this sense States are bound by customary rules even if they have not specifically assented to them. But this presumption is liable to be rebutted by proof of persistent objection, which may release a State from obligations contained in those rules.

The second consequence of the determinative role of consent as the basis of obligation in customary law is that it is unnecessary to have recourse to the general practice of States in order to create a presumption that a particular State is bound by a rule if it can be proved that that State has in fact consented to the rule. Furthermore, individual States may consent to rules which have not been generally accepted, with the result that they become bound by them. So, for example, the first few States to claim a twelve-mile territorial sea were bound *inter se* to admit its legality, even though States in general did not at that time recognise claims of more that three miles in breadth. As we noted above, such twelve-mile claims would not have been opposable to States persistently objecting to them. This phenomenon is sometimes explained by writers and courts in terms of the existence of local or regional rules of customary international law; while it is often the case that States in a region will adopt the same position on questions such as the breadth of the territorial sea, in reality the point is much wider than those terms imply, since there is no need for States consenting to the rule in question to come from the same region.

Consent to rules may be found in the form of legislative claims based upon the rule, declarations of Ministers and so on. In principle, there is no reason why support for United Nations resolutions should not evidence such consent, but in fact most States do not intend — which is the crucial test — their support to be taken as consent to any rule of law which the resolution may purport to lay down, and in the absence of such intention an affirmative vote for a resolution is merely a declaration of political intent and not an assumption of legal obligation. The International Court carried this reasoning further in the *Nuclear Tests* cases (1974), by holding that unilateral declarations in which French Ministers undertook to cease atmospheric nuclear weapons tests were, if made with the intention of binding France, binding in law.

It will be apparent that customary international law is not a monolithic body of general rules uniformly binding upon all States alike, but rather that the existence of customary law obligations between particular States is ultimately a question of opposability. Thus customary law may develop by shifts in the patterns of opposability. For instance, at a time when most States claimed only three- or twelve-mile fishery zones, but a few Latin American States claimed 200 mile fishery zones, it could be said that the 'general' rule — using 'general' in a descriptive rather than a prescriptive sense — was that international law admitted fishery jurisdiction only up to three or twelve miles from shore, and that as an exception 200 mile claims were opposable to the Latin American States alone. But as more and more States have moved to the Latin American position and claimed 200 mile zones the balance has shifted, so that the 'general' rule now admits the legality of such claims, even though they would not be opposable to any States which have persistently objected to them. It is in this sense that we refer in this book to 'general' rules and practices.

While the foregoing account is believed both to be correct and to represent the generally accepted view, the nature of customary law is a controversial matter.[3] In particular, it is necessary to note that it has sometimes been argued that rules of customary law may create truly general obligations, which States cannot escape by persistent opposition. One example of such an argument of relevance to this book is the claim by Professor De Visscher that the legal concept of the continental shelf is not, strictly speaking, the product of customary law, developed according to the processes which we have described, but is rather the expression of the direct and irresistible operation of certain facts — the extension of a State's land mass below the adjacent waters — upon the formation of international law.[4] Although the International Court has occasionally given 'objective' force, *erga omnes*, to certain types of legal status, such as the legal personality of the United Nations in the *Reparations case* (1949), it is questionable how far this view may properly be adopted. Thus, although it is arguable that De Visscher's approach, deriving universally applicable rules from the *effectiveness* of claims rather than from their recognition by other States, may be applicable to other maritime claims such as claims to archipelagic and historic waters, this argument is at best highly controversial. Unfortunately, shortage of space precludes its further examination in the book.

Evidence of State practice, sought in connection with the proof of customary law, can be found in many places, including States' legislation, the decisions of their courts, and the statements of their official government and diplomatic representatives. Sometimes requests for statements of practice emanating from international organisations or conferences produce replies containing comprehensive statements of practice upon a particular point. Thus national statute books, law reports, parliamentary debates, collections of diplomatic material, and the records of international conferences will yield evidence of practice. States involved in international litigation will also frequently explain their practice and opinion on the law in pleadings before the court or tribunal concerned. Further details on these sources will be found at the end of this chapter.

It is necessary to exercise some care when dealing with State practice. Claims appearing on the statute book may have been quietly abandoned or may never have been enforced, and therefore may not represent the actual 'practice' of the State. In this context it is also necessary to bear in mind the basic distinction between two kinds of jurisdiction: legislative, and enforcement, jurisdiction. Legislative jurisdiction is the right to prescribe laws. It may be limited *ratione loci* (i.e. limited in the geographical area within which the law applies — for example, fishery jurisdiction is in general limited to 200 miles from the coast); *ratione personae* (i.e. limited in its application to certain classes of person — for example, some customs laws may apply only to nationals and ships flying the flag of the legislating State); and *ratione materiae* (i.e. limited to certain kinds of matter — for example, States have jurisdiction in respect of the natural resources of that part of the continental shelf which lies more than 200 miles from shore, but not over other uses of the sea in that area). In the case of legislative jurisdiction, statutes can be taken more or less at face value (it is always necessary to take account of the municipal rules of statutory interpretation which may, for example, provide that statutes be presumed to apply only within territorial limits): a claim to legislate for, say, coastal fisheries is a claim to legislative jurisdiction whether or not it is enforced in practice. Enforcement jurisdiction is the right actually to enforce laws. It often coexists with legislative jurisdiction. For example, States may not only legislate for fishery matters, but also actually enforce those laws, throughout their 200 mile fishery zones.

But they do not always go together. For instance, although a State may legislate for its ships wherever they might be, it will not enforce its laws against its ships when they are in a foreign State's internal or territorial waters, because to do so would violate the other State's sovereignty: if it wishes to take enforcement action against such ships, it must wait until they leave the foreign waters. Thus legislation is a fallible guide to claims to enforcement jurisdiction.

General principles of international law

The rather vague category of 'general principles of international law' is not of great significance for the law of the sea. Its presence in article 38 of the International Court's Statute allows the Court to fill gaps in treaty and customary law by applying principles of law common to the major legal systems of the world, such as estoppel. General principles of a slightly different kind have more relevance. Such rules as the freedom of the high seas, and the exclusiveness of flag State jurisdiction over ships on the high seas, are sometimes described as general principles of law, in the sense that in the absence of clear proof of, for example, a right under treaty for a State other than the flag State to exercise jurisdiction over ships on the high seas, no such right will exist. Here any doubt over the existence of the non-flag State's rights is settled in favour of the exclusiveness of the flag State's jurisdiction, by reference to the general principle: it thus functions as a residual presumption for the resolution of doubtful claims. But such principles are better regarded as rules of customary law, albeit rules having a particular and fundamental importance.

Judicial decisions and the writings of publicists

The final paragraph of article 38(1) refers to judicial decisions and the writings of publicists as a subsidiary means for the determination of rules of law. This puts their role into a proper perspective. They cannot *create* law: only States can do that, through the formation of treaty and customary rules and general principles of law. They serve merely to aid the identification of rules created by States. The value of a statement by a judge or a legal author on a point of international law is dependent upon his or her standing, and the thoroughness with which he or she has researched the appropriate materials.

It will be clear that international law is a complex subject. The collection and analysis of State practice is a difficult task, compounded by the fact the States often feel it unnecessary to explain why they act as they do. Writers have a crucial role in researching State practice and articulating the legal rules on which it is based and which it generates. In addition, they perform the service of tracing the development of the law, and identifying divergences in State practice, and of describing the network of legal obligations resulting from the enormous body of overlapping rules of customary and treaty law. We refer at the end of each chapter to some of the most important specialist monographs on individual topics within the law of the sea, but it is appropriate to mention here the work of writers such as Colombos, and McDougal and Burke, who have prepared general expositions of the subject, and, towering above all, the monumental work of Gilbert Gidel, *Le droit international public de la mer* (3 vols, Paris, 1932–34), a book of outstanding scholarship which remains of great value and interest. In addition, the volumes of *New Directions in the Law of the Sea*, though containing little analysis, represent an invaluable collection of recent treaties and State practice on the law of the sea, as do the relevant volumes of the *United Nations Legislative Series*. From time to time the enormous task of bringing together all the basic rules on the law of the sea has been essayed, and it is to these codification efforts that we now turn.

Attempts at codification

There have been many attempts to codify the rules of customary international law applicable to the seas. Most of these, especially in the decades preceding the establishment of the United Nations, were undertaken by non-governmental learned societies. Four such bodies have made particularly notable contributions. The International Law Association has, since its inception in 1873, produced several reports and sets of resolutions, and held lengthy and detailed discussions, on various topics such as territorial waters, marine pollution, the sea bed and its resources, international waterways, deep sea bed mining, piracy, and port State jurisdiction. Apart from the participation of distinguished lawyers, which has preserved a high standard of legal scholarship, and of interest, in its work, the Association has also been enriched by the participation of non-lawyers, such as shipowners, politicians and economists, concerned with the topics under review. The more prestigious (if only because its membership is strictly limited) Institute of International Law was also founded in 1873. It has always selected its members from among the most eminent international lawyers of the day, and its deliberations and reports are accorded the highest respect. It has adopted resolutions on such matters as international waterways, the high seas, the regime of merchant ships, submarine cables, marine resources, the territorial sea and internal waters, marine pollution, and, in a rare flight of fancy, the creation of an International Waters Office. Unlike the Association, whose main language is English, a large proportion of its business has been transacted, and reported, in French. The third body is the Harvard Law School, which prepared notable reports on territorial waters and piracy in the first part of this century. The final body is the American Law Institute, whose *Restatement of the Law* includes a volume on the

Foreign Relations Law of the United States, which is of enormous influence upon United States courts faced with questions of international law.

Several other organisations have produced draft articles on aspects of the international law of the sea, and in addition some individuals, such as Domin–Petrushevecz, Bluntschli, Fiore, and Internoscia, have undertaken the codification of international law single-handed — although enthusiasm for such projects seems to have died out after the First World War. Apart from the incidental interest which all model codes, collective and individual, have as reflections of prevailing approaches to the law of the sea, their main value lies in the careful collection and analysis of State practice which is (or at least should have been) associated with their preparation. It is this that gives the work of the Association and Institute, and the Harvard Research, its especially influential position in the development of the law.

There have been four major official attempts to codify the peacetime rules of the international law of the sea. The first was instigated by the League of Nations. In 1924 the League appointed a Committee of Experts to draw up a list of subjects ripe for codification. Territorial waters, piracy, exploitation of marine resources and the legal status of State-owned merchant ships were among the subjects considered, and the committee circulated 'Questionnaires' to governments on the first three of them. Subsequently, a Preparatory Commission was set up to prepare three topics — nationality, State responsibility and territorial waters — for codification. These preparations involved the circulation of a 'Schedule of Points' to governments, and, after replies had been received, the drafting of 'Bases of Discussion' on which the Codification Conference could base its work. There were also reports drawn up for the Committee and Preparatory Commission, notably those prepared by the German lawyer, Schücking. These reports, and the replies of governments, are of enormous interest, and represent an unrivalled survey of State practice and policy of the period.

Unfortunately, the conference, which convened at the Hague in 1930, did not succeed in adopting a convention on territorial waters. A committee was set up to study the subject, and its rapporteur, François, produced a report setting out such agreement as had been reached. This included draft articles on matters such as the nature and extent of coastal States' rights over the territorial sea, and of the right of innocent passage. However, it was not possible to reach agreement on the crucial question of the breadth of territorial waters. Accordingly, the conference decided to do no more than refer the draft articles to governments, in the hope that agreement could be reached at some later date.

The Hague draft articles were, however, not without influence. When the League of Nations was replaced by the United Nations in 1945, it was thought desirable to provide for the establishment of a body charged with the 'progressive codification' of international law. This body is the International Law Commission (hereafter, ILC), a body of thirty-four eminent lawyers, serving in individual capacities but nominated and elected by governments, whose first members were elected in 1948. During its early years the ILC embarked on the preparation of draft articles on the high seas and the territorial sea. Its rapporteur, François, who had prepared the 1930 conference report, drew heavily on the Hague articles. By 1956 the ILC had, at the request of the UN General Assembly, produced a report covering all aspects of the law of the sea of contemporary importance. This report, the product of painstaking analysis and careful drafting and illuminated by the observations of governments on its early drafts, formed the basis of the work of the first United Nations Conference on the Law of the Sea (hereafter UNCLOS I), held at Geneva in 1958.

UNCLOS I was attended by eighty-six States — almost double the number at the 1930 conference. It succeeded in adopting four conventions: the Convention on the Territorial Sea and the Contiguous Zone; the Convention on the High Seas; the Convention on the Continental Shelf; and the Convention on Fishing and Conservation of the Living Resources of the High Seas. The first three of these have been ratified by substantial numbers of States, and are also based in large measure upon customary international law, as presented in the ILC's reports. Consequently, these conventions form the core of the generally accepted rules of the law of the sea concerning maritime zones, and hence of the discussion in the earlier chapters of this book. The fourth convention, and an optional protocol on dispute settlement, have proved less popular, perhaps partly because they went further than the existing obligations which customary law imposed on States: they, too, are discussed below (see chapters fourteen and nineteen). The one major problem which the 1958 conference could not solve was that which had defeated the 1930 conference: the breadth of the territorial sea. Accordingly a second conference, UNCLOS II, was convened in 1960 to discuss that problem, and also the associated question of fishery limits. It failed, by only one vote, to adopt a compromise formula providing for a six-mile territorial sea plus a six-mile fishery zone. Agreement on the breadth of the territorial sea had to await the preparation of the convention drawn up by the third United Nations Conference on the Law of the Sea (UNCLOS III) more than half a century after the first attempt at the Hague.

UNCLOS III had its origins in the Sea Bed Committee established in 1967 by the United Nations General Assembly to examine the question of the deep sea bed lying beyond the limits of national jurisdiction over the continental shelf, following a proposal by Dr Arvid Pardo, the Maltese ambassador. The 1958 conference had not made any special provision for the legal regime of the deep sea bed, because at the time its great mineral wealth was not appreciated, nor did the technology necessary for its exploitation

exist. As we shall see in chapter twelve, many States were keen to have the
deep sea bed and its resources declared the 'common heritage of mankind'.
This involved defining the limits of national jurisdiction over the sea bed
and therefore the revision of parts of the 1958 Convention on the Continental Shelf, as well as of the Convention on the High Seas. But other States
were reluctant to review the law of the sea which had been so laboriously
codified in the 1950s. However, the presence in the United Nations of
many newly independent States, which had had no say in the formulation
of the 1958 conventions, provided a substantial majority in favour of reviewing the earlier law. Moreover, many States were increasingly concerned about the problems of overfishing and marine pollution off their
coasts, neither of which could satisfactorily be controlled within the narrow
jurisdictional limits on which the 1958 regime was based. The existence of
these factors, and the recognition that the various parts of the law of the
sea were inextricably interrelated, led to widespread support for a review
of the whole of the law of the sea. It was agreed in 1970, in General Assembly Resolution 2570, to convene a United Nations conference with the
task of producing a comprehensive Convention on the Law of the Sea.

The conference held its first session in 1973, and worked for several
months each year until it finally adopted a convention in 1982. It was divided, as was the Sea Bed Committee, which from 1971 to 1973 was engaged
in preparatory work for the conference, into three main committees. Committee One dealt with the problem of the legal regime of the deep sea bed;
Committee Two dealt with the regimes of the territorial sea and contiguous
zone, the continental shelf, exclusive economic zone, the high seas, and
fishing and conservation of the living resources of the high seas, as well as
with specific aspects of these topics, such as the questions of straits and
archipelagic States; Committee Three dealt with the questions of the preservation of the marine environment and scientific research. In addition,
smaller *ad hoc* groups considered other detailed questions on behalf of the
conference. In contrast with the 1930 Hague Conference and the first two
UN Law of the Sea conferences, UNCLOS III had no 'Bases of Discussion'
or ILC report to aid its work: it was, from the time of the establishment of
the Sea Bed Committee, seen as a political rather than a narrowly legal enterprise — indeed, the issue was from the outset assigned to the United Nations
First (Political and Security) rather than Sixth (Legal) Committee. The at-
tendance of about 150 States, each with its own interests to promote and
defend, made negotiations difficult, but a number of loose groupings soon
emerged. The most prominent were the 'Group of 77', as the group of developing States (in fact numbering around 120 States) is known, and the
groups of Western capitalist and of east European socialist States. Indeed,
the Group of 77, whose coherence is remarkable in view of the diversity of
its members, achieved a notable diplomatic triumph in leaving its imprint

clearly upon the Convention text. But there were many other special interest groups coexisting with these broad blocs; for example, the groups of land-locked and geographically disadvantaged States, of archipelagic, and of straits States, and of 'coastal' and 'maritime' States, all played important roles during negotiations on at least some parts of the Convention.

The positions of States at the outset of UNCLOS III were too far apart on many issues for the preparation of even an agreed basis for discussion to have been a practical possibility. It was appreciated, however, that there was little point in adopting measures by vote, where the major maritime States, on whose acceptance the efficacy of the Convention would depend, could be easily outvoted by other participants. It was therefore agreed to proceed by way of 'consensus' procedures, searching for areas of maximum agreement without formal votes. The conference worked for the whole of its time on this basis, except when it came to adopting the final text of the Convention, when a vote was forced by the United States, which could not accept some of the Convention's provisions. This 'consensus' approach led, from 1975 onwards, to the production of a series of 'negotiating texts', containing draft articles on all of the topics under consideration by the conference, by the chairmen of the conference's three main committees. The early texts represented in part an emerging consensus among delegates, and in part the aspirations of their drafters. But the subsequent texts evidenced an increasing level of agreement on most of the essential issues, such as the extent of the territorial sea, the legal regimes of the territorial sea, contiguous zone, continental shelf, exclusive economic zone and high seas, and the regulation of scientific research and marine pollution. Provisions in these texts began to be incorporated into national legislation, and so to exert an influence upon the development of customary international law.

Difficulties in securing agreement upon a few matters, chief among which were some details of the legal regime of the deep sea bed, delayed the preparation of a final text until 1982, when it was adopted, together with four resolutions, by 130 votes to four, with seventeen abstentions.[5] Its failure to secure unanimous support illuminates the hybrid nature of the Convention. In part — the section dealing with the deep sea bed — it is an exceptionally precise, detailed instrument closer in appearance to a commercial contract or concession than an international treaty. The unacceptability of some of these details was the main cause of negative votes and abstentions on the adoption of the Convention. The other parts are more in the nature of a framework treaty or *loi-cadre*, leaving the elaboration of precise rules to other bodies, such as national governments and international organisations, and to dispute settlement procedures or future international negotiations. Perhaps because of the flexibility inherent in this approach, these parts did command general support. On 10 December 1982 the United Nations Convention on the Law of the Sea (hereafter we refer to it as the Law of the

Sea Convention; abbreviation, LOSC) was opened for signature in Jamaica by States and international organisations, such as the EEC, to which States have delegated competence in matters touching upon the Convention (LOSC, art. 305–7).[6] It will enter into force, for the States and organisations party to it, twelve months after it has been ratified by sixty States (LOSC, art. 308), and will then constitute a comprehensive statement of the basic rules of the law of the sea.

The Convention was open for signature for a period of two years: at the end of this time it had been signed by 159 States and other entities (including the EEC). Among the major non-signatories are the Federal Republic of Germany, the United Kingdom and the United States, all of which are opposed essentially only to parts of the Conventional regime for the deep sea-bed. By the end of 1986 the Convention had been ratified by thirty-one States, nearly all of which are developing countries, and by the UN Council for Namibia (for a complete list, see appendix). The Convention remains open indefinitely for ratification by signatories, and for accession by States or other entities which did not sign the Convention within the prescribed period.

The Convention is some way from entering into force. Nonetheless, preparations for the implementation of some parts of the Convention have begun. Under Resolution I, adopted by UNCLOS III at the same time as the convention text, a Preparatory Commission for the International Sea Bed Authority and for the International Tribunal for the Law of the Sea, known as PrepCom in UNCLOS *argot*, consisting of representatives of the signatory States (although States which have signed the Final Act but not the Convention may only participate as observers, and not vote on decisions), was to be convened when fifty States had signed the Convention. The first meeting of PrepCom was held in 1983, when it began its work on the drafting of rules and a provisional agenda for the Authority, and on the administration of the interim 'preparatory investment' regime for deep sea-bed mining (see chapter twelve). PrepCom operates though plenary sessions and through four Special Commissions, dealing respectively with the problems of developing land-based producer States whose economies might be adversely affected by the recovery of sea-bed minerals, with ensuring that the Enterprise is able to carry out activities in the International Seabed Area in such a manner as to keep pace with States and other entities exploiting the Area, with the interim rules governing sea-bed mining, and with the International Tribunal for the Law of the Sea (see further, chapter twelve). PrepCom has, therefore, an important role in relation to the most controversial matters regulated by the Convention, reflected in the decision which it took that its major decisions — which it will be difficult for the Authority to overturn — should be reached by consensus; and even signatory States which have announced that they have no present intention to ratify the

Convention have participated in its work. The Commission will cease to exist at the end of the first session of the Authority's Assembly.

In keeping with the consensus approach adopted during its negotiation, the Convention does not permit any reservations to it to be made (LOSC, art. 309). Nevertheless, a number of States have made declarations (which are permitted as long as they do not purport to exclude or modify provisions of the Convention: see LOSC, art. 310) when signing and/or when ratifying the Convention, setting out their understanding of the effect of specific provisions of the Convention. These declarations, and statements made by other States in exercise of their right of reply, evidence substantial disagreement over some issues: they are discussed at appropriate points in later chapters.

International organisations

Finally, we must mention the role of international organisations in developing the law of the sea, beginning with those in the United Nations 'family'. As will be seen is subsequent chapters, many organisations make some contribution to the subject, although they are not primarily concerned with maritime matters. For example, the International Atomic Energy Agency was responsible for preparing a Convention on Civil Liability for Nuclear Damage, which is applicable to damage caused by nuclear-powered ships, and the World Health Organisation has prepared regulations concerning sanitary and quarantine matters affecting international shipping. Other organisations have clearer interests in maritime matters but, not being primarily regulatory agencies, have a less direct influence on the development of the law. Thus the Food and Agriculture Organisation has made a great contribution to fishery science and to the understanding of conservation techniques. Its activities include reviewing world fisheries generally, through its Committee of Fisheries, the establishment of regional fishery bodies to advise on fisheries management, and providing assistance to many poorer countries in developing their fishing industries. The organisation which has probably had the most substantial direct effect upon the law of the sea as such is the IMO — the International Maritime Organisation. The IMO was established in 1958, when its constitutive treaty, signed in 1948, came into force: until 1982 it was known as IMCO — the Intergovernmental Maritime Consultative Organisation. It has a wide competence in matters affecting shipping and has adopted a detailed and technical approach to its work. Its committees, such as the Maritime Safety Committee, the Legal Committee and the Marine Environment Protection Committee, have played a prominent role in drawing up regulations concerning navigation and pollution. Some of these are presented to the IMO Council, which is composed of the representatives of thirty-two States with the largest interests in the provision of shipping services and in international seaborne trade and other special interests in maritime transport or navigation, and which in turn passes them on to the IMO Assembly, in which all member States — at present numbering about 130 — have a seat. The Assembly may then decide to recommend that members comply with the proposals. Such recommendations are not binding. Alternatively, the IMO may seek a more formal arrangement by having measures adopted in the form of a convention at a diplomatic conference convened under its auspices. More than two dozen conventions, many of which have attracted a high number of ratifications, have been concluded in this way (see table 3). Some of these conventions provide that they may be amended by resolutions adopted by the IMO Assembly: such amendments, in most cases, come into force after a certain period of time unless objected to.

Organisations outside the UN 'family', whose competence is limited to certain matters and certain regions, fulfil a crucial role, and often have a much greater and more direct influence upon particular maritime activities within their competence than their more wide-ranging international counterparts. Notable examples are regional bodies such as the EEC and wider alliances such as the OECD, both active in advancing the causes of resource management and environmental protection, and *ad hoc* bodies such as the Oslo and Paris Commissions, which are concerned with marine pollution. In the fisheries field, major contributions have been made by the regional fisheries commissions and the International Council for the Exploration of the Sea. These, and other, international organisations have a considerable part to play in the development of the law. Apart from recommendations and conventions which they may make or initiate, the constant and detailed surveillance which they exercise over maritime matters, and the reports which they prepare, exert a great influence on States' perceptions of what is happening in the seas, and so upon the formulation of national maritime policies which are ultimately expressed in the practice of States.

The present legal regime

From the description of various sources of the law of the sea it will have become evident that there is no single text containing the whole of that law. The 1958 Conventions provided a basic framework for most of the law of the sea, but these are in the process of being replaced by the 1982 Law of the Sea Convention. Although that Convention will not enter force until ratified by sixty States, all 159 States and other entities which have so far signed it are nevertheless obliged to refrain from acts which would defeat its object and purpose unless they make clear that they do not intend to proceed to ratification,[7] and those intending to ratify will obviously tend, in general, to conform to its terms — or, at least, its spirit — before it enters into force. Furthermore, as we shall see, some parts of the Law of the Sea Convention reflect pre-existing customary international law, and other parts which went beyond previous practice have already passed into customary law: in both cases such provisions may, as customary law, bind States whether parties to the Convention or not and whether the Convention has entered into force or not.[8] States parties to the 1958 Conventions will remain bound by those Conventions until they lawfully denounce them or become parties to the new Convention, which is expressly stated to prevail over the 1958 conventions;[9] but until that time, though their hands may be tied by the old rules, their eyes will be set on the new.

In addition to the basic conventional framework described above, rules of customary law, such as those concerning historic bays, and other international conventions concerning, for example, pollution and navigation, are and will continue to be of enormous importance in determining the detailed rights and duties of States. In the following chapters we have sought to bring all these sources together, so as to give a bird's eye view of the present complex web of the law, and of the major developments which have brought it to its present state. Inevitably we have had to omit much detail. This is particularly the case, and particularly regrettable, in our accounts of customary law: we offer generalisations based on our knowledge of State practice but in such a short book can give only examples to illustrate, rather than comprehensive surveys to justify, our statements.

Much has been written on the law of the sea, especially in recent years. Nevertheless, there remain wide areas, particularly in customary law, which stand in need of detailed and precise analysis and in which valuable and scholarly research can be undertaken. While this book attempts no such task itself, we hope that through it others may be helped to do so.

Notes

1 [1969] ICJ Rep. 3, at 39.
2 [1951] ICJ Rep. 116, at 131.
3 For a fuller account of this matter see A. V. Lowe, 'Do general rules of international law exist?', 9 *Review of International Studies* 207–13 (1983), and T. Stein 'The approach of the different drummer: the principle of the persistent objector in international law', 26 *Harvard International Law Journal* 457–82 (1985). For another view, see J. I. Charney, 'The persistent objector rule and the development of customary international law', 56 *BYIL* 1–24 (1985).
4 C. De Visscher, *Problèmes de confins en droit international public*, Paris, 1969, pp. 148ff, and *Les effectivités du droit international public*, Paris, 1967.
5 Israel, Turkey, the United States and Venezuela voted against; Belgium, Bulgaria, Byelorussia, Czechoslovakia, the German Democratic Republic, the Federal Republic of Germany, Hungary, Italy, Luxembourg, Mongolia, the Netherlands, Poland, Spain, Thailand, the Ukraine, the USSR and the United Kingdom abstained. Votes against and abstentions were explained by the

delegations concerned at the meeting on 30 April 1982, and recorded in UNCLOS III, *Official Records*, vol. XVI, pp. 152–67.

6 Adherence by international organisations is governed by art. 305 and Annex IX. Organisations to which member States have transferred competence over matters governed by the Convention may sign the Convention if the majority of their member States have done so, and may ratify it under similar conditions. Participation of the organisation does not increase its member States' entitlement to representation by, for example, giving the organisation a separate vote in the International Sea Bed Authority; nor does such participation confer any rights on member States not party to the Law of the Sea Convention. Namibia, represented by the UN Council for Namibia, and self- governing associated States and self-governing territories with treaty- making competence over matters governed by the Convention, may also become parties to the Convention (LOSC, arts. 305–7). National liberation movements which have participated in the work of UNCLOS III may sign the Final Act in their capacity as observers (LOSC, Resolution IV), and may participate as observers in meetings arranged under the Convention, such as meetings of the Authority (LOSC, art. 156 (3)); they may not ratify the Convention.

7 Vienna Convention on the Law of Treaties, 1969, art. 18. See further, G. M. White, 'UNCLOS and the modern law of treaties: selected issues', in W. E. Butler, (ed.), *The Law of the Sea and International Shipping: Anglo–Soviet Post–UNCLOS Perspectives*, New York, London, Rome, 1985.

8 See, e.g., H. Caminos and M. R. Molitor, 'Progressive development of international law and the package deal', 79 *AJIL* 871–90 (1985), and W. E. Butler, 'State practice and the development of the international law of the sea', in W. E. Butler (ed.), *The Law of the Sea and International Shipping: Anglo–Soviet Post–UNCLOS Perspectives*, New York, London, Rome, 1985.

9 Article 311.

Further reading

A convenient introduction to the materials of public international law can be found in chapter eight of J. Dane and P. A. Thomas, *How to Use a Law Library*, London, 1979, to which reference should be made for details concerning the use of legal materials.

Treaties.   There are three major collections of international treaties: the *Consolidated Treaty Series*, ed. C. Parry, covering the period from 1648 to the early years of the present century; the *League of Nations Treaty Series*, covering the period from 1920 to the Second World War, and the *United Nations Treaty Series*, covering post-war treaties. Several States maintain collections of treaties to which they are party, such as the *United Kingdom Treaty Series* and the *United States Treaty* series. Texts of major treaties are also reproduced in the volumes of *New Directions in the Law of the Sea* (11 vols, 1973–81, and in its second, loose-leaf edition, 2 vols., London, Rome, New York, 1983–   ), and the bi-monthly *International Legal Materials* produced by the American Society of International Law (1962–   ) both of which also include texts of significant national legislation, United Nations resolutions, etc. All the series named above include index volumes. In addition, there are three other useful indices: the invaluable *Index of Multilateral Treaties on the Law of the Sea*, edited by P. de Cesari *et al.*, Milan, 1985, which also contains the texts of reservations, declarations and statements made by signatory States; the

World Treaty Index, by P. H. Rohn, 5 vols., Santa Barbara and Oxford, 1984, and *Multilateral Treaties. Index and Current Status* by M. J. Bowman and D. J. Harris, London, 1984.

Customary international law.   State practice is often published, in the form of the texts of decrees or statutes, law reports, or volumes of diplomatic correspondence. Several States collect their practice: the leading collections are the annual *Digest of United States Practice in International Law* (1973 to date), following on from the *Digests* prepared by M. M. Whiteman (15 vols., 1963–74), G. H. Hackworth (8 vols., 1940–44) and J. B. Moore (8 vols., 1906). United Kingdom practice has, since 1978, been included in a section of the *British Yearbook of International Law*, as is the case with the practice of other States in other national *Yearbooks*.

In addition to *New Directions in the Law of the Sea* and *International Legal Materials*, much practice concerning the law of the sea is collected in certain volumes of the *United Nations Legislative Series* (bearing the UN document code UN Doc. ST/LEG/SER.B/1, 2, 6, 8, 15, 16, 18 and 19 respectively). The issues of the United Nations *Law of the Sea Bulletin* (1983 onwards) also include the texts of selected recent legislation, treaties and decisions relating to the law of the sea.

Codification.   Records of the proceedings of the conferences on the law of the sea, and of the committees which prepared for them, have been published by the League of Nations (in the case of the 1930 Hague Conference) and the United Nations (in the case of UNCLOS I, II and III.) The Hague papers have been conveniently re-printed in *The Progressive Codification of International Law (1925–28)* 2 vols., Dobbs Ferry, N.Y., 1972, and *League of Nations Conference for the Codification of International Law* (1930), 4 vols, Dobbs Ferry, N.Y., 1975, both edited by S. Rosenne. The proceedings of the International Law Commission are published in the Commission's annual *Yearbooks*. The papers of the UN Sea Bed Committee have been reprinted under the title *Seabed*, ed. M. Y. Sachs, by Worldmark Inter-national Documentation (many vols., 1970 onwards), as well as in the official records of the United Nations General Assembly. Concise accounts of the work of all United Nations bodies can be found in the annual *Yearbook of the United Nations*. The more important documents published by international organizations and relating to the Law of the Sea are collected in *International Organizations and the Law of the Sea Documentary Yearbook*, Dordrecht, 1985–   .

The most important papers of UNCLOS I, II, and III are published by the United Nations in the *Official Records* of those conferences. A fuller set of UNCLOS III papers is reprinted in R. Platzöder, *Third United Nations Conference on the Law of the Sea*, 12 vols., Dobbs Ferry, NY, 1982–87. The Office of the Special Represen-tative of the Secretary-General for the Law of the Sea, at the United Nations in New York, has also begun publishing material on the Law of the Sea. Apart from its occasional *Law of the Sea Bulletin* (which includes not only State practice but also summaries of national elaims, declarations and statements made by signatories of the Law of the Sea Convention, and regular lists of States which have signed or ratified the Convention) it has published a *Master File Containing References to Official Documents of the Third United Nations Conference on the Law of the Sea*, New York, 1985 and a list of *Multilateral Treaties Relevant to the United Nations Convention on the Law of the Sea*, New York, 1985. Other publications are men-tioned at appropriate points in this text. Finally, mention must be made of the massive project undertaken by the University of Virginia under the direction of M. H. Nordquist, for the production of an article-by-article commentary and legislative history of the Convention. Volume 1 has appeared, under the title *United Nations Convention on the Law of the Sea 1982: A Commentary*, Dordrecht, Boston, Lancaster, 1985. In view of the relative paucity of *travaux préparatoires* of the Convention, and the distinction of the contributors to that series, it will undoubtedly enjoy an unusual authority on the subject.

Judicial decisions. Judgments of courts appear in the reports of the court concerned, notably those of the Permanent Court of International Justice and the International Court of Justice, and national collections of law reports. Many arbitral tribunal awards are collected in the *United Nations Reports of International Arbitral Awards*. The *International Law Reports* reproduce notable decisions of international and municipal tribunals.

Publicists. The writings of publicists, which often contain valuable collections and analyses of State practice and treaty law, are manifold. N. Papadakis, *International Law of the Sea. A bibliography*, Aalphen an den Rijn, 1980 and Supplement, 1984 is a very useful introduction to them, as is the periodical *Marine Affairs Bibliography* (Dalhousie, Canada, 1980–, with its cumulative volume for 1980–85, Dordrecht, 1987). The United Nations has published *Law of the Sea: A Select Bibliography*, New York, 1985. Among the learned journals which frequently carry articles concerning the law of the sea are the *International Journal of Estuarine and Coastal Law*, *Marine Policy*, *Ocean Development and International Law*, *Ocean Management*, *Maritime Policy and Management*, *Ocean Yearbook* and, more generally, the *American Journal of International Law*, the *International and Comparative Law Quarterly* and the *Reports* of the conference proceedings of the Law of the Sea Institute, the International Law Association and the Institut de droit international.

Among the leading international law textbooks are I. Brownlie's *Principles of Public International Law*, 3rd ed., Oxford, 1979; D. W. Greig's *International Law*, 2nd ed., London, 1976; and D. P. O'Connell's *International Law*, 2nd ed., 2 vols., London, 1970

Special works on the law of the sea

Two works constitute particularly suitable complements to this work. First, *New Directions in the Law of the Sea*, with its collection of source materials and, in volume three (1973), of essays on the subject. Secondly, R. P. Barston and Patricia Birnie (eds.), *The Maritime Dimension*, London, 1980, which contains essays on the various uses of the seas, provides a most helpful background to the legal issues treated in the present work. In addition, M. M. Sibthorp (ed.), *The North Sea. Challenge and Opportunity*, London, 1975, contains much valuable material on maritime activities in one of the world's most heavily used seas, as well as useful accounts of the rules of international and United Kingdom laws which regulate them. It has now been succeeded by a more recent survey, *The Waters around the British Isles: Their Conflicting Uses*, by R. B. Clark (ed.), Oxford, 1987.

Classical writings on the law of the sea

C. van Bynkershoek, *De Dominio Maris Dissertatio*, Leyden, 1744; trans. R.V.D. Magoffin and ed. J. B. Scott, New York, 1923.

H. Grotius, *Mare Liberum*, 1608; trans. R.V.D. Magoffin and ed. J. B. Scott, New York, 1916.

J. Selden, *Mare Clausum: seu, De Dominio Maris Libri Duo*, London, 1635.

E.de Vattel, *Le Droit des gens ou Principes de la loi naturelle appliqués à la conduite et aux affaires des Nations et des Souverains*, London, 1758; trans. and ed. A. de Lapradelle, Washington, D.C.,1916.

W. Welwood, *The Abridgement of all the Sea Lawes*, London, 1613

Modern monographs on the law of the sea

R. P. Anand, *Origin and Development of the Law of the Sea*, The Hague, 1982.

D. Bardonnet and M. Virally (eds.), *Le nouveau droit international de la mer*, Paris, 1983.

D. Bowett, *Law of the Sea*, Manchester, 1967.

C. J. Colombos, *The International Law of the Sea*, 6th ed., London, 1967.

R–J. Dupuy and D. Vignes (eds.), *Traité du Nouveau Droit de la Mer*, Paris, Bruxelles, 1985.

O. de Ferron, *Le droit international de la mer*, 2 vols., Paris, 1958.

G. Gidel, *Le droit international public de la mer*, 3 vols., Paris, 1932–34.

Hague Academy of International Law/United Nations University, *The Management of Humanity's Resources. The Law of the Sea* (Workshop, 1981), The Hague, 1982.

M. S. McDougal and W. T. Burke, *The Public Order of the Oceans*, New Haven, Conn., 1962.

G. J. Mangone, *Law for the World Ocean*, London, 1981.

D. P. O'Connell, *The International Law of the Sea*, 2 vols., Oxford, 1982, 1984.

S. Oda, *The Law of the Sea in our Time*, 1, *New Developments, 1966–1975*, Leyden, 1977 (Vol. II of this title, *The United Nations Seabed Committee, 1968–73*, Leyden, 1977, also by S. Oda, summarises the work of the Sea Bed Committee).

H. A. Smith, *The Law and Custom of the Sea*, 3rd ed., London, 1959.

National and regional studies and collections of documents

F. V. Garcia Amador, *Latin America and the Law of the Sea*, Law of the Sea Institute, University of Rhode Island, Occasional Paper No. 14, 1972.

L. Bouony, 'Les Etats arabes et le nouveau droit de la mer', 90 *RDGIP* 849–875 (1986).

W. E. Butler, *The Soviet Union and the Law of the Sea*, London, 1971.

—, *The USSR, Eastern Europe and the Development of the Law of the Sea*, 2 vols., London, Rome, New York, 1986.

F. Durante and W. Rodino, *Western Europe and the Development of the Law of the Sea*, 3 vols., Dobbs Ferry, N.Y., 1979.

A. A. el-Hakim, *The Middle Eastern States and the Law of the Sea*, Manchester, 1979.

J. Greenfield, *China and the Law of the Sea, Air and Environment*, Alphen aan den Rijn, 1979.

A. L. Hollick, *U.S. Foreign Policy and the Law of the Sea*, Princeton, 1981.

B. Johnson and M. W. Zacher (eds.), *Canadian Foreign Policy and the Law of the Sea*, Vancouver, 1977.

R. D. Lumb, *The Law of the Sea and Australian Offshore Areas*, 2nd ed., St Lucia, Queensland, 1978.

J. L. Malone, 'The United States and the law of the sea', 24 *VJIL* 785–807 (1984).

N. S. Rembe, *Africa and the International Law of the Sea*, The Hague, 1980.

V. Sebek, *The Eastern European States and the Development of the Law of the Sea*, 2 vols., Dobbs Ferry, N.Y., 1977.

A. Szekely, *Latin America and the Development of the Law of the Sea*, 2 vols., Dobbs Ferry, N.Y., 1976.

P. Tangsubkul, *ASEAN and the Law of the Sea*, Singapore, 1982.

UNCLOS III

The *American Journal of International Law* has published a series of useful articles reviewing the work of the sessions of UNCLOS III, by B. H. Oxman and J. R. Stevenson. They appear as follows: Stevenson and Oxman, 68 *AJIL* 1–32 (1974), 69 *AJIL* 1–30, 763–97 (1975); Oxman, 71 *AJIL* 247–69 (1977), 72 *AJIL* 57–83 (1978), 73 *AJIL* 1–41 (1979), 74 *AJIL* 1–47 (1980), 75 *AJIL* 211–56 (1981), and 76 *AJIL* 1–23 (1982).

For an analysis of the Conference procedure, see B. Buzan, 'Negotiating by consensus. Developments in technique at the United Nations Conference on the Law of the Sea', 75 *AJIL* 324–48 (1981), and J. K. Sebenius, *Negotiating the Law of the Sea*, Cambridge, Mass., 1984.

For an account of the workings of PrepCom, see W. Goralczyk, 'Preparatory measures for the implementation of the Convention on the Law of the Sea', XIV *Polish Yearbook of International Law* 7–42 (1985).

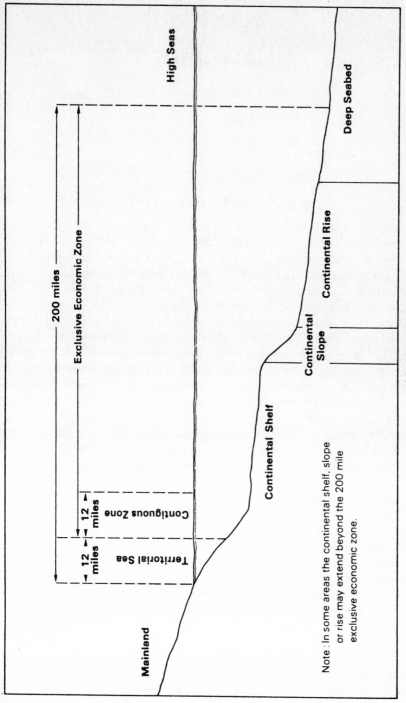

Maritime zones

Note : In some areas the continental shelf, slope
or rise may extend beyond the 200 mile
exclusive economic zone.

CHAPTER TWO
Baselines

Introduction

In determining the extent of a coastal State's territorial sea and other maritime zones, it is obviously necessary first of all to establish from what points on the coast the outer limits of such zones are to be measured. This is the function of baselines. The baseline is the line from which the outer limit of the territorial sea and other coastal State zones (the contiguous zone, the exclusive fishing zone and the exclusive economic zone (EEZ) is measured.[1] The waters on the landward side of the baseline are known as internal waters (see chapter three). Thus the baseline also forms the boundary between internal waters and the territorial sea. While this boundary does not mark the outer limit of a State's territory, since in international law the territorial sea forms part of a State's territory, it does represent the demarcation between that maritime area (internal waters) where other States enjoy no general rights, and those maritime areas (the territorial sea and other zones) where other States do enjoy certain general rights. Baselines may also be relevant in drawing maritime boundaries: where two neighbouring States agree that the boundary between their maritime zones is to be a line equidistant from both States, it is from the baselines of each State that such equidistance is normally calculated.

Traditionally both writers and international conventions (including the Law of the Sea Convention) have treated the rules relating to baselines as part of the body of law relating to the territorial sea. This was justifiable at the time when the territorial sea was the only zone of coastal State jurisdiction. But since the baseline is now used to measure not only the outer limit of the territorial sea, but also the outer limits of the contiguous zone, the exclusive fishing zone and the EEZ, and in some circumstances the continental shelf, it no longer seems appropriate to consider baselines simply as part of the law relating to the territorial sea. Thus in this book we deal with baselines as a separate topic.

The question of baselines was considered at the 1930 Hague Codification Conference. As we saw in the previous chapter, this conference did not succeed in adopting any convention on the law of the sea.[2] Nevertheless, the work done by the conference in respect of baselines formed a useful basis for the International Law Commission (ILC) when it came to consider the topic as part of its study on the law of the sea in the early 1950s. The Commission's deliberations resulted in a number of articles dealing with baselines being included in the 1958 Geneva Convention on the Territorial Sea and the Contiguous Zone. These provisions — articles 3–11 and 13 — set out the current law dealing with baselines: not only are they binding on the thirty-seven coastal States parties to the Convention, but in most respects they may also be considered, for reasons which will be explained later, as representing the rules of customary international law. Thus it is not surprising to find that the Law of the Sea Convention — in articles 4–14 and 16 — simply repeats most of the 1958 Convention's provisions verbatim, making only a few slight additions to cover geographical situations not considered by the ILC or the 1958 Geneva conference. At the same time it is regrettable that greater effort was not made in the Law of the Sea Convention to resolve the ambiguities and fill in the gaps in the 1958 rules: suggestions for improvements have not been lacking from commentators.[3]

If all coastlines were relatively straight and unindented, the question of ascertaining the baseline would be a simple one. All that would be necessary would be to select the high or low tide mark as the baseline. In practice, however, the position is not nearly so straightforward: many coasts are not straight, but are indented or penetrated by bays, and have islands, sandbanks and harbour installations off them. It is necessary, therefore, to have rules on baselines which deal with a wide variety of geographical circumstances. At the same time, it is desirable that the rules should be formulated in as precise and objective a way as possible, so that two cartographers, asked to draw the baselines along a particular stretch of coast, would both arrive at the same result. It is also desirable that the waters enclosed by baselines should be of such a nature that the regime of internal waters is as or more appropriate to them than the regime of the territorial sea or EEZ. These desiderata should be borne in mind in the discussion of the rules that follows. If the rules are not sufficiently precise, it may be quite possible for a State to draw its baselines in a generous manner, thus pushing the outer limit of its territorial sea and other zones farther seawards and bringing greater areas of sea within internal waters.

Article 3 of the Territorial Sea Convention and article 5 of the Law of the Sea Convention provide in identical words that 'the normal baseline for measuring the breadth of the territorial sea is the low-water line along the coast as marked on large-scale charts officially recognised by the coastal State'. The effect of choosing the low-water line,[4] rather than the high-tide line, is to push the outer limit of the territorial sea and other zones farther seawards, particularly on coasts where there is an extensive tidal range.

The rules in articles 3 and 5 apply particularly, as suggested earlier, to coasts which are relatively straight and unindented. The low-water line is described in both the Territorial Sea and Law of the Sea Conventions as the 'normal baseline', but the variety of geographical circumstances for which special provisions are laid down makes it doubtful whether in practice the low-water line is the normal baseline for most States. The Law of Sea Convention appears to recognise this situation, for in article 14 it provides that 'the coastal State may determine baselines in turn by any of the methods provided for ... to suit different conditions'.

The special geographical circumstances for which particular rules are laid down in the Geneva and Law of the Sea conventions are: (i) straight baselines for coasts deeply indented or fringed with islands; (ii) bays; (iii) river mouths; (iv) harbour works (v) low-tide elevations; (vi) islands; and (vii) reefs. Each of these will now be considered in turn; in the discussion of each type of baseline, it may be found useful to refer to fig. 2 on p. 34.

Straight baselines

Customary rules. Much of the coast of Norway is penetrated by fjords and fringed by countless islands, islets, rocks and reefs, known as the *skjaergaard* (a Norwegian work meaning literally rock rampart). In theory it would be possible to draw the baseline along the Norwegian coast by following the low-water mark around all the fjords and islands and by drawing lines across bays, but in practice this would be very cumbersome, and it would be difficult to ascertain the outer limit of the Norwegian territorial sea. Instead, from the mid-nineteenth century onwards, Norway used as the baseline a series of straight lines connecting the outermost points on the *skjaergaard*. In the 1930s the United Kingdom began to object to this method of drawing the baseline, arguing that it was contrary to international law. The United Kingdom's objections were motivated by the fact that the effect of using such straight lines as the baseline, rather than the low-water mark, was to extend farther seawards the outer limit of the Norwegian territorial sea, thus reducing the area of high seas open to fishing by British vessels. The ensuing dispute, which centred on a Norwegian decree of 1935 delimiting straight baselines north of 66°28.8' north, was referred by the United Kingdom to the International Court of Justice in 1949.

In its judgment in the *Anglo-Norwegian Fisheries* case (1951), the Court held that the Norwegian straight baseline system was in conformity with international law. The Court was much influenced by the geographical circumstances of the case. It observed that the *skjaergaard* was but an extension of the Norwegian mainland, and that it was the outer limit of the *skjaergaard*, not the mainland, that constituted the real dividing line between the land and the sea. The low-water mark to be used for constructing the baseline was therefore not that of the mainland, but the outer line of the *skjaergaard*. The Court then noted that 'three methods have been contemplated to effect the application of the low-water mark rule'[5] — the *tracé parallèle* (i.e. drawing the outer limit of the territorial sea by following the coast in all its sinuosities), the *courbe tangente* (i.e. drawing arcs of circles from points along the low-water line) and straight baselines. Where a coast was deeply indented or fringed by islands, then, according to the Court, neither the *tracé parallèle* nor the *courbe tangente* method was appropriate. Instead, 'the baseline becomes independent of the low-water mark, and can only be determined by means of a geometric construction'.[6] The straight baseline was such a geometrical construction, and had been used by several States without objection.[7] In this connection the Court considered it of some importance that no objection had been made to the Norwegian system by the United Kingdom or other States between 1869 (when Norway had first begun applying a detailed system of straight baselines) and 1933 (when the United Kingdom had first objected to the system).

Although it upheld the validity of straight baselines in international law, the Court made it clear that the coastal State does not have an unfettered discretion as to how it draws straight baselines, and it laid down a number of conditions governing the drawing of such baselines. First, such lines must be drawn so that they do 'not depart to any appreciable extent from the general direction of the coast'.[8] Secondly, they must be drawn so that the 'sea areas lying within these lines are sufficiently closely linked to the land domain to be subject to the regime of internal waters'.[9] Thirdly — and here the Court seems to have been considering the way in which individual lines are drawn rather than the system as a whole — it is legitimate to take into account 'certain economic interests peculiar to a region, the reality and importance of which are clearly evidenced by a long usage.'[10]

Conventional rules.   At the time it was given, the Court's judgment was widely regarded as a piece of 'judicial legislation'. However, the rules enunciated by the Court were taken up by the ILC and eventually incorporated in the Territorial Sea Convention (art. 4), which closely follows the language of the Court's judgment. While the Court suggests that straight baselines are simply a special application of the low-water mark principle of constructing the baseline, the Territorial Sea and Law of the Sea Conventions more realistically recognise straight baselines as a distinct method of construction.

Under the Territorial Sea and Law of the Sea Conventions, a system of straight baselines 'may' be used 'in localities where the coastline is deeply indented and cut into, or if there is a fringe of islands along the coast in its immediate vicinity' (TSC, art. 4(1); LOSC, art. 7 (1)). It is clear from the use of the word 'may' that even where a coast fulfils the requisite conditions a State has a choice as to whether it uses straight baselines or not. The USA, for example, does not use straight baselines on the coast of Alaska, although it is entitled to do so. In practice, however, most States do exercise their option and draw straight baselines, because the use of such lines is likely to place their baseline (and hence the outer limit of their various maritime zones) farther seawards than other methods of drawing the baseline, and makes the drawing of the outer limit of the territorial sea (and other zones) more straightforward.

Having established the situation where the use of straight baselines is permissible, the Territorial Sea and Law of the Sea Conventions go on to lay down a number of conditions governing the way in which straight baselines may be drawn. First:

[straight] baselines must not depart to any appreciable extent from the general direction of the coast, and the sea areas lying within the lines must be sufficiently closely linked to the land domain to be subject to the regime of internal waters. [TSC, art. 4(2); LOSC, art. 7(3)]

This provision follows the *Anglo-Norwegian Fisheries* case almost verbatim. Secondly, straight baselines may not be drawn to and from low-tide elevations, unless lighthouses or similar installations which are permanently above sea level have been built on them, or, the Law of the Sea Convention adds, 'in instances where the drawing of baselines to and from such elevations has received general international recognition' (TSC, art. 4(3); LOSC, art. 7(4)). The point of this provision is presumably to prevent baselines being drawn too far seawards of the coast, and thus to reinforce the first condition. Thirdly, a State may not draw straight baselines in such a way as to cut off from the high seas (or, the Law of the Sea Convention adds, the EEZ) the territorial sea of another State (TSC, art. 4(5); LOSC, art. 7(6)). This provision deals with highly exceptional situations, where a smaller territory is embedded in a larger territory (e.g. Monaco in France) or where small islands belonging to one State lie close to the coast of another State (e.g. Southern Yemen's Karaman Island, which lies close to the coast of North Yemen). Finally, a State utilising a straight baseline system must clearly indicate the lines on charts to which 'due publicity' must be given (TSC, art. 4(6); LOSC, art. 16).

Both the Territorial Sea and Law of the Sea Conventions follow the *Anglo-Norwegian Fisheries* case in providing that in determining particular baselines, 'account may be taken ... of economic interests peculiar to the region concerned, the reality and the importance of which are clearly evidenced by a long usage' (TSC, art. 4(4); LOSC, art. 7(5)). The most obvious such economic interest, and the interest at issue in the *Anglo-Norwegian Fisheries* case, is fishing. Neither the Territorial Sea Convention nor the Law of the Sea Convention contains any provision limiting the length of individual baselines (apart from 'archipelagic' baselines: see chapter six), although an unsuccessful attempt was made at UNCLOS I to introduce a maximum length of fifteen miles for any one baseline. In the *Anglo-Norwegian Fisheries* case the longest line, whose validity was upheld by the Court, was forty-four miles. (In this chapter, as elsewhere in this book, all references to 'miles' are to nautical miles unless otherwise stated). It would seem, therefore, that there is in principle no restriction on the length of individual baselines, although obviously in practice the necessity for compliance with the general conditions set out above will be a restraining factor.

The Law of the Sea Convention contains a provision, dealing with a rather exceptional geographical situation, which has no equivalent in the ~~deltas~~ Territorial Sea Convention. Article 7(2) provides that, 'Where because of the presence of a delta and other natural conditions the coastline is highly unstable, the appropriate points [between which straight baselines may be drawn] may be selected along the furthest seaward extent of the low-water line'. This provision, inspired by a Bangladeshi proposal, is not very well drafted. It is not clear if this provision is laying down a third type of coastline, in addition to deeply indented coasts and coasts fringed with islands, where straight baselines may be drawn, or whether it applies only to deltas along coasts which fall into the first two categories. The former seems more likely. Nor is it clear whether the use of the 'furthest seaward extent of the low-water line' is subject to the general rules about the use of low-tide elevations as basepoints for straight baselines, contained in article 7(4), or is an exception to such rules. Furthermore, the meaning of the phrase 'and other natural conditions' which qualifies deltas is obscure. In practice, no State appears yet to have drawn straight baselines utilising this provision, although some deltas are enclosed within straight baselines drawn on the basis of other criteria. Article 7(2) goes on to provide that where straight baselines are drawn along the furthest seaward extent of the low-water line of deltas, then 'notwithstanding subsequent regression of the low-water line, the straight baselines shall remain effective until changed by the coastal State in accordance with [the] Convention'. This provision was inserted for the benefit of States such as Egypt: part of the delta of the Nile is retreating at the rate of about forty metres a year.

State practice. Although both the International Court of Justice in the *Anglo-Norwegian Fisheries* case and the Territorial Sea and Law of the Sea Conventions regard the use of straight baselines as being limited to exceptional geographical circumstances, and although few States have a coastline that is anywhere near as indented or fringed with islands as that of Norway, some 45–55 States have in fact drawn straight baselines along all or part of their coasts,[11] and a further fourteen States have adopted enabling legislation to draw straight baselines but have not yet drawn them.

As we have seen, the rules governing the use of straight baselines laid down in customary and conventional law are relatively imprecise, and thus allow States a considerable latitude in the way they draw straight baselines. Some States, however, do appear to have gone beyond the spirit and the vague wording of these rules. Studies by the Geographer of the US Department of State (in the *Limits in the Seas* series) and by Prescott (*op. cit.* in 'Further reading') suggest that of the straight baseline systems so far drawn, over half depart from the rules of international law in one way or another. First, some States (such as Albania, Cuba, Italy, Senegal and Spain) have drawn straight baselines along coasts which are not deeply indented. A particularly good example is Colombia, which has drawn a single straight baseline 131 miles in length along part of its Caribbean coast and enclosed a smooth coast with no fringing islands.[12] A second form of departure is the drawing of straight baselines along coasts which possess some offshore islands but which do not form a fringe in the immediate vicinity of the coast. This has been done by, among others, Ecuador, Iceland, Iran, Italy, Malta and Thailand. Perhaps the most extreme example is Vietnam, which has used the isolated islet of Hon Hai, lying seventy-four miles from the mainland coast, as a basepoint for its straight baseline system, and connected it northwards to Hon Doi islet and southwestwards to Bay Canh islet, each of which is 161 miles away.[13] A third form of breach is to draw straight baselines which depart to a considerable extent from the general direction of the coast. For example the straight baselines of Burma and Ecuador are in some places at an angle of 60° to the general direction of the coast[14] (by comparison in the Norwegian baseline system, generally regarded as the standard model, the angle of deviation is never more than about 15°). Fourth, baselines are sometimes drawn so that the sea areas inside the lines are insufficiently closely linked to the land to be subject to the regime of internal waters. Again the Burmese system is a good illustration: the 222-mile long line across the Gulf of Martaban is at one point seventy-five miles from the nearest land, and in the Burmese system as a whole the ratio of land (i.e. islands lying within the baselines) to water is less than 1:50 (in comparison, the ratio in the Norwegian system is 1:3.5). Fifth, some States appear to accept the use of low-tide elevations as basepoints, regardless of whether lighthouses or similar installations have been built on them: see, for example, the enabling legislation of Egypt, Saudi Arabia and Syria.[15] Sixth, in spite of the obligation not to draw straight baselines in such a way as to cut off the territorial sea of another State from the high seas or EEZ, Morocco's straight baselines appear to do just that in respect of Spain's North African enclaves of Ceuta and Melilla.[16] Seventh, in spite of the obligation to publicise baselines, Haiti, North Korea and Malaysia have drawn the outer limit of their territorial sea in a way which presupposes that it is measured from straight baselines, even though such lines have not been published. Finally, some States have located basepoints for straight baselines in the sea. The leading example here is Bangladesh, which has drawn a straight baseline system all of whose basepoints are in the sea. For most of its course the line lies close to the ten-fathom isobath and in places is 50 miles from the nearest land.[17] Less objectionable is the practice of some States in locating the terminus of their baseline system in the sea but on the boundary with the neighbouring State. Other anomalies in the drawing of straight baselines are the bizarre practice of locating the terminus of a system in another State's territory (as Ecuador has done in Colombia and Venezuela in Guyana); and not anchoring a straight baseline to the mainland coast, so that it is possible to sail into internal waters without crossing the baseline (as has been done by, amongst others, Bangladesh, North Korea and Norway (in Spitsbergen)). Surveying State practice, Prescott concludes that abuse of the rules relating to straight baselines has been such that 'it would now be possible to draw a straight baseline along any section of coast in the world and cite an existing straight baseline as a precedent'.[18] On the other hand, it should be noted that some of the straight baselines referred to above have drawn objections from other States: for example, Burma and India have objected to Bangladesh's baselines, and France, Singapore, Thailand and the USA to those of Vietnam. The question of the legality of baselines which do not appear to conform to the rules is further considered at the end of this chapter.

The effect of drawing straight baselines, even strictly in accordance with the rules, is often to enclose considerable bodies of sea as internal waters: for example, the whole of the Minches, lying between the Inner and Outer Hebrides off the west coast of Scotland, is enclosed by straight baselines and thus is internal waters. It should, however, be noted that in some such internal waters, including the Minches, there is a right of innocent passage: see pp. 51–2.

Bays

Pre-1958 customary rules. International law has always recognised that bays have a close connection with land and that it is more appropriate that they should be considered as internal waters rather than territorial sea. Customary international law had therefore in principle recognised that the baseline could be drawn across the mouth of bays, enclosing them as internal waters. But customary international law failed to provide clear rules on two essential points: the criteria by which an indentation of the coast would be recognised as a bay, and the maximum length of the closing line across a bay. As regards the first point, the deficiencies of customary international law can be seen in the *North Atlantic Coast Fisheries* case (1910), where the Permanent Court of Arbitration found that there was no general principle

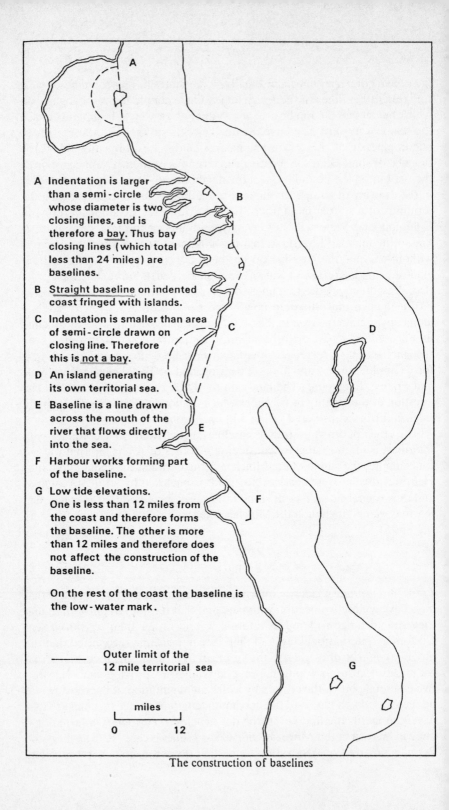

A Indentation is larger than a semi-circle whose diameter is two closing lines, and is therefore a bay. Thus bay closing lines (which total less than 24 miles) are baselines.

B Straight baseline on indented coast fringed with islands.

C Indentation is smaller than area of semi-circle drawn on closing line. Therefore this is not a bay.

D An island generating its own territorial sea.

E Baseline is a line drawn across the mouth of the river that flows directly into the sea.

F Harbour works forming part of the baseline.

G Low tide elevations. One is less than 12 miles from the coast and therefore forms the baseline. The other is more than 12 miles and therefore does not affect the construction of the baseline.

On the rest of the coast the baseline is the low-water mark.

——— Outer limit of the 12 mile territorial sea

miles

0   12

The construction of baselines

of international law which described a bay: factors to be taken into account in deciding whether an indentation was a bay included the penetration of the bay inland and the security and economic interests of the coastal State therein. As regards the maximum length of closing lines for bays, the United Kingdom in the *Anglo-Norwegian Fisheries* case argued that customary international law had established ten miles as the maximum length for closing lines. This contention was rejected by the Court on the ground that there was no uniformity of State practice on the question.

Conventional rules.   The Territorial Sea Convention, in article 7, established clear and precise rules for determining both these hitherto uncertain points, and these rules are repeated almost verbatim in the Law of the Sea Convention (art. 10). At the outset it should be noted that these rules do not apply to cases where straight baselines are used (see above), or to historic bays or bays whose coasts belong to more than one State (which are considered below). To establish whether an indentation is a bay in the legal sense the Conventions lay down the following geometric test. First, a line should be drawn between the natural entrance points of the indentation. Next, a semicircle having the diameter of this line should be constructed and its area measured. (Where the presence of islands means that an indentation has more than one mouth, the diameter of the semicircle is a line as long as the sum total of the lengths of the lines across the different mouths.) Then the area of water between the line across the indentation and the low-water mark around the indentation should be calculated: for this purpose any islands within the indentation are to be included in the area of water. If the area of water is larger than the area of the semicircle, the indentation is a bay. Conversely, if the area of water is smaller, the indentation is not a bay. Once an indentation has been established as being a bay, a closing line can be drawn across it. If the length of the line between the natural entrance points of the bay (in the case of bays with more than one mouth, the total of the lengths of the lines across the different mouths) is less than twenty-four miles, this line is the closing line and, therefore, the baseline. If the line or lines are more than twenty-four miles in length, then a straight line of twenty-four miles is drawn within the bay in such a way as to enclose the greatest amount of water possible: this line then forms the baseline. Around the unenclosed part of the bay the baseline will be the low-water mark (unless any of the features that justify a different baseline are present).

These provisions are obviously a great improvement on previous customary international law, but their practical application is not wholly free from difficulties. The main difficulty is that often it is not obvious which are the 'natural entrance points' of an indentation. An example of this problem can be seen in *Post Office* v. *Estuary Radio* (1968), where the English Court of Appeal had to decide whether the Thames estuary was legally a bay. Estuary Radio argued that the natural entrance points of the estuary were Orfordness and the North Foreland (in which case the estuary would not have been a bay because it would have failed the semicircle test). The Post Office, on the other hand, argued that the natural entrance points were the Naze and Foreness (in which case the estuary was a bay). Although the Court of Appeal accepted the Post Office's contention, neither set of points seems very obviously to be the 'natural entrance points' of the estuary. Similarly, difficulties may arise in determining the extent to which rivers running into a bay, or other subsidiary features such as lagoons, should be taken into account in calculating the area of water in the bay; the application of the rules to bays with islands fringing, or lying just seaward of, the mouth may also be problematic.[19]

Even where the application of article 7 of the Territorial Sea Convention is free from difficulty, some States parties to the Convention have nevertheless failed to act in conformity with it. Thus, the Dominican Republic has drawn closing lines across four bays which do not meet the semicircle test, while the closing line in a Portuguese bay exceeds twenty-four miles.[20]

Historic bays.   We must now turn to consider the two types of bay to which the provisions of article 7 of the Territorial Sea Convention and article 10 of the Law of the Sea Convention do not apply — historic bays and bays whose coasts belong to more than one State. Neither the Territorial Sea Convention nor the Law of the Sea Convention contains any provisions dealing with historic bays, although UNCLOS I had before it a memorandum on the subject prepared by the UN Secretariat (see the reference in 'Further reading' at the end of this chapter) and a draft article proposed by Japan,[21] and UNCLOS III had a draft article proposed by Colombia.[22] UNCLOS I did, however, adopt a resolution requesting the UN to arrange for the study of the juridical regime of historic waters, including historic bays.[23] Such a study was published by the UN Secretariat in 1962 (see the reference in 'Further reading'), but it has not led to any international legislative action. The position is therefore governed by customary international law. In the *Tunisia/Libya Continental Shelf* case the International Court stated that 'general international law ... does not provide for a *single* 'régime' for 'historic waters' or 'historic bays', but only for a particular régime for each of the concrete, recognised cases of 'historic waters' or 'historic bays'[24]: thus, in one case only exclusive 'historic' fishing rights might exist, whereas in another the coastal State might enjoy full sovereignty. Accordingly, claims to historic title must be approached with circumspection. However, the general criteria for the establishment of an historic title were addressed in the 1962 UN Secretariat study, according to which a State may validly claim title to a bay on historic grounds if it can show that it has for a considerable period of time claimed the bay as internal waters and effectively exercised its authority therein, and that during this time the claim has received the acquiescence of other States. The United States Supreme Court has subsequently applied these criteria in *US* v. *Louisiana* (1969) and *US* v. *Alaska* (1975). Where title to an historic bay has been acquired, a closing line may be drawn across the mouth of the bay which will then form the baseline. There appear to be no rules as to the maximum permissible length of such lines, and it would seem that, if good title has been acquired, the closing line may be of any length.

The need for authority to have been effectively exercised over a claimed historic bay for a considerable period of time is a condition which is objected to by many recently independent developing States, which argue that it is impossible for them to produce evidence of an uninterrupted exercise of authority. While in fact it would seem possible for such States to cite the practice of both the colonial and pre-colonial period (Sri Lanka's claim to Palk Bay as historic waters is based not only on acts of the British, Dutch and Portuguese colonial administration but also on authority exercised by the pre-colonial kings of Ceylon), some developing States have argued for a theory of 'vital bays' under which vital security or economic interests would justify title to a bay independently of any true historic title. Such a doctrine, whose origins can be traced back to the early part of the twentieth century, has naturally been rejected by the traditional maritime States, such as the United Kingdom and USA, because of the ease with which it would allow a State to claim large areas of sea as internal waters, at the expense of the international community.

In the case of historic bays strictly so called, the question of whether a State has acquired good title to a claimed historic bay is likely to depend largely on whether other States have acquiesced in its claim. At the present time over twenty States claim historic bays. Examples of such claims include those by the USSR to the Sea of Azov and Peter the Great Bay (although several States, including the United Kingdom and the USA, do not accept the latter as an historic bay);[25] by Canada to Hudson Bay (although the USA does not accept it as an historic bay);[26] by the USA to Chesapeake and Delaware Bays; and by Vietnam to parts of the Gulfs of Thailand and Tonkin (to which claim France, Thailand and China have objected).[27] As these examples show, historic bays are likely to be larger than bays governed by article 7 of the Territorial Sea Convention and article 10 of the Law of the Sea Convention, partly because in the case of smaller bays it is simpler for a State to close a bay under the conventional rules than risk a claim to historic status that may be disputed.

Perhaps the most controversial claim to a bay on historic grounds is that of Libya to the Gulf of Sidra (Sirte). In 1973 Libya claimed the Gulf as an historic bay and drew a closing line across it which is 296 miles in length.

This action evoked protests from several States, including the United Kingdom, USA and USSR. The USA not only sent a note of protest but passed through the Gulf with a naval squadron. Further displays of naval strength by the USA to demonstrate its objections to the Libyan claim and its assertion that the Gulf remains high seas have taken place subsequently, notably in 1981 (when two Libyan aircraft were shot down by the USA) and in 1986 (prior to the US bombing of the Libyan mainland, though the latter was unconnected with Libya's claim to the Gulf of Sidra, being justified by the USA as an act of self-defence in response to claimed Libyan attacks on US nationals in West Germany and elsewhere). There seems little evidence to support Libya's claim to have exercised sovereignty over the Gulf 'through history' and much evidence of objections from other States. The conclusion must be, therefore, that the Gulf of Sidra is not an historic bay. Conceivably it might be claimed as a 'vital bay', but such a claim would only have any validity as against those States that accept the doctrine of vital bays.[28] Lest it be thought that such claims are confined to recently independent States, it may be noted that the Italian claim to the Gulf of Taranto is in many respects similar to this Libyan claim, and has elicited rejections from States such as the United Kingdom.

Bays bordered by more than one State.   As with historic bays, bays which are bordered by more than one State are not dealt with by either the Territorial Sea Convention or the Law of the Sea Convention. There are over forty such bays in the world. Examples include Lough Foyle (bordered by Ireland and the United Kingdom), the Bay of Figuier (France and Spain) and Passamaquoddy Bay (Canada and the USA). The normal rule of customary international law in relation to such bays would appear to be that, unlike bays governed by article 7 of the Territorial Sea Convention and article 10 of the Law of the Sea Convention, or historic bays, they cannot be closed by a line drawn across their mouth. Instead the baseline is constituted by the low-water mark around the shores of the bay. The matter, however, is not free from controversy. Exceptionally it may be possible for the riparian States to show that the position is different by reason of historic title. Such is the case with the Gulf of Fonseca, bordered by El Salvador, Honduras and Nicaragua. In *El Salvador* v. *Nicaragua* (1917) the now defunct Central American Court of Justice held that the Gulf was an historic bay, thus having the character of internal waters, and that the three riparian States were co-owners of its waters except for the innermost three miles which was the exclusive property of each.

River mouths

Article 13 of the Territorial Sea Convention and article 9 of the Law of the Sea Convention provide in almost identical wording that:

If a river flows directly into the sea, the baseline shall be a straight line across the mouth of the river between points on the low-water line of its banks. [LOSC, art. 9. TSC has 'low-tide']

No limit is placed on the length of such a river closing line. The provision, in the absence of any qualification to the contrary, would appear to apply both to rivers with a single riparian State as well as to rivers with two riparian States, although the latter application is apparently not accepted by some States, such as the USA.[29]

Estuaries. It should be noted that articles 13 and 9 apply only to rivers that flow 'directly' into the sea. Most large rivers do not flow directly into the sea, but enter it via estuaries. In such cases the question of the baseline should be governed by the provisions concerning bays (as we earlier saw was done with the Thames estuary in *Post Office* v. *Estuary Radio*). The original ILC draft did in fact contain a specific provision in this regard, but it was deleted at UNCLOS I because of the difficulty of defining an estuary.

It may not always be easy to distinguish between a river entering the sea directly and one entering the sea via an estuary, and in any case the distinction is open to abuse. An example of this problem can be seen in the action of Argentina and Uruguay in 1961 in drawing a line 120 miles in length across the mouth of the river Plate between Punta del Este in Uruguay and Cabo San Antonio in Argentina.[30] This action, which has met with protests from a number of other States, including the United Kingdom and the USA, is said by Argentina and Uruguay to be based on article 13,[31] although few cartographers would be likely to choose the location of the above line as the mouth of the river Plate or indeed say that the river entered the sea 'directly': furthermore, the river Plate estuary has in the past been claimed, inconsistently with the present claim, as an historic bay.[32]

Deltas. Where a river enters the sea via a delta, it is unlikely that articles 13 and 9 will be applicable. Instead the baseline is likely to be constituted by the low-water mark or in some cases by straight baselines (as the Law of the Sea Convention with its provision on deltas and other unstable coastlines, referred to above, appears to contemplate.) In addition, in many instances, the provisions on low-tide elevations and islands (considered below) will be applicable.

Harbour works

Article 8 of the Territorial Sea Convention provides that the 'outermost permanent harbour works which form an integral part of the harbour system' (such as piers and breakwaters) are to be regarded as forming part of the coast and hence can serve as the baseline. Article 11 of the Law of the Sea Convention repeats article 8 almost verbatim, but makes it clear that harbour works must be attached (or at least very close) to the coast if they are to be used as baselines, by adding that 'off-shore installations and artificial islands shall not be considered as permanent harbour works'. Although the Conventions do not make provision for such an eventuality, it would seem reasonable for coastal States to be able to draw a straight line across the mouth of a harbour (although such a line would normally have a negligible influence on the extent of the territorial sea). Support for such a position is provided by article 50 of the Law of the Sea Convention which permits archipelagic States to draw closing lines across harbours (see p. 103 below).

Where roadsteads which are 'normally used for the loading, unloading and anchoring of ships' lie not only beyond the baseline but also wholly or partly outside the territorial sea, they are included in the territorial sea, though they do not otherwise affect its delimitation (TSC, art. 9; LOSC, art. 12). Strictly speaking these provisions (which appear to have very limited practical application) have nothing to do with baselines, and are only included here for the sake of completeness.

Low-tide elevations

A low-tide elevation is defined in the Conventions as 'a naturally formed area of land which is surrounded by and above water at low tide but submerged at high tide' (TSC, art. 11 (1); LOSC, art. 13(1)). Low-tide elevations are often referred to in older books and treaties as 'drying rocks' or 'banks'. The effect of low-tide elevations on the delimitation of the territorial sea was uncertain under customary international law before 1958, but clear rules are laid down in article 11 of the Territorial Sea Convention, which are repeated verbatim in article 13 of the Law of the Sea Convention. Under these provisions:

Where a low-tide elevation is situated wholly or partly at a distance not exceeding the breadth of the territorial sea from the mainland or an island, the low-water line on that elevation may be used as the baseline for measuring the breadth of the territorial sea.

Where, however:

a low-tide elevation is wholly situated at a distance exceeding the breadth of the territorial sea from the mainland or an island, it has no territorial sea of its own.

This is so, even if such a low-tide elevation is situated at a distance less than the breadth of the territorial sea from another low-tide elevation, which in turn is situated less than the breadth of the territorial sea from the mainland, i.e. it is not possible to 'leapfrog' from one low-tide elevation to another. The now general recognition of a twelve-mile territorial sea will give low-tide elevations a much greater potential for extending the baseline sea-wards than when the territorial sea was more commonly three miles in breadth. Thus, in an extreme case, where a low-tide elevation is twelve miles from the mainland, the outer limit of the territorial sea will be twenty-four miles from the mainland: furthermore, in such a case the twelve miles between the mainland and the low-tide elevation, might not, if the elevation were an isolated one, truly have the characteristics of internal waters.

Finally, it should be noted that in limited cases low-tide elevations can be used as basepoints in constructing a straight baseline system (see above).

Islands

An island is defined in the Conventions as 'a naturally formed area of land, surrounded by water, which is above water at high tide' (TSC, art. 10(1); LOSC, art. 121(1)). This definition removes the doubts which had existed in customary international law before 1958 as to whether in addition an island had to be capable of effective occupation, by making it clear that this is not a necessary condition. The Conventions go on to provide that the territorial sea of an island is measured in accordance with the general rules on baselines (TSC, art. 10(2); LOSC, art. 121(2)). This means that every island has a territorial sea, no matter what its size (which appears also to have been the position in customary international law before 1958). With large islands, such as Australia, Great Britain or Greenland, there are obviously no problems. But it also means that every islet or rock, no matter how small in size, has a territorial sea, i.e. the islet or rock, or rather the low-water mark around it, will serve as part of the baseline. The question then arises whether this is the baseline for the territorial sea only, or the baseline for all maritime zones. The Territorial Sea Convention mentions only the territorial sea specifically, but by implication also includes the contiguous zone (see TSC, art. 24(2)). State practice since 1958 suggests that it also includes the twelve-mile exclusive fishing zone.[33] (The continental shelf, the only other kind of maritime zone in existence before UNCLOS III, is not, under customary international law or the Continental Shelf Convention, measured from the baseline.) The Law of the Sea Convention, on the other hand, specifically provides that all islands in principle can serve as the baseline for all maritime zones, viz. the territorial sea, contiguous zone, EEZ and continental shelf[34] (LOSC, art. 121(2)), but makes a partial exception for 'rocks which cannot sustain human habitation or economic life of their own': such islands can serve as the baseline only for the territorial sea and contiguous zone, but not for the EEZ or continental shelf (LOSC, art. 121(3)). This provision is poorly drafted. It does not define what a 'rock' is or suggest any dividing line between 'rocks' and other islands. In addition, the question of whether any particular 'rock' can sustain 'human habitation' or 'economic life' is one that may admit of more than one answer because of the vagueness of the phrases used[35]. The effect of article 121(3), which is further analysed in chapters eight and nine (see pp. 127 and 135–6), is to create a situation — the one situation — where the baseline is not the same for all maritime zones. It also has the rather anomalous result that a low-tide elevation can sometimes generate an exclusive economic zone, whereas an uninhabitable 'rock' cannot, even though the latter will usually be a much more visible manifestation of land. On the other hand, it would appear permissible to use an uninhabitable 'rock' as a basepoint in constructing a straight baseline or archipelagic baseline system, and in such a case the limitations of article 121(3) could be circumvented. In practice most 'rocks' lie immediately offshore, and thus if article 121(3) is applied and they are discounted as basepoints for delimitation of the EEZ and continental shelf, the extent of those zones will not be greatly affected. However the few isolated oceanic 'uninhabitable rocks' that do exist (and exactly how many will depend on what criteria, if any, emerge as to the size and habitability of 'rocks') — such as Rockall (off the United Kingdom), St Peter and St Paul Rocks (off Brazil) and L'Espérance Rock (off New Zealand) (all less than 0·01 square miles in area) — are likely to or have already given rise to difficulties and disputes (see further chapter nine).

Archipelagos.   Where islands are grouped so as to form an archipelago, the Law of the Sea Convention provides that, in addition to any baselines drawn along individual islands to delimit internal waters, straight lines may be drawn around the outermost points of the archipelago itself (archipelagic baselines). Such archipelagic baselines form the baseline from which the territorial sea and other zones are measured. This matter is discussed more fully in chapter six.

Artificial islands.   The definition in the Conventions of an island as being 'naturally-formed' excludes artificial islands, although the distinction between a 'naturally-formed' and an 'artificial' island may not always be easy to make in practice: e.g. if a State constructs some kind of barrier in the sea so that sand being moved by currents piles up against it, with the result that eventually an island is formed, is this a 'naturally-formed' or an artificial island? The only provision on artificial islands in the 1958 Geneva Conventions is article 5(4) of the Continental Shelf Convention, which provides that installations connected with the exploration and exploitation of the shelf's natural resources and located on the continental shelf have no territorial sea nor do they affect its delimitation. The implication would seem to be that no artificial island is entitled to a territiorial sea or, therefore, to serve as a basepoint. The Law of the Sea Convention reinforces this conclusion. First, article 11 provides, as we have already seen, that 'offshore installations and artificial islands shall not be considered as permanent harbour works' and therefore do not, *qua* harbour works, form part of the baseline. Secondly, articles 60(8) and 80 provide that artificial islands and installations constructed in the EEZ or on the continental shelf have no territorial sea of their own nor does their presence affect the delimitation of the territorial sea, EEZ or continental shelf. Thirdly, even though the construction of artificial islands on the high seas is now recognised as a freedom of the high seas (LOSC, art. 87), the prohibition on States from subjecting any part of the high seas to their sovereignty (LOSC, art. 89) prevents the establishment of any maritime zones around artificial islands on the high seas. This principle is spelt out for that part of the high seas overlying the International Sea Bed Area. Under article 147(2) stationary installations used for the conduct of activities in the Area have no territorial sea of their own, nor do they affect the delimitation of the territorial sea, EEZ or continental shelf.

Reefs

The coral reefs of atolls present a problem in that they may be continuously submerged or, if exposed at low tide, may be situated from the islands of the atoll at a distance greater than the breadth of the territorial sea: in neither case, therefore, under the rules so far considered could such reefs serve as the baseline. And yet it is desirable for a variety of reasons, principally ecological, that the territorial sea should be measured from the outer limit of the reef so that the lagoon inside the reef has the status of internal waters. The problem of coral reefs was recognised and discussed by the ILC in the earlier stages of its work[36] but no provision on the subject was contained in its final draft, nor does the matter appear to have been discussed at UNCLOS I. With the emergence into independence since 1958 of many States formed of atolls in the Caribbean and Indian and Pacific Oceans, such as the Bahamas, the Maldives and Nauru, there has come greater political impetus for a specific rule for coral reefs, and such a rule is now contained in the Law of the Sea Convention. Article 6 provides that:

In the case of islands situated on atolls or of islands having fringing reefs, the baseline for measuring the breadth of the territorial sea is the seaward low-water line of the reef, as shown by the appropriate symbol on charts officially recognized by the coastal State.

A number of points may be noted about this provision. First, it is not limited in its application to atolls or coral reefs (unlike an early draft provision in the ILC). Secondly, it suggests that only reefs exposed at low tide, and not wholly submerged reefs, may be used as baselines (again unlike the early

ILC draft, which had provided that 'the edge of the reef as marked on . . . charts, should be accepted as the low-water line'). Thirdly, it is not clear how far from the island the fringing reef may lie before it ceases to be eligible to serve as the baseline. It may be that 'fringing reef' is used in its technical geographical sense as meaning a reef extending outwards from the shore, from which it is not separated by a channel (as opposed to a barrier reef, which lies at some distance from the shore). On the other hand, a literal reading of article 6 would suggest that it could apply to the Great Barrier Reef, which can be said to fringe the island of Australia: yet the reef is at points 150 miles from the coast. It must be assumed that article 6 is not intended to apply to this situation, and it therefore seems desirable that, if the term is not used in its technical geographical sense, some limit should be placed on the distance a fringing reef which is to serve as a baseline may lie from the coast of an island. A further problem is that article 6 does not specify what is to happen where there is a gap in the fringing reef. The obvious solution is to draw a straight line across the gap, and this appears to be the growing practice of States: see, for example, the legislation of Fiji,[37] Nauru[38] and of New Zealand in respect of the Tokelau Islands.[39] Finally, many atolls form part of archipelagos. In such cases it will often be simpler and more advantageous for the archipelagic State to use archipelagic baselines as the baseline (see chapter six) than to construct baselines in accordance with the provisions of article 6.

Charts and publicity

Under the Territorial Sea Convention the only baselines which the coastal State is required to indicate on charts and publicise are straight baselines (TSC, art. 4(6)). Under the Law of the Sea Convention this obligation is extended to closing lines across river mouths and bays, and there is now an obligation to deposit a copy of a chart showing such baselines (or alternatively a list of geographical co-ordinates) with the UN Secretary General (LOSC, art. 16). Presumably the reason why the list of baselines to be indicated on charts and publicised has not been extended to the low-water line and low-tide elevations is partly because such features are constantly changing as the result of tides and currents, and partly because the low-water line is the normal baseline which the coastal State must adopt if it does not choose man-made baselines such as river and bay closing lines and straight baselines: in any case the low-water line must be marked on 'large-scale charts officially recognised by the coastal State' (TSC, art. 3; LOSC, art. 5).

Article 16 of the Law of the Sea Convention should introduce greater precision and certainty into the drawing of baselines: this is particularly important for mariners and fishermen wanting to know whether they are

in any of a coastal State's maritime zones and, if so, which. The requirement of publicity may also help to reduce some of the past abuse of straight
baselines and river mouth and bay closing lines which we have noted above.

Present-day customary international law relating to baselines

In discussing the conventional rules on baselines, brief mention was made
of the pre-1958 customary rules. In some cases, such as the low-water line
and straight baselines, these customary rules were the same as the provisions
of the Territorial Sea Convention. In other cases, notably bays, islands and
low-tide elevations, there was considerable uncertainty as to what the customary rules were. The question we must now consider is whether the customary rules on baselines have been clarified or have changed since 1958.
This question is particularly important given that only about a quarter of all
coastal States are parties to the Territorial Sea Convention and that the
Law of the Sea Convention is not yet in force.

There is in fact considerable evidence to suggest that today the customary
rules on baselines are identical with the conventional rules. There are three
main aguments to support this thesis. First, the Territorial Sea Convention's
provisions on baselines were incorporated *in toto* and unchanged into the
Law of the Sea Convention, with little discussion and no opposition at
UNCLOS. All UNCLOS did was to make some minor additions. Secondly, the Territorial Sea Convention's rules on baselines have been incorporated by reference into other treaties, the parties to which include States
which are not parties to the Territorial Sea Convention.[40] Thirdly, the
legislation of many, though not all, States not party to the Territorial Sea
Convention generally reflects its provisions (practice on straight baselines
reflects the provisions less faithfully than practice on other matters). We
have been able to examine the legislation of some seventy-one of the approximately 100 coastal States which are not parties to the Convention.

Of these States, only a dozen (e.g. Ireland,[41] Kuwait,[42] New Zealand,[43]
Samoa,[44] Sri Lanka[45] and Sudan[46]) have legislation which refers to most or
all of the types of baseline dealt with by the Territorial Sea Convention: in
these cases the legislation is generally in accordance with the Convention's
provisions. The majority of States, however, simply refer in their legislation to the low-water mark and/or straight baselines. Of individual types
of baseline, we have already commented on the legislation relating to
straight baselines earlier in this chapter. As regards bays, only four States
(New Zealand,[47] Papua New Guinea,[48] Samoa[49] and Vanuatu[50]) incorporate the Territorial Sea Convention's provisions. In the case of the other
nineteen States whose legislation mentions bays, the legislation either fails
to define a bay and/or fails to prescribe the maximum limit of the closing
line. One should not conclude from this, however, that the practice of these

States is necessarily contrary to the Territorial Sea Convention. What is essential in determining this question is how these States in practice draw baselines across bay mouths, and on this we have very little information. Two cases, however, have come to our attention where closing lines appear to have been drawn across bays contrary to the rules of the Convention. These are certain of the bay closing lines utilised by Argentina and France.[51] In the case of river-mouth closing lines, only seven States have legislation referring to such baselines and all but possibly one of these pieces of legislation (that of Cameroon[52]) is in accordance with the Convention. Fourteen States have legislation dealing with harbour works: in each case the legislation conforms to the Convention. Of the thirteen States whose legislation refers to low-tide elevations, eleven follow the Convention, while two Arab States (Egypt[53] and Saudi Arabia[54]) appear to allow low-tide elevations wherever situated to generate a territorial sea. Sixteen States have legislation dealing with islands: generally it follows the Convention (although in some cases an island is not defined), but two Arab States (Egypt[55] and Saudi Arabia[56]) allow artificial islands to generate a territorial sea. Finally, it may be noted that five States (Kiribati,[57] Nauru,[58] New Zealand — in respect of Niue and the Tokelau Islands[59] — Southern Yemen[60] and Tuvalu[61]) have legislation concerning fringing reefs which is in accordance with article 6 of the Law of the Sea Convention.

Validity of baselines

In those cases where a State either has a discretion as to which kind of baseline it chooses and/or has to construct an artificial line as the baseline — namely, straight baselines, bay and river-mouth closing lines and low-tide elevations — the coastal State's action in exercising its discretion and constructing lines remains subject to international law. As the International Court of Justice put it in the *Anglo-Norwegian Fisheries* case in an oft-quoted dictum:

The delimitation of sea areas has always an international aspect; it cannot be dependent merely upon the will of the coastal State as expressed in its municipal law. Although it is true that the act of delimitation is necessarily a unilateral act, because only the coastal State is competent to undertake it, the validity of the delimitation with regard to other States depends upon international law.[62]

Thus where a baseline is clearly contrary to international law, it will not be valid, certainly in respect of States which have objected to it, though a State which has accepted the baseline (for example in a boundary treaty) might be estopped from later denying its validity. In border-line cases — for example, where there is doubt as to whether a State's straight baseline system conforms to all the criteria laid down in customary and conventional law — the attitude of other States in acquiescing in or objecting to the baseline is likely to prove crucial in determining its validity.[63] Having said this, it must, however, be pointed out that few doubtful baselines have encountered active opposition or led to serious disputes, the Norwegian straight baseline system prior to 1950 and the Gulf of Sidra closing line being notable exceptions. It may be that the widespread toleration of much of the practice described in this chapter which clearly appears to contravene the relevant rules of international law (particularly as regards straight baselines) will in time lead to a modification of those rules themselves.

Notes

1 One recent, and so far as is known unique, exception to using the baseline as the point from which the outer limit of maritime zones is measured, is the 150-mile Falkland Islands fishing zone established in 1986, which is measured from a single point in the middle of the Falkland Islands. See Proclamation No. 4 of 1986 of the Governor of the Falkland Islands, 9 *LOSB* 19 (1987).
2 The report of the conference's Committee on Territorial Waters contained a set of draft articles on the territorial sea. Six of these articles were concerned with the problems of baselines, and dealt with the low-water line, low-tide elevations, bays, harbour works, islands and river mouths. These draft articles are reproduced in S. Rosenne (ed.), *League of Nations Conference for the Codification of International Law [1930]*, Dobbs Ferry, N.Y., 1975, pp. 833–6.
3 See, for example, the works by Hodgson and Alexander, and Hodgson and Smith, referred to in 'Further reading'.
4 There appears to be no uniformity in State practice as to whether the low-water line is represented by the mean low-water spring tide, the lowest low-water mark or some other low-water line. See *Whiteman*, Vol. IV, p. 141; and *O'Connell* Vol. I, pp. 171–85.
5 [1951] ICJ Rep. 116, at 128.
6 *Ibid.*, at p. 129.
7 The Court itself gave no examples of such States. States utilising straight baselines prior to the Court's judgment include Ecuador, Egypt, Iran, Saudi Arabia and Yugoslavia. See *Whiteman*, Vol. IV, p. 148, and Waldock, *op. cit.*, in 'Further reading', p. 148.
8 [1951] ICJ Rep. 116, at 133.
9 *Ibid.*
10 *Ibid.*, and cf. the Court's discussion of individual baselines of the Norwegian system at p. 142.
11 The reason for the lack of precision about the number is because it is not always possible to tell if the use by a State of a straight line as the baseline is intended to be a straight baseline *stricto sensu* or as a bay or river closing line. Most straight baselines are depicted, and reference to their legislative source given, in *Atlas of the Straight Baselines* and/or *Limits in the Seas, op. cit.* in 'Further reading'.
12 See *Limits in the Seas* No. 103 (1985).
13 See *Limits in the Seas* No. 99 (1983).
14 See *Limits in the Seas* No. 14 (1970) (Burma) and No. 42 (1972) (Ecuador).

Minor amendments were made to the Burmese system in 1977: see *UN Leg. Ser.* B/19, p. 42.

15   See *Limits in the Seas* Nos. 22 (1970), 20 (1970) and 53 (1973) respectively.
16   See *Atlas of the Straight Baselines*, p. 99.
17   *Ibid.*, p. 19.
18   Prescott, 'Straight and Archipelagic Baselines', *op. cit.* in 'Further reading', p. 38.
19   For a discussion of these and other problems, see the works cited in the general section of 'Further reading' by Beazley (pp. 12–23), Hodgson and Alexander (pp. 3–21), Prescott (pp. 51–60) and O'Connell (pp. 396–406).
20   See *Limits in the Seas* Nos. 5 (1970) and 27 (1970) respectively. There are also doubts as to whether the Portuguese bay meets the semicircle test.
21   UNCLOS I, *Official Records*, Vol. III, p. 241.
22   UNCLOS III, *Official Records*, Vol. V, p. 202. Cf. also the discussion of historic bays in Vol. II, pp. 100–11 and Vol. IV, p. 196.
23   *Op. cit.* in n. 21, Vol. II, p. 145.
24   [1982] ICJ Rep. 18, at 74 (emphasis in the original).
25   See *Whiteman*, Vol. IV, pp. 250–7.
26   *Ibid.*, pp. 236–7.
27   See *Limits in the Seas* No. 99 (1983).
28   For fuller discussion of Libya's claim, see F. Francioni, 'The Gulf of Sidra Incident (*United States* v. *Libya*) and international law' 5 *Italian Yearbook of International Law* 85–109 (1980–81); *ibid.* in Symposium on Historic Bays of the Mediterranean, *op. cit.* in 'Further reading'; and J. M. Spinnato, 'Historic and vital bays: an analysis of Libya's claim to the Gulf of Sidra', 13 *ODIL* 65 (1983).
29   See *Whiteman*, Vol. IV, p. 343.
30   Text of the Argentina–Uruguay Declaration in *Limits in the Seas*, No. 44 (1972).
31   In fact, however, neither Argentina nor Uruguay is a party to the Territorial Sea Convention, although both have signed it.
32   See *Whiteman*, Vol. IV, pp. 240, 342–3.
33   Although Ireland objected to the United Kingdom claiming a twelve-mile fishing zone around the miniscule islet of Rockall. See Symmons, *op. cit.* in 'Further reading', pp. 101–2.
34   Under the Law of the Sea Convention, unlike the Continental Shelf Convention or customary international law, the outer limit of the continental shelf is in many, but not all, cases measured from the baseline. See art. 76 and the discussion in chapter 8, pp. 124–7.
35   For a fuller discussion of the meaning of art. 121(3), see E. D. Brown, 'Rockall and the limits of national jurisdiction of the UK', 2 *Marine Policy* 181 (1978), at pp. 205–8.
36   See *Whiteman*, Vol. IV, pp. 297–300, 306.
37   See *Limits in the Seas* No. 101 (1984), which, however, questions whether in some cases this has not been done somewhat arbitrarily, particularly because of the use of submerged reefs.
38   Interpretation Act, 1971. *UN Leg. Ser.* B/16, p. 19.
39   Tokelau (Territorial Sea and Exclusive Economic Zone) Act, 1977, s. 5. *ND* VII, p. 468.
40   For example, the 1962 and 1969 amendments to the International Convention of the Prevention of Pollution of the Sea by Oil, Annex A and art. II

respectively; the 1964 European Fisheries Convention, art. 6; and the 1971 Treaty on the Prohibition of the Emplacement of Nuclear Weapons and Other Weapons of Mass Destruction on the Seabed and Ocean Floor, art. II.

41 Maritime Jurisdiction Acts, 1959 and 1964. *UN Leg. Ser.* B/15, p. 90.
42 Decree of 17 December 1967 regarding the Delimitation of the Breadth of the Territorial Sea of Kuwait. *UN Leg. Ser.* B/15, p. 96.
43 Territorial Sea and Exclusive Economic Zone Act, 1977. *UN Leg. Ser.* B/19, p. 65.
44 Territorial Sea Act 1971. *UN Leg. Ser.* B/18, p. 33.
45 Maritime Zones Law No. 22 of 1976 and Presidential Proclamation of 15 January 1977. *UN Leg. Ser.* B/19, pp. 120, 124.
46 Territorial Waters and Continental Shelf Act, 1970. *UN Leg. Ser.* B/16, p. 30.
47 *Op. cit.* n 43, ss. 2 and 6.
48 National Seas Act, 1977, Schedule 1. *ND* VII, p. 486.
49 *Op. cit.* n 44, ss. 2 and 6.
50 Maritime Zones Act No. 23 of 1981, ss. 1 and 4. *Smith*, p. 471.
51 Prescott, *The Maritime Political Boundaries of the World*, pp. 279, 313.
52 Decree No. 71/DF/416 of 26 August 1971, art. 1 *UN Leg. Ser.* B/19, p. 131. It is not clear whether the lines drawn across certain specified river mouths are river-mouth closing lines, bay closing lines, straight baselines or an illegitimate use of roadsteads as the baseline.
53 Royal Decree concerning the Territorial Waters of the Kingdom of Egypt, 1951, arts. 1 and 6. *Limits in the Seas*, No. 22 (1970).
54 Royal Decree concerning the Territorial Waters of the Kingdom of Saudi Arabia (Royal Decree No. 33 of 16 February 1958), arts, 1 and 5. *UN Leg. Ser.* B/15, p. 114.
55 *Loc. cit.* n. 53
56 *Loc. cit.* n. 54.
57 Maritime Zones (Declaration) Act 1983, s. 2. *Smith*, p. 245.
58 *Loc. cit.* in n. 38.
59 Territorial Sea and Exclusive Economic Zone Act 1978, s. 6 (Niue). *Smith*, p. 335; *loc. cit.* in 39 (Tokelau Islands).
60 Act No. 45 of 1977 concerning the Territorial Sea, Exclusive Economic Zone, Continental Shelf and other Marine Areas, art. 5. UN *Leg. Ser.* B/19, p. 21.
61 Marine Zones (Declaration) Ordinance 1983, s. 2. *Smith*, p. 459.
62 [1951] ICJ Rep. 116, at 132.
63 For an example of this, see the *Anglo-French Continental Shelf* case (1977), paras. 121–44, where France was estopped from denying that Eddystone Rock (whose status as an island was in doubt) could be used as a basepoint because of its previous acquiescence in the use of the Rock as a basepoint.

Further reading

General

L. M. Alexander, 'Baseline delimitations and maritime boundaries', 23 *VJIL* 503–36 (1983).

P. B. Beazley, *Maritime Limits and Baselines*, Hydrographic Society, Special Publication No. 2. 2nd ed., 1978.

R. D. Hodgson and L. M. Alexander, *Towards an Objective Analysis of Special Circumstances. Bays, Rivers, Coastal and Oceanic Archipelagos and Atolls*, Law of the Sea Institute, University of Rhode Island, Occasional Paper No. 13, 1972.

R. D. Hodgson and R. W. Smith, 'The informal single negotiating text (Committee II). A geographical perspective', 3 *ODIL* 225–59 (1976).

D. P. O'Connell, *The International Law of the Sea*, Vol. I, Oxford, 1982, chapters 5 and 9–11.

J. R. V. Prescott, *The Maritime Political Boundaries of the World*, London, 1985.

M. Voelckel, 'Les lignes de base dans la Convention de Genève sur la mer territoriale', 19 *AFDI* 820–37 (1973).

Straight baselines

G. Marston, 'Low tide elevations and straight baselines', 46 *BYIL* 405–23 (1972–73).

G. Francalanci, D. Romano and T. Scovazzi (eds.), *Atlas of the Straight Baselines*, Milan, 1986.

J. R. V. Prescott, 'Straight and archipelagic baselines' in G. Blake (ed.), *Maritime Boundaries and Ocean Resources*, London, 1987, pp. 38–51.

J. R. V. Prescott, 'Straight baselines: theory and practice' in E. D. Brown and R. R. Churchill (eds.), *The UN Convention on the Law of the Sea: Impact and Implementation*, Honolulu, Hawaii, 1987, pp. 288–318.

C. H. M. Waldock, 'The Anglo-Norwegian Fisheries Case', 28 *BYIL* 114–71 (1951).

The Geographer, US Department of State, *Limits in the Seas*. The straight baselines legislation of about forty States has so far been reproduced and analysed in this series.

Bays

L. J. Bouchez, *The Regime of Bays in International Law*, The Hague, 1963.

M. P. Strohl, *The International Law of Bays*, The Hague, 1963.

Symposium on Historic Bays of the Mediterranean, 11 *Syracuse Journal of International Law and Commerce* 205–415 (1984).

UN Secretariat, 'Historic Bays'. First UN Conference on the Law of the Sea, *Official Records*, Vol. I, pp. 1–38.

UN Secretariat, 'Juridical regime of historic waters, including historic bays', *ILC Yearbook*, 1962, Vol. 2, pp. 1–26.

G. Westerman, *The Juridical Bay*, Oxford, 1987.

Islands

D. W. Bowett, *The Legal Regime of Islands in International Law*, Dobbs Ferry, N.Y., 1979.

H. Dipla, *Le régime juridique des îles dans le droit international de la mer*, Paris, 1984.

N. Papadakis, *The International Legal Regime of Artificial Islands*, Leyden, 1977.

C. R. Symmons, *The Maritime Zones of Islands in International Law*, The Hague, 1979.

CHAPTER THREE
Internal waters

Definition

Internal, or national, or interior, waters are those waters which lie on the landward side of the baseline from which the territorial sea and other maritime zones are measured (TSC, art. 5(1); LOSC, art. 8; see chapter two). Thus, as we saw in the previous chapter, internal waters of a maritime character mostly comprise bays, estuaries and ports, and waters enclosed by straight baselines. Waters enclosed by the baseline drawn around the outermost islands of an archipelagic State have a special status, which is considered in chapter six; but each separate island in the archipelago is entitled to its own baseline, drawn according to the normal principles, so that its ports, bays and so on may be constituted as internal waters (LOSC, art. 50).

Legal status

The baseline serves, with rather more precision, the same purpose in defining the limits of a State's territory as did the more arbitrary test used by Hale in the seventeenth century, albeit for the rather different purpose of defining the limits of the jurisdiction of the common law courts in municipal law: 'That arm or branch of the sea which lies within the *fauces terrae*, where a man may reasonably discern between shore and shore is or at least may be within the body of a county'. This view of internal waters as an integral part of the coastal State remains unaltered today, and for this reason they are not the subject of detailed regulations in the Law of the Sea Conventions. The coastal State enjoys full territorial sovereignty over them. Consequently, there is no right of innocent passage through internal waters such as exists through the territorial sea. The single exception to this rule is that where straight baselines are drawn along an indented coast, enclosing as internal waters areas which had not previously been considered as such, a right of innocent passage continues to exist through those waters, at least for parties to the Territorial Sea and Law of the Sea Conventions (TSC, art. 5 (2); LOSC, art. 8(2)). That is the position under the Conventions: the position if such lines are drawn in exercise of rights under customary law is unclear, the *Anglo–Norwegian Fisheries* case making no reference to the preservation of rights of innocent passsage in these circumstances.

Two particular aspects of coastal States' sovereignty over internal waters have given rise to much State practice, and will be considered separately. These are the questions of access to ports, and of the exercise of jurisdiction over foreign ships in ports.

The right of access to ports and other internal waters

The existence of sovereignty over internal waters and absence of any general right of innocent passage through them logically implies the absence of any right in customary international law for foreign ships to enter a State's ports. There is, indeed, very little support in State practice for such a right, except for ships in distress seeking safety, which enjoy a right of entry recognised in cases such as the *Creole* (1853) and the *Rebecca* (1929). A much quoted *dictum* from the award in the *Aramco* arbitration in 1958 stated that 'According to a great principle of public international law, the ports of every State must be open to foreign vessels and can only be closed when the vital interests of the State so require.'[1] While it is undoubtedly true that the international ports of a State are presumed to be open to international merchant traffic (the right to exclude foreign warships is undoubted), it is very doubtful whether this presumption has acquired the status of a *right* in customary law. Moreover, any such right would be subject to substantial restrictions.

First, it is clear that States have the right to nominate those of their ports which are to be open to international trade — that is, to those ships which the State chooses or binds itself by treaty to admit to its ports. This rule, which can be traced back at least as far as *Bates* case (UK) in 1610, often finds expression in laws designating ports of entry for customs and immigration purposes.

Secondly, it is generally admitted that a State may close even its international ports to protect its vital interests without thereby violating customary international law, and it would be difficult to establish that any interests invoked by a State were inadequate to justify closure. Furthermore, States have a wide right to prescribe conditions for access to their ports. The International Court in the *Nicaragua* case noted that internal waters are subject to the sovereignty of the State and that it is 'by virtue of its sovereignty that the coastal State may regulate access to its ports'[2]. Similarly, the US Supreme Court in *Patterson* v. *Bark Eudora* (1903), stated that 'the implied consent to enter our harbours may be withdrawn, and if this consent may be wholly withdrawn, it may be extended upon such terms and conditions as the government sees fit to impose'[3]. It is, however, possible that closures or conditions of access which are patently unreasonable or discriminatory might be held to amount to *abus de droit*, for which the coastal State might be internationally responsible even if there were no right of entry to the port.

If there is no general right of entry into ports for foreign merchant ships in customary law, the position in treaty law is very different, for many treaties confer rights of entry. Most commonly, such rights are found in bilateral treaties of 'Friendship, Commerce and Navigation', whose numbers run into many hundreds. Sometimes, more specific agreements have been concluded: for example, bilateral agreements giving rights of entry were made in connection with the voyages of the United States Nuclear Ship *Savannah* in 1964.[4] In addition, the multilateral Convention and Statute on the International Regime of Maritime Ports, 1923, provides for a reciprocal right of access to, and equality of treatment within, maritime ports; it has not, however, been widely ratified. The provisions of the EEC Treaty on non-discrimination and free movement of goods would seem to give the twelve Member States a similar reciprocal right of access to each other's ports[5]. Thus, despite the absence of any clearly established right of entry to ports in customary law, most States enjoy such rights under treaty.

Finally, it should be mentioned that although rights of access, to the extent that they exist, imply a right to leave ports, the right of exit is subject to important limitations. Thus States are entitled to arrest ships in port, in accordance with their normal legal processes — for example, seizure of vessels for customs offences. Similarly, ships in port are liable to arrest as security in civil actions or actions *in rem* against the ship itself, though under the 1952 Brussels Convention on the Arrest of Sea-going Ships, ships of party States are subject to civil arrest only in the case of maritime claims. Furthermore, States may detain ships which are in an unseaworthy condition, or otherwise unfit to proceed to sea. States may also require foreign ships to obtain clearing papers from the port authorities, certifying compliance with customs and health formalities, before they leave port. These rights flow from the sovereignty of the State in its ports, and submission to them is arguably an implied condition of admission to the ports. It should be noted that port State jurisdiction is considerably extended in the case of pollution offences by the Law of the Sea Convention: the relevant provisions are discussed in chapter fifteen.

Foreign ships may also seek access to navigable rivers and canals in a State. These, too, constitute internal waters, but are in practice treated differently from ports. Thus, while there is no right of access to navigable rivers situated wholly within the boundaries of a single State, in the case of international rivers, which flow through the territory, or constitute the boundary, of more than one State, wider rights exist. Following the precedent set in the Final Act of the Congress of Vienna in 1815, the major international rivers in Europe are subject to free navigation established by treaty. The regulation of river traffic was at one time largely in the hands of commissions, such as those responsible for the Rhine, the Elbe and the Oder — though these last two do not now exist. The difficulties attending the revision of the convention concerning the Danube illustrate many of the problems of fluvial law. When the 1948 Belgrade Convention replaced the 1921 Definitive Statute of the Danube, it preserved freedom of navigation but deprived non-riparian users, among them the United Kingdom, the United States and France, of their participation in the control of river traffic, leading those States to withhold recognition of the reconstituted Danube Commission. Treaties or unilateral declarations allowing free navigation, subject always to regulations imposed by riparian States, have at various times been made in respect of many major rivers around the world, and a multilateral treaty to this effect — the Barcelona Convention on the Regime of Navigable Waterways of International Concern — was concluded in 1921, although it has not been widely ratified. But, although the matter is not free of controversy, it seems that the predominant view is that, in the absence of a subsisting treaty right, ships — or at least the ships of non-riparian States — do not enjoy a right of access to any river, national or international.

Canals are in principle to be treated in the same manner as natural waterways, but again the practical importance of the interoceanic canals has resulted in their express 'internationalisation'. Thus, in the 1977 Panama Canal Treaties, and the 1957 Declaration in which Egypt affirmed its intention to respect the terms of the 1888 Convention of Constantinople concerning the Suez Canal, all States are declared to have the right of free navigation through the canals, which remain, however, under the sovereignty of the State concerned — although in the case of the Panama Canal the United States of America has been given the right to manage the canal until the year 2000, in continuation of the extensive powers which it formerly enjoyed under the 1903 Hay-Bunau-Varilla Treaty.

Jurisdiction in internal waters

By entering foreign ports and other internal waters, ships put themselves within the territorial sovereignty of the coastal State. Accordingly, that State is entitled to enforce its laws against the ship and those on board, subject to the normal rules concerning sovereign and diplomatic immunities, which arise chiefly in the case of State-owned ships. But since ships are more or less self-contained units, having not only a comprehensive body of laws — those of the flag State — applicable to them while in foreign ports, but also a system for the enforcement of those flag State laws through the powers of the captain and the local consul, coastal States commonly enforce their laws only in cases where their interests are engaged; matters relating solely to the 'internal economy' of the ship are left to the authorities of the flag State.

While the details of enforcement policy may vary from State to State, the foregoing statement is a serviceable summary of the general practice of States. However, States have given different explanations for the adoption of this practice, and a distinction is commonly drawn between Anglo-American and French positions on the matter. The Anglo-American position, summarised in the United Kingdom reply to the Hague 'Questionnaire' of 1929 and in American cases such as *Cunard S. S. Co.* v. *Mellon* (1923), is that the coastal State's jurisdiction over foreign ships in its ports is complete, but that it may, as a matter of policy, choose to forgo the exertion of its jurisdiction. France, on the other hand, is said to adopt the system of 'partial désintéressement', according to which the coastal State has in law no jurisdiction over purely internal affairs on foreign ships in its ports. This view derives from the *Avis* of the Conseil d'Etat in the case of the *Sally* and the *Newton* in 1806, on which subsequent French practice was modelled. It was held there that two intercrew assaults were within the sole jurisdiction of the flag State consul. That *Avis* has been taken as setting out a general rule of customary international law, although, as Charteris points out, there was in any event in force at the time a convention with the United States (under whose flag the *Sally* and the *Newton* sailed) which aimed to delimit coastal and consular jurisdiction, and gave consuls competence over incidents confined to the interiors of their ships. Moreover it should be remembered that this case, and almost all others cited in support of the 'French doctrine', were decided at a time when the sovereignty of the coastal State over internal and territorial waters was not a settled part of French jurisprudence (cf. chapter four, below, and the case of the *Johmo* (France, 1970)).

Despite any differences between the theoretical bases of French and Anglo-American practice, it is clear that the practice of these States, and of States in general, is remarkably consistent. Thus local jurisdiction will be asserted when the offence affects the peace or good order of the port either literally (for example, customs or immigration offences), or in some constructive sense. A French court, no doubt a little more sensitive to violence than the court in 1806 had been, decided in the *Tempest* (1859) that some crimes, such as homicide, had an intrinsic gravity which, apart from any actual disturbance to the port resulting from their commission, warranted local intervention. Other States have taken the same view: for example, the United States in the cases of *Wildenhus* (1887) (homicide) and *People* v. *Wong Cheng* (1922) (opium smoking), and Mexico in the case of *Public Minister* v. *Jensen* (1894) (shipwreck due to master's imprudence did not compromise tranquillity of port).

Coastal States will also assert jurisdiction where their intervention is requested by the captain, or consul of the flag State, of the ship. The Belgian
cases of *Watson* (1856) and *Sverre* (1907), both involving thefts on board
foreign ships, illustrate this point; and the Costa Rican case of *State* v.
Dave Johnson Plazen (1927), in which local authorities intervened after the
victim of a murder on board a foreign ship was transferred to a hospital on-
shore, was decided on a similar ground, although it could equally well have
been decided on the 'gravity' principle.

Thirdly, coastal authorities commonly intervene in cases where a non-
crew member is involved. This ground was recognised in the decisions in
the *Cordoba* (1912) in France and the *Redstart* (1895) in Italy, for instance.
Some States, such as Japan, have asserted the right to intervene in cases involving their nationals. Others claim the right to remove 'wanted persons'
from foreign ships in their ports. This was done in 1949 when one *Eisler*,
wanted by the British police for extradition to the United States, was removed from a Polish ship lying off Southampton, despite protests by the
captain and the flag State authorities; and the United States, approving the
removal of one *Menez* from an American ship in 1884, of which he was a
crew member, while it was in a Cuban port, noted that American police
frequently went on board foreign ships in their ports to arrest people accused
of crimes under United States law.[6]

The United States asserted an even wider right in the *Medvid* incident in
1985. Medvid, a crew member of a Soviet freighter, apparently tried to
escape from the ship while it was in a United States port, in order to seek
asylum. While the local immigration authorities released him for return to
the ship after interviewing him and concluding that he was not seeking
asylum, the United States government asserted that it had a clear right to
remove him from the ship, by force if necessary, if it was suspected that he
was being taken from the United States against his will.[7]

Coastal States will, of course, exercise their jurisdiction in matters which
do not concern solely the 'internal economy' of foreign ships. Pollution,
pilotage and navigation laws are routinely enforced against such vessels
and, as we have noted, ships may be arrested in the course of civil proceedings in the coastal State. But, with the exception of the categories described
above, States do not exercise their jurisdiction in respect of the internal affairs of foreign ships in their ports even though, as a matter of strict law,
they would be entitled to do so because of the voluntary entry of those ships
within their territorial jurisdiction. Indeed, it is common practice for States
to conclude bilateral consular conventions providing for the reservation of
jurisdiction over matters of internal discipline, etc., to the authorities of
the flag State.[8]

This reasoning will clearly not apply to ships driven into internal waters
by *force majeure* or distress, and accordingly international law demands that

they be given a degree of immunity from coastal State jurisdiction. They are entitled to be excused liabilities which arise inevitably from their entry in distress — for example, liability to pay import duties on their cargoes, or liability to arrest (see, for example, the *Rebecca* or *Kate A. Hoff* case (1929), the *Brig Concord* (USA, 1815)). It has even been held, in the *Creole* arbitration (1853), that a coastal State had no right to release slaves on board a foreign ship driven into its ports by distress, even though its laws prohibited slavery; however it is most unlikely that the monstrous illegality of slavery would today be considered to be protected by the essentially humanitarian distress rule. Ships in distress must comply with some laws, which it is reasonable to expect them to observe once they reach the relative calm of the port. In the Canadian case of *Cushin and Lewis* v. *R.* (1935), for example, such ships were held bound to observe regulations concerning the reporting-in of cargo on arrival at a port. There is also some authority, such as the *Carlo Alberto* case (France, 1832), for the view that vessels forced to seek refuge in the port of a State in which they had intended to made an unlawful landing enjoy no immunity at all from local jurisdiction.

The essential ground for the application of local law to visiting ships is the temporary allegiance which they owe to the territorial sovereign. Sometimes the coastal State has sought to impose on foreign ships obligations which, if they are to be complied with in the State's ports, must be complied with throughout the voyage. Notable examples are the United States liquor laws of the 1920s, prohibiting the carriage of alcohol in American waters; laws subjecting foreign shipping companies serving United States ports to a wide range of duties to disclose details of their trade, in América and elsewhere, and to American anti-trust laws; and laws regulating the employment of seamen on foreign ships frequenting American ports (see the *Incres Steamship* case (USA, 1963)). All these exercises of jurisdiction have been vigorously protested by the flag States concerned, with varying degrees of success. They are objectionable both on the ground that they offend against the rule of comity concerning the 'internal economy' of visiting ships and, more seriously, that in some respects at least they exceed the limits of jurisdiction which can properly be claimed on the basis of the temporary allegiance owed by foreign ships in ports.

Notes

1 27 *ILR* 167, at 212. See further Lowe, *op. cit.*, in 'Further reading'.
2 [1986] ICJ Rep. 14, at 111.
3 190 US 169, at 178.
4 *ND* II, p. 654.
5 See the *Mary Poppins* case; cf., *O'Connell*, vol. II, p. 850
6 For the *Eisler* incident, see 26 *BYIL* 468 (1949); for the *Menez* incident, see Moore, *Digest*, II, p. 278.

7   See 80 *AJIL* 622–627 (1986).
8   See, e.g., the British Consular Relations Act 1968, and Orders made there-under implementing bilateral consular treaties.

Further reading

Ports and other internal waters

A. H. Charteris. 'The legal position of merchantmen in foreign ports and national waters', 1 BYIL 45–96 (1920).

V. D. Degan, 'Internal waters', 17 *NYIL* 3–44 (1986).

P. Fedozzi, 'La condition juridique des navires de commerce', 10 *Receuil des Cours* 5–222 (1925).

F. Francioni, 'Criminal jurisdiction over foreign merchant vessels in territorial waters', 1 *Italian Yearbook of International Law* 27–41 (1975).

P. C. Jessup, *The Law of Territorial Waters and Maritime Jurisdiction*, New York, 1927.

R. Laun, 'Le régime international des ports', 15 *Receuil des Cours* 1–143 (1926).

J. L. Lenoir, 'Criminal jurisdiction over foreign merchant ships', 10 *Tulane Law Review* 13–35 (1935).

A. V. Lowe, 'The right of entry into maritime ports in international law', 14 *San Diego Law Review* 597–622 (1977).

Rivers and canals

R. R. Baxter, *The Law of International Waterways, with particular regard to Inter-oceanic Canals*, Cambridge, Mass., 1964.

H. Fortuin, 'The regime of navigable waterways of international concern and the Statute of Barcelona' 7 *Netherlands International Law Review* 125–43 (1960).

S. Gorove, *Law and Politics of the Danube. An Interdisciplinary Study*, The Hague, 1964.

R. Zacklin and L. Caflisch (eds.), *The Legal Regime of International Rivers and Lakes*, Dordrecht, 1981.

CHAPTER FOUR
The territorial sea

Development of the concept

In this section we outline the development of the concept of the territorial sea as a maritime zone. The questions of the status of the sea bed underlying the territorial sea and of the air space above it arose separately from the question of the status of the waters themselves, and accordingly we defer consideration of them to the following section.

Although the recent legislation of several States, such as Guyana, Pakistan and the Seychelles, declares that the State's sovereignty 'extends and has always extended' to its territorial sea,[1] such statements are historically incorrect: the true picture of the development of the concept is rather more complex.

Since the replacement of the Holy Roman Empire by a system of independent sovereign States having definite boundaries — what has been termed the 'birth of territoriality', in the sixteenth century — it has been generally accepted that coastal States enjoy some rights to regulate in their own interests activities in the seas adjoining their coasts. Even during the great debates in the seventeenth century between Grotius, as advocate of the freedom of the seas, and the proponents of 'closed seas' (see chapters one and eleven), this much was agreed. Grotius, for example, did not claim that all the seas were open to use by all men. Borrowing a distinction drawn by the Italian civil lawyer Baldus in the fourteenth century, between rights of property (*dominium*) and rights of jurisdiction or control (*imperium*) in the sea, Grotius argued that there could be no property rights in the high seas but seems to have admitted the existence of jurisdiction without property rights in coastal waters which could be effectively controlled from the land.

Grotius' position was developed during the seventeenth century by writers such as Pontanus in Holland, Welwood in Scotland, and Meadows in England, who abandoned his distinction between property and jurisdictional rights in the marginal belt. On the basis that property rights demand the existence of jurisdiction for their protection and that the right to exclude, for example, foreign fishermen by the exercise of jurisdiction is tantamount to the existence of property rights, the idea gained ground of a simple distinction between high seas, free and open to all, and coastal waters susceptible to appropriation by the adjacent State. By the end of that century this idea was well established: for instance, the influential work by Bynkershoek, *De dominio maris dissertatio*, published in 1702, was based upon the twin pillars of the freedom of the high seas and the 'sovereignty' of the coastal State over its adjacent sea.

Although Bynkershoek himself regarded this 'sovereignty' as complete, and as including the right to deny foreign ships passage through the territorial sea, his view was not generally shared and was not to survive. Vattel, whose treatise *Le droit des gens* was published in 1758, took the part of earlier writers such as Grotius and Gentilis, and declared that ships of all States enjoyed a right of innocent passage through the territorial sea. While the exact scope of this right has been questioned in several respects, such as its extension to warships, its existence has not been seriously challenged since the early nineteenth century.

As the distinction between high seas and the territorial sea (or 'territorial waters', as it was, and is, commonly known) crystallised, two matters remained unresolved: first, the question of the width of those waters, which we consider below, and secondly, the question of the precise juridical nature of coastal States' rights over the territorial sea. Some writers claimed that coastal States either had proprietorial rights in their territorial seas, or at least enjoyed sovereignty or plenary jurisdiction over them. The practice of many States supported this view: for example, by the early nineteenth century British and American jurisdictional claims were premised upon the existence of a belt of maritime territory surrounding a State, and the civil codes adopted in the middle of that century by several Latin American States treated territorial seas as integral parts of the State. On the other hand, States such as France and Spain did not claim ownership or sovereignty over the territorial sea, but merely jurisdictional competence over adjacent waters for specific purposes — notably defence and the regulation of customs and fishing. These claims had not then been consolidated into a single claim to maritime territory — indeed, the distances over which jurisdiction was claimed often varied according to the subject matter of the regulation (see chapter seven). This approach was more easily reconciled with the existence of a right of innocent passage than the sovereignty doctrine, and found some enthusiastic advocates. The theory was expounded in various forms — neatly summarised, along with other theories, in Fauchille's *Traité de droit international public* (1925) — but found its classic exposition in an article by La Pradelle in 1898.[2] He argued that States enjoyed only a 'bundle of servitudes' (*faisceau de servitudes*) over coastal waters, permitting them to exercise jurisdiction in the measure necessary for the protection of their interests, and accepted the corollary that if the existence of a right of jurisdiction were to be questioned the burden lay upon the coastal State to prove that it did exist — quite the opposite of the presumption flowing from the 'sovereignty' doctrine.

These two broad approaches coexisted for several decades. They were considered by the English Court for Crown Cases Reserved in the *Franconia* case (*R v. Keyn* (1876)), in which the question of the status of the territorial sea arose. Keyn was the commander of the German ship *Franconia*, which collided with the British ship *Strathclyde* two and a half miles off Dover beach, causing the death of thirty-eight of the *Strathclyde*'s passengers. Keyn was prosecuted for manslaughter and convicted by an English court. He appealed on the ground that the court lacked jurisdiction to try him, because he was a foreigner and at the material time sailing on a foreign ship on the high seas. The Crown maintained that the collision, having occurred within three miles of the shore, had occurred within the realm and so within British jurisdiction. After an extensive review of the conflicting authorities, contained in a set of judgments of great learning, the Court of Crown Cases Reserved decided, by a majority of seven to six (a fourteenth judge would have joined the majority, but died before judgment was given) to allow the appeal. The common thread running through the majority judgments was the view that even though Great Britain might be entitled to claim a territorial sea, it had not expressly done so, and until legislation repaired the omission British jurisdiction did not extend to foreigners and foreign ships beyond British shores. Some judges went further and argued that Britain could not, consistently with international law, apply the whole of its criminal law to foreigners in the territorial sea.

The *Franconia* decision was clearly not expected by the British government, and two years later English law was brought back into line with the view of international law which Great Britain had taken throughout the nineteenth century, by the enactment of the Territorial Waters Jurisdiction Act, 1878. That Act reaffirmed the 'rightful jurisdiction' of the Crown over territorial waters, which were 'deemed by international law to be within the territorial sovereignty of Her Majesty'. This position has been consistently adhered to ever since, although, as will be seen, the Act was the subject of much critical comment, and there were occasional doubts on the question expressed privately within the British government.

Doubts concerning the juridical nature of the territorial sea survived into the present century. States such as France, Italy, Russia and the Ottoman Empire continued to claim separate jurisdictional zones for various purposes, rather than sovereignty and plenary jurisdiction over a belt of maritime territory as was claimed, for example, by the countries of the British Empire (which had agreed upon a single three-mile limit for all jurisdictional purposes at the 1923 Imperial Conference), the United States, the

Netherlands and the Scandinavian States. Jurists were similarly divided in
their views, as is evident, for instance, from the debates of the International
Law Association and of the Committee of Experts preparing for the Hague
Codification Conference, both in the 1920s. With hindsight it is possible to
see that the trend in doctrine and State practice was steadily towards recognition of coastal States' sovereignty over their territorial seas. Governments had repeatedly had the question of the juridical status of those waters
put before them directly, in the context of various diplomatic exchanges
from the early nineteenth century onwards, and indirectly through the deliberations of influential bodies such as the Institute of International Law.
And in the twenty years preceding the 1930 Hague Conference the question had arisen in several connections — notably in relation to the limits of
neutrality and naval warfare during World War I; the work of the 1919
Conference on Aerial Navigation (see below); the dispute over the application of the United States' liquor laws to foreign ships (see chapter seven);
and the preparation for the Hague Conference itself. In each case, it was
evident that support for the principle of coastal State sovereignty over the
territorial sea was growing.

The replies of governments to the Schedule of Points circulated before
the Hague Conference showed that most respondents preferred the sovereignty doctrine. Some, such as France and Poland, considered the juridical
status of the territorial sea unsettled; and other States which had not replied
to the Schedule, such as Greece and Czechoslovakia, argued at the conference against the ascription of sovereignty to the coastal State. But it was
clear that, despite some reluctance to use a word so burdened with implications and overtones deriving from its use in connection with land territory, there was general agreement that the principle of coastal sovereignty
should be included in any draft treaty. The final text forwarded to the conference by its Territorial Waters Committee accordingly provided that:

The territory of a State includes a belt of sea described in this Convention as the
territorial sea. Sovereignty over this belt is exercised subject to the conditions prescribed by the present Convention and the other rules of international law.[3]

The text was not adopted as a convention, mainly because of a failure to
agree on the vital question of the breadth of the territorial sea. Nonetheless, there has been no serious challenge to the principle of coastal sovereignty over the territorial sea since the Hague Conference, and the 1930
conference may fairly be regarded as the occasion when the doubts over
that sea's juridical status, which had persisted right up to the preceding decade, were finally dispelled.

In the years following the Hague Conference, the few States which had
not espoused the sovereignty doctrine came to do so, as did States gaining
their independence. That is not to say that the municipal law of every State

treats the sea in the same way as the land, so that, for example, municipal laws automatically apply there. Thus British territorial waters remain outside the 'realm', and British laws apply therein only to the extent specifically provided.[4] But for the purposes of international law, States have sovereignty, and the plenary jurisdiction which is its concomitant, over the territorial sea. This principle was sufficiently well established in State practice for François to adopt it in his first report to the ILC in 1950, and for it to survive, almost unquestioned, throughout the ILC debates and the 1958 Geneva Conference. Such discussion as there was centred upon the relationship between coastal State sovereignty and the right of innocent passage, which we consider below. In order to emphasise that the right of innocent passage rendered coastal States' rights less extensive than those over their land territory, the Hague formula was amended so as to provide that:

(1) The sovereignty of a State extends, beyond its land territory and its internal waters, to a belt of sea adjacent to its coast, described as the territorial sea.
(2) This sovereignty is exercised subject to the provisions of these articles and to other rules of international law. [TSC, art. 1]

A substantially similar provision, in which there has been inserted a reference to archipelagic waters after that to internal waters, appears in the Law of the Sea Convention (art. 2(1), (3)).

Legal status of the bed, subsoil and superjacent air space of the territorial sea

We have seen that during the first three decades of this century the sovereignty of States over their territorial seas, subject to the existence of the right of innocent passage for foreign ships through those seas, gained general acceptance. Although claims to sovereignty over the superjacent air space and subjacent sea bed gained acceptance at about the same time, this development was distinct from the consolidation of the sovereignty theory in respect of the waters themselves: thus States which had for many years claimed sovereignty over the waters did not at first claim sovereignty over the air and sea bed in the zone.

The question of the status of the air space above States' territory and territorial sea arose following the use of balloons during the Franco-Prussian war in 1870–71. In the period following that war, jurists divided in their views on the question: some, such as Fauchille, proposed that the air be treated as high seas, free for the use of all, subject to rights of 'conservation' up to a height of 1,500 m; others, such as Mérighnac, thought that States should enjoy sovereignty in their air space. This division mirrored the contemporary doctrinal dispute over the status of the territorial sea itself. Although an international congress in 1910 failed to resolve the question, the practice during the First World War was to treat the air space as subject to the sovereignty of the State. Some States had taken this position earlier, as the United Kingdom had in its Aerial Navigation Act of 1911. Agreement was reached at the 1919 Paris Conference on a Convention for the Regulation of Aerial Navigation, article 1 of which provided that:

The High Contracting Parties recognize that every Power has complete and exclusive sovereignty over the air space above its territory.

For the purpose of the present Convention, the territory of a State shall be understood as including the national territory ... and the territorial waters adjacent thereto.

This convention was also a significant step towards the general recognition of sovereignty over the territorial sea itself. Since 1919 sovereignty over the superjacent air space has been a firm principle of international law, enshrined in article 2 of the 1944 Convention on International Civil Aviation, article 2 of the Territorial Sea Convention, and article 2(2) of the Law of the Sea Convention. No right of innocent passage for aircraft has ever been admitted, the dangers to the coastal State inherent in their speed and ability to avoid detection being considered to preclude such a right.

The question of the status of the bed of the territorial sea was ignored for the most part until the present century, it being assumed either that the bed was subject to the coastal State's sovereignty, or that it was not, according to each writer's views concerning the status of the waters of the territorial sea. The lack of any significant interest in use of the sea bed — apart from the construction of piers and submarine mines at relatively short distances from the shore — resulted in there being little attention paid to the bed as a separate legal concept and little State practice from which rules of international law concerning the bed might have been deduced. While this shortage of practice was recognised by the drafters of the 1930 Hague Conference text on the territorial sea, it was agreed that there should be included an article stating that 'the territory of a coastal State includes also the air space above the territorial sea, as well as the bed of the sea, and the subsoil'.[5] Again, no provision was made for a right of 'innocent passage' through the subsoil, for the obvious reason that such a right would amount to a freedom to mine and tunnel the subsoil. Sovereignty over the bed and subsoil, once articulated and accepted at the Hague Conference, was readily incorporated into international law, and was reiterated without opposition in the Territorial Sea Convention (art. 2) and the Law of the Sea Convention (art. 2(2)). Nevertheless, the question of the time at which this right of sovereignty became established for particular States has arisen in a number of cases in federal jurisdictions where ownership of the bed has been disputed between the federal and provincial governments. Such cases have not, however, provided definitive answers to the question.[6]

Thus, although the extension of sovereignty to bed, waters and air space alike was recognised by 1930, and is now taken as one of the basic rules of the law of the sea, the process by which this came about was more complex: as Marston has put it:

... the rule for the bed and subsoil of the territorial sea was conceived later than the corresponding rule for the superjacent waters and later even than that for the superjacent airspace, although the subsequent crystallization process resulted in a unitary customary rule and not three separate rules.[7]

The breadth of the territorial sea

Throughout the entire history of the territorial sea, the question of its breadth has been a matter of controversy. Early practice and doctrine, in the sixteenth and seventeenth centuries, used vague criteria such as the limits of visibility to determine the extent of the waters over which control was claimed. Later, writers such as Grotius and Bynkershoek did much to promote the tendency, already evident in the practice of some States, to replace this unsatisfactory criterion with the rule that coastal States' rights over marginal waters extended up to the point at which those waters could be controlled by shore-based cannon. This 'cannonshot' doctrine was probably not intended to support the establishment of a continuous belt of maritime territory along the whole coast, but rather to acknowledge the possibility of 'pockets' of control by actual cannon present at various places on shore, this being in accordance with Dutch and Mediterranean State practice of the day. Scandinavian States, on the other hand, did not employ the cannonshot rule, but claimed maritime *dominium* over fixed distances from the shore along the whole coastline, regardless of the presence or absence of shore batteries. These distances were progressively narrowed from those claimed around the sixteenth century, and had largely settled at the four-mile Scandinavian 'league' by the mid-eighteenth century.

The 'cannonshot' and 'fixed distance' approaches coexisted for several generations, and eventually came together. The decisive move towards fusion of the two approaches came at the end of the eighteenth century. In 1782 Galiani suggested that it would be reasonable to adopt a three-mile limit along the whole coast, rather than await the establishment of coastal batteries at any particular point. The distance was chosen as a matter of reasonableness and convenience, cannon of the day having a range of under three miles: it was not chosen as the precise range of actual cannon. The three-mile limit was adopted for neutrality purposes by the United States at the beginning of the War of the Coalition in 1793. Thenceforward the 'cannonshot' principle was commonly treated as generating a continuous belt of maritime territory three miles in breadth, although this belied its origin. The three-mile rule gained widespread and rapid acceptance; it was recognised, for example, by Lord Stowell in *The Anna* (Great Britain, 1805). The survival of this distance throughout the nineteenth century, despite increases in the range of artillery, is explicable by the interest of the major naval powers, which were its main supporters, in preserving the maximum freedom of navigation for their merchant fleets and warships.

Although the three-mile limit was adhered to by most of the major powers throughout the last century, it was never unanimously accepted. The Scandinavian countries consistently claimed four miles, and several other countries, such as Spain, claimed zones of more than three miles for specific purposes (see chapter seven). Indeed, shortly before the First World War, France, Italy, Russia, Spain and the Ottoman Empire all claimed the right to jurisdiction up to any distance from shore reasonable for the control of specific activities such as fishing or smuggling, within the overall limit of the actual range of coastal artillery — claims which evidenced growing dissatisfaction with the three-mile limit and which the British Foreign Office thought might lead to its demise as a rule of law. But these wider claims were not publicly admitted by States claiming only three miles. Great Britain for example, until the late 1960s, when the practice seems to have been abandoned, often issued protests saying that 'His Majesty's Government are obliged to place firmly on record that they do not recognise territorial jurisdiction over waters outside the limit of three miles from the coast; nor will they regard British vessels engaged in their lawful pursuits on the high seas as being subject to any measures which the [coastal State] Government may see fit to promulgate,'[8] or something similar. The effect of such 'persistent objection' was that the wider claims were not 'opposable' to the objecting State. Consequently, it is meaningless to speak of a single limit for territorial sea claims existing at any one time. Between three-mile States the three-mile rule operated; between States claiming, say, six miles that distance was recognised. Between different groups many disputes arose, of which the Anglo-Spanish dispute (which ran throughout most of the nineteenth and early twentieth centuries) described by Masterson is but one of many examples. This difficulty persists to the present day, and we return to it below.

The 1930 Hague Conference attempted to reach agreement upon the width of the territorial sea, and failed. At the final meeting of its Territorial Waters Committee, twenty States sought territorial seas of three miles, twelve sought six miles, and the four Scandinavian States sought recognition of their own historic four-mile claim; of these States, several wanted the right to claim contiguous zones beyond the territorial sea. No general agreement was reached. Consequently Gidel, writing four years later, expressed the view that there was no rule of international law fixing the limit of the territorial sea, except in the negative sense that the validity of claims of up to three miles could not be denied. Subsequently, both the First (1958) and the Second (1960) UN Conferences on the Law of the Sea tried to agree upon a limit, without success.

Although a proposal for a six-mile territorial sea coupled with an additional six-mile fishery limit failed to adopted at the second UN conference by only one vote, it is evident that such a compromise would have been short-lived even if it had been adopted. Whereas in 1960 the great majority of States claimed territorial seas of less than twelve miles, by the closing stages of UNCLOS III the position was dramatically reversed, and the great majority of States claimed territorial seas of twelve miles or more (see appendix for current claims). It should, however, be noted that some of the wider 'territorial sea' claims have a juridical content different from that embodied in the Territorial Sea Convention: for example, Uruguay allows full freedom of navigation and overflight in the outer 188 miles of its 200 mile territorial sea.[9] The steady shift towards wider territorial seas, especially among newly independent States, is a reflection of the desire to bring coastal waters — and the fishing, pollution and so on conducted, often by foreign vessels, within them — under national control. Indeed, many of the States claiming three-or twelve-mile territorial seas also claim jurisdiction over matters such as fishing and pollution out to much greater distances. The trend towards wider jurisdiction would seem irresistible.

The Law of the Sea Convention sets the limit of territorial waters at twelve miles (art. 3) in accordance with the clearly dominant trend in State practice. Accordingly, the present position in international law appears to be as follows. For parties to the Law of the Sea Convention, and all other States recognising the lawfulness of territorial sea claims up to at least twelve miles, the twelve-mile limit will prevail. Wider claims will not be recognised, except as between States making or otherwise recognising such claims: thus, for example, 200 mile claims would be opposable to Argentina and Brazil, both of whom claim 200 mile territorial seas, but not to, say, India, which claims only twelve miles. In theory, States making narrower claims, notably the remaining three-mile States, would not be bound even by the twelve-mile claims in so far as they have persistently objected to them. However, since the United States announced in 1983 that it would respect claims of up to twelve miles which accord to other States their rights and freedoms under international law[10] — chiefly rights of passage — it seems unlikely that there is any State in the position of a persistent objector in this matter.

The twelve-mile limit is now firmly established in international law, and it is likely that the practice, if not always the legislation, of all States will in the near future be brought into line with this limit. One legal aspect of this development is the existence of duties owed by coastal States to foreign vessels in their territorial seas. Thus Judge Fitzmaurice in his separate opinion in the *Fisheries Jurisdiction* case (1973) said:

The territorial sea involves responsibilities as well as rights, ... for example policing and maintaining order; buoying and marking channels and reefs, sandbanks and other obstacles; keeping navigable channels clear and giving notice of danger of navigation; providing rescue services, lighthouses, lightships, bell-buoys, etc.[11]

Such reasoning had earlier led Judge McNair to state, in his dissenting opinion in the *Anglo-Norwegian Fisheries* case (1951):

International law does not say to a State: 'You are entitled to claim territorial waters if you want them.' No maritime State can refuse them. International law imposes upon a maritime State certain obligations and confers upon it certain rights arising out of the sovereignty which it exercises over its maritime territory. The possession of this territory is not optional, not dependent upon the will of the State, but compulsory.[12]

This notion of a territorial sea automatically appurtenant to coastal States, which had been expressed by the Permanent Court of Arbitration in the *Grisbadarna* case as early as 1909, is also implicit in both the 1958 Territorial Sea Convention, article 1 of which, as we have seen, prescribes the extension of sovereignty to that sea, rather than simply leaving it to States to claim such sovereignty, and the Law of the Sea Convention (art. 2) which follows the 1958 text. Similarly, the requirement that a State 'give appropriate publicity to any danger to navigation, of which it has knowledge, within its territorial sea' (TSC, art. 15(2); LOSC, art. 24(2)), by imposing duties in respect of the territorial sea, suggests that there should be a zone within which this duty must be discharged. It follows, therefore, that international law should lay down a *minimum* breadth for the territorial sea, within which coastal States must fulfil their duties towards foreign shipping. While the theoretical basis of this view has not been adequately explored, it is evident that the many jurists who subscribe to it regard three miles as the minimum breadth, that distance being the smallest claimed for the territorial sea during modern times. The time may come, however, when customary international law moves beyond the Law of the Sea Convention and regards twelve miles not merely as the maximum, but as the minimum, mandatory limit for the territorial sea.

One anomalous development which should be noted here is the extension by the Federal Republic of Germany of its territorial sea in 1984.[13] The normal three-mile limit was abandoned in the Heligoland Bight in favour of an area of territorial sea defined by geographical coordinates, creating a 'box' extending approximately sixteen miles from the coastline. However, it is unlikely that this heralds a major threat to the twelve-mile limit: the measure was designed for the limited purpose of facilitating the prevention of tanker accidents by subjecting the heavily-used waters in question to German control.

The right of innocent passage

The existence of a right of innocent passage through the territorial sea for foreign ships was, as we noted above, widely conceded throughout the period in which the concept of the territorial sea began to crystallise, and particularly since the time of Vattel. This was no well defined right, around which notions of coastal sovereignty collected; rather, the concepts of innocent passage and coastal sovereignty developed in parallel, each helping to mould the other.

'Passage'

The definition of 'passage' is a relatively easy matter. It includes not only actual passage through the territorial sea, but also stopping and anchoring in so far as this is incidental to ordinary navigation or rendered necessary by *force majeure* or distress (TSC, art. 14(3)). The Law of the Sea Convention expressly extends the distress exception to cases where one ship seeks to assist another ship, person or aircraft in danger or distress (LOSC, art. 18(2)). Otherwise, ships are not allowed to 'hover' or cruise around in the territorial sea, because, regardless of whether or not they are 'innocent' — and under the Law of the Sea Convention they certainly would not be innocent, because they would be engaging in activity not having a direct bearing on passage — they would not be engaged in passage: passage must be 'continuous and expeditious' (LOSC, art. 18(2)). All submarines and other underwater vehicles must navigate on the surface (TSC, art. 14(6); LOSC, art. 20). These conventional definitions are in accordance with a long and consistent general practice among States.

The 1930 Hague Conference articles introduced a new element into the definition of passage, not previously adopted in State practice, by including ships travelling through the territorial sea to or from internal waters within the scope of the right of innocent passage. This was not because there was considered to be any right, analogous to innocent passage, to enter or leave internal waters; thus coastal States retained the right to take, impose and enforce conditions for admission to internal waters (TSC, art. 16(2)); LOSC, art. 25(2)). Rather, it was done for the convenience of bringing such ships within the legal regime of ships in innocent passage, for general purposes of coastal State control and jurisdiction. The Territorial Sea Convention adopted the same position, in article 14(2), and that article has been carried over into the Law of the Sea Convention, modified slightly so as to include also ships navigating the territorial sea in order to call at roadsteads or port facilities outside internal waters, within the scope of 'passage' (LOSC, art. 18(1)). The extension of the right of innocent passage to voyages to and from ports was regarded by the International Court in the *Nicaragua* case (1986) as now being established in customary law.[14]

'Innocence'

For long the criterion of innocence lacked any clear definition, and probably any clear meaning. Thus, during the nineteenth and early twentieth centuries, Anglo-American practice and some jurists, such as Schücking,

whose reports prepared the ground for the 1930 Hague Conference, appear
to have regarded innocence as a question distinct from that of compliance
with coastal State laws. From their point of view it was not necessary that
any coastal law should have been violated in order that innocence be lost; it
was enough that vital coastal interests, such as security, be prejudiced.
Conversely, it would seem to follow that not all infractions of coastal laws
would deprive passage of its innocent character, but only those which did
have such a prejudicial effect. Furthermore, if prejudice to coastal interests
were the criterion, it would not be necessary to point to any particular act
of the foreign ship as being incompatible with innocence, and the mere presence of the ship could be enough to threaten the coastal State. On the other
hand, other States, and most other jurists, drew no such distinction, either
expounding the law as if the duty to comply with local laws was in essence
the same as the duty to remain 'innocent' during passage, or taking no clear
position on the question.

The 1930 Hague Conference adopted a text somewhere between these
views; it read:

Passage is not *innocent* when a vessel makes use of the territorial sea of a coastal
State for the purpose of doing any act prejudicial to the security, to the public
policy or to the fiscal interests of that State[15]

Here no breach of any coastal law was required, but arguably some act of
the foreign ship, other than mere passage, was. State practice after 1930
showed a tendency to follow the Hague formulation — for example, the
Bulgarian Decree Law of 25 August 1935,[16] and the Japanese case of *Japan
v. Kulikov* (1954) — as did international arbitral practice, in cases such as
the *David* (1933).

The question received full discussion in the *Corfu Channel* case (1949),
before the International Court of Justice. That case concerned the denial
of passage through the Corfu Channel to British warships, and is discussed
in more detail in chapter five. The important point for present purposes is
that, in defining the right of innocent passage, the Court referred to the
manner of passage as the decisive criterion, holding that as long as the passage was conducted in a fashion which presented no threat to the coastal
State it was to be regarded as innocent. The whole tenor of the judgment
makes clear that innocence is a quality capable of objective determination,
and that a coastal State's view will not necessarily be conclusive. It follows
that a breach of a coastal State's law will not *ipso facto* deprive passage of
its innocent character. The Court's view was, therefore, close to that adopted
in early Anglo-American practice.

Although the more flexible approach of the International Court was
fresh in the minds of the International Law Commissioners when they began
preparing draft articles on the territorial sea, most of them preferred the

approach adopted in the 1930 Hague draft, in which non-innocence was defined by reference to acts prejudicing coastal State interests. Some disagreed. Lauterpacht, for instance, proposed that, except in the case of acts prejudicing coastal State security, only acts violating specific coastal State laws could deprive passage of its innocence. Fitzmaurice, on the other hand, suggested that passage could, where it prejudiced coastal security, be non-innocent irrespective of any act of the vessel. However, the final Commission text provided that passage was innocent so long as the ship did not commit 'any acts prejudicial to the security of the coastal State or contrary to the present rules, or to other rules of international law'.[17] The term 'present rules' was understood, as the commentary makes clear, to refer to the duty which was imposed by another of the draft articles to comply with coastal State legislation on matters such as public health, immigration, customs and fiscal matters, navigation, fishing and the protection of the products of the territorial sea, these being the interests which the coastal State was entitled to protect in its territorial sea.

The Commission's draft article was not accepted by the 1958 conference. The United States proposed an amendment stating that 'passage is innocent so long as it is not prejudicial to the security of the coastal State . . .'. Other States objected to this on two main grounds: first, that deletion of the reference to acts of the passing ship gave too much latitude to the coastal State in the determination of innocence and (which is more difficult to accept) was contrary to existing international law; and secondly, that interests other than security deserved protection. A compromise text was eventually adopted as article 14(4) of the Territorial Sea Convention, which reads:

(4) Passage is innocent so long as it is not prejudicial to the peace, good order or security of the coastal State. Such passage shall take place in conformity with these articles and with other rules of international law.

This final text, which seems to be consistent with the actual practice of States, and so with customary law, clearly does not require the commission of any particular act, or violation of any law, before innocence is lost. Nor does violation of a coastal law necessarily remove innocence, unless the violation actually prejudices the coastal interests. This latter rule is subject to one exception: according to article 14(5):

Passage of foreign fishing vessels shall not be considered innocent if they do not observe such laws and regulations as the coastal State may make and publish in order to prevent these vessels from fishing in the territorial sea.

Such laws could deal not only with actual fishing but also with, for example, storage of nets while the vessel was in transit. This provision was adopted at the 1958 conference with the express purpose of introducing an additional element into the criterion of innocence applicable to fishing vessels.

It represents the only case in which breach of a coastal State law *ipso facto* deprives passage of its innocent character.

Despite the acceptance of the Territorial Sea Convention by almost fifty States, and the incorporation of the terms of the 'innocent passage' provisions in several municipal laws, such as the Burmese Territorial Sea and Maritime Zones Law, 1977,[18] the Pakistan Territorial Waters and Maritime Zones Act, 1976,[19] and the Yugoslavian Law of 22 May 1965,[20] the definition of innocent passage has been substantially amended in the Law of the Sea Convention. Article 19 of the Convention retains, as paragraph 1, the text of the 1958 article 14(4), quoted above. But the article goes on to provide in paragraph (2) that 'passage of a foreign ship shall be considered to be prejudicial to the peace, good order or security of the coastal State, if in the territorial sea it engages in any of the following activities', and there follows a list including weapons practice; spying; propaganda; launching or taking on board aircraft or military devices; embarking or disembarking persons or goods contrary to customs, fiscal, immigration or sanitary regulations; wilful and serious pollution; fishing; research or survey activities; and interference with coastal communication or other facilities. The list is completed by two rather wider categories of activity:

(a) any threat or use of force against the sovereignty, territorial integrity or political independence of the coastal State, or in any other manner in violation of the principles of international law embodied in the Charter of the United Nations; . . .
(1) any other activity not having a direct bearing on passage. [LOSC, art. 19(2)(a), (1)]

The comparatively simple definition of innocence in the 1958 Convention was replaced by these detailed provisions in the 1982 Convention in the hope of producing a more objective definition, allowing coastal States less scope for interpretation, and so less opportunity for abuse of their right to prevent non-innocent passage. It is not clear exactly what, if any changes in the substance of the right of innocent passage have been imported by the 1982 Convention. On the one hand, the reference to *activities* suggests that the mere presence or passage of a ship could not, under the Convention, be characterised as prejudicial to the coastal State, unless it were to engage in some activity: this would, at least in theory, widen the scope of the right. On the other hand, the addition of a list of proscribed activities must, at least if it is non-exhaustive (as the retention of the general 1958 formula as article 19(1), and the phrasing of article 19(2)(1) imply), have narrowed the right of innocent passage, if it has changed the law at all. Under article 19(2) commission of any of the listed acts — which means, following paragraph (2)(1), *any* activity not having a direct bearing on passage — will automatically render the passage non-innocent, whereas under the 1958 rules it would have been necessary to show that such activities actually prejudiced the peace, good order or security of the coastal State. Furthermore, the reference in subparagraph (a), quoted above, to threats of force is wide enough to encompass threats directed against States other than the coastal State, although the 1958 formula would not have rendered such threats incompatible with innocence, at least in the absence of some link, such as a mutual defence treaty, between the coastal State and the threatened State. Otherwise, the list of 'protected interests' appears to be little more than an express statement of the protected interests which were implicit in the 1958 obligation to conduct passage in accordance with 'these articles and other rules of international law' (TSC, art. 14(4)). The 1958 provision concerning fishing vessels has become subsumed within this general scheme, and has anyway lost much of its importance following the massive extension of fisheries jurisdiction since the time of the first Law of the Sea Conference. Thus, while the 1982 definition of innocence has adhered to the basic approach in the 1958 Territorial Sea Convention of defining innocence by reference to prejudice to coastal State interests, whether or not it involves any violation of coastal State laws, it has also introduced doubts as to whether or not non-innocence must turn on activities of the ship, and whether or not certain activities may automatically deprive passage of its innocence.

Already State practice is demonstrating the influence of the reformulation of innocent passage, with lists of activities incompatible with innocence, based on earlier drafts prepared by UNCLOS III, appearing in municipal laws such as the Act concerning the territorial sea and other maritime zones enacted by Southern Yemen in 1977.[21] Other States are now incorporating the substance of the definition in the 1982 Convention into their laws: the French decree of 1985 is an example.[22] As these and other claims are made, the revised definition begins its passage into customary international law.

The right to deny and suspend passage

The territorial sea is subject to the sovereignty of the coastal State, and the only right which foreign ships have to be in the territorial sea of the State, apart from any specific treaty provisions which might exist, is the right of innocent passage. In consequence, if the foreign ship ceases to be innocent, or steps outside the scope of passage, it may be excluded from the territorial sea. Accordingly, it is provided that 'the coastal State may take the necessary steps in its territorial sea to prevent passage which is not innocent.' (TSC, art. 16(1); LOSC, art. 25(1)). There is no express provision setting out the right to exclude vessels not engaged in passage, but this right undoubtedly exists in customary law, and hovering vessels would almost certainly be deemed non-innocent, so providing a further justification for their exclusion. In addition, as we shall see below, ships which have stepped outside the right of innocent passage are subject to the full jurisdiction of the coastal State and may (subject to the usual exception for warships and other vessels enjoying sovereign immunity) be arrested by the coastal State for any violation of its laws.

It is a logical consequence of this right that States should have the right to suspend passage altogether where the passage of *any* ship would prejudice its peace, good order or security. States have commonly exercised this right so as to exclude foreign ships from zones in front of naval dockyards, for example. It appears in the Territorial Sea Convention in the following form:

... the coastal State may, without discrimination amongst foreign ships, suspend temporarily in specified areas of its territorial sea the innocent passage of foreign ships if such suspension is essential for the protection of its security. [TSC, art. 16(3)]

This right has been interpreted rather liberally, as is often the case where rights protect security interests. This is reflected in the corresponding provision in the Law of the Sea Convention, which adds to the quoted words: 'including weapons exercises' (LOSC, art. 25(3)). This inelegant formula underlines the fact that it is not only that which is necessary, but also that which is expedient for the protection of coastal security, which is seen as justifying the temporary suspension of passage.

States may not suspend, even temporarily, innocent passage through straits. We consider this point in chapter five.

Warships and nuclear-powered ships

The question of the right of warships to innocent passage has long been one of the most controversial aspects of the law of the sea. The argument against their enjoying this right was succinctly put by Elihu Root, counsel for the United States in the *North Atlantic Coast Fisheries* arbitration in 1910:

Warships may not pass without consent into this zone, because they threaten. Merchant ships may pass and repass because they do not threaten.[23]

Ironically, Root had previously been the Secretary of State of the country which, in recent times, has been one of the stoutest defenders of the right of innocent passage for warships. The source of the controversy is clear: the major naval powers (among which the United States could not be counted before the First World War) seek maximum freedom of manoeuvre for their warships in order to secure their interests, whereas other States seek to deny foreign warships close access to their shores in order to protect their security.

This stark division of interests has prevented the adoption of any clear rules on the matter. The 1930 Hague Conference text provided:

As a general rule, a coastal State will not forbid the passage of foreign warships in its territorial sea and will nor require a previous authorisation or notification.[24]

While the *Corfu Channel* case settled the right of warships to innocent passage through straits, it did not deal expressly with their rights in the territorial sea *simpliciter*. Accordingly, the question remained open at the 1958 Geneva conference. The International Law Commission, noting that the laws of many States required previous authorisation or notification, proposed that the Convention should allow such requirements. The proposed text was adopted by one of the conference's committees, being supported by States which sought a requirement of authorisation and by those which, though not seeking authorisation, did demand prior notification. In plenary session the latter group joined with those States seeking an unrestricted right of innocent passage for warships and secured the deletion of the authorisation requirement, leaving a text under which only prior notification could be required. However, this resulted in those States demanding authorisation joining with those objecting even to prior notification in voting to reject the amended article, with the consequence that the Territorial Sea Convention contains no express provision on the matter.

Different conclusions are drawn from this background to the 1958 Convention. Some argue that, since article 14(1), which reads:

Subject to the provisions of these articles, ships of all States, whether coastal or not, shall enjoy the right of innocent passage through the territorial sea.

appears under the rubric 'Rules applicable to all ships', both merchant and warships enjoy the right.[25] Others regard the matter as unregulated by the Convention, and some States, such as Czechoslovakia, Hungary, Roumania and the USSR, have entered declarations accompanying their ratifications of the Territorial Sea Convention to this effect,[26] claiming the right to require authorisation for the passage of foreign warships.

Untidy as this result is, it appears to have the virtue of acceptability. Since the 1958 conference, as before it, State practice has contrived to avoid any direct confrontation over the issue. Where a coastal State requires no authorisation or notification, it seems that the naval powers give none. Where some requirement is laid down, low-level contacts between naval attachés and local navy officers, on a rather informal basis, seem to be favoured. Any such contact occurs against the general diplomatic background of consistent denials by 'naval' States of the legality of requirements of prior authorisation for passage. In this way the principles of both sides remain intact because neither side is willing to force the issue, although there have been cases in which force has been used to assert rights of passage through archipelagic waters and straits. Given this background of unenthusiastically enforced laws, and the determination to preserve rights of passage for warships, it is not wholly surprising that UNCLOS III decided to adopt the ambiguous 1958 'solution', and leave the matter open once more. Although the emergence of many new States since 1958 might well have produced a majority in favour of authorisation or notification, the Soviet Union, which had argued strongly for such requirements in 1958, now sees its naval interests rather differently, and there seems to be a general sense that the question is, for all practical purposes, best left without a clear answer.

One point which is clear is that submarines passing through the territorial sea must navigate on the surface. This rule has been accepted for as long as submarines have been used as naval vessels, although, as we shall see, the injunction seems not always to be applied to passage through international straits. Needless to say, this rule, though included in both the Territorial Sea Convention, as article 14(6), and the Law of the Sea Convention, as article 20, is not always observed. In recent years submerged foreign submarines have been located and pursued on several occasions in Swedish and other territorial waters. Depth-charges have been used against them after warnings to leave the area had been given, in exercise of the right to take necessary steps to prevent non-innocent passage. In October 1981 one such submarine ran aground near a Swedish naval base. It was Russian: despite the position taken by the USSR at the 1958 conference, it seems that no notification was given or authorisation sought before the submarine entered Swedish waters.

A problem analogous to that of warships has arisen in the form of nuclear-powered ships. Some States regard these vessels as inherently threatening to their peace and good order. Spain, for example, enacted legislation in 1964 stating that the passage of nuclear ships through territorial waters was to be considered an exception to the right of innocent passage.[27] For their part the flag States of nuclear-powered vessels have been cautious in sending them through foreign waters. Before the United States Nuclear Ship *Savannah* visited the United Kingdom in 1964, for instance, an elaborate agreement regulating its passage through British territorial waters had been concluded between the two governments. Similar agreements were made with other States whose waters the *Savannah* entered.[28] The fears of coastal States seem, however, to have diminished, since the right of passage for such ships is recognised in the Law of the Sea Convention, article 23 of which requires them, and ships carrying nuclear or other inherently dangerous or noxious substances, to carry documents and observe internationally agreed precautionary measures (such as those included in the 1974 SOLAS Convention, discussed in chapter thirteen) when exercising their right to innocent passage. Coastal States are also specifically authorised to require such ships to confine their passage to any sea lanes which they might have designated in their territorial seas (LOSC, art. 22(2)).

Rights and duties of the coastal State

State practice and doctrine on the question of the extent of a coastal State's rights to enact legislation — its legislative, as opposed to its enforcement, jurisdiction — varied according to whether the territorial sea was regarded as a mere 'bundle of servitudes' or as a belt of maritime territory under the plenary jurisdiction of the State. The aim, in all cases, was to reconcile the right of innocent passage with the legitimate interests of coastal States in the enforcement of their laws in the territorial sea.

Those adhering to the former view considered that States had jurisdiction only in respect of certain specific matters, of which the most commonly accepted were navigation, customs, fishing, sanitation and security. The general law of a State was not regarded as extending to foreign ships in the territorial sea. This view was close to that taken in respect of ships in port under the 'internal economy' doctrine, which we considered in chapter three, according to which only acts on foreign ships which had effect beyond the ship were subject to the coastal State's law. Indeed, it is arguable that the real concern of States and jurists adopting this position was to limit the occasions for coastal State interference with foreign vessels, which is a question of enforcement, rather than legislative, jurisdiction. Nonetheless, the laws of several States incorporate limitations upon their actual application to foreign vessels, suggesting a limitation upon legislative jurisdiction proper: Cuba, Roumania and Spain,[29] among others, incorporated such limitations in their laws. For such States, matters which belonged to the internal economy of foreign ships were for the flag State alone to deal with, although it should be noted that there is a curious ambivalence in this position: since even these States accepted the right to intervene in matters of internal economy when requested to do so by the authorities of the flag State, it would seem that they must have accepted that their laws *could* be applied in full to foreign ships when a request was made, again suggesting that the limitation sounded only in enforcement jurisdiction.

States claiming plenary jurisdiction, as a consequence of their claims to sovereignty over the territorial sea, allowed no such limitations upon coastal State legislative jurisdiction as a matter of law. The United Kingdom has held to this position throughout the nineteenth and twentieth centuries, giving it clear expression in the Territorial Waters Jurisdiction Act of 1878, which extended the ambit of all indictable offences (that is, offences triable by jury, rather than summarily before magistrates) to all vessels in the territorial sea. That Act met with considerable opposition within Parliament, and from other States and jurists, who regarded it as exceeding the limited jurisdiction allowed to coastal States under international law. But the British government held fast to its view that there was no limit on States' legislative jurisdiction in law, and the Act was passed. Thus, for example, during the dispute with the United States in the 1920s arising from the enforcement of American prohibition laws against British ships in the American territorial sea, the British government was careful not to challenge the ultimate right of the United States to legislate for those ships. However, this attitude was tempered in two ways. First, the consequences of the British view, which was shared by some other Sates, were not always insisted upon. For instance, although children born on foreign ships in British ports automatically acquired British nationality under British law, the Law Officers of the Crown advised, in an opinion dated 10 November 1897, that this would not apply to a child born of foreign parents on a foreign ship merely passing through British waters. Similarly, during discussions arising from the case of *Savarkar* in 1910 the Lord Chancellor stated that where a prisoner was carried on a foreign ship into British waters the British government would not be entitled, or at least would not choose, to demand that extradition procedures be complied with before the ship and its prisoner left British waters.[30] This latter example overlaps with the second concession, which is that, even where legislative jurisdiction does exist, its exercise or enforcement will be restrained where interests of comity so demand. In these ways the more inconvenient implications of plenary jurisdictional claims were largely avoided.

Attempts at the codification of the law applicable to the territorial sea have failed to resolve this divergence in State practice, except perhaps by implication. Thus the 1930 Hague Draft included an article obliging foreign ships to 'comply with the laws and regulations enacted in conformity with international usage by the coastal State', adding in particular, as regards 'those concerning navigation, pollution and the resources of the territorial sea' (Hague Draft article 6). The presence of a list might be taken to imply that legislative jurisdiction was limited to specific purposes, but it will be recalled that the Hague Draft upheld the principle of sovereignty over territorial waters, and this, coupled with the absence of any specific limitations on legislative jurisdiction apart from those prohibiting discriminatory laws (Hague Draft article 6) and the levying of charges upon ships for merely passing through the territorial sea (Hague Draft article 7), suggests that no such limitations were intended to be imposed as a matter of law. Again, the considerations of international comity would nevertheless engender some restraint in the exercise of jurisdiction, especially in respect of ships in innocent passage.

The International Law Commission adopted a similarly uncertain position. Noting that no list of matters on which States might legislate could be exhaustive, it proposed an article providing:

Foreign ships exercising the right of innocent passage shall comply with the laws and regulations enacted by the coastal State in conformity with these articles and other rules of international law and, in particular, with such laws and regulations relating to transport and navigation.

This provision was eventually adopted as article 17 of the Territorial Sea Convention, but without it being made clear in the process whether there were any limitations *ratione materiae* on legislative jurisdiction implicit in the article.

The Law of the Sea Convention has modified the coastal State's legislative competence. Article 21 allows the coastal State to adopt laws 'in respect of all or any of the following'–the following topics being, broadly, navigation, protection of cables and pipelines, fisheries, pollution, scientific research, and customs, fiscal, immigration and sanitary regulations. The coastal State must give due publicity to all such laws (LOSC, art. 21(3)). These laws may not affect the design, construction, manning or equipment of foreign vessels unless they conform to generally accepted international standards — a significant limitation upon coastal State legislative competence — but otherwise foreign ships are bound to comply with them, as they are with sea lanes designated by the coastal State (LOSC, arts. 21(4), 22). In addition, foreign ships must comply with 'all generally accepted international regulations relating to the prevention of collisions at sea', apparently regardless of whether the flag or coastal State is a party to the conventions containing those regulations (LOSC, art. 21(4)). The most important regulations are those in the 1972 Collisions Regulations Convention. Although the Law of the Sea Convention strongly suggests that coastal State legislative jurisdiction is limited, since the listed topics are not even presented as examples, as they had been in the 1930 and 1958 texts, there is still some doubt. As we shall see, the Law of the Sea Convention provides for the enforcement of general criminal jurisdiction in some circumstances, under article 27, and the existence of general enforcement jurisdiction clearly presupposes the existence of general legislative jurisdiction.

In the light of this uncertainty, it seems that the present legal position can best be put as follows. States may not legislate so as to hamper (TSC, art. 15(1); LOSC, art. 24(1)) or levy charges upon innocent passage (TSC, art. 18(1); LOSC, art. 26). They may charge for specific services rendered, such as rescue or pilotage services, but not in a manner which discriminates among ships of different foreign flags (TSC, art. 18(2); LOSC, art. 26(2)). Similarly, other legislation may not discriminate against ships of any State or against ships carring cargoes to, from or on behalf of any State (LOSC, art. 24(1)(b)). They may legislate for such matters as navigation, pollution, fishing, etc., listed in article 21 of the Law of the Sea Convention and implicit in article 17 of the Territorial Sea Convention, and all ships, whether in innocent passage or not, must comply with such laws while in the territorial sea. It is also well established in State practice that ships not engaged in innocent passage, either because they are not passing, or are passing but not innocent, are subject to all coastal State laws. Beyond this, it seems a legitimate inference from the principle of coastal sovereignty over territorial waters that States retain the right to extend any other legislation apart from that dealing with navigation and so on, to foreign ships in their waters, but that they will normally be expected, as a matter of comity, to refrain from doing so.

The question of the extent of coastal States' rights of enforcement juris-diction has many parallels with the question of their legislative jurisdiction; the two being commonly, though wrongly, regarded as covered by the single question of the extent of coastal State control over foreign vessels. Hence the same basic division exists in the doctrine and State practice between States such as the United Kingdom, which has regarded itself for well over a century as entitled in strict law to enforce any of its laws against foreign vessels in its waters, and States which considered themselves entitled only to enforce specific laws on matters such as customs and fishing against foreign ships. Both views admitted of exceptions.

Thus States claiming full enforcement jurisdiction were conscious that comity required restraint in its exercise. It was mainly on the basis of comity and usage that the enforcement of the American liquor laws was challenged by other States, for instance, rather than on the basis of any legal limits upon American rights to enforce those laws. Generally, indeed, enforce-ment jurisdiction was only actually exercised in limited circumstances: pri-marily when the offence disturbed the peace of the port or involved a stranger to the crew of the foreign ship; where coastal Sate intervention was requested by the flag State; to arrest a person sought by the coastal State; or where a specific law applying to the conduct of the ship in customs, navigation, fishing, etc., matters was breached. Ships in innocent passage were other-wise not the object of enforcement measures. In turn, these limitations, accepted as a matter of comity by Great Britain and similarly minded States, were regarded by States claiming only limited jurisdiction as being as a matter of law the only occasions on which coastal States might inter-vene.

This doctrinal divergence was evident in the replies of governments to the Schedule of Points circulated before the 1930 Hague Conference. But it was also evident that the actual enforcement practice of States was more or less uniform, and that the difference between the British doctrine of plenary jurisdiction and the doctrine of limited jurisdiction espoused by Belgium, France, Norway and others was theoretical rather than practical. Accord-ingly, it was not difficult to reach agreement on draft articles which provided that States must not exercise enforcement jurisdiction on board foreign passing vessels unless the peace of the coastal State was compromised, or the flag State requested coastal State intervention. In addition, States could enforce laws concerning navigation, pollution and fishing, even against passing vessels, and other laws where the ship was lying in the territorial sea or passing through it having left the internal waters of that State.[31] Otherwise, no enforcement jurisdiction existed, although violations of coastal laws in the territorial sea could, of course, be prosecuted if the violator subsequently appeared in the internal waters or territory of the State concerned.

In the years between the 1930 and 1958 conferences State practice adhered broadly to the Hague formula, but without the underlying doctrinal dispute being resolved. The case of the *David*, before the US-Panama Claims Commission in 1933, shows this continuing uncertainty, with a majority of the arbitrators holding that innocent passage conferred, in the absence of any clear preponderance of authority, no immunity from coastal enforcement jurisdiction, and the minority holding that such immunity did exist.

The International Law Commission proposed draft articles on the matter which followed the 1930 articles in excluding coastal rights of enforcement as a matter of law, except in certain circumstances. The main exception was that States had a right to enforce laws of particular concern to the territorial sea as a consequence of the legislative jurisdiction which they were given under what became article 17 of the Territorial Sea Convention. This was accepted by the conference, and there is no doubt that States may enforce these laws against foreign ships, whether passing or stationary, in the territorial sea. Other laws could be enforced on foreign ships only if their violation had disturbed the peace of the coastal State or local intervention was requested. But this was not accepted by the conference. The United States proposed an amendment with the specific purpose of reasserting the full jurisdiction of the coastal State by replacing the mandatory requirement that States 'may not' exercise jurisdiction except in the stated circumstances with the exhortatory suggestion that they 'should not' do so. This was accepted, with the result that although States should, as a matter of comity, not enforce their laws in respect of crimes committed on passing ships unless the consequences extend to the coastal State, or disturb the peace of the country or the good order of the territorial sea, or coastal State intervention is requested by the flag State, or (an exception not then evident in State practice, but added by the conference) to suppress drug trafficking, they nonetheless retain the ultimate legal right to do so if they so wish (TSC, art. 19(1)). Enforcement jurisdiction is excluded in law in only one case: where the crime was committed before the ship entered the territorial sea and the ship is merely passing through the sea without entering internal waters (TSC, art. 19(5)). Coastal States are expressly given the right to take enforcement measures in respect of crimes committed on ships passing through the territorial sea after leaving internal waters (TSC, art. 19(2)), and impliedly retain the right, which flows from their sovereignty over that sea, to enforcement jurisdiction over ships not engaged in passage but lying in the territorial sea. Where it is proposed that jurisdiction be exercised, due regard must be paid to the interests of navigation (TSC, art. 19(4)), and, if the action is taken under the 'peace of the port' provisions of article 19(1)(a) and (b), the flag State authorities must be notified if the captain of the foreign ship so requests.

Civil jurisdiction was treated similarly in the 1958 Convention. Article 20(1) provides that passing ships should not be stopped or diverted in order to exercise civil jurisdiction against a person on board. Paragraph 2 of that article prohibits the arrest of ships for civil proceedings, except in relation to obligations or liabilities assumed by the ship itself in the course of or for the purpose of its voyage through the territorial sea, but here coastal State jurisdiction is reserved in the case of ships lying in the territorial sea or passing through it after leaving internal waters.

It should be noted that for the States, now numbering over two dozen, parties to the 1952 Brussels Conventions on Penal Jurisdiction in Matters of Collision, and on the Arrest of Sea-going Ships, this basic jurisdictional framework is overlain by more specific rules. The Convention on Penal Jurisdiction, for example, accords exclusive jurisdiction in collisions to the authorities of the flag State: unless a State party exercises its right to declare that the Convention will not apply to its territorial waters, the jurisdiction allowed to it under the 1958 Convention will clearly be limited by the provisions of the 1952 Convention. On the other hand, the 1958 rules on the exercise of civil jurisdiction appear to be more restrictive that those of the 1952 Convention on the Arrest of Sea-going Ships, which allow arrest for the purpose of any maritime claim, and not merely those claims arising from the voyage through territorial waters.

The 1958 rules have been taken over, almost verbatim, without any serious debate on their substance, as articles 27 and 28 of the Law of the Sea Convention. The present position under treaty law is, therefore, that coastal enforcement jurisdiction in the territorial sea is in principle complete, except for (*a*) jurisdiction over crimes committed before a ship, merely passing through the territorial sea, entered that sea; and (*b*) jurisdiction in civil matters to arrest a ship in connection with liabilities not incurred in connection with its voyage through the territorial sea. The Law of the Sea Convention requires that coastal State laws should not discriminate in form or in fact — that is, as a matter of legislative or enforcement jurisdiction — against ships of any State or ships carrying cargoes to, from or on behalf of any State (art. 24(1)(b)). In addition rules of comity require that jurisdiction should not be exercised over passing ships except in the circumstances set out in article 19 of the Territorial Sea Convention and article 27 of the Law of the Sea Convention. The Law of the Sea Convention provisions on pollution (art. 220) have also resulted in minor limitations upon coastal enforcement jurisdiction, as we shall see in chapter fifteen.

These rules apply to all foreign merchant vessels, but specific provision is made for ships operated by foreign governments and foreign warships, to take account of their right to sovereign immunity. Government ships operated for commercial purposes are treated like all other merchant ships (TSC, art. 21; such ships are included in the general jurisdictional provisions of Part II, section 3(B) of the Law of the Sea Convention). This follows the approach of the 1926 Brussels Convention on the Immunity of State-owned Ships, and current trends in the law of State immunity: nonetheless, several East European States entered reservations when ratifying the Territorial Sea Convention, claiming full immunity for all government-operated ships, whether or not commercial. Government ships operated for non-commercial purposes, like warships, are not subject to the enforcement jurisdiction of the coastal State, because of the immunity which they enjoy under customary international law (TSC, art. 22(2); LOSC, art. 32). However, both warships and other government-operated non-commercial ships are subject to the legislative jurisdiction of the coastal State, it being only the enforcement of law against them which is precluded by reason of their immunity. Hence they are under an obligation to respect coastal laws, and under customary law, and under article 31 of the Law of the Sea Convention, the flag State is responsible for loss to the coastal State arising from non-compliance by such ships with laws concerning passage through the territorial sea. Responsibility would also attach, under customary law, to the flag State for breach of any other laws which the ship was obliged to obey. Warships which violate coastal laws concerning passage through the territorial sea and which ignore requests for compliance may be required to leave the territorial sea (TSC, art. 23; LOSC, art. 30), and the coastal State may use any force necessary to compel them to do so. This will allow the upholding of laws on matters such as customs, navigation, pollution and fishing: other laws, such as the general criminal law of the coastal State, cannot be upheld in this way under the treaty provisions, the warship retaining its right to pursue its passage unmolested. Though the treaties are silent, and there is a dearth of State practice on the point, it seems reasonable to extend this right of exclusion to non-commercial government-operated ships, since their legal status can, for these purposes, be assimilated to that of warships.

It should also be recalled that some breaches of coastal laws may involve a loss of innocence, depriving the ship of its right of innocent passage and entitling the coastal State to take any necessary steps to prevent what has become non-innocent passage through its territorial sea (TSC, art. 16(1); LOSC, art. 25(1)). In some cases this right to exclude the offending vessel from the territorial sea may be a convenient alternative to arresting it and instituting proceedings before municipal courts: it also offers a remedy where the ship has not violated a coastal law, but has gone outside its right of innocent passage by threatening coastal interests in the manner described above.

Finally, it may be noted in passing that States enjoy a general right of self-defence in international law and, if they are facing an imminent attack from foreign vessels in their territorial sea and have no other means of protection, may use any necessary force against the vessels in order to defend themselves.

We have already discussed the most important duties incumbent upon coastal States in respect of their territorial seas. In the discussion concerning the breadth of the territorial sea it was noted that States must give notice of known navigational hazards. This duty exists both in customary law, as was recognised in the *Corfu Channel* case (1949) and under treaty (TSC, art. 15(2); LOSC, art. 24(2)). It must also provide basic navigational services such as lighthouses and rescue facilities.

Again, States must not hamper innocent passage (TSC, art. 15 (1); LOSC, art. 24(1)). This rule has been seen in the context of limitations upon coastal State jurisdiction, but is of general application and would, for example, operate so as to prevent unreasonable interference with innocent passage by the establishment of installations in the territorial sea.

In addition to these specific duties States are, of course, subject to all the other rules of international law which may apply to their dealings with the territorial sea. For example, disputes over the delimitation of maritime boundaries must be settled by peaceful means, and no unnecessary force must be used in enforcing coastal State rights against foreign ships in the territorial sea. These general rules apply equally to other States concerned.

Notes

1 Guyana, Maritime Boundaries Act, 1977, s. 5, *UN Leg. Ser* B/19, p. 33, *ND* VII, p. 112; Pakistan, Territorial Waters and Maritime Zones Act, 1976, s. 2(1), *UN Leg. Ser.* B/19, p. 85, *ND* VII, p. 478; Seychelles, Maritime Zones Act, 1977, s. 3(1), *UN Leg. Ser.* B/19, p. 102, *ND* VIII, p. 11.

2 A. G. de Lapradelle, 'Le droit de l'Etat sur la mer territoriale', 5 *RGDIP* 264–84, 309–47 (1899). Cf. P. Fauchille, *Traité de droit international public*, 4 vols, Paris, 1925, Vol. 1.II, pp. 128–73.

3 League of Nations Doc. C. 351(b). M. 145(b). 1930. v., p. 212. Reproduced in S. Rosenne, *League of Nations Conference for the Codification of International Law (1930)*, Dobbs Ferry, N. Y., 1975, p. 1414.

4 See *R.* v. *Keyn* (1876). See, too, the French case of *Minister of Defence et. al.* v. *Starr and the British Commonwealth Insurance Co. (the 'Johmo')* (1970).

5 League of Nations Doc. C. 351(b). M. 145(b). 1930. v., p. 213; Rosenne, *op. cit.* n. 3, p. 1415.

6 Cf. the cases of *U.S.* v. *California* (1947); *U.S.* v. *Louisiana* (1950); *U.S.* v. *Texas* (1950); *U.S.* v. *Maine* (1975); Reference re *Offshore Mineral Rights of British Columbia* (Canada, 1967); *New South Wales* v. *The Commonwealth* (Australia, 1975).

7 G. Marston, 'The evolution of the concept of sovereignty over the bed and subsoil of the territorial sea', 48 *BYIL* 321, at 332 (1976–77).

8 See the example quoted in A. V. Lowe, 'The development of the concept of

the contiguous zone', 51 *BYIL* 109, at 149 (1981).

9   See the discussion in L. D. M. Nelson, 'The patrimonial sea', 22 *ICLQ* 668, at 679 (1973).
10 Presidential Proclamation of 10 March 1983, XXII *ILM* 461 (1983).
11 [1973] ICJ Rep. 3, at 27 n. 8.
12 [1951] ICJ Rep. 116, at 160.
13 See the Decree of 12 November 1984, 7 *LOSB* 9–22 (1986).
14 [1986] ICJ Rep. 12, at 111.
15 League of Nations Doc. C. 351 (b). M. 145(b). 1930. v., p. 213; Rosenne, *op. cit.* n.3, p. 1415.
16 *UN Leg. Ser.* B/1, p. 53 (art. 4).
17 *Yearbook of the International Law Commission, 1956,* Vol. II, p. 272.
18 *UN Leg. Ser.* B/19, p. 8, *ND* VII, p. 356 (chapter 2).
19 *UN Leg. Ser.* B/19, p. 85, *ND* VII, p. 478 (s. 3).
20 *UN Leg. Ser.* B/15, p. 188, *ND* I, p. 35 (art. 12).
21 *UN Leg. Ser.* B/19, p. 21, *ND* VIII, p. 57 (art. 6).
22 Decree No. 85/185, see 6 *LOSB* 14 (October, 1985); and see the 1984 Rules for Navigation and Sojourn of Foreign Warships in the Territorial Waters (Territorial Sea) of the USSR and the Internal Waters and Ports of the USSR, XXIV *ILM* 1715 (1985).
23 North Atlantic Coast Fisheries Arbitration, *Proceedings*, Vol. II, p. 2007.
24 League of Nations Doc. C. 351(b). M. 145(b). 1930. v., p. 217; Rosenne, *op. cit.* n. 3, p. 1418.
25 Cf. the similar provision in art. 17 of the Law of the Sea Convention. It is also argued that because it is expressly provided in article 14 of the Territorial Sea Convention, which is concerned with innocent passage, that submarines must navigate on the surface (art. 14(6)), and because, at present, all submarines are warships, it follows that warships were intended to have a right of innocent passage.
26 See the entry for the Territorial Sea Convention in the annual *Lists of Signatures, Ratifications, Accessions, etc., of Multilateral Treaties in Respect of which the Secretary-General Performs Depository Functions*, published by the United Nations. See also *Smith*, p. 10, for a list of States requiring prior authorisation or notification for the passage of warships and nuclear-powered ships.
27 Act No. 25/64, 29 April 1964, art. 7, *UN Leg. Ser.* B/16, p. 45.
28 *ND* II, p. 654.
29 Cuba, Code of Social Defence, 1936, art. 7, *UN Leg. Ser.* B/2, p. 29; Roumania, Penal Code, 1936, art. 7, *ibid.*, p. 99; Spain, Code of Military Justice, 1945, art. 9(1), *ibid.*, p. 108.
30 Lord Loreburn's opinion of 10 September 1910, in *Law Officers' Opinions to the Foreign Office*, microfilm, Dobbs Ferry, N. Y.
31 League of Nations Doc. C. 357(b). M. 145(b). 1930. v., pp. 214–15; Rosenne, *op. cit.*, n. 3, pp. 1416–17.

Further reading

P. Allott, 'Language, method and the nature of international law', 45 *BYIL* 79–135 (1971).

W. E. Butler, 'Innocent passage and the 1982 Convention: the influence of Soviet law and policy', 81 *AJIL* 331–47 (1987).

C. C. Emanuelli, 'La pollution maritime et la notion de passage inoffensif', 11

Canadian Yearbook of International Law 13–36 (1973).

P. T. Fenn, 'Origins of the theory of territorial waters', 20 *AJIL* 465–82 (1926).

E. Franckx, 'The USSR position on the issue of innocent passage of warships through foreign territorial waters', 18 *JMLC* 33–65 (1987).

T. W. Fulton, *Sovereignty of the Seas. An Historical Account of the Claims of England to the Dominion of the British Seas*, Edinburgh and London, 1911.

P. C. Jessup, *The Law of Territorial Waters and Maritime Jurisdiction*, New York, 1927.

H. S. K. Kent, 'Historical origins of the three-mile limit' 48 *AJIL* 537–53 (1954).

L. T. Lee, 'Jurisdiction over foreign merchant ships in the territorial sea. An analysis of the Geneva Convention on the Law of the Sea', 55 *AJIL* 77–96 (1961).

A. Manin, 'L' échouement du Whisky 137 dans les eaux suédoises', 27 *AFDI* 689–710 (1981).

CHAPTER FIVE

Straits

Definition

'Strait' is not a term of art, and it is not defined in any of the conventions produced by the United Nations Conferences on the Law of the Sea. It bears its ordinary meaning, describing a narrow natural passage or arm of water connecting two larger bodies of water. It is the legal status of the waters constituting the strait and their use by international shipping, rather than any definition of 'strait' as such, that determines the rights of coastal and flag States. Because the legal regime of straits has been substantially revised in the Law of the Sea Convention, the 1958 rules will be first considered separately.

The regime under customary law and the Territorial Sea Convention

The rights of passage through straits depend primarily, under the 1958 rules, upon whether the waters of the strait are high seas or territorial sea. If they are high seas, then foreign ships enjoy the same freedom of navigation, free from coastal jurisdiction or control, through the strait as they enjoy in any other part of the high seas. If, on the other hand, the strait is comprised of territorial waters of one or more States, then foreign ships enjoy only the right of innocent passage (TSC, art. 16(4)). This right, as has been seen in chapter four, can be suspended temporarily by the coastal State if that is essential for the protection of its security. But were passage to be suspended in straits connecting areas of the high seas, such as the Straits of Gibraltar or Malacca, the freedom of navigation which exists on the high seas would be undermined, as Vattel had pointed out in the eighteenth century. Accordingly, a rule of international law emerged providing that innocent passage could not be suspended in straits used for international navigation between one part of the high seas and another. This rule was recognised by the International Court of Justice in the *Corfu Channel* case in 1949, and was subsequently incorporated in article 16(4) of the Territorial Sea Convention.

In the *Corfu Channel* case, as we saw in the previous chapter, the United
Kingdom asserted its right to passage through international straits by sending a naval force through the Corfu Channel, without complying with Albanian regulations requiring prior authorisation. Albania claimed that its
sovereignty had been violated by the passage and, concerning the status of
the channel, argued that it was not a strait used for international navigation, because it was only an alternative route between the Adriatic and the
Aegean Seas and it was used almost exclusively by local traffic. This argument was rejected by the Court, which held that 'the decisive criterion is
rather its geographical situation as connecting two parts of the high seas
and the fact of its being used for international navigation', and noted its
'special importance to Greece by reason of the traffic to and from the port
of Corfu'. Its secondary importance as a sea route, and the actual volume
of traffic through the Channel, were irrelevant to its legal status. Accordingly, although the high degree of tension in Greco-Albanian relations
(Greece considered itself technically at war with Albania) would have
justified the regulation of the passage of warships for security reasons,
passage through the strait could not actually be prohibited. Thus either of
the coastal States could, for example, have limited the number of foreign
ships traversing its waters within the strait at any one time, or have prohibited passage during hours of darkness, had such measures been necessary for the protection of its security in the prevailing circumstances: but
neither State was entitled to suspend passage through the strait completely,
or to deny the existence of the right of passage by subjecting it to a requirement of special authorisation.

The case itself established that, as a matter of customary law, warships
(and hence, *a fortiori*, merchant ships) had a right of innocent passage
through international straits which could not be suspended by the coastal
State. But some jurists[1] and, indeed, delegates of some of the maritime
powers to UNCLOS III have argued that the right under customary law is
rather wider than this, amounting to a freedom of navigation unlimited by
any criterion of 'innocence'. Unlike innocent passage, which extends only
to ships, this alleged 'right of transit', as it is sometimes called, includes a
right of overflight of foreign aircraft. In support of this argument, it is said
that overflight and naval manoeuvres, both of which fall outside the scope
of innocent passage, take place in straits such as Gibraltar, apparently without the prior consent or subsequent protests of the littoral States. Furthermore, the 1979 Treaty of Peace between Egypt and Israel refers to the right
of all nations to 'unimpeded and non-suspendable freedom of navigation
and overflight' through the Strait of Tiran and Gulf of Aqaba.[2] On the
other hand, it must be said that, both inside UNCLOS III and outside it in
declarations such as the 1971 statement of Indonesia, Malaysia and Sing-

apore on the Malacca Straits[3], several littoral States seem to hold to the view that the only right is that of non-suspendable innocent passage. This divergence is partly explicable on the basis that some maritime States had refused to recognise the extension by littoral States of their territorial waters so as to cover passages which were formerly high seas — the United States, for example, assumed that a high-seas passage existed in the Strait of Gibraltar, which narrows to a width of only eight miles, despite the historic six-mile claim by Spain and the extension of Moroccan territorial waters from three to twelve miles in 1973, neither of which was recognised by the United States, which adhered to the old three-mile rule. In so far as there is a core of disagreement on the precise legal status of international straits, the balance of juristic opinion seems to favour the conclusion that customary law accords only a non-suspendable right of innocent passage through them. This, at least, was the position until the later stages of UNCLOS III: the question whether the position changed subsequently is discussed below.

The earlier view was adopted in article 16(4) of the Territorial Sea Convention, which provides:

There shall be no suspension of the innocent passage of foreign ships through straits which are used for international navigation between one part of the high seas and another part of the high seas or the territorial sea of a foreign State.

While the nature of the right of passage here follows customary law, the definition of straits within which that right subsists arguably does not. In rejecting the ILC proposal that only straits 'normally' used for international navigation' should be included, the 1958 conference was simply reflecting the decision in the *Corfu Channel* case; but in extending the article to include not only straits connecting two areas of the high seas, as the ILC had proposed, but also straits connecting the high seas with the territorial sea of another State, the conference was moving beyond mere codification. It is clear that article 16(4) was primarily intended to secure the right of access to the Israeli port of Eilat, situated at the end of the Gulf of Aqaba, through the Straits of Tiran, which were then under Arab control. It did not achieve this aim because the Arab States, reluctant to accept the article, did not sign the Territorial Sea Convention. Nonetheless, Western States have declared on several occasions, in the face of an actual or threatened closure of the Straits of Tiran to Israeli shipping, that the Straits (and, indeed, the waters of the Gulf of Aqaba, the whole of which consists of territorial waters of the littoral States) constitute an international waterway in which no State has the right to prevent free and innocent passage. This view implies that customary law includes an obligation identical to that in article 16(4), and support for this can be drawn from the unanimous Resolution 242 of the UN Security Council in 1967 affirming the necessity for guaranteeing freedom of navigation through international waterways in the Middle East; but the status of the right in customary law remains controversial.

The regime under the Law of the Sea Convention

In the years between UNCLOS I and the close of UNCLOS III many States made claims to wider coastal jurisdiction, notably in the form of extended territorial seas, economic zones and the enclosure of archipelagic waters. While these claims are not inconsistent with the preservation of rights of passage through international straits, they signal a growing reluctance to regard passing foreign ships as beyond the jurisdictional reach of coastal States whose security, environmental or economic interests those ships might adversely affect. The major maritime States, on the other hand, consider that their economic well-being and security — particularly in relation to the deployment, and pursuit, of submarines carrying strategic nuclear missiles — depend upon continuing guarantees of passage through international straits such as Dover, Gibraltar, Hormuz, Bab el Mandeb and Malacca. A compromise was reached, based on the creation of two new legal rights of passage: 'transit passage' through international straits, which is discussed below, and 'archipelagic sea lanes passage' through archipelagic waters, which is discussed in chapter six. Both new categories allow less coastal State control over passing vessels than does innocent passage, but fall far short of granting the same freedom of navigation as would have existed had the waters of the straits constituted high seas. The regime of transit passage applies to 'straits which are used for international navigation between one part of the high seas or an exclusive economic zone and another part of the high seas or an exclusive economic zone' (LOSC, art. 37). Excluded from this definition are, first, cases where a high-seas route or a route through an exclusive economic zone of similar convenience with respect to navigational and hydrographical characteristics exists through the strait (LOSC, art. 36: the so-called Florida Strait between the USA and Cuba would be an example); and, secondly, cases where the strait is formed by an island bordering the strait and its mainland and a route of similar navigational and hydrographic convenience exists through the exclusive economic zone or high seas seaward of the island (LOSC, art. 38(1): the Corfu Channel would be an example).

In the first of these exceptional cases, which can apply only in straits more than twenty-four miles wide, there exists freedom of navigation through the economic zone or high seas route, and the right of innocent passage through the bands of territorial seas which lie on either side of it. In the second case, there exists a non-suspendable right of innocent passage between the island and the mainland, as there does in the third exceptional case, of straits connecting an area of the high seas or an exclusive economic zone with the territorial sea of a third State, as in the Straits of Tiran (LOSC, art. 45). In all other international straits, unless they are the subject of some special treaty such as the Montreux Convention, which regulates the Dardanelles and Bosphorus, the Law of the Sea Convention gives a right of transit passage.

It has been suggested that the transit passage regime is subject to two modifications. First, Iraq takes the view that the regime also applies to passage between islands situated near to international straits if the IMO has designated shipping lanes lying near such islands (as it has in the Straits of Hormuz): this seems to involve no more than a clarification of where the international strait is considered to lie.[4] Secondly, Greece has stated that where the presence of many islands creates a multiplicity of potential straits (as, for example, in the Aegean), the coastal State may designate those in which the right of transit passage is to exist — much as it may designate passages through archipelagic waters.[5]

Transit passage is the exercise of freedom of navigation and overflight solely for the continuous and expeditious transit of the strait between one area of high seas or economic zone and another, or in order to enter or leave a State bordering the strait (LOSC, art. 38(2)). While there is no criterion of 'innocence' to be satisfied, ships and aircraft exercising this right are bound to refrain from the threat or use of force against States bordering the straits or in any other manner which violates the principles of international law embodied in the UN Charter (LOSC, art. 39(1)(b)). Moreover, there is an obligation to refrain from any activities other than those incidental to their normal modes of continuous and expeditious transit unless rendered necessary by *force majeure* or distress (LOSC, art. 39(1)(c)), and it is provided that any activity which is not an exercise of the right of transit passage remains subject to the 'other applicable provisions' of the Convention (LOSC, art. 38(3)). Accordingly, any activity threatening a coastal State would bring the ship or aircraft under the general regime of innocent passage, in which case passage could be denied for want of innocence. In the absence of such 'activity', the only remedy for any threat of force — for example, a threat which may be implicit in the mere fact of the passage of a large number of warships — would appear to be is to pursue the matter as a breach of international law through diplomatic channels and dispute settlement procedures: there is no right to impede the passage. Similarly, transit passage cannot be suspended for security or any other reasons (LOSC, art. 44). Of course, in extreme cases coastal State action might be justifiable on the basis of the right of self defence.

While in transit ships must comply with generally accepted international regulations, procedures and practices for safety at sea and for the prevention of pollution from ships (LOSC, art. 39(2)). Thus standards in, for example, SOLAS conventions and the IMO pollution conventions would be applicable to ships in the strait even if their flag States were not parties to those conventions. Aircraft, too must comply with international standards whilst exercising their right of overflight (LOSC, art. 39(3)). In this way coastal State interests can be protected without imposing unreasonable burdens on passing ships and aircraft, for although the coastal State may legislate for passing craft in these matters, it may only apply internationally agreed standards in its legislation (LOSC, art. 42(1)). This precludes the exposure of merchant ships to a mass of differing, and possibly inconsistent, regulations as they sail around the world. In the same way coastal States may prescribe sea lanes and traffic separation schemes in the strait, but these must first have been adopted by the competent international organisation — that is, the IMO (LOSC, art. 41). The duty to comply with international safety and pollution standards is independent of coastal legislation: the advantage of implementing them in such legislation is that they then become directly enforceable by the coastal State authorities, whereas the duty of compliance would allow only an international claim through diplomatic channels for breach of the treaty obligation, and the international conventions themselves leave enforcement in the hands of the flag State. There is, in addition, a specific duty to refrain from research and survey activities during passage unless the prior authorisation of the States bordering the strait is obtained — even, it seems, if the passage is entirely within the waters of only one of them (LOSC, art. 40).

Apart from the right to implement international safety and pollution standards, coastal States may legislate for passing vessels only in respect of fishing and the taking on board or putting overboard for any commodity, currency or person in violation of local customs, fiscal, immigration or sanitary regulations (LOSC, art. 42(1)). No international standards are imposed here but these laws, like all others, must not discriminate among foreign ships or have the practical effect of impairing the right of transit passage (LOSC, art. 42(2)). Laws on other matters may not be extended to passing ships. So far, we have been concerned with the right to extend the geographical ambit of coastal laws to vessels in transit passage — that is, with legislative jurisdiction. The Convention is silent on the question of the enforcement of these laws against such ships; accordingly the general territorial sea rules apply (LOSC, art. 34), under which enforcement *should*, as was seen in chapter four, only be exercised where the good order of the territorial sea or coastal State is disturbed or the flag State requests assistance. On the other hand, the express provision for the exercise of enforcement jurisdiction in case of pollution causing or threatening major pollution (LOSC, art. 233) may be evidence of a general understanding that enforcement jurisdiction *must* be confined to such cases, notwithstanding the wider coastal State powers enjoyed under the territorial sea regime. Were this interpretation to prove correct, coastal State laws could in general be enforced against foreign ships only when they put into the State's ports. There is, however, a general duty to comply with all laws made within the legislative competence allowed under the Convention to straits States (LOSC, art. 42).

The rights of transit passage described above extend to all ships and aircraft, both military and commercial. As far as submarines are concerned, their apparently common practice of transiting some international straits while submerged seems to be recognised in the requirement that passing vessels engage only in activities 'incident to their *normal mode* of continuous and expeditious transit' (LOSC, art. 39(1)(c); emphasis added). This, at least, is the interpretation adopted by the maritime States, and it is consistent with the *travaux préparatoires* of UNCLOS III: it underlines the importance of transit passage for submarines, which must normally pass through the territorial sea on the surface. Similarly, transit passage is of great importance to aircraft, which have no right of innocent passage over the territorial sea.

The LOSC regime and customary law

Since the end of UNCLOS III, it has been argued by some of the major maritime States, notably the United States and the United Kingdom,[6] neither of which has signed the Law of the Sea Convention, that the right of transit passage given by the Convention is now part of customary international law. A number of arguments have been advanced in support of this view.[7] First, it is argued that a right of passage similar to transit passage existed in customary law before the Convention was drawn up. It was suggested earlier that the balance of opinion was against the existence of such a customary rule. Furthermore, many of the delegates at UNCLOS III, including those of the United States, considered transit passage to be a new concept in international law.[8] Secondly, it is argued that the provisions of the Convention relating to navigation represent a consensus among participating States as to what State practice is or should be. But while there was by the end of UNCLOS III a consensus on the navigational provisions, that consensus would seem to relate to the provisions as components of the Convention, rather than of customary law — a view reflected in the Iranian declaration made on signing the Convention,[9] and borne out by the package-deal nature of UNCLOS III. A third argument is that since the Convention states that 'all' ships and aircraft enjoy the right of transit passage (art. 38(1)), ships and aircraft of non-Party States must enjoy the right. It is doubtful, however, whether the drafters of the Convention actually did intend to accord such rights to third States, as article 36(1) of the Vienna

Convention on the Law of Treaties requires if third parties are to enjoy rights under treaties.

It might be argued that practice since the end of UNCLOS III has generated a right of transit passage in customary law. Undoubtedly, the ships of the major maritime States have sailed, and continue to sail, through straits in what was and is intended to be an exercise of a right corresponding to the conventional right of transit passage. This practice has, however, a certain ambivalence. As far as surface vessels are concerned, it will usually be impossible to tell merely by observing their conduct whether they are engaging in innocent or transit passage. In the case of submarines transiting a strait submerged, the strait State(s) will often be unaware of their presence. In some cases it is probably reasonable to assume that straits States, especially where allies of the flag State in question, have acquiesced in such passage or accepted that passage through the strait was indeed transit passage. Some strait States have explicitly granted a right of transit passage. For example, the United Kingdom announced, during passage of the 1987 Territorial Sea Act (which extends the United Kingdom territorial sea from three to twelve miles, so abolishing the high seas corridor in straits such as the Straits of Dover), that rights equivalent to a right of transit passage would be afforded to other States in the Straits of Dover and certain other straits adjoining the United Kingdom.[10]

The conclusion which emerges is that a general right of transit passage has not yet become established in customary international law. However, through certain straits of particular importance to international navigation, such as the Straits of Dover and probably the Straits of Gibraltar, a right akin to transit passage does in fact exist, either because the States bordering the straits have explicitly granted such a right to third States, or because they have acquiesced in the exercise of such a right.

Special regimes

The Law of the Sea Convention rules on transit passage do not oust those applicable under long-standing international conventions which regulate passage through particular straits in whole or in part (LOSC, art. 35(c)). Though this principle is simply stated, the implications of its application remain to be sorted out. For example, a treaty made in 1881 between Argentina and Chile provides that 'the Straits of Magellan are neutralised for ever, and free navigation is guaranteed to the flags of all nations', but does not elaborate upon the nature of this right of 'free navigation'.[11] Similarly, the 1904 Anglo-French Declaration respecting Egypt and Morocco speaks of the securing of the 'free passage of the Straits of Gibraltar' — although that declaration is arguably concerned only with the neutralisation of the shore, and not with the regime of passage at all. Since 'free navigation' and 'free passage' are, and were, not terms of art clearly distinguished from, for

example, non-suspendable innocent passage, it seems that the best interpretation of the Law of the Sea Convention is that its straits regime would
apply to these straits, there being no special rules on passage to oust it, but
that the neutrality obligations would survive.

More difficult are conventions such as the 1857 Treaty of Copenhagen,
stated by Sweden to fall within the scope of article 35(c). The Treaty includes in relation to the Baltic the provision that 'No vessel shall hence-
forth, under any pretext whatsoever, be subjected, in its passage of the
Sound or Belts, to any detention or hindrance'. Here the right of passage
appears to be supplemented by an immunity from coastal State enforcement jurisdiction. In this case the effect would seem to be that rules in the
Law of the Sea Convention dealing with, for example, the scope of coastal
States' legislative competence would be applicable, but that the rules on
enforcement jurisdiction would not. The Finnish and Swedish governments
have similarly stated that the straits off the Aaland Islands fall within article
35(c), the applicable conventions in this case being the 1921 Convention
on the Non-Fortification and Neutrality of the Aaland Islands, which limits
the access of warships to the territorial seas of the islands, and the 1940
Agreement on the demilitarisation of the islands concluded by Finland and
the Soviet Union. Apart from the constraints upon warships, these conventions would have very little practical impact upon the general regime
set out in the 1982 Convention.[12]

The most detailed of the specific international conventions is the Montreux Convention of 1936 concerning the Turkish Straits of the Bosphorus
and Dardanelles. This convention, the latest of a series concerning the
straits beginning with a Russo-Turkish treaty of 1774, gives during peacetime 'complete freedom of transit and navigation' to merchant vessels and
'freedom of transit' during daylight hours for certain light warships which
give prior notification to the Turkish government. The provisions concerning warships are detailed. Broadly speaking, they must be under 10,000
tons, and no more than nine warships, which must not exceed 15,000 tons
in all, may pass at any one time; however, the Black Sea littoral States have
wider rights and may send capital ships of any tonnage through the straits,
one at a time, and may in some circumstances send submarines through.
These provisions confining the right of passage to certain classes of ship,
and imposing conditions such as prior notification on that right, would continue to apply despite the entry into force of the Law of the Sea Convention. But again, the Law of the Sea Convention provisions on coastal legislative jurisdiction would apply to the Turkish straits, since the Montreux
Convention does not deal with this question.

The restrictive rules of the Montreux Convention are, however, under
some pressure. Aircraft carriers are expressly excluded from the right of
passage under the Convention, but in 1976 the USSR sent the warship
Kiev through the straits. The *Kiev* is equipped with a dozen aircraft, two

dozen helicopters and a flight deck six hundred feet long; but according to the Soviet Union it is not an aircraft carrier but an 'antisubmarine cruiser', like its British counterparts in the *Invincible* class. In fact warships are allowed to carry flight decks so long as they are not 'designed or adapted primarily for the purpose of carrying and operating aircraft at sea', but it is difficult to accept that this was not the intended role of the *Kiev*, even while functioning as an 'antisubmarine cruiser'. The ship was allowed through by Turkey. This underlines the need for the revision of the Montreux Convention, of which there is no immediate prospect, and may signal the practical demise of some of the limitations imposed by that Convention. However, this does not affect the present point, which is that the detailed rules of the Montreux Convention would coexist with the provisions of the Law of the Sea Convention concerning matters outside the scope of the Montreux Convention.

Notes

1 See, e.g., *O'Connell*, vol. I, p. 327.
2 See further R. Lapidoth, 'The Strait of Tiran, the Gulf of Aqaba, and the 1979 Treaty of Peace between Egypt and Israel', 77 *AJIL* 84–108 (1983); M. ElBareidi, 'The Egyptian-Israeli Peace Treaty and access to the Gulf of Aqaba: a new legal regime', 76 *AJIL* 532–54 (1982).
3 *ND* IV, p. 330
4 5 *LOSB* 15 (1985)
5 *Ibid.*, p. 13.
6 See the Statement of the President on United States Ocean Policy, 10 March 1983, XXII *ILM* 464 (1983), and the US Diplomatic Note to Algeria, as protecting power for Iran, 12 July 1984, 78 *AJIL* 884 (1984). And see the British *Parliamentary Debates* (Hansard), House of Lords, Vol. 484, col. 382, 5 February 1987.
7 See, for instance, R. B. Krueger and S. A. Riesenfeld (eds.), *The Developing Order of the Oceans*, Honolulu, 1985, pp. 661–730; R. D. Neubauer and J. S. Shi, 'Establishing the non-seabed provisions of the UNCLOS III Treaty as customary international law', *Ocean Policy Study Series*, 1 (1984), p. 1; J. M. Van Dyke (ed.), *Consensus and Confrontation: The United States and the Law of the Sea Convention*, Honolulu, 1985, pp. 292–301.
8 See *DUSPIL 1974*, 347–52; *DUSPIL 1975*, 431–2.
9 5 *LOSB* 42 (1985).
10 *Parliamentary Debates* (Hansard), House of Lords, Vol. 484, col. 382, 5 February 1987. Cf., French Law No. 71–1060 of 1971, which enables regulations to be made for 'free maritime and aerial navigation' through the straits bordered by France: (English translation in XI *ILM* 153 (1972)).
11 See now article 10 of the Argentina–Chile Treaty of Peace and Friendship, 1984, under which the parties agree that their boundary in the Straits in no way affects the 1881 Treaty, and Argentina 'assumes the obligation to maintain at all times and under any circumstances, the right of ships of all flags to navigate expeditiously and without obstacles through the jurisdictional waters towards and away from the Straits of Magellan'.
12 5 *LOSB* 10 (Finland), 22 (Sweden) (1985).

Further reading

General

R. P. Anand, 'Transit passage and overflight in international straits', 26 *IJIL* 72–105 (1986).

R. R. Baxter, *The Law of International Waterways*, Cambridge, Mass., 1964.

E. D. Brown, *Passage through the Territorial Sea, Straits Used for International Navigation, and Archipelagos*, London, 1974.

E. Brüel, *International Straits*, 2 vols., Copenhagen, 1947.

K. L. Koh, *Straits in International Navigation. Contemporary Issues*, London, 1982.

R. Lapidoth, *Les détroits en droit international*, Paris, 1972.

J. N. Moore, 'The regime of straits and the Third United Nations Conference on the Law of the Sea', 74 *AJIL* 77–121 (1980).

W. M. Reisman, 'The regime of straits and national security. An appraisal of international lawmaking', 74 *AJIL* 48–76 (1980).

Particular straits

A. R. Deluca, *Great Power Rivalry at the Turkish Straits. The Montreux Conference and Convention of 1936*, New York, 1981.

F. D. Froman, 'Kiev and the Montreux Convention', 14 *San Diego Law Review* 681–717 (1977).

L. Gross, 'The Geneva Conference on the Law of the Sea and the right of innocent passage through the Gulf of Aqaba', 53 *AJIL* 564–94 (1959).

D. H. N. Johnson, 'Some legal problems of international waterways, with particular reference to the Straits of Tiran and the Suez Canal' 31 *Modern Law Review* 153–64 (1968).

T. L. McDorman, 'In the wake of the *Polar Sea*: Canadian jurisdiction and the Northwest Passage', 10 *Marine Policy* 243–257 (1986).

D. Pharand, 'Innocent passage in the Arctic', 6 *Canadian Yearbook of International Law* 3–60 (1968).

F. Vali, *The Turkish Straits and NATO,* Stanford, Cal, 1972.

A series of detailed monographs, each written by a specialist, is currently being published under the general editorship of G. J. Mangone. The volumes published at present are as follows:

G. Alexandersson, *The Baltic Straits*, Alphen aan den Rijn, 1982.

W. E. Butler, *The Northeast Arctic Passage*, Alphen aan den Rijn, 1978.

L. Cuyvers, *The Straits of Dover,* Alphen aan den Rijn, 1986.

R. Lapidoth, *The Red Sea,* Alphen aan den Rijn, 1981.

M. Leifer, *Malacca, Singapore and Indonesia,* Alphen aan den Rijn, 1978.

D. Pharand and L. Legault, *Northwest Passage: Arctic Straits*, Alphen aan den Rijn, 1984.

R. K. Ramazani, *The Persian Gulf and the Strait of Hormuz*, Alphen aan den Rijn, 1979.

C. L. Rozakis and P. N. Stagos, *The Turkish Straits*, Alphen aan den Rijn, 1987.

S. K. Truver, *The Strait of Gibraltar and the Mediterranean,* Alphen aan den Rijn, 1980.

CHAPTER SIX
Archipelagos

Development of a special regime for archipelagos

We saw in chapter two that every island can generate a territorial sea and that most islands can generate all other maritime zones. In the case of an archipelago (that is, a group of islands), the question of whether this rule should apply, or whether an archipelago should enjoy a special regime which would recognise and reinforce its unitary nature (for example, by drawing baselines around and enclosing the archipelago), was debated extensively, but inconclusively, between 1930 and 1958. Thus neither the 1930 Hague conference, nor the ILC in preparing its draft articles for the 1958 conference, nor that conference itself — in spite of having before it an excellent memorandum on the subject by the Norwegian jurist Jens Evensen (see the reference in 'Further reading') — were able to agree on any provisions dealing specifically and comprehensively with archipelagos.

The 1958 conference, however, did deal with one type of archipelago, the so-called 'coastal' archipelago. Article 4 of the Territorial Sea Convention, it may be recalled (see chapter two), provides that straight baselines may be drawn around islands fringing a coast. It is therefore possible, using this provision, to draw straight baselines around the outermost points of a coastal archipelago and 'tie' it to the mainland coast. This is what Norway had done, and the United Kingdom disputed, in the *Anglo-Norwegian Fisheries* case (1951); and since then similar action has been taken by other States, e.g. by the United Kingdom in respect of the Hebrides,[1] and by the Federal Republic of Germany in respect of the Frisian islands.[2]

It was unsuccessfully argued by some at the 1958 conference, notably Indonesia, the Philippines, Denmark and Yugoslavia, that the rules on straight baselines, which deal with coastal archipelagos, could be applied by analogy to 'mid-ocean' archipelagos such as Tonga and the Philippines. This distinction between 'coastal' and 'mid-ocean' archipelagos is one that is commonly made, and although it is in general terms easy to see the difference between the two types, it is sometimes difficult in practice to apply the distinction: for example, is Iceland's straight baseline system in effect tying offshore islands to a mainland coast (and so governed by the rules on straight baselines), as Iceland claims, or is it in reality a system of straight lines drawn around the islands of a mid-ocean archipelago? This difficulty in distinguishing between the two broad categories of archipelago points to a further factor: the great geographical diversity of archipelagos, even within each broad group, which has made it difficult to draw up a set of agreed rules of general application.

The main advocates of a special regime for archipelagos at the 1958 conference were Indonesia and the Philippines. Shortly before the conference, in 1957 and 1955 respectively, these two States announced that they would enclose the whole of their archipelagos by straight lines and treat the waters thus enclosed as internal waters.[3] These claims were followed by detailed legislation in 1960 and 1961.[4] The reasons for these claims, which met with protests from a number of States (including the United Kingdom and the USA)[5] were primarily security and, in the case of Indonesia, to stress the unity and integrity of its vast and heterogenous island territory.

The principal opposition at UNCLOS I to a special regime for archipelagos came from the major maritime States. They feared that such a regime would result in areas which had previously been high seas or territorial seas becoming internal waters, with the consequent loss of navigational rights for both their naval and commercial vessels, especially in the case of archipelagos such as the Bahamas, Fiji, Indonesia and the Philippines, which straddle important shipping routes. Until UNCLOS III these maritime States consistently took the view that the normal regime of islands should apply to mid-ocean archipelagos, thus leaving territorial sea or high seas routes between most islands.

Since 1958 many archipelagic States in the Caribbean and Indian and Pacific Oceans have become independent, and this has increased the pressure for the adoption of a special regime for mid-ocean archipelagos to meet the interests of archipelagic States. These interests are economic (fishing and the control of inter-island traffic); political (promoting the unity of the archipelago); security; preventing smuggling and illegal entry; and the control of pollution. The question of a special archipelagic regime was taken up and vigorously pursued at UNCLOS III by a group of archipelagic States (Fiji, Indonesia, Mauritius and the Philippines), and as a result the Law of the Sea Convention contains a special regime for mid-ocean archipelagos in Part IV. Coastal archipelagos are covered by the provisions on straight baselines — although it should be noted that the Convention does not use the terms 'mid-ocean' or 'coastal', nor does it distinguish directly between the two.

The essential features of the new regime laid down in Part IV (which is now to some extent being reflected in State practice, discussed below) are, first, that it permits straight 'archipelagic baselines' to be drawn around the outermost islands of archipelagos, thus meeting the wishes of archipelagic States, and, secondly, that it creates a new legal concept of 'archipelagic waters' for the waters thus enclosed of such a nature that it should accommodate the navigational interests of maritime States. Before looking at these two aspects in detail, it is necessary to consider the definition of an archipelago and an archipelagic State.

Definition of an archipelago and an archipelagic State

Only an archipelagic *State* can draw archipelagic baselines around an archipelago (LOSC, art. 47). It is therefore important to know what an archipelagic State is. Article 46 defines an archipelagic State as 'a State constituted wholly by one or more archipelagos and may include other islands'. An archipelago is defined in the same article as:

a group of islands, including parts of islands, interconnecting waters and other natural features which are so closely interrelated that such islands, waters and other natural features form an intrinsic geographical, economic and political entity, or which historically have been regarded as such.

A number of points should be noted about these definitions. First, archipelagic States do not include mainland States which possess non-coastal archipelagos e.g. Denmark (with the Faroes), Ecuador (the Galapagos Islands), Norway (Spitsbergen) and Portugal (the Azores). This means that archipelagic baselines cannot be drawn around such archipelagos, nor in many cases would it appear to be justifiable under the Law of the Sea Convention to construct straight baselines around them. This seems an unnecessary and unreasonable restriction. It may be noted, however, that some archipelagos of this type, such as the Faroes and Galapagos, are bounded at present by a series of straight lines which serve as the baselines.[6] The validity of these claims under customary international law will be discussed below.

Secondly, the definition of an archipelagic State would appear to embrace a number of States which do not normally consider themselves to be archipelagic States, such as Japan, New Zealand and the United Kingdom. While it is not clear whether States have a choice as to whether they consider themselves as archipelagic States, they certainly do have an option as to whether they draw archipelagic baselines — and the capacity to draw such baselines appears to be the only consequence of a State being designated an archipelagic State — since article 47 says, 'an archipelagic State *may* draw straight archipelagic baselines' (emphasis added). In any case most of these non-traditional archipelagic States will in practice be unable to draw archipelagic baselines because of the rules governing the drawing of such lines, discussed in the next section.

Even if we exclude States which would not consider themselves to be archipelagic States (like Japan and the United Kingdom), there are still quite a number of States — somewhere between twenty-five and thirty-five — which fall within the definition of an archipelagic State. Although the definition of an archipelago (and thus an archipelagic State) is rather wide and imprecise (for example, nothing is said about the number of islands or their size and proximity relative one to another), some of the difficulties which might arise as a result are in practice avoided by the fact that the extent to which archipelagic baselines may be drawn around archipelagos is, as we shall see in a moment, much more clearly and strictly formulated. The effect is to deprive some archipelagic States altogether of the possibility of drawing archipelagic baselines.

Archipelagic baselines

Article 47(1) provides that 'an archipelagic State may draw straight archipelagic baselines joining the outermost points of the outermost islands and drying reefs of the archipelago'. These lines then serve as the baseline from which the breadth of the archipelagic State's territorial sea, contiguous zone, exclusive economic zone and continental shelf is measured (LOSC, art. 48). The drawing of archipelagic baselines is subject to a number of conditions, of which two are precise and mathematical, and the remainder (many of which parallel the conditions governing the drawing of straight baselines) more general and less precise. These conditions are as follows:

1. Archipelagic baselines must be so drawn that the ratio of land to water within the lines is not more than 1 : 1 and not less than 1 : 9 (LOSC, art. 47(1)). For the purpose of computing this ratio, 'land' may include 'waters lying within the fringing reefs of islands and atolls, including that part of a steepsided oceanic plateau which is enclosed or nearly enclosed by a chain of limestone islands and drying reefs lying on the perimeter of the plateau' (LOSC, art. 47(7)). The maximum ratio of 1 : 1 prevents archipelagic States which consist predominantly of one large island or a few large islands close together (such as Cuba, Iceland, Madagascar, New Zealand and the United Kingdom) from drawing archipelagic baselines (although why this is thought to be necessary is unclear): often in such cases, however, it will be possible for the State concerned to draw straight baselines along all or part of the coast of the main island and tie in offshore islands in this way, as has been done notably by Cuba[7] and Iceland.[8] The minimum ratio of 1 : 9 prevents archipelagic baselines being drawn around very distant islands in an archipelago or being drawn at all around widely dispersed archipelagos consisting of small islands, such as Kiribati and Tuvalu. Nevertheless, these figures accommodate the main archipelagic claims — as they were intended to do. By way of illustration, the ratio of

land to water in the Indonesian and Philippine claims is 1 : 1·2 and 1 : 1·8 respectively.

2. Archipelagic baselines must not exceed 100 miles in length, except that up to three per cent of the total number of lines may be between 100 and 125 miles in length (LOSC, art. 47(2)). These figures are generous to the archipelagic State, and the fact that they changed quite considerably during successive versions of the negotiating text suggests that their choice is not based on any objective geographical, ecological or oceanographical factors. By way of illustration again, it is of interest to note that the Indonesian system is made up of 196 lines, of which five are between 100 and 125 miles in length and the remainder less than 100 miles; while the Philippine system has eighty lines, of which two are between 100 and 125 miles in length, one is 140 miles and the remainder less than 100 miles.

3. The main islands of the archipelago must be included within the archipelagic baselines (LOSC, art. 47(1)).

4. The drawing of archipelagic baselines must not 'depart to any appreciable extent from the general configuration of the archipelago' (LOSC, art. 47(3)). Whether most archipelagos have an ascertainable 'configuration' may be doubted. In any case, it is the archipelagic baselines themselves, by being drawn around the outermost islands of the group, which largely determine the configuration of the archipelago.

5. Archipelagic baselines 'shall not be drawn to and from low-tide elevations, unless lighthouses or similar installations which are permanently above sea level have been built on them or where a low-tide elevation is situated wholly or partly at a distance not exceeding the breadth of the territorial sea from the nearest island' (LOSC, art. 47(4)).

6. Archipelagic baselines must not be drawn in such a way as to cut off the territorial sea of another State from the high seas or its exclusive economic zone (LOSC, art. 47(5)). The Indonesian baseline system would seem to have this effect on the territorial sea of Singapore. On the other hand, even without the Indonesian system, it is doubtful whether Singapore would have been able to generate an exclusive economic zone. In a case like this, where the result appears to be the same whether the rule in article 47(5) is applied or not, it would seem not unreasonable for the archipelagic State to be allowed to draw archipelagic baselines, even though a strict reading of article 47(5) might suggest that no such baselines should be drawn in this situation.

7. The archipelagic State must clearly indicate its archipelagic baseline system on charts of an adequate scale. Alternatively, it may list the geographical co-ordinates of the points to and from which archipelagic baselines are drawn. In either case, due publicity must be given to such charts or lists. Furthermore, a copy of each chart or list must be deposited with the UN Secretary General (LOSC, art. 47(8), (9)).

It is not necessary for an archipelagic State to attempt to enclose all the islands making up that State in a single system of archipelagic baselines, since, according to its definition in article 46, an archipelagic State can consist of a number of archipelagos (as, for example, is the case with the Solomon Islands and Mauritius). In such cases, archipelagic baselines can be drawn around each of the archipelagos making up the archipelagic State (provided, of course, that the above conditions are fulfilled), as indeed the Solomon Islands have done.

Archipelagic waters

Archipelagic waters comprise all the maritime waters within archipelagic baselines. One qualification must, however, be made. *Within* archipelagic baselines an archipelagic State can draw closing lines across river mouths, bays and ports on individual islands in accordance with the normal rules on base-lines. The waters so enclosed are internal waters, not archipelagic waters (LOSC, art. 50). Since article 50 does not refer to the possibility of drawing closing lines across gaps in the coral reefs of atolls, lagoons lying within such reefs appear to be archipelagic waters, rather than internal waters, notwithstanding the fact that they are regarded as 'land' for the purpose of calculating the land — water ratio within archipelagic baselines (LOSC, art. 47(7) — discussed above) and that under the ordinary rules on baselines they would be internal waters. It would seem logical that they should always be treated as internal waters and archipelagic States permitted to draw closing lines across gaps in reefs, as in fact Fiji has done in its archipelagic baseline system.[9]

The concept of archipelagic waters is a new one in international law. Such waters are neither internal waters nor territorial sea, although they bear a number of resemblances to the latter. An archipelagic State has sovereignty over its archipelagic waters, including their superjacent air space, subjacent sea bed and subsoil, and 'the resources contained therein' (LOSC, art. 49). This sovereignty is, however, subject to a number of rights enjoyed by third States. First, an archipelagic State must 'respect' rights enjoyed by third States deriving from existing agreements (LOSC, art. 51(1)). This provision was presumably inserted to avoid any possible conflict between an archipelagic State's rights under the Law of the Sea Convention and its obligations under prior agreements. Secondly, an archipelagic State must:

recognise traditional fishing rights and other legitimate activities of the immediately adjacent neighbouring States in certain areas falling within archipelagic waters. The terms and conditions for the exercise of such rights and activities, including the nature, the extent and the areas to which they apply, shall, at the request of any of the States concerned, be regulated by bilateral agreements between them. Such rights shall not be transferred to or shared with third States or their nationals. [LOSC, art. 51(1)]

Furthermore, in circumstances such as exist in relation to Indonesia and Malaysia, where part of an archipelagic State's archipelagic waters:

lies between two parts of an immediately adjacent neighbouring State, existing rights and all other legitimate interests which the latter State has traditionally exercised in such waters and all rights stipulated by agreement between those States shall continue and be respected. [LOSC, art. 47(6)]

In implementation of article 47(6), for whose benefit and at whose prompting the provision was inserted in the Convention, Indonesia and Malaysia signed a bilateral agreement in February 1982.[10] The agreement has provisions guaranteeing navigation and overflight between East and West Malaysia (discussed below), deals with cables linking East and West Malaysia and passing through Indonesian waters (also discussed below), and permits Malaysian fishermen to fish by traditional methods in part of Indonesia's archipelagic waters east of the Anambas Islands, an area where Malaysian fishermen have fished for decades.

The third obligation on an archipelagic State is to:

respect existing submarine cables laid by other States and passing through its waters without making a landfall. An archipelagic State shall permit the maintenance and replacement of such cables upon receiving due notice of their location and the intention to repair or replace them. [LOSC, art. 51(2)]

It should be noted that this provision applies only to cables, and not pipelines, and then only to existing cables. The laying of new cables and new pipelines by other States is thus totally dependent on the consent of the archipelagic State. As far as existing pipelines are concerned, the question arises as to whether an archipelagic State can require their removal. Where the State owning the pipeline is a party to the Law of the Sea Convention, articles 49 and 51(2) would appear to suggest that this is possible. Where the pipeline State is not a party, however, legal relations between the pipeline State and the archipelagic State will be based on customary international law. If the pipeline has been laid in an area that according to custom is high seas, then it would seem that the archipelagic State may not interfere with the pipeline and take away the other State's acquired rights. This point may of course be of only theoretical interest as far as pipelines passing through archipelagos are concerned, but the point is a general one which may have practical application in other areas. The Indonesia–Malaysia agreement, referred to above, in its provisions on cables essentially repeats the provisions of article 51(2), but in addition also permits Malaysia to lay new cables through Indonesian waters and requires Indonesia to ensure the security of existing cables, for example by establishing safety zones around them where appropriate.

Finally, and most important, there are the navigational rights of other States. The ships of all States enjoy in archipelagic waters the same right of innocent passage as they enjoy in the territorial sea (LOSC, art. 52(1)). This right may only be suspended, temporarily and in specified areas, for security reasons, after due notice has been given (LOSC, art. 52(2)). In addition, foreign ships and aircraft enjoy the rather more extensive right of 'archipelagic sea lanes passage' in sea lanes and air routes designated by the archipelagic State in consultation with the 'competent international organisation' (by which presumably is meant the IMO) (LOSC, art. 53(1), (2), (9)). Such lanes and routes, which may be up to fifty miles in width, shall cross both archipelagic waters and the territorial sea beyond, and shall include all normal passage routes used for international navigation or overflight (LOSC, art. 53(4), (5)). Archipelagic sea-lanes passage is essentially the same as transit passage through straits (discussed in chapter five), and the rights and duties of foreign States and the archipelagic State in respect of archipelagic sea-lanes passage are the same, *mutatis mutandis*, as the rights and duties of foreign States and straits States in respect of transit passage (LOSC, arts. 53, 54). On this latter point the Convention simply cross-refers to the articles on transit passage through straits (LOSC, art. 54): a similar technique is also used earlier when dealing with innocent passage in archipelagic waters (LOSC, art. 52(1)). This has one unfortunate effect as far as the jurisdiction of the archipelagic State over foreign shipping in archipelagic waters is concerned. While the general jurisdictional competence — both legislative and enforcement — of the coastal State is set out in the provisions of the Law of the Sea Convention on innocent passage and transit passage (and by cross-reference applies to innocent passage in archipelagic waters and archipelagic sea-lanes passage), the Convention in its provisions on pollution gives the coastal State additional enforcement jurisdiction in respect of pollution over foreign vessels in its territorial sea and straits (see LOSC, arts. 220, 233). This additional jurisdiction does not apply in archipelagic waters. The result, therefore, is that in its archipelagic waters an archipelagic State has less enforcement jurisdiction over foreign vessels in matters of pollution than a non-archipelagic State in its territorial sea or straits (or than the archipelagic State itself has in its own territorial sea lying *beyond* its archipelagic waters). This seems anomalous and undesirable, and may possibly be an oversight in drafting.

Article 53(12) provides that 'if an archipelagic State does not designate sea lanes or air routes, the right of archipelagic sea lanes passage may be exercised through the routes normally used for international navigation'. This provision, assuming it applies to aircraft (and the wording is rather ambiguous because of the omission of a reference to overflight at the end of the sentence), is most important, for without it aircraft would have no guaranteed right to overfly archipelagos, since aircraft, unlike ships, enjoy no right of innocent passage.

Under the Indonesia–Malaysia agreement referred to above, Indonesia has designated two corridors of twenty miles in width (not fifty miles as in the Convention) for Malaysia to exercise archipelagic sea lanes passage between East and West Malaysia. On the other hand, in such sea lanes Malaysia has the right (not enjoyed by other States) to conduct naval or aerial manoeuvres so long as such manoeuvres do not infringe Indonesia's security. In addition, Malaysian civilian aircraft can continue to use existing air routes through Indonesia's archipelagic waters.

In general, the rights accorded to foreign States in archipelagic waters should satisfy the navigational and communciations interests of maritime States. It is, however, anomalous that these rights are somewhat more extensive than the rights foreign States enjoy in an archipelagic State's territorial sea, which lies seaward of its archipelagic waters.

Recent State practice

Although there appears to have been general consensus at UNCLOS III on the legal regime for archipelagos since about 1977, recent State practice is rather diverse and not always in accordance with the Law of the Sea Convention. A number of trends can be discerned. First, several archipelagic States have drawn archipelagic baselines and accorded the enclosed waters the status of archipelagic waters in a manner that appears to be in accordance with the provisions of the Convention. These States include Antigua and Barbuda,[11] Fiji,[12] Papua New Guinea,[13] São Tomé e Príncipe,[14] the Solomon Islands,[15] Trinidad and Tobago[16] and Vanuatu.[17] Secondly, there are three States — Kiribati,[18] St Vincent[19] and Tuvalu[20] — which have enacted legislation for an archipelagic regime whose provisions appear to be in conformity with the Convention as regards the status of archipelagic waters but which have not yet drawn the necessary archipelagic baselines. Prescott suggests that it is impossible for Kiribati and Tuvalu to draw archipelagic baselines while respecting the Convention's minimum ratio of land to water of 1:9, but adds that Kiribati and some other archipelagic States 'regard the formulae and measurements in article 47 as arbitrary and without binding force for those archipelagic States which were too poor to involve themselves in the negotiations which produced those rules.'[21]

Thirdly, there are some archipelagic States which have adopted archipelagic legislation which in one way or another is not in conformity with the Convention. Such States include Cape Verde[22] (two out of a total of fourteen archipelagic baselines are in excess of 125 miles, the ratio of land to water is less than 1:9, and although a 'freedom of innocent passage and overflight along established navigation routes' through archipelagic waters is given, this may not equate to archipelagic sea lanes passage); Comoros[23] (a right of innocent passage is given through archipelagic waters, but the legislation makes no mention of archipelagic sea lanes passage); Indonesia (which has retained its orginal archipelagic legislation[24] which accords the waters enclosed by archipelagic baselines the status of internal waters, through which there is a right of innocent, but not archipelagic sea lanes, passage); and Mauritius[25] (which has delimited its maritime zones *inter alia* from straight lines drawn around the Chagos Archipelago but these lines are described in the legislation, wrongly it would seem, as straight baselines, not archipelagic baselines, and there is no provision concerning the legal status of the waters enclosed by these lines.) Most notable of these States is perhaps the Philippines, which has retained its original archipelagic legislation[26] which accords the waters enclosed by archipelagic baselines (more than three per cent of which are over 100 miles and one of which is over 125 miles in length) the status of internal waters and says nothing about other States' navigational rights therein, although according to a Philippine *note verbale* of 1955[27] there is a right of innocent passage. When ratifying the Law of the Sea Convention the Philippines made a declaration that the 'provisions of the Convention on archipelagic passage through sea lanes do not nullify or impair the sovereignty of the Philippines as an archipelagic State over the sea lanes and ... that the concept of archipelagic waters is similar to the concept of internal waters under the Constitution of the Philippines, and removes straits connecting these waters with the economic zone or high seas from the rights of foreign vessels to transit passage for international navigation'.[28] This declaration has been objected to by Czechoslovakia, the USSR and Bulgaria on the grounds that it exceeds the permissible scope of declarations given by article 310 of the Convention and is in reality an impermissible reservation and that it indicates an intention by the Philippines to contravene the Convention.[29] On the other hand, no protest appears to have been made in respect of the length of the Philippines' archipelagic baselines.

A fourth trend is that some obviously archipelagic States have not utilised archipelagic baselines in their recent maritime zones legislation but may do so in the future (e.g. the Seychelles[30] and Tonga[31]). Finally, some States not falling within the definition of archipelagic States claim to draw baselines enclosing mid-ocean archipelagos. These lines cannot be archipelagic baselines as that term is used in the Law of the Sea Convention, nor do they appear to be justifiable as straight baselines. Examples of States making such claims are Denmark (in respect of the Faroes);[32] Ecuador (in respect of the Galapagos Islands);[33] Spain (in respect of the Canaries);[34] and Australia (in respect of the Houtman Abrolhos Islands).[35] On the other hand, some non-archipelagic States have recently rejected the opportunity, when enacting maritime zones legislation, to draw lines enclosing mid-ocean archipelagos. Examples of such States include the USA (in respect of Micronesia)[36] and New Zealand (in respect of the Cook Islands and the Tokelau Islands).[37]

The question arises as to the validity of these various claims, pending the entry into force of the Law of the Sea Convention. As with most maritime claims, the answer turns on the issue of opposability (see chapter one). In other words, an archipelagic claim will be valid *vis-à-vis* those States that acquiesce in the claim or definitely accept it (as, for example, the EEC, Norway and the USSR appear to have done when concluding agreements with Denmark permitting their vessels to fish in the Faroese 200 mile fishing zone[38] and as Malaysia has done in its 1982 agreement with Indonesia, referred to above). The claim will not, however, be valid as against States which have persistently objected to it (but see pp. 9–10). As regards the important question of navigational rights in the vicinity of archipelagos, it therefore follows that where an archipelagic claim has been recognised, States recognising that claim enjoy whatever navigational rights through archipelagic waters are accorded by the claim. Where, on the other hand, a claim is not accepted, the status of the waters between the islands of the archipelago will not be archipelagic but territorial sea or high seas: consequently other States' navigational rights will be those of innocent passage or high seas freedom of navigation.

Hodgson and Smith[39] question whether the concept of an archipelagic State is really necessary with the introduction of the exclusive economic zone. They point out that the use of archipelagic baselines will only marginally increase the size of the exclusive economic zone (compared with measuring the zone from each individual island), and that the gain in the waters enclosed by baselines becoming archipelagic rather than territorial sea or exclusive economic zone 'may be more psychological than real'. On the other hand, these factors should help to make the concept of an archipelagic State acceptable to the maritime State. And for an archipelagic State, as Anand points out,[40] 'the psychological feeling of its various islands and sea between them being universally accepted as one unit is no mean gain'.

Notes

1 Territorial Waters Order in Council, 1964. S. I. 1965, p. 6452A; *UN Leg . Ser.* B/15, p. 129.
2 *Limits in the Seas*, No. 38 (1974).
3 See Indonesian communiqué of 14 December 1957, Whiteman, Vol. IV, p. 284; and Philippine *note verbale* of 7 March 1955 to the UN Secretary General, UN Doc. A/2934 (1955), pp. 52–3. These were really the first specific claims to a special status for archipelagos, although rather unclearly formulated claims had been made earlier by Ecuador (in respect of the Galapagos Islands), Tonga and Bermuda. For details, see D. P. O' Connell, *op. cit.* in 'Further reading', pp. 23–4, 45–7 and 51.

4   Indonesia: Act No. 4 concerning Indonesian Waters, 18 February 1960. *Limits in the Seas*, No. 35 (1971). Philippines: Act No. 3046 of 17 June 1961 to define the Baselines of the Territorial Sea of the Philippines (as amended by Act No. 5446 of 18 September 1968). *ND* I, p. 27; *UN Leg. Ser.* B/15, p. 105; *Limits in the Seas*, No. 33 (1971).

5   See Whiteman, Vol. IV, pp. 283–5

6   For the Faroese legislation, see n. 32. For the legislation relating to the Galapagos, see Ecuador, Supreme Decree No. 959-A of 28 June 1971 prescribing Straight Baselines for the Measurement of the Territorial Sea. *UN Leg. Ser.* B/18, p. 15; *Limits in the Seas*, No. 42 (1972).

7   Act of 24 February 1977 (Decree No. 1) concerning the Breadth of the Territorial Sea. *ND* VII, p. 23; *UN Leg. Ser.* B/19, p. 16; *Limits in the Seas,* No. 76 (1977); *Smith*, p. 109.

8   Law No. 41 of 1 June 1979 concerning the Territorial Sea, the Economic Zone and the Continental Shelf. *UN Leg. Ser.* B/19, p. 43; *Smith* p. 209. But note that neither the Cuban nor the Icelandic baselines are wholly in conformity with the Convention's provisions on straight baselines: see J. R. V. Prescott, *The Maritime Political Boundaries of the World*, London, 1985, pp. 260 and 337.

9   See n. 12.

10 Treaty relating to the Legal Regime of Archipelagic State and the Rights of Malaysia in the Territorial Sea, Archipelagic Waters and the Territory of the Republic of Indonesia lying between East and West Malaysia. We have not been able to locate the text of this Treaty. The account of its provisions that follows is taken from the article by Hamzah, *op. cit.* in 'Further reading'.

11 Territorial Waters (Amendment) Act 1986.

12 Marine Spaces Act, 1977. *ND* VII, p. 391; *Smith*, p. 129; *Limits in the Seas* No. 101 (1984).

13 National Seas Act, 1977. *ND* VII, p. 485; *Smith*, p. 363.

14 Decree-Law No. 14/78 of 16 June 1978. *ND* VII, p. 50; *UN Leg. Ser.* B/19, p. 101; as amended by Decree Law No. 48/82, 1 *LOSB* 39 (1983); *Limits in the Seas* No. 98 (1983).

15 Delimitation of Marine Waters Act, 1978. *Smith*, p. 413; and Declaration of Archipelagos of Solomon Islands, 1979, and Declaration of Archipelagic Baselines, 1979. *UN Leg. Ser.* B/19, pp. 106, 107.

16 Archipelagic Waters and Exclusive Economic Zone Act, 1986. 9 *LOSB* 6 (1987). But note that the Act makes provision specifically only for innocent passage in archipelagic waters: archipelagic sea lanes passage may be provided for by regulations (see s. 22(s)). Furthermore, the Act does not specify the exact location of archipelagic baselines: this is to be published later (s.6). Prescott, *op. cit.* in 'Further reading', p. 47, suggests that Trinidad and Toabago would be unable to draw archipelagic baselines so as to satisfy the 1:1 maximum ratio of land to water.

17 Maritime Zones Act, 1981. 1 *LOSB* 64 (1983); *Smith*, p. 471.

18 Maritime Zones (Declaration) Act, 1983. *Smith*, p. 245.

19 Maritime Areas Act, 1983. *Smith*, p. 399.

20 Maritime Zones (Declaration) Ordinance, 1983. *Smith*, p. 459.

21 Prescott, *op. cit.* in 'Further reading', p. 48.

22 Decree No. 126/77. *Smith*, p. 95 (replacing Decree No. 14/75, *UN Leg. Ser.* B/19, p. 13).

23 Law No. 82–005. *Smith*, p. 103. It is not clear whether Comoros has yet drawn the archipelagic baselines for which its legislation provides.

24 See n. 4; and see also Presidential Decree No. 8 concerning Innocent Passage of Foreign Vessels in Indonesian Waters, 1962. Tangsubkul, *op. cit.* in 'Further reading', p. 73.

25 Maritime Zones Act, 1977 and Notice No. 199 of 1984. *Smith*, pp. 288 and 292. Note that the Chagos Archiepalgo is regarded by the United Kingdom as being part of British Indian Ocean Territory.

26 See n. 4.

27 See n. 3.

28 5 *LOSB* 62–3 (1985).

29 6 *LOSB* 10 and 12 (1985); 7 *LOSB* 7 (1986).

30 Maritime Zones Act, 1977 and Exclusive Economic Zone (No.2) Order, 1978. *Smith*, pp. 407 and 411.

31 Territorial Sea and Exclusive Economic Zone Act, 1978. *Smith*, p. 441.

32 Order No. 598 of 21 December 1976 on the Fishing Territory of the Faroes. *ND* V, p. 111; *UN Leg. Ser.* B/19, p. 192. Order No. 599 of 21 December 1976 on the Boundary of the Sea Territory of the Faroes. *ND* V, p. 112.

33 See n. 6.

34 Law No. 15/78 of 20 February 1978 on the Economic Zone. *ND* VIII, p. 19; *UN Leg. Ser.* B/19, p. 250; *Smith*, p. 425; and Royal Decree No. 2510/1977. *UN Leg. Ser.* B/19, p. 112.

35 Proclamation of 4 February 1983. *Commonwealth of Australia Gazette* No. 29 of 9 February 1983. On the other hand, the lines drawn around the Furneaux Islands would appear to be justifiable as straight baselines. On the claims referred to in this and the preceding three notes, see J. R. V. Prescott, 'Straight baselines: theory and practice' in E. D. Brown and R. R. Churchill (eds.), *The UN Convention on the Law of the Sea: Impact and Implementation*, Honolulu, Hawaii, 1987, pp. 288–318.

36 Micronesia. Fishery Zones Jurisdiction Act, 1977. *ND* VII, p. 143.

37 Cook Islands. Territorial Sea and Exclusive Economic Zone Act, 1977. *ND* VII, p. 374; *Smith*, p. 325. Tokelau. Territorial Sea and Exclusive Economic Zone Act, 1977. *ND* VII, p. 468; *Smith*, p. 341.

38 See Denmark-EEC Agreement on Fisheries, 1977; Faroes-Norway Agreement on Mutual Fishery Rights, 1979; and Denmark-USSR Agreement on Mutual Fishery Relations between the Faroes and the USSR, 1977.

39 R. D. Hodgson and R. W. Smith, 'The informal single negotiating text (Committee II). A geographical perspective', 3 *ODIL* 225 (1976), at 244.

40 R. P. Anand, *op. cit.* in 'Further reading', p. 254.

Further reading

C. F. Amerasinghe, 'The problem of archipelagos in the international law of the sea', 23 *ICLQ* 539–75 (1974).

R. P. Anand, 'Mid-ocean archipelagos in international law. Theory and practice', 19 *IJIL* 228–56 (1979).

D. Andrew, 'Archipelagos and the law of the sea', 2 *Marine Policy* 45–64 (1978).

D. W. Bowett, *The Legal Regime of Islands in International Law*, Dobbs Ferry, N.Y., 1979, chapter 4.

J. Evensen, 'Certain legal aspects concerning the delimitation of the territorial waters of archipelagos', *First UN Conference on the Law of the Sea, Official Records*, Vol. I, pp. 289–302.

B. A. Hamzah, 'Indonesia's archipelagic regime. Implications for Malaysia', 8 *Marine Policy* 30–43 (1984).

L. L. Herman, 'The modern concept of the off-lying archipelago in international law', XXIII *Canadian Yearbook of International Law* 172–200 (1985).

R. D. Hodgson and L. M. Alexander, *Towards an Objective Analysis of Special Circumstances. Bays, Rivers, Coastal and Oceanic Archipelagos and Atolls*, Law of the Sea Institute, University of Rhode Island, Occasional Paper No. 13, 1972, pp. 45–52.

R. Lattion, *L'archipel en droit international*, Lausanne, 1984.

D. P. O'Connell, 'Mid-ocean archipelagos in international law', 45 *BYIL* 1–77 (1971).

J. R. V. Prescott, 'Straight and archipelagic baselines' in G. Blake (ed.), *Maritime Boundaries and Ocean Resources*, London, 1987, pp. 38–51.

P. E. J. Rogers, *Midocean Archipelagos and International Law*, New York, 1981.

P. Tangsubkul, *The Southeast Asian Archipelagic States: Concept, Evolution and Current Practice*, Honolulu, Hawaii, 1984.

P. de Vries Lentsch, 'The right of overflight over strait States and archipelagic States' XIV *NYIL* 165–225 (1983).

CHAPTER SEVEN
The contiguous zone

Development of the concept

The contiguous zone is a zone of sea contiguous to and beyond the territorial sea in which States have limited powers for the enforcement of customs, fiscal, sanitary and immigration laws. It has its origins in the eighteenth century 'Hovering Acts' enacted by Great Britain against foreign smuggling ships hovering within distances of up to eight leagues (i.e. twenty-four miles) from the shore. These Acts, which had effect from 1736 until their repeal by the 1876 Customs Consolidation Act, were at the time regarded as permitted by 'the common courtesy of nations for their convenience', as Lord Stowell put it in the case of *Le Louis* in 1817. However, this was at a time when practice had not yet given the three-mile limit for the territorial sea the force of a rule of law.

A dispute with Spain in the early years of the nineteenth century over seizures of British ships within the six-mile Spanish customs zone, among other incidents, focused attention on the extent of maritime claims. By mid-century the three-mile limit for the territorial sea, combined with the exclusivity of flag State jurisdiction on the high seas beyond, was well established in Anglo-American practice and served well the interests of free navigation. Great Britain recognised that its wider customs zones were inconsistent with the three-mile rule. The seizure of the French ship the *Petit Jules* twenty-three miles off the Isle of Wight in 1850 was the last occasion on which the Hovering Acts were enforced against a foreign vessel beyond the marine league.[1] Indeed, the British Law Officers advised that the seizure was impermissible under international law, and the one member of the crew who had been captured was set free. From then on, the three-mile rule was applied in Britain and its dominions and colonies. But this rule was subject to two qualifications allowing the exercise of jurisdiction against foreign vessels at greater distances from shore.

First, according to the doctrine of constructive presence, where a ship beyond the marine league sent its boats within that limit, such as occurred for the purpose of illegal fishing in the case of the *Araunah* (1888) and for the purpose of releasing prisoners in Australia in the *Catalpa* incident (1877), no distinction was drawn between the ship and its boats, and the ship was liable to be seized for the violation of the local law.[2] According to later refinements of the doctrine, illustrated, for example, by some of the diplomatic exchanges concerning the seizure of the *Henry L. Marshall* for violation of the American liquor laws in 1922 and by the Italian case of the *Sito* in 1957, it had no application where a foreign ship communicated with the shore not by means of its own boats but by means of boats sent out from the shore. Here the exclusive jurisdiction of the flag State over its ships on the high seas remained intact. The second exception was the doctrine of hot pursuit. This provided that when a ship was found within the territorial sea of a State, and there was good reason to believe that it had violated the local law, it could be pursued and arrested on the high seas. The doctrine, which was incorporated in the Geneva Conventions as article 23 of the High Seas Convention, is discussed in more detail in chapter eleven. What is important for present purposes is the fact that it, like the doctrine of constructive presence, allowed a measure of enforcement jurisdiction beyond the three-mile limit, which was otherwise adhered to more or less strictly.

Other States adopted different approaches. Several, mostly in Europe, did not claim united territorial seas as such but, as was noted in chapter four, claimed a variety of jurisdictional zones. The width of the zones was fixed at whatever distance the State concerned thought was necessitated by the purpose for which the zone was established. For example, France maintained three-mile zones for fishery and general policing purposes, but a six-mile neutrality zone and a twenty-kilometre customs zone. Belgium, Italy, Greece and Spain and, outside Europe, Cuba and Turkey were among other States adopting this position. While exact widths varied from State to State, customs and security zones were usually more extensive than other zones.

The practice of a third group of States was much closer to the concept of the contiguous zone as it is recognised today. Several Latin American States claimed a one-league belt as the public property of the State, and beyond that zone of sovereignty a second zone, of a further three leagues, in which the State enjoyed the right of policing for customs and security purposes only. The 1855 Chilean Civil Code contained such a provision, as did the laws of, for example, Argentina, Ecuador, Honduras and Mexico. While some non-American States such as Egypt, Latvia and Norway followed this practice, the most notorious claims were those advanced by the United States in its 1922 Tariff Act. Under this Act, foreign ships within twelve miles of the United States' coasts were subjected to its laws on the prohibition of alcohol, which had been introduced by the Volstead

Act in 1919. The American liquor laws provoked a great deal of opposition from foreign States, partly because they were apparently much
more vigorously enforced against foreign ships than were the laws of other
States and partly because the policy enforced was not one which was
shared by the States concerned. Sufficient wrath was raised in the British
Foreign Office for the idea of banning American ships and all ships
trading from American ports from British ports to be suggested: wisely, no
attempt was made to implement the notion. Despite the strong opposition
to the unilateral enforcement of American law beyond the marine league,
there was some sympathy with the general aim of preventing hovering
vessels from violating the prohibition. Both these sentiments were satisfied
by the 1924 Anglo-American 'Liquor Treaty', which began by reaffirming
the importance of the three-mile limit and went on to provide that the
British government would raise no objection to the searching of British
vessels within one hour's steaming of the American coast, thus satisfying
the American demands without conceding its right to act in the absence of
the specific treaty agreement. Similar treaties were concluded by the USA
with most European States, as well as with Panama, Chile and Japan, and
there was a comparable arrangement between the Baltic States in the 1925
Helsingfors Treaty.

Thus by the early part of the twentieth century there were three main
approaches to the question of jurisdiction beyond the three-mile limit.
First, States which denied that such jurisdiction existed, except where
given by treaty or under the doctrines of hot pursuit and constructive presence. This group included Britain and the dominions, Germany, Denmark, Sweden, Japan and the Netherlands, as the replies to the Hague
Codification Conference's 'Schedule of Points' in 1929 showed. Second,
States which claimed a variety of jurisdictional zones; and, third, States
which claimed a jurisdictional zone, usually for customs and security
purposes, which was clearly distinct from the territorial sea.

The idea of using the contiguous zone beyond a narrow territorial sea as
a basis for compromise between such groups of States and for resolving the
question of the breadth of the territorial sea, had been put forward by
Renault during the discussion of neutrality zones by the Institute of International Law in 1894. The idea was taken up more generally by the learned
societies in the years before the Hague conference, but despite the considerable interest shown in proposals to include a zone of extended customs,
sanitary and security jurisdiction in the 1930 Hague conference text, none
was in fact agreed upon, doubtless largely as a result of the same failure to
agree upon the width of the territorial sea which prevented the text from
being adopted as a treaty.

In the years between the Hague and Geneva conferences, State practice
remained divided between those States, such as the United Kingdom,

which did not recognise the validity of contiguous zone claims, and the increasing number of States which made such claims. During this period the notion of a territorial sea distinct from other jurisdictional zones became generally accepted, although a few States, such as Cuba, Spain and Greece, still kept to the idea of a 'territorial sea' whose width varied according to the purpose for which jurisdiction was exercised. But most States claimed special customs and security, and sometimes sanitary and immigration, zones on the high seas contiguous to their territorial sea. Claims to fishery zones also became commonplace, and State practice does not seem to have distinguished between the legal character of these zones and that of other contiguous zones. However, Gidel did distinguish between them, requiring the establishment of fishery zones by treaty while admitting the legality of unilateral claims to other contiguous zones. The distinction was preserved in the reports which François made to the International Law Commission during its consideration of the law of the sea, and in the reports of the Commission itself, and at the Geneva Conference, where the question of fishery zones was allotted to a special committee.

The 1958 conference eventually agreed upon the establishment of a contiguous zone within which:

... the coastal State may exercise the control necessary to:
(a) Prevent infringement of its customs, fiscal, immigration or sanitary regulations within its territory or territorial sea;
(b) Punish infringement of the above regulations committed within its territory or territorial sea. [TSC, art. 24(1)]

A substantially identical provision appears as article 33(1) of the Law of the Sea Convention.

Breadth of the contiguous zone

Under both the 1958 and 1982 Conventions a State may choose whether to claim a contiguous zone, and the majority of States have chosen not to claim such a zone (see appendix). Under the Territorial Sea Convention the contiguous zone may not extend more than twelve miles from the baseline (TSC, art. 24(2)), or, unless there be agreement to the contrary between the States concerned, farther than the median line equidistant from the nearest points on the baselines where two States are opposite or adjacent to each other (TSC, art. 24(3)). No agreement on the breadth of the territorial sea was reached at the 1958 conference, and the practice of States in the years immediately following varied, some claiming a three-mile territorial sea and nine-mile contiguous zone, others a six-mile territorial sea and six-mile contiguous zone.

None of these claims modelled on the wording of article 24 of the 1958 Convention now survives (although one or two related claims to twelve-mile customs or anti-liquor smuggling zones remain), largely because most States now claim a twelve-mile territorial sea. In the light of these territorial sea claims, UNCLOS III decided to move the contiguous zone seaward, setting the outer limit at twenty-four miles from the baseline (LOSC, art. 33), so allowing a twelve-mile zone. Since the purpose of the zone is essentially the protection of the shore, it must be doubted whether a contiguous zone is necessary once a twelve-mile territorial sea is conceded. Unlike the Territorial Sea Convention, the Law of the Sea Convention contains no provision on the delimitation of the contiguous zone between opposite and adjacent States, probably because its delimitation would (for States claiming an EEZ) amount to a delimitation of the EEZ, and is therefore dealt with as such: see chapter ten. However, Yugoslavia, when ratifying the Convention, declared that delimitation of the contiguous zone should be governed by 'the principles of customary international law, codified in article 24, paragraph (3) of the 1958 Convention'.[3]

The wave of new claims to maritime zones since the late 1970s has included many to contiguous zones. As of mid-1987, twenty-six States had claimed a twenty-four mile contiguous zone (although, as is noted below, some claims are for purposes wider than those set out in the conventions), and six other States had claimed a contiguous zone of between twelve and twenty-four miles.

Legal status of the contiguous zone

The early unilateral claims had asserted both the right to prescribe regulations to operate in the extended zones and the right to enforce them; in other words, both legislative and enforcement jurisdiction. The literal wording of article 24 of the Territorial Sea Convention (and now article 33 of the Law of the Sea Convention), however, ascribes only enforcement jurisdiction to the coastal State. Action may be taken only in respect of offences committed within the territory or territorial sea of a State, not in respect of anything done within the contiguous zone. This seems to have been the intention of the 1958 conference. The ILC had proposed a text identical to that adopted, but a Polish amendment which deleted the reference to infringements committed within the territory or territorial sea in order to 'make provision for action to deal with possible infringement within the contiguous zone' was adopted by the First Committee at Geneva. That proposed article also included a right to protect security interests; this was opposed, despite the prevalence of security zones in State practice, by some State which saw in that right a danger to free navigation in the zone. The amended article was rejected in plenary session and replaced by the original ILC text, to which immigration had been added as a protected interest, and which had clearly been considered to create a zone of enforcement jurisdiction only. Indeed, this seems a necessary result of the 1958 scheme, for article 19(5) of the Territorial Sea Convention (and now article 27 of the Law of the Sea Convention) forbids the arrest of ships passing through the territorial sea for offences committed before they enter that sea. If legislative jurisdiction were to exist in the contiguous zone, so that ships could commit offences there, they would be able to achieve a greater degree of immunity from coastal State jurisdiction by fleeing to the territorial sea than by fleeing to the high seas or economic zone, since in the latter case they could be seized after hot pursuit (HSC, art. 23; LOSC, art. 111).

Article 33 of the Law of the Sea Convention has followed article 24 of the Territorial Sea Convention almost verbatim as far as the legal status of the contiguous zone and list of purposes are concerned. In addition, it should be noted that by a legal fiction the contiguous zone has been extended to archaelogical and historical objects. Article 303(2) provides that 'in order to control traffic in such objects, the coastal State may, in applying article 33, presume that their removal from the sea-bed in the [contiguous] zone . . . without its approval would result in an infringement within its territory or territorial sea of the laws and regulations referred to in that article'.

State practice since 1958 has not always followed the conventional provisions on the status of the zone. Some States quite clearly claim both enforcement and legislative jurisdiction.[4] More States claim contiguous zones for purposes other than those listed in the conventions, notably for security purposes (see appendix). Such claims to security and legislative jurisdiction do not appear to have evoked significant international opposition in practice, although neither is sanctioned by the Territorial Sea or Law of the Sea Conventions. Support for the view that customary law is wider than the conventional regime was given by a United States court in the controversial case of the *Taiyo Maru* (1974), a Japanese vessel pursued from the nine-mile fishery zone contiguous to the three-mile American territorial sea. It was held that article 24 of the Territorial Sea Convention was merely permissive, not exhaustive, and that contiguous zones, apparently including both enforcement and legislative jurisdiction, could be established for purposes other than those detailed in the article. Similarly, in the case of *US* v. *Gonzalez* (1985), a United States court held that the 'protective' principle of jurisdiction in international law justified the exercise of jurisdiction over foreign ships on the high seas in order to enforce narcotics legislation, although in this case no limit *ratione materiae* was set to such jurisdiction: the case is discussed further in chapter eleven.[5]

The difficulty of resolving the problem of the legal status of the contiguous zone has, indeed, increased with the adoption of the Law of the Sea Convention. Under the Geneva rules and under the earlier practice, at least of those States which did not claim a 'variable' territorial sea, the contiguous zone was a part of the high seas. It followed that, unlike the case of the territorial sea, where the sovereignty of the coastal State resulted in a presumption in favour of the existence of that State's jurisdiction in case of doubt, the presumption in the contiguous zone was against the existence of coastal State jurisdiction over foreign ships: coastal State rights were to be strictly construed. But under the Law of the Sea Convention the contiguous zone falls not within the high seas but within the EEZ. The consequence is that the presumption against coastal State jurisdiction is removed, and in cases where a dispute arises concerning a claim by a coastal State to jurisdictional rights not expressly granted under the Convention, the question is to be resolved, as will be seen in chapter nine, 'on the basis of equity' and 'taking into account the respective importance of the interests' of the parties concerned and of the world at large. It is unclear what effect, if any, this change will have, but it is likely to make the extension of contiguous zone rights *ratione materiae*, and the inclusion of both enforcement and legislative jurisdiction, more easy to defend than formerly.

Notes

1 For details of and references to this and other cases, and to pre-1958 legislation, see Lowe, *op. cit*,. in 'Further reading'.
2 *Ibid*.
3 *LOSB*, Special Issue I, (1987), p. 9.
4 See, e.g., India, Territorial Waters, Continental Shelf, Exclusive Economic Zone and Other Maritime Zones Act, 1976, *UN Leg. Ser.* B/19, p. 47, *ND* V, p. 305, *Smith*, p. 213; Pakistan, Territorial Waters and Maritime Zones Act, 1976, *UN Leg. Ser.* B/19, p. 85, *ND* VII, p. 478, *Smith*, p. 357; Sri Lanka, Maritime Zones Law, 1976, *UN Leg. Ser.* B/19, p. 120, *Smith*, p. 427.
5 Cf. the practice of the Italian courts reported in *O'Connell*, vol. II, p. 1059.

Further reading

L. Caflish, 'Submarine antiquities and the law of the sea', 13 *NYIL* 3–32 (1982).

E. D. Dickinson, 'Jurisdiction at the maritime frontier', 40 *Harvard Law Review* 1–29 (1926).

Sir Gerald Fitzmaurice, 'Some results of the Geneva Conference on the Law of the Sea', 8 *ICLQ* 73–121 (1959).

G. Gidel, 'La mer territoriale et la zone contiguë', 48 *Receuil des Cours* 241–73 (1934).

P. C. Jessup, *The Law of Territorial Waters and Maritime Jurisdiction*, New York, 1927.

A. V. Lowe, 'The development of the concept of the contiguous zone', 52 *BYIL* 109–69 (1981).

W. E. Masterson, *Jurisdiction in Marginal Seas*, New York, 1929.

S. Oda, 'The concept of the contiguous zone', 11 *ICLQ* 131–53 (1962).

A. Pazarci, 'Le concept de zone contiguë dans la convention sur le droit de la mer de 1982', 18 *Revue belge de droit international* 249–271 (1984–85).

S. A. Riesenfeld, *Protection of Coastal Fisheries under International Law*, Washington, D.C., 1942.

CHAPTER EIGHT
The continental shelf

Introduction

Physically, the sea bed adjacent to the coast is usually comprised of three separate sections. First, that section which slopes down gradually from the low-water mark to a depth, averaging about 130 metres, at which the angle of slope increases markedly: this is the continental shelf proper. Second, the section bordering the shelf and having the steeper slope, going down to around 1,200 to 3,500 metres: this is known as the continental slope. Third, beyond the slope in many places there is a gentler falling away of the sea bed, there composed mainly of sediments washed down from the continents, called the continental rise, which descends to around 3,500 to 5,500 metres. Together these three sections form the continental margin, which constitutes about one fifth of the sea floor. (See figs. 1, 3.)

The continental margin — and especially the continental shelf — is rich in natural resources. Most important are the extensive oil and gas reserves, which represent over ninety per cent of the total value of minerals taken from the sea bed. Offshore exploitation of oil and gas on a commercial scale did not begin until shortly before the Second World War. By 1984 offshore oil and gas production each accounted for about one quarter of total world production. These proportions are expected to rise in the future as improvements in technology and the relative cost of offshore production make the exploitation of more and more fields economically attractive. Other minerals are also important. Increasing interest is being shown in 'placer' deposits of heavy minerals containing metals such as titanium, tin, chromium and zirconium. Pools of brine in the subsoil, notably under the Red Sea, contain concentrations of lead, zinc, gold and silver, and may become an important source of these metals, and perhaps of thermal energy. Exploitation of all these offshore resources is likely to become increasingly attractive. This is partly because of the increasing cost of traditional sources of these minerals, resulting from their growing scarcity, but also because of an increasing desire among developed countries for greater self-sufficiency, prompted to some extent by what is perceived as an increasing instability in traditional supplies of these minerals.

As well as mineral resources, there are also important fisheries on the continental shelf for sedentary species, such as oysters and clams, and lobsters and crabs (although the classification of the two latter organisms as 'sedentary' is controversial). In some areas, notably the Pacific, these fisheries make an important contribution to the economies of the littoral States.

The existence of such a rich diversity of resources therefore makes the legal status of the continental shelf an important practical question. This chapter outlines the rules of international law relevant to the determination of that status. The delimitation of the continental shelf between opposite and adjacent States is discussed in chapter ten.

The legal status of the continental shelf

In the early years of the present century, in the period leading up to the Hague Codification Conference of 1930, it became generally accepted that possession of a territorial sea bestowed on the coastal State proprietary rights over the resources of that sea, including its bed and subsoil. There were much older claims to the resources of the subsoil, exploited by tunnelling from the shore: the United Kingdom, for example, had long claimed such a right in relation to the submarine mines off Cornwall. But the significance of the twentieth-century development of the law on this matter was that it drew a clear distinction between the bed of the territorial sea, which automatically appertained to the coastal State, and the bed of the high seas, which did not. The bed of the high seas could, however, be the subject of effective occupation by a State, which was sufficient to give that State title to its resources. Mining from the coast was one way of achieving effective occupation, resulting in proprietorial rights to parts of the subsoil. Regular exploitation of, and the assertion of rights of control over, specific areas of the surface of the bed could similarly give such rights to such areas. This was fairly common practice. The United Kingdom, for example, claimed sovereign rights in respect of pearl and chank fisheries off Ceylon, and France in respect of sponge fisheries beyond the territorial sea off Tunis. Such claims were widely recognised, and did not compromise the legal regime of the high seas, since the freedoms of fishing and navigation in the superjacent waters were unaffected. However, some authorities disputed the right of States to appropriate areas of the sea bed, on the grounds that it was in law *res communis*, and therefore incapable of unilateral appropriation, rather than *res nullius*, in which case it would have been open for appropriation by the first State establishing effective occupation. Nevertheless, exclusive rights to harvest the resources of specific areas of the sea bed, apart from claims to ownership of the bed itself, seem to have been generally admitted.

The question of jurisdiction and property rights over marine resources was proposed for examination by the Hague conference, but not discussed by the conference. Nonetheless, the practical importance of sea-bed resources was such that it was inevitable that States would soon take action to arrogate to themselves the sea bed adjacent to their coasts. The first step was cautious. In 1942 the United Kingdom, on behalf of Trinidad, and Venezuela concluded a Treaty relating to the Submarine Areas of the Gulf of Paria. Under this treaty the sea bed beyond territorial waters in the gulf was divided into two sectors. In one sector the United Kingdom agreed not to assert any claim to sovereignty or control and to recognise any rights of sovereignty or control lawfully acquired by Venezuela, while Venezuela gave a corresponding undertaking in respect of the other sector. Although the treaty bound only the two signatories, its effect was tantamount to the division of the bed of the Gulf of Paria between them, since it was most improbable that any other State would have sought to build up a title based on effective occupation of a zone which the coastal States were actively engaged in developing. Thus the treaty clearly defined the sectors within which each party was to make no claim to sovereignty, but did not itself assert the sovereignty of the other party over such sectors: sovereignty still had to arise from occupation. So the 1942 treaty succeeded in delimiting the continental shelf before the legal concept of the continental shelf itself was established.

It is customary to regard the proclamation made by President Truman of the USA in 1945 at the first clear assertion of the idea that a continental shelf belongs to the coastal State. The proclamation stated that:

... the Government of the United States regards the natural resources of the subsoil and seabed of the continental shelf beneath the high seas but contiguous to the coasts of the United States as appertaining to the United States, subject to its jurisdiction and control.[1]

In its preamble the proclamation justified this claim on the basis of contiguity and reasonableness.

The Truman Proclamation was followed by similar claims on the part of many other States. These varied in their precise nature: some claimed jurisdiction and control over the resources of the shelf, while others claimed sovereignty over the shelf as such. Yet other claims, made by a number of Latin American States, extended not only to the shelf but also to the superjacent waters, and in some cases even to the air space above those waters. The inconsistency of early practice, both as regards the nature and the geographical extent of the claims, was such that in 1951, in his award in the arbitration between Petroleum Development Ltd and the Sheik of Abu Dhabi, Lord Asquith stated that the doctrine could not claim to have 'assumed hitherto the hard lineaments or the definitive status of an established rule of international law'.[2]

Throughout the following years more and more States laid claim to some kind of jurisdiction over the shelf. By the time of the 1958 Geneva conference about twenty States, some acting both in their own right and on behalf of dependent territories, had made such claims. At the conference the idea that coastal States should enjoy certain rights over their continental shelves was generally accepted. The Continental Shelf Convention adopted by the conference provided that these rights should be sovereign rights for the purpose of exploring and exploiting the resources of the continental shelf (CSC, art. 2). So firmly was the principle of coastal State rights over the continental shelf established that in 1969, only eighteen years after the *Abu Dhabi* award, the ICJ stated in its judgment in the *North Sea Continental Shelf* cases that:

[T]he rights of the coastal State in respect of the area of continental shelf that constitutes a natural prolongation of its land territory into and under the sea exist *ipso facto* and *ab initio*, by virtue of its sovereignty over the land, and as an extension of it in an exercise of sovereign rights for the purpose of exploring the seabed and exploiting its natural resources. In short there is here an inherent right.[3]

It is not clear whether or not the International Court intended to rewrite legal history, so that the *ab initio* appurtenance of the shelf of the coastal State would, in retrospect, be said to have attached the continental shelf to Abu Dhabi by 1951, for example. But it is quite clear that the doctrine of the continental shelf was firmly established in international law by 1958, and that its position has not weakened since then.

However, while the doctrine of the continental shelf may not have weakened, a certain amount of duplication and possible confusion has arisen recently with the emergence of the concept of the exclusive economic zone at UNCLOS III. As we shall see in chapter nine, under the Law of the Sea Convention the coastal State has sovereign rights over all the natural resources of its EEZ, including sea-bed resources (LOSC, art. 56). Thus there are now two legal bases for coastal State rights in relation to the sea bed. The first is the classical doctrine of the continental shelf as formulated in the Continental Shelf Convention and customary international law. The second is the newer concept of the EEZ. The second basis will at present only apply to those States which accept that the EEZ is already part of customary international law or recognise claims based on the concept. It is important to keep these two bases separate. Their origins are quite different, and, while they will often apply to the same geographical area, this is by no means always the case: the EEZ has a breadth of 200 miles, which may be greater or less than the breadth of the continental shelf under the classical doctrine. In this chapter we concentrate primarily on the classical continental shelf doctrine, looking first at the area to which it applies and secondly at the nature of coastal States' rights.

The seaward limit of the continental shelf

The inner or landward limit of the continental shelf has never been contentious. It has always been regarded as being the outer limit of the territorial sea (even though the exact breadth of the territorial sea has been controversial). However, it has been less easy to attain an agreed definition of the outer limit of the continental shelf. The Truman Proclamation did not fix in terms of miles or depth a seaward limit for the claim which it advanced to the continental shelf (although an accompanying memorandum by the State Department Legal Advisor noted that 'The continental shelf is usually defined as that part of the undersea land mass adjacent to the coast, over which the sea is not more than 100 fathoms (600 feet) in depth').[4] But by referring to the continental shelf as 'an extension of the land mass of the coastal State and thus naturally appurtenant to it' the proclamation, like other claims which referred to rights over the 'continental shelf' to an unspecified distance, was clearly confined to the continental margin as the physical continuation of the land mass; but it is not clear whether it was more limited than that and confined, for example, to the continental shelf in the strict geomorphological sense.

The continental shelf claims were the first claims to jurisdiction in time of peace extending beyond the comparatively modest belt of coastal waters since the abandonment of grandiose claims over the high seas in the early nineteenth century (see chapter eleven). It was therefore natural that there should at some point be felt, among lawyers and governments alike, a desire to limit the extent to which these claims intruded upon the area of high seas and its traditional freedoms. Unfortunately, the few (Latin American) States which did fix seaward limits for their continental shelf claims put the limit, usually of 200 miles, often beyond the furthermost reach of their continental margins.

In the early stages of the development of the concept of the continental shelf the question of the seaward limit was less important than it became in later years as a result of developments in offshore technology. When the ILC first addressed itself to the task of drafting an article establishing a conventional limit, it proposed that the legal definition of the shelf should include all the sea bed contiguous to the coast where the depth of the superjacent waters admitted of the exploitation of the resources of the sea bed and subsoil. A number of governments suggested that this exploitability criterion was too vague, and might lead to international conflicts, and the ILC accordingly replaced it with the more precise limit of the 200 metre isobath in its 1953 report. It was thought that, for practical purposes and for the foreseeable future, that limit would satisfy national interests in the shelf. However, reconsidering the question in the light of the resolutions of the Inter-American Specialised Conference on Conservation of

Natural Resources, held at Cuidad Trujillo in 1956, a majority of the ILC followed the lead of that conference in reintroducing the 'exploitability' criterion, in addition to the 200 metre isobath, as an alternative limit. This allowed exploitation of shelf resources by coastal States in cases where such was possible at depths greater than 200 metres. Although there was considerable opposition to this dual criterion at the Geneva Conference, the ILC proposal was eventually approved. Thus Article 1 of the 1958 Continental Shelf Convention defined the continental shelf as being:

the seabed and subsoil of the submarine areas adjacent to the coast but outside the area of the territorial sea, to a depth of 200 metres or, beyond that limit, to where the depth of the superjacent waters admits of the exploitation of the natural resources of the said areas ...

In the *North Sea Continental Shelf* cases the International Court said that this article also represented customary law (although the Court also laid stress on the continental shelf as being the 'natural prolongation' of the coastal State's land mass). The definition of the continental shelf contained in the Convention has also been adopted by many States, a number of which are not parties to the Convention, in their national legislation (see Appendix).

In spite of the widespread adoption of the Convention's definition of the continental shelf, the definition is not free of difficulties. Even at the 1958 conference it was recognised that the addition of the exploitability test rendered the seaward limit dangerously imprecise. It was clear that new technology would push the limit farther and farther from the shore, and that 'exploitability' — which could mean anything from the ability to drag up a basket of sedentary fish to the ability to establish a full-scale profit-making oil well complex — was itself an elusive criterion. Moreover, it was never clear whether it was the ability of the coastal State, or of any other State — or even all other States — which was in question. The use of the word 'adjacent' also raised questions: was it intended to restrain the seaward limit of exploitability, or did it simply mean that, to qualify as continental shelf, the sea bed must be one continuous mass, unbroken by troughs or depressions? In the years following the 1958 conference attention was increasingly given to the resources of the deep sea bed (see chapter twelve). It became clear that, given sufficient investment, there were few, if any, areas of the ocean bed which could not be exploited in some form. The fear was that the consequence of continued adherence to the exploitability test in the face of rapidly developing technology would be the extension of coastal claims to continental shelves so as to cover the entire ocean floor. This would in practice have benefited only those few States with the technology necessary to exploit the deep ocean bed, and it so happened that the geographical distribution of States over the globe was such that, were national claims to be established into the mid-ocean and delimited by the use of median lines (see chapter ten), the developed States would be the major benficiaries of the carving up of the sea bed. This, as will be seen in chapter twelve, led to calls for the internationalisation of the deep sea bed, placing the mineral resources of that area beyond the reach of unilateral claims. However, this in turn necessitated the fixing of a definite limit for national claims to jurisdiction over the sea bed.

There was considerable difficulty in reaching agreement on this outer limit at UNCLOS III. While the consolidation of the emergent rules on the EEZ automatically imported acceptance of a limit of at least 200 miles (which brought about thirty-six per cent of the sea bed within national jurisdiction, including in some areas parts of the sea bed lying beyond the physical continental margin), a number of States, including the UK, USA and USSR, have continental margins which extend beyond the 200 mile limit, and were therefore reluctant to give up any claims to the resources in the outermost portions of the margin. Other States with a narrower shelf wished to secure agreement on the 200 mile limit or some other basis which would leave the greatest possible area of sea bed beyond the permissible scope of national jurisdiction.

The Law of the Sea Convention provides that:

The continental shelf of a coastal State comprises the sea-bed and subsoil of the submarine areas that extend beyond its territorial sea throughout the natural prolongation of its land territory to the outer edge of the continental margin, or to a distance of 200 nautical miles from the baselines from which the breadth of the territorial sea is measured where the outer edge of the continental margin does not extend up to that distance. [LOSC, art. 76(1)]

Thus the legal definition of the shelf is quite distinct and different from the geographical definition: areas of the sea bed which lie beyond the continental margin are included, so long as they are within 200 miles of the coast. Where the continental margin (defined in article 76(3) as consisting of the shelf, slope and rise and excluding the deep oceanic floor with its oceanic ridges) extends beyond 200 miles, the outer limit of the legal continental shelf is *either* a line connecting points not more than sixty miles apart, at each of which points the thickness of sedimentary rocks is at least one per cent of the shortest distance from such point to the foot of the continental slope, *or* a line connecting points not more than sixty miles apart, which points are not more than sixty miles from the foot of the slope. In each case the points referred to are subject to a maximum seaward extent: they must be either within 350 miles of the baseline or within 100 miles of the 2,500 metre isobath (LOSC, art. 76(4), (5); and see Annex II of the Final Act of UNCLOS III for an exception to the rules for the Bay of Bengal). These limits would allow the inclusion within national jurisdiction of substantially the whole of the continental margin.

In order to avoid disputes over the limits of the shelf, States are obliged to notify the outer limit established in accordance with the rules described above, to the Commission on the Limits of the Continental Shelf provided for in Annex II of the Convention, and to the Secretary General of the United Nations, who will give due publicity to them (LOSC, art. 76(7), (8), (9)). The Commission may make recommendations to States concerning the delimitation; and 'the limits of the shelf established by a coastal State on the basis of these recommendations shall be final and binding' (LOSC, art. 76(8)). It is not clear how far delimitations not so based must be regarded as valid.

Although the Convention is not yet in force, its provisions on the outer limit of the continental shelf have a growing importance in State practice. By mid-1987, no less than twenty-two States had defined the outer limit of their continental shelves in terms closely modelled on article 76(1); and a further three States had defined the outer limit as being the edge of the continental margin, 350 miles, and 100 miles beyond the 2,500 metre isobath, respectively (see Appendix).

The continental shelves of islands

Under the Continental Shelf Convention, islands are entitled to their own continental shelves (CSC, art. 1(b)). While the term 'island' is not defined in that Convention, it would seem reasonable to assume that the draftsmen intended the term to have the same meaning as it has in the Territorial Sea Convention, i.e. 'a naturally-formed area of land, surrounded by water, which is above water at high tide'. In order to overcome some of the inequities which might be thought to result from the ability of small, isolated islands to generate possibly extensive continental shelves, the Law of the Sea Convention provides that:

Rocks which cannot sustain human habitation or economic life of their own shall have no exclusive economic zone or continental shelf. [LOSC, art. 121(3)]

The poor drafting of this provision, and the problems that it is likely to give rise to, were discussed in chapter two (see pp. 41–2; and see chapter nine, pp. 135–6). However, it might be noted that the report of the Conciliation Commission concerning the continental shelf of Jan Mayen island regarded the provisions of the article as 'reflecting the present status of international law on the subject',[5] although no evidence was given to support this statement.

The rights of the coastal State

Since the continental shelf was originally the bed of an area which remained high seas (CSC, art. 3), it was inevitable that coastal State rights in the area should be strictly limited. This position has been modified by the establishment of the EEZ as an area of maritime jurisdiction, and it is now necessary to consider separately coastal State rights over the shelf within the 200 mile zone (where the continental shelf regime and EEZ regime coexist) and beyond the 200 mile zone (where only the continental shelf regime applies, as it does in cases where the coastal State does not claim an EEZ).

Rights within the 200 mile zone

The basic principle which has always governed coastal State rights is that these rights are limited to the exploration of the shelf and exploitation of its natural resources. In other words, the shelf is not regarded as part of the territory of the coastal State. Rights to all the natural resources of the bed do, however, attach to the coastal State. The sovereign rights attaching to the coastal State cover all the natural resources of the shelf, that is:

... the mineral and other non-living resources of the seabed and subsoil together with living organisms belonging to sedentary species, that is to say, organisms which, at the harvestable stage, either are immobile on or under the sea-bed or are unable to move except in constant physical contact with the sea-bed or the subsoil. [CSC, art. 2(4); LOSC, art. 77(4)]

Thus oil and gas are included, as are sedentary species such as oysters, clams and abalone. Species such as crabs and lobsters have remained controversial candidates for inclusion, giving rise to several disputes: for example, the USA-Japan dispute over the king crab fishery in the eastern Behring Sea and the Franco-Brazilian dispute over the lobster fishery off the Brazilian coast. However, within the 200 mile EEZ such disputes will now be of only historical importance, since all rights to exploit resources (including fish) within the zone belong to the coastal State (LOSC, art. 56(1)), the former freedom to take non-sedentary species from what was originally the high seas having been supplanted. Nevertheless, it remains true that non-natural 'resources' are not the subject of coastal State rights merely because they are found on the continental shelf, so that, for example, wrecks lying on the shelf are still excluded.

The coastal State has sovereign rights for the purpose of exploring the shelf and exploiting its natural resources (CSC, art. 2(1); LOSC, arts. 56(1), 77(1)). These rights are exclusive in the sense that no State can undertake such activities without the coastal State's consent (CSC, art. 2(2); LOSC, art 77(2)), and the rights do not depend on occupation or proclamation but automatically attach to the coastal State (CSC, art. 2(3); LOSC, art. 77(3)). It follows that it is for the coastal State, through its own laws and regulations, to define the conditions under which such exploration and exploitation are to be conducted. A wealth of such legislation, particularly in relation to offshore oil and gas and sedentary fisheries, exists. The coastal State's rights are not, however, unlimited. In earlier practice (and under the Continental Shelf Convention) the superjacent waters were high seas, and freedom of navigation and fishing were preserved; now the latter freedom has disappeared in the EEZ, but it is still provided that:

The exercise of the rights of the coastal State over the continental shelf must not infringe or result in any unjustifiable interference with navigation and other rights and freedoms of other States as provided for in this Convention. [LOSC, art. 78(2)]

Plainly it is inevitable that some interference with navigation will result. The establishment of drilling platforms and other installations for the exploitation of offshore resources, which the coastal State alone may authorise (CSC, art. 5(2); LOSC, arts. 60(1), 80), and over which it has full rights of jurisdiction and control (CSC art. 5(4); LOSC, arts. 80, 60(2)), must to some degree impede freedom of navigation. But as a right consequent upon the right to exploit, the establishment of such installations, and of safety zones around them, is expressly permitted (CSC, art. 5; LOSC, arts. 80, 60). The Conventions permit safety zones of up to 500 metres, measured from the outer limits of the installations, although some States, such as Norway, have forbidden certain navigational and fishing practices in wider areas; in practice even a cluster of 500 metre zones can effectively curtail such activities in the interstitial waters.

On the other hand, no installations may be erected 'where interference may be caused to the use of recognised sea lanes essential to international navigation' (CSC, art. 5(6); LOSC, art. 60(7)). While the 1958 Convention requires the complete removal of abandoned installations (CSC, art. 5(5)), the 1982 Convention does not, but merely requires that they be removed 'to ensure safety of navigation' and taking account of generally accepted international standards (such as those being developed by the IMO) and having due regard to other interests such as fishing and the marine environment, with appropriate publicity being given to installations only partly removed (LOSC, art. 60(3)). State practice on this point is divided, but there are signs of a shift towards requiring partial removal only, even on the part of States Parties to the Continental Shelf Convention — an instance of the 1982 Convention modifying not only customary law, but also antecedent treaty obligations.

A further limitation on coastal States' rights results from the obligation to permit, subject to measures to protect rights of exploration and exploitation and to other reasonable conditions, the laying of submarine pipelines and cables by other States on the shelf (CSC, art. 4; LOSC, art. 79). Conditions may relate to the course of cables and pipelines, and the prevention of pollution from or by them, and to other matters where the pipes or cables enter the territorial sea of the coastal State.

For the sake of completeness, it should be noted that the coastal State is expressly given the right to exploit shelf resources by tunnelling (CSC, art. 7; LOSC, art. 85), although this provision is probably redundant in view of ·the wider rights given elsewhere.

Rights beyond the 200 mile zone

Coastal State rights over the shelf beyond the 200 mile zone are slightly different, since the superjacent waters are in that area high seas, rather than part of the coastal State's EEZ. Generally the same rights exist in relation to exploration and exploitation, and the establishment of installations, and the same obligations regarding respect for the freedoms of pipeline and cable laying and of navigation. But there are significant differences nevertheless. First, in relation to living resources, the question of what is comprised within the category of sedentary species becomes critical. While sedentary species still remain exclusively under the rights of the coastal State, non-sedentary species fall under the regime of free fishing, as one of the freedoms of the high seas. Accordingly, if commercial fisheries are found at such distances from land, disputes over whether a particular species is sedentary could arise as they have done in the past. Secondly, and more important, exploitation of non-living resources is subject to additional restrictions under the Law of the Sea Convention. Where such resources are exploited in this outer portion of the shelf, the coastal State — which, of course, has the exclusive right to engage in such exploitation — would have to pay to the International Sea Bed Authority (on which see chapter twelve) a proportion of the value or volume of the production at the site after the first five years of exploitation. The proportion would rise from one per cent in the sixth year to seven per cent in the twelfth and following years. The Authority would distribute any such payments to States parties to the Convention:

on the basis of equitable sharing criteria, taking into account the interests and needs of developing States, particularly the least developed and the land-locked among them. [LOSC, art. 82(4)]

Developing countries which are net importers of the minerals exploited would be exempt from the obligation to pay (LOSC, art. 82(3)). This scheme is a kind of *quid pro quo* for the diminution of the resources of the International Sea Bed Area consequent upon allowing jurisdiction over the shelf beyond the 200 mile limit.

Non-independent territories

Special provision is made in the Law of the Sea Convention concerning the beneficial ownership of the resources of maritime zones of non-independent territories: this point is discussed in the next chapter.

Notes

1 *ND* I, p. 106.
2 18 *ILR* 144, at 155.
3 [1969] ICJ Rep. 3, at 23.
4 A. L. Hollick, *U. S. Foreign Policy and the Law of the Sea*, New Jersey, 1981, p. 49.
5 Report of the Conciliation Commission established by the Governments of Iceland and Norway, concerning the continental shelf area between Iceland and Jan Mayen, XX *ILM* 797, at 803 (1981).

Further reading

J. Andrassy, *International Law and the Resources of the Sea*, New York and London, 1970.

B. B. L. Auguste,*The Continental Shelf. The Practice and Policy of the Latin American States, with special reference to Chile, Ecuador and Peru*, Geneva and Paris, 1960.

E. D. Brown, *Sea-Bed Energy and Mineral Resources and the Law of the Sea, vol. 1: The Areas Within National Jurisdiction*, London, 1984, and *ibid.*, vol. 3, *Selected Documents, Tables and Bibliography*, London, 1986.

R. R. Churchill, 'The conflict between oil and fisheries: a survey of Norwegian and United Kingdom law and practice', in G. Ulfstein, P. Andersen, and R. R. Churchill, *Proceedings of the European Workshop on the Regulation of Fisheries*, Council of Europe, Strasbourg, 1987, pp. 197–213.

T. C. Daintith and G. D. M Willoughby, *A Manual of United Kingdom Oil and Gas Law*, London, 1984.

L. F. E. Goldie, 'Sedentary fisheries and article 2(4) of the Continental Shelf Convention', 63 *AJIL* 86–97 (1969).

Sir C. J. B. Hurst, 'Whose is the bed of the sea?', 4 *BYIL* 34–43 (1923–24).

J. A. C. Gutteridge, 'The 1958 Convention on the Continental Shelf', 35 *BYIL* 102–23 (1959).

D. N. Hutchinson, 'The seaward limit to continental shelf jurisdiction in customary international law', 56 *BYIL* 133–87 (1985).

H. Lauterpacht, 'Sovereignty over submarine areas', 27 *BYIL* 376–433 (1950).

M. W. Mouton, *The Continental Shelf*, The Hague, 1952, and 85 *Receuil des Cours* 343–465 (1954).

B. H. Oxman, 'The preparation of article 1 of the Convention on the Continental Shelf', 3 *JMLC* 245–305, 445–72, 683–723 (1971–72).

Z. J. Slouka, *International Custom and the Continental Shelf*, The Hague, 1968.

D. Vallée, *Le plateau continental dans le droit positive actuel*, Paris, 1971.

M. M. Whiteman, 'Conference on the Law of the Sea. Convention on the Continental Shelf', 52 *AJIL* 629–60 (1958).

R. Young, 'The legal status of submarine areas beneath the high seas', 45 *AJIL* 225–39 (1951).

See also the further reading recommended in chapter ten.

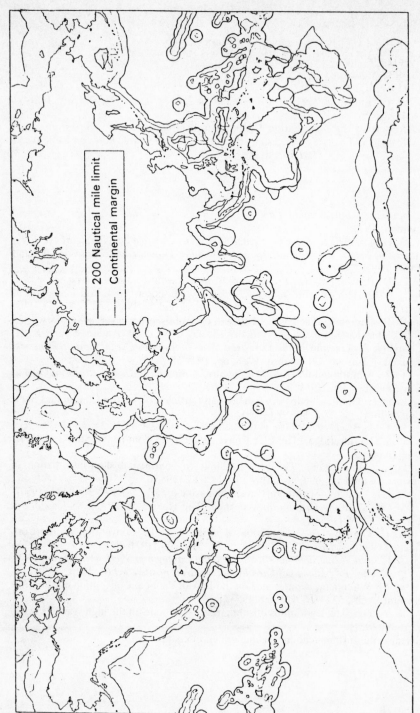

The 200 mile limit and continental margin

CHAPTER NINE
The exclusive economic zone

Evolution of the EEZ

The exclusive economic zone (EEZ) is a zone extending up to 200 miles from the baseline, within which the coastal State enjoys extensive rights in relation to natural resources and other jurisdictional rights, and third States enjoy the freedoms of navigation, overflight by aircraft and the laying of cables and pipelines. The EEZ is a concept of recent origin. While its historical roots lie in the growing trend since 1945 to extend the limits of coastal State jurisdiction ever seawards (particularly the Truman and other continental shelf proclamations, and the resource-oriented claims of Latin American and African States to broad territorial seas and fishing zones), its more direct and immediate origins lie in the preparations for UNCLOS III. The concept of the EEZ was put forward for the first time by Kenya to the Asian-African Legal Consultative Committee in January 1971, and to the UN Sea Bed Committee in the following year. Kenya's proposal received active support from many Asian and African States.[1] At about the same time many of the Latin American States began to develop the rather similar concept of the patrimonial sea.[2] The two lines of approach had effectively merged by the time UNCLOS began, and the new concept — the EEZ being the preferred name — had attracted the support of most developing States and was beginning to attract support from some developed coastal States such as Canada and Norway. The EEZ is a reflection of the aspiration of the developing countries for economic development and the desire to gain greater control over the economic resources off their coasts, particularly fish stocks, which in many cases were largely exploited by the distant-water fleets of developed States. At the same time the EEZ could be seen as something of a compromise between those States that claimed a 200 mile territorial sea (some Latin American and African States) and those developed States (e.g. Japan, USSR and USA) which were hostile to extended coastal State jurisdiction. The fact that the EEZ could be seen as a compromise proposal led to its rapid acceptance in principle at UNCLOS by most States, although many landlocked and geographically disadvantaged States were, at least initially, rather reserved towards the EEZ because it reduced the area of high seas open to use by all States.

The main provisions of the Law of the Sea Convention dealing with the EEZ are contained in Part V of the Convention. However, it is necessary to examine not only the Convention but also State practice. By about 1976 the idea of the EEZ had become so firmly accepted by most UNCLOS participants that since then a growing number of States — some seventy-four as of 1987 — have unilaterally claimed EEZs without waiting for UNCLOS to end or the Convention to come into force. In addition, a further fifteen States have claimed, largely relying on the position at UNCLOS, a 200 mile fishing zone, rather than — for reasons which will be explained later — a 200 mile EEZ.

The universal establishment of 200 mile EEZs would embrace about thirty-six per cent of the total area of the sea. Although this is a relatively small proportion, the area falling within 200 mile limits contains over ninety per cent of all presently commercially exploitable fish stocks, about eighty-seven per cent of the world's known submarine oil deposits, and about ten per cent of manganese nodules (see, further, table 1 below). Furthermore, a large proportion of marine scientific research takes place within 200 miles of the coast, and virtually all the major shipping routes of the world pass through the EEZs of States other than those in which the ports of departure and destination are situated. In view of these extensive activities conducted within 200 miles of land, the legal regime of the EEZ provided for in the Law of the Sea Convention is obviously of crucial importance.

This chapter begins by looking at the way in which the EEZ is delimited, and then considers the legal nature of the EEZ by examining the rights which coastal States and other States enjoy therein. Finally it deals with the legal implications of the unilateral claims that have already been made.

Delimitation of the EEZ

Outer limit. The inner limit of the EEZ is the outer limit of the territorial sea (LOSC, art. 55). The zone's outer limit 'shall not extend beyond 200 nautical miles from the baselines from which the breadth of the territorial sea is measured' (LOSC, art. 57). The wording of this provision suggests that, while 200 miles is the maximum breadth of the EEZ, it would be quite possible for a State, if it so wished, to claim an EEZ of some lesser breadth. In many regions, of course, coastal States will have no option but to claim less than 200 miles because of the presence of neighbouring States' EEZs. It may be wondered why the figure of 200 miles was chosen as the maximum breadth for the EEZ. The reasons are historical and political:

200 miles has no general geographical, ecological or biological significance. At the beginning of UNCLOS the most extensive zones claimed by coastal States were the 200 mile claims of some Latin American and African States. Since it would have been very difficult to persuade those States to accept some lesser limit than 200 miles, it was thought — correctly, as it turned out — that it would be easiest to reach agreement on the outer limit of the EEZ by choosing the figure that represented the broadest existing claims. However, there remains the question as to why the figure of 200 miles was originally chosen by the first State to claim a zone of this breadth — Chile. According to Professor Hollick (see the reference in 'Further reading' at the end of this chapter), the figure of 200 miles seems to have been something of an accident. Chile's claim was motivated by a desire to protect its then new offshore whaling operations. The whaling industry only wanted a fifty-mile zone, but was advised that some precedent was necessary. The most promising precedent appeared to be the security zone adopted in the 1939 Declaration of Panama. This zone was wrongly thought to have been 200 miles in breadth: in fact it varied and was nowhere less than 300 miles.

Boundaries. In many regions States will be unable to claim a full 200 miles zone because of the presence of neighbouring States, and it will therefore — and in many cases has already — become necessary to delimit the EEZ of opposite and adjacent States. The international law governing such boundary delimitation is discussed in the next chapter.

Islands. In principle all land territory can generate an EEZ. However, three qualifications must be made to this statement. First, although islands normally generate an EEZ, article 121(3) of the Law of the Sea Convention provides that 'rocks which cannot sustain human habitation or economic life of their own shall have no exclusive economic zone or continental shelf'. The poor drafting of this provision was criticised in chapter two. So far the provision seems to have had little impact on State practice. As far as can be ascertained, only one of the seventy-four or so States at present claiming an EEZ — Mexico[3] — has incorporated provisions modelled on article 121(3) in its domestic legislation. On the other hand, a number of States have claimed EEZs around islands which could conceivably be regarded as uninhabitable rocks, e.g. France (in respect of various tiny islands in the Pacific and Indian Ocean)[4] and Fiji (in respect of the island of Ceva-i-Ra)[5]. And even Mexico itself has claimed an EEZ around tiny islets, such as Clarion and Guadalupe in the Pacific.[6] However, the 200 mile fishing zone (and continental shelf) claimed by the United Kingdom around the minute islet of Rockall has met with protests and counterclaims from Denmark (in respect of the Faroes), Iceland and Ireland, which have invoked article 121(3) in support of their case[7] (and see chapter eight, p. 127).

Non-independent territories. The second qualification relates to territories which have not attained either full independence or some other self-governing status recognised by the UN, and to territories under colonial domination. Resolution III, adopted by UNCLOS III at the same time as the Convention text, declares that in the case of such territories 'provisions concerning rights and interests under the Convention shall be implemented for the benefit of the people of the territory with a view to promoting their well-being and development.' This resolution replaced a transitional article at the end of earlier drafts of the Convention text, which had proposed to vest the resources of the maritime zones of such territories in their inhabitants. The transitional article presented formidable legal and political difficulties, and was opposed by most States which are administering powers — although it is noteworthy that New Zealand adopted legislation for the Tokelau Islands which is in keeping with its spirit.[8] Resolution III avoids the major difficulties inherent in its predecessor, but it is still not entirely clear which territories it applies to, or what the precise obligations of the administering powers might be. In practice 200 mile EEZs or fishing zones have been established by administering powers for nearly all dependent territories.

Antarctica. Finally, it should be noted that the effect of article IV of the 1959 Antarctic Treaty would seem to be that EEZs cannot be claimed off territory lying within the area to which that Treaty applies, namely the area south of 60° South.

The legal status of the EEZ

During the earlier stages of UNCLOS there was considerable discussion as to the exact legal nature of the EEZ. Many maritime States argued, because of a fear of 'creeping jurisdiction', that the EEZ should have a residual high seas character, i.e. any activity not falling within the clearly defined rights of the coastal State would be subject to the regime of the high seas. This approach did not find favour with the majority of UNCLOS participants, and articles 55 and 86 of the Law of the Sea Convention make it clear that the EEZ does not have a residual high seas character. Equally it is clear that the EEZ does not have a residual territorial sea character, which would have created a presumption that any activity not falling within the clearly defined rights of non-coastal States would come under the jurisdiction of the coastal State — as was desired by some UNCLOS participants (notably those Latin American States claiming a 200 mile territorial sea). Instead, the EEZ must be regarded as a separate functional zone of a *sui generis* character, situated between the territorial sea and the high seas. The *sui generis* legal character of the EEZ has three principal elements: (1) the rights and duties which the Law of the Sea Convention accords to the coastal State; (2) the rights and duties which the Convention accords to other States; and (3) the formula provide by the Convention for regulating activities which do not fall within either of the two previous categories. We now examine each of these three elements in turn.

The rights and duties of the coastal State in the EEZ

The coastal State's rights and duties are set out in broad terms in article 56 of the Law of the Sea Convention, and amplified in later articles. The coastal State's rights relate essentially to the natural resources of the EEZ, and fall under six broad headings.

1. Non-living resources. First, the coastal State has 'sovereign rights for the purpose of exploring and exploiting, conserving and managing' the non-living natural resources of the sea bed and subsoil and the superjacent waters. With the exception of the provisions relating to 'conserving and managing' and 'superjacent waters', the rights accorded to the coastal State are exactly the same as it enjoys in respect of sea bed resources under the 1958 Geneva Convention on the Continental Shelf and customary international law. Furthermore, these rights are to be exercised in accordance with the provisions of the Law of the Sea Convention relating to the continental shelf (see chapter eight). Had it not been for a strong desire on the part of many coastal States, now reflected in the provisions of the Law of the Sea Convention, to include within the legal continental shelf those parts of the continental margin extending beyond 200 miles, the legal regime of the continental shelf could have been subsumed within the EEZ.

The reference to the coastal State 'conserving and managing' non-living resources seems to be a question of drafting rather than of substance. The whole phrase 'sovereign rights for the purpose of exploring and exploiting, conserving and managing' applies to both living and non-living resources: presumably the reference to 'conserving and managing' is intended to apply primarily, if not exclusively, to living resources, since the Convention contains no provisions relating to the conservation or management of non-living resources. The reference to the non-living resources of the superjacent waters relates to the various minerals which can be extracted from sea water.

2. Living resources. Article 56 provides that the coastal State has 'sovereign rights for the purpose of exploring and exploiting, conserving and managing' the living natural resources of the sea bed and subsoil and the superjacent waters. These rights, together with certain duties imposed on the coastal State, are spelt out in detail in articles 61–73. We will examine these provisions in chapter fourteen. It may be noted here, however, that the Convention, unlike the position in regard to non-living resources, gives the coastal State generally more extensive rights, exercisable in a greater area, than it enjoyed under customary international law in respect of its exclusive fishing zone.

3. Other economic resources.   Article 56 gives the coastal State 'sovereign rights ... with regard to other activities for the economic exploitation and exploration of the zone, such as the production of energy from the water, currents and winds'. This provision gives the coastal State quite new rights, and reflects — and is phrased so as to permit the coastal State to take advantage of — developments in technology. The production of energy will usually require the construction of installations of some kind (e.g. wave barrages), so that this aspect of the right must be read in conjunction with the next right.

4. Construction of artificial islands and installations.   In respect of this and the following two rights the Law of the Sea Convention confers on the coastal State, not 'sovereign rights' (as with the first three rights), but the more limited 'jurisdiction'. Article 56 provides that the coastal State has 'jurisdiction as provided for in the relevant provisions of this Convention with regard to ... the establishment and use of artificial islands, installations and structures'. The 'relevant provisions' referred to are to be found in article 60. This article gives the coastal State:

the exclusive right to construct and to authorise and regulate the construction, operation and use of:

(a) artificial islands;
(b) installations and structures for the purposes provided for in article 56 and other economic purposes;
(c) installations and structures which may interfere with the exercise of the rights of the coastal State in the zone.

The coastal State has exclusive jurisdiction over such artificial islands, installations and structures, and has the right to establish safety zones, which are normally not to exceed 500 metres in breadth, around them (LOSC, art. 60(2), (4), (5)). The distinction between the rights of the coastal State to construct 'artificial islands' for any purpose, and the right to construct 'installations and structures' for more limited purposes, seems tenuous, since, in the absence of a definition of an 'artificial island', an 'installation' or 'structure' could be regarded as being an 'artificial island'. On the other hand, since the Convention does make a distinction between 'artificial islands' and 'installations and structures', the categories are presumably not intended to overlap. It is paradoxical that 'artificial islands' can be constructed for any purpose, unlike 'installations and structures', when 'artificial islands' are presumably larger and thus create a greater impediment to other uses of the EEZ. Artificial islands might be established to serve, for example, as deep-water ports, offshore air-ports, mining platforms or even — as in a Dutch proposal — for the siting of a near self-contained industrial 'town'.

The rights of the coastal State in respect of artificial islands, installations and structures are subject to certain duties. Thus the coastal State must give due notice of the construction of artificial islands, installations and structures, must maintain permanent means for giving warning of their presence and must remove, in whole or in part, those installations and structures no longer in use, to ensure safety of navigation (LOSC, art. 60(3)). Furthermore, the coastal State must not construct artificial islands, installations and structures 'where interference may be caused to the use of recognised sea lanes essential to international navigation' (LOSC, art. 60(7)).

The rights which the coastal State is given in respect of artificial islands, installations and structures in its EEZ are similar to the rights the coastal State is given under the continental shelf regime in respect of structures for exploring and exploiting the natural resources of the continental shelf (see the previous chapter), but are wider, since they may be exercised for a broader range of purposes.

5. *Marine scientific research.* Article 56 gives the coastal State 'jurisdiction as provided for in the relevant provisions of this Convention with regard to ... marine scientific research'. The 'relevant provisions' of the Convention are to be found in Part XIII. Article 246(1) provides that the coastal State has 'the right to regulate, authorise and conduct' scientific research in its EEZ. The coastal State must normally give its consent to pure research by other States in its EEZ, but it may withhold its consent to resource-oriented research (LOSC, art. 246(3), (5)). In either case, those wishing to undertake research in another State's EEZ are subject to various obligations. These provisions are discussed in more detail in chapter sixteen.

The powers of control over scientific research in its EEZ which the coastal State is given by the Law of the Sea Convention are broadly similar to the powers the coastal State is given by the Continental Shelf Convention to regulate research on its continental shelf, except that here, of course, the powers are wider, since they relate not just to the sea bed but also to the superjacent column of water.

6. *Pollution control.* Article 56 confers on the coastal State 'jurisdiction as provided for in the relevant provisions of this Convention with regard to

... the protection and preservation of the marine environment'. The 'relevant provisions' of the Convention are to be found in Part XII. This part gives the coastal State legislative and enforcement competence in its EEZ to deal with the dumping of waste (LOSC, arts. 210(5), 216), other forms of pollution from vessels (LOSC, arts. 211 (5–6), 220, 234), and pollution from sea-bed activities (LOSC, arts. 208, 214). These provisions are discussed in detail in chapter fifteen.

Apart from its competence to regulate pollution from sea-bed activities, which is broadly similar to the powers which a coastal State has hitherto enjoyed under the continental shelf regime, the powers to control pollution in the EEZ given to a coastal State by the Law of the Sea Convention are quite novel. Hitherto the only powers which coastal States have enjoyed in areas beyond the territorial sea have been those powers to take action against maritime casualties threatening or causing serious oil pollution which are given by the 1969 International Convention relating to Intervention on the High Seas in Cases of Oil Pollution Casualties (discussed in chapter fifteen).

The above six rights are set out in article 56(1), sub-paragraphs (a) and (b). Article 56(1) goes on, however, in sub-paragraph (c), to state that in addition to these rights the coastal State also has in its EEZ 'other rights and duties provided for in this Convention'. The principal rights which would appear to be referred to here are those which the coastal State has in its contiguous zone (LOSC, art. 33; and see chapter seven) — for the contiguous zone is coterminous with the inner twelve miles of the EEZ — and the right to hot pursuit (LOSC, art. 111; and see chapter eleven).

We have seen that, in relation to each of the six principal rights outlined above, the Convention imposes a number of duties on the coastal State. In addition, article 56(2) lays down a general duty on a coastal State:

in exercising its rights and performing its duties under this Convention in the exclusive economic zone, ... [to] have due regard to the rights and duties of other States and [to] act in a manner compatible with the provisions of this Convention.

The rights and duties of other States in the EEZ

The rights and duties of other States are set out in article 58 of the Law of the Sea Convention. They are all essentially concerned with international communications and are those high seas freedoms that have survived the demands of coastal States. Of the four freedoms specifically mentioned in the High Seas Convention, fishing in the EEZ has come within the jurisdiction of the coastal State, while the other three remain open to all States, although — as we shall see — subject to greater limitations than on the high seas. We now consider each of these three rights of other States in turn.

1. Navigation. Article 58 provides that all States enjoy 'freedoms referred to in article 87 of navigation' in the EEZ, and 'other internationally lawful uses of the sea related to' this freedom compatible with the other provisions of the Convention. This freedom is subject to a number of limitations. First, the freedom may possibly be subject to the general limitation governing all freedoms of the high seas — namely, that these freedoms must be exercised 'with due regard for the interests of other States in their exercise of the freedom of the high seas' (LOSC, art. 87(2)). The uncertainty arises because of the rather oblique and ambiguous reference to article 87, which concerns the high seas, in article 58. Secondly, freedom of navigation in the EEZ is subject to the provisions of articles 88–115 of the Convention and the other relevant rules of international law which deal with navigation on the high seas (see chapters eleven and thirteen), in so far as they are not incompatible with the Convention's provisions on the EEZ. There are two further limitations not explicitly mentioned in the Convention but implicit in its provisions. First, foreign shipping is subject to the coastal State's powers of pollution control (discussed above). Secondly, foreign ships may be affected by the presence of artificial islands and installations — although, as we have seen, such structures may not be placed in 'recognised sea lanes essential to international navigation'. It must also not be forgotten that shipping in the inner twelve miles of the EEZ will be in the coastal State's contiguous zone and therefore subject to the jurisdiction which the coastal State enjoys in that zone.

In general terms these provisions appear reasonably adequate for guaranteeing unhampered navigation by foreign shipping through coastal States' EEZs. It may be wondered, however, exactly how extensive the rights of warships are: in particular, can warships engage in naval manoeuvres or practise using their weapons? Naval manoeuvres, and perhaps weapons practice, are clearly 'uses of the sea related to' navigation, but there might be argument over the extent to which they are 'internationally lawful' (a majority of writers take the view that such uses of the high seas have been lawful in the past), or compatible with other provisions of the Convention — notably article 88, which provides that the high seas 'shall be reserved for peaceful purposes'. This question is discussed further in chapter seventeen (see pp. 310–11).

2. Overflight. Article 58 provides that all States enjoy freedom of overflight in the EEZ, and 'other internationally lawful uses of the sea related to' this freedom compatible with the provisions of the Convention. This freedom is subject to the two explicit limitations to which the freedom of navigation is subject, namely due regard for other States and articles 88–115, etc. (although many of these articles have no application to aircraft). In addition, the freedom is implicitly subject to two further possible limitations. First, the coastal State's right to construct artificial islands and installations might effectively prevent low flying in the vicinity of such structures. Secondly, aircraft are subject to the coastal State's competence to regulate the dumping of waste. There may also be some uncertainty about the use of the EEZ by foreign military aircraft for the purpose of military exercises.

There is one further matter of importance about which there is also uncertainty, and that is the rules of the air which apply to aircraft in the EEZ. Under article 12 of the Convention on International Civil Aviation, 1944, aircraft over the 'high seas' must comply with the Rules of the Air laid down by the International Civil Aviation Organisation (ICAO). Over a State's territory and territorial sea, however, aircraft must comply with that State's regulations, which can diverge from ICAO rules (art.38). In this context, is the EEZ to be regarded as high seas or territorial sea? The Law of the Sea Convention gives no direct answer, but it would seem reasonable to argue that article 12 is one of the 'pertinent rules of international law' which by virtue of article 58(2) apply to the EEZ. There is considerable support for this view in articles 39(3) and 54 of the Law of the Sea Convention, which provide that aircraft exercising a right of transit passage over straits or archipelagic sea-lanes passage over archipelagic waters, i.e. *landwards* of the EEZ, must observe ICAO rules. If it is correct that ICAO rules do apply in the EEZ, this position might require modification where a coastal State built an airport on an artificial island in its EEZ.

3. Laying of submarine cables and pipelines. Finally, all States enjoy the freedom of laying submarine cables and pipelines in the EEZ, and 'other internationally lawful uses of the sea related to' this freedom compatible with the other provisions of the Convention. This freedom is subject to the two explicit limitations to which the freedom of navigation is subject, namely due consideration for the interests of other States and articles 88–115 of the Convention. While many of these articles have no application to cables and pipelines, articles 112–15 are specifically concerned with them, dealing principally with the question of their being broken or damaged. In addition, there is a further explicit limitation contained in article 79. Although this article is in the part of the Law of the Sea Convention dealing with the continental shelf, it must also apply to the EEZ, since the sea bed of the EEZ is coterminous with the continental shelf. Article 79(3) provides that 'the delineation of the course for the laying of' pipelines (but not cables) is 'subject to the consent of the coastal State'. Article 79(4) empowers the coastal State to lay down conditions for cables and pipelines entering its territorial sea, and to establish its jurisdiction over cables and pipelines constructed on or used in connection with the exploration and exploitation of its continental shelf[9] or the operations of artificial islands and installations under its jurisdiction. How far article 79(3) is compatible with a freedom to lay pipelines may be questioned, and to use the term 'freedom' here is perhaps misleading.

The effect of the above provisions is that the rights of other States to navigate, overfly and lay cables and pipelines in a coastal State's EEZ are less extensive than their corresponding rights on the high seas. Furthermore, article 58(3) obliges other States when exercising their rights in a coastal State's EEZ to:

have due regard to the rights and duties of the coastal State and ... comply with the laws and regulations adopted by the coastal State in accordance with the provisions of this Convention and other rules of international law in so far as they are not incompatible with Part V of the Convention (on the EEZ).

Relationship between the rights of the coastal State and the rights of other States

It is clear from the enumeration given above of the rights expressly attributed to the coastal State and to other States that there is considerable potential for conflict between these two groups of rights. The regulation of such conflict is in some cases expressly provided for in the Convention. Thus, for example, the provisions of article 60 (quoted above) are designed to avoid conflicts between the construction of artificial islands or installations by the coastal State and foreign shipping. Similarly the coastal State's powers of pollution control are carefully spelt out in Part XII in order to minimise interference with foreign shipping. But in some cases the Convention contains no specific rules to avoid conflicts of use. Thus, for example, it is unclear whether and to what extent a coastal State can (as part of its sovereign rights to exploit and manage living resources) regulate foreign shipping in order to minimise conflicts with fishing in its EEZ, e.g. by requiring ships to avoid areas where there are standing nets or which are important spawning and nursery grounds for fish. In such cases the only guidance (if it can be called that) given by the Convention is the mutual obligation of coastal States and other States to have 'due regard' to each other's rights. In some cases other treaties will help to regulate conflicting uses: for example, the 1972 Convention on the International Regulations for Preventing Collisions at Sea governs the relationship between vessels which are fishing and other vessels.[10]

The attribution of other rights in the EEZ

The Law of the Sea Convention, in attributing rights in the EEZ to the coastal State and other States, has covered most of the more obvious uses of the EEZ. There may, however, be some uses of the EEZ which do not fall within the rights of either the coastal State or other States. Possible examples include the emplacement of underwater listening devices for submarines (see chapter seventeen); the recovery of historic wrecks beyond the contiguous zone (for the position within the contiguous zone see article 303 of the Convention and chapter seven); and jurisdiction over buoys used for pure scientific research (discussed in chapter sixteen): developments in technology may produce further examples. What is the position in relation to such uses? Which States are to have the competence to enjoy and regulate them? The Convention does not give a precise answer: instead it provides, in article 59, a general formula for attributing rights in such cases. Article 59 reads as follows:

In cases where this Convention does not attribute rights or jurisdiction to the coastal State or to other States within the exclusive economic zone, and a conflict arises between the interests of the coastal State and any other State or States, the conflict should be resolved on the basis of equity and in the light of all the relevant circumstances, taking into account the respective importance of the interests involved to the parties as well as to the international community as a whole.

Article 59 thus makes it clear that, in the case of unattributed rights, there is no presumption in favour of either the coastal State or other States: each case, as it arises, will have to be decided on its own merits on the basis of the criteria set out in article 59. As far as the machinery for deciding such cases is concerned, this will be determined by the provisions of the Convention dealing with the settlement of disputes (discussed in detail in chapter nineteen). Essentially this means that there must first be an attempt at settlement by diplomatic means: if this is unsuccessful, the dispute must be referred to one of the judicial bodies listed in article 287, unless the dispute relates to military activities and one of the parties has made a declaration under article 298 exempting itself from settling such disputes by compulsory third-party means.

Unilateral claims to EEZs

At the beginning of this chapter it was pointed out that, notwithstanding the fact that the Law of the Sea Convention has not yet come into force, a considerable number of States — about seventy-four as of 1987 — have unilaterally claimed EEZs, fortified by the support shown for the EEZ concept at UNCLOS: nearly two-thirds of these claims were made in the period 1976 — 79. The States which have made such claims can be seen from the table of claims in the Appendix. These States come from all the major geographical regions of the world; and while the great majority of claimants are developing States, some developed States have claimed EEZs. On the other hand, a number of developed States, such as Canada, Japan and the United Kingdom, have preferred to claim a 200 mile exclusive fishing zone (EFZ) rather than a 200 mile EEZ. The reason for this seems to be that a 200 mile EFZ, together with the exclusive rights over sea-bed resources which they already have under the continental shelf regime, give these States all that they at present want from an EEZ. They are less certain about the other principal rights of the coastal State in the EEZ — the regulation of research and pollution control — and at the time they made their claims to a 200 mile EFZ (in 1977 in most cases) preferred not to prejudice negotiations at UNCLOS over the content of coastal State jurisdiction over pollution and research by claiming such jurisdiction themselves. It is also noteworthy that a number of States which originally claimed a 200 mile EFZ in 1977 or so, e.g. Senegal, the USSR and the USA, have subsequently changed their claim to an EEZ.

Of the seventy-four or so claims to an EEZ that have so far been made, the majority are modelled on the provisions of the Law of the Sea Convention or the various negotiating texts which preceded it. Most claims have been made in broad terms, with the legislation often repeating or paraphrasing articles 56 and 58. Few States have issued the detailed regulations — except for fisheries — necessary to implement their laws fully. (The detailed regulations which have been issued by States for fisheries, pollution and research are considered in the later chapters dealing with those topics.) It is thus difficult to identify the precise juridical content of many of the EEZs which have been claimed and to establish how far the claims conform to the provisions of the Convention. Nevertheless, even with respect to the basic jurisdictional claim, the legislation of some States does diverge significantly from the provisions of the Convention. Thus the Maldives[11] and Portugal[12] accord to foreign shipping the right, not of freedom of navigation, but of innocent passage (and Mauritania[13] claims to be able to 'amend' foreign vessels' freedom of navigation where its rights and security are 'adversely affected'). Possible unjustifiable interference with navigation may result from the legislation of Guyana[14] India,[15] Mauritius,[16] Pakistan[17] and the Seychelles,[18] each of which claims the competence to designate certain areas of its EEZ for resource exploitation: within such areas provision may be made for 'entry into and passage through the designated area of foreign ships by the establishment of fairways, sealanes, traffic separation schemes or any other mode of ensuring freedom of navigation which is not prejudicial to the interests' of the coastal State concerned. Furthermore, these five States claim to be able to extend any law in force to the EEZ and to regulate the conduct of any person in the EEZ:[19] a somewhat similar claim is found in the legislation of Bangladesh,[20] Barbados,[21] Grenada,[22] Samoa,[23] Sri Lanka,[24] and Vanuatu.[25] Nigerian law provides that, to protect any installation in designated areas of its EEZ, the Nigerian authorities may prohibit ships from entering without consent a specific part of the zone.[26] Haiti claims to be able to exercise in its EEZ 'any control which it deems necessary to' ensure navigational safety, prevent violations of health, fiscal, customs and immigration laws, and prevent pollution.[27] Finally, Morocco requires advance authorisation for any archaeological exploration in its EEZ.[28] These claims give rise to concern that what many hoped the Law of the Sea Convention would achieve, namely a clear demarcation of coastal States' rights and an end to 'creeping jurisdiction', will be undermined. In contrast to the broad claims just described, a small number of States (e.g. Mozambique[29] and Togo[30]) claim only sovereign rights over natural resources, and their legislation makes no mention of jurisdiction relating to artificial islands, pollution control or scientific research.[31]

The question arises as to the legal validity of these claims, given that there is at present no convention in force which authorises them. The number of claims to an EEZ, coupled with an almost complete absence of protest, strongly suggests that the right to a 200 mile EEZ has now become part of customary international law, and indeed in the *Libya/Malta Continental Shelf* case (1985) the International Court said that it is 'incontestable that ... the EEZ ... is shown by the practice of States to have become part of customary law'.[32] Of course, a State which has persistently objected to EEZ claims would not be bound by this new rule of customary law (see chapter one), but in practice there do not appear to be any such States. It would seem that what is part of customary international law are the provisions of articles 56 and 58 of the Law of the Sea Convention. It is much more doubtful whether the obligations in the articles relating to the exercise of coastal State jurisdiction over fisheries, pollution and research have passed or are likely quickly to pass into customary international law. This reflects a tendency for rights to pass more quickly into custom than duties. It is also partly because of a lack of claims embodying the duties of the Convention, partly because there is some divergence between State practice and the Convention, and partly because some of the conventional rules would not seem to have the 'fundamentally norm-creating character' necessary for the creation of a rule of customary international law (see chapter one). This question is considered further in the later chapters dealing with fisheries, pollution and research.

Significance of the EEZ

The extension of coastal State jurisdiction by means of 200 mile EEZs from what had previously generally been narrow coastal State limits to encompass areas which had formerly been high seas — areas containing the major proportion of the ocean's resources and being the site of most ocean activities — represents a major change in the regulation of and access to ocean activities. It is a move away from open access to resources and regulation based primarily on flag State jurisdiction, to near-exclusive coastal State access to resources and regulation based primarily — though not exclusively — on coastal State jurisdiction. As yet it is too soon to say how effective a means of regulating ocean activities in practice the EEZ regime will turn out to be: whether it will be any better at managing fish stocks and preventing pollution than the previous narrow coastal State jurisdiction/ high seas regime. It should be noted, however, that in many cases the responsibility for managing the resources of the EEZ assumed by the coastal State, together with the necessary enforcement machinery, represent for many coastal States a significant new undertaking as well as a new form of expenditure (which may, of course, be more than offset by an increase in revenue from the resources of the EEZ).

As regards the question of whether the EEZ will represent any fundamental redistribution of the ocean's resources — as many developing countries have argued it would and should — one or two observations can already be made. First, it seems that few developing countries will be among the main beneficiaries of EEZs. Only about thirty States stand to gain significantly from establishing an EEZ, at least in terms of area (the resources of the area are not, of course, necessarily commensurate with its size), and these States are those that front the great oceans of the world: as a quick glance at an atlas will show, many such States are developed, not developing. African States, in particular, come off badly. The fifteen leading beneficiaries of EEZs, together with some indication of the resources of their zones, are shown in table 1. Secondly, one would have expected the widespread introduction of 200 mile EEZs and EFZs in the late 1970s to have led to a reduction in the catches of distant-water fishing nations and an increase in the catches of the States off whose coasts they fished. If one compares the catches for 1981 — 83 with the catches for 1973 — 75 (before the general introduction of 200 mile zones), it can be seen that this has not altogether been the case. The catches of both the two distant-water nations, Japan and the USSR, have in fact slightly increased. Of the less important distant-water nations, a number (e.g. East Germany, Portugal and Bulgaria) have been badly hit, but by no means all (e.g. South Korea and Roumania, both of which have increased their catches) (and see further table 4 in chapter fourteen). These differing fortunes are perhaps largely due to the success or otherwise of distant-water nations in negotiating access to the 200 mile limits of other States. On the other hand, many of those States which have successfully reduced foreign fishing off their coasts by the introduction of a 200 mile limit have significantly increased their catches (e.g. the USA, Canada, Iceland, Mexico and New

Table 1. *Leading EEZ beneficiaries*

State	Area of 200 mile zone (square nautical miles)[34]	Offshore daily average crude oil production 1986 ('000 of barrels)	Offshore natural gas production 1986 (million cubic feet per day)	Fish catches or estimated potential (EP) in 200 mile zone (million tonnes)
1. USA	2,831,400	1,257·0		2·8 (1985)
2. France (including overseas departments and territories)	2,083,400	—	12,781·0	Not available
3. Indonesia	1,577,300	391·9	663·7	2·2 (EP)
4. New Zealand	1,409,500	14·0	369·0	0·6 (EP)
5. Australia	1,310,900	384·1	1,448·6	1·5 (EP)
6. USSR	1,309,500	165·0	1,300·0	5·0 (1979)
7. Japan	1,126,000	1·4	55·0	8·4 (1980)
8. Brazil	924,000	376·0	215·0	0·7 (1984)
9. Canada	857,000			1·5 (1984)
10. Mexico	831,500	1,700·0	950·0	1·0 (1984)
11. Kiribati	770,000			Not available
12. Papua New Guinea	690,000			0·1 (EP)
13. Chile	667,300	11·3		4·5 (1984)
14. Norway	590,500	780·6	3,011·0	2·9 (1979)
15. India	587,600	621·0	240·6	2·0 (EP)
Total all states	37,745,000	13,478·8	33,831·9	73·1 (1984)

Source. Cols 1 and 2: *Limits in the Seas*, No. 36, 4th revision (1981), p. 12; Cols 3 and 4: *Offshore*, May 1987, pp. 51–2; Col 5: a variety of EEC, FAO and OECD publications.

Zealand). In the case of some developing countries which have substantially increased the size of their catch in recent years, e.g. Guinea-Bissau, Indonesia, Malaysia, Pakistan and Sri Lanka, the increase may be due as much to improvements in technology and greater investment in the fishing industry as to phasing out foreign fishing off their coasts. Even where a developing country has not reduced foreign fishing off its coasts, it may nevertheless have benefited economically from establishing a 200 mile zone through being able to impose licensing fees on foreign vessels fishing in the zone. To an extent, therefore, the establishment of 200 mile EEZs and EFZs had led to some redistribution of resources. This redistribution has largely been from distant-water fishing States to the States off whose coasts they fished. Although the former are nearly all developed States, the latter are by no means exclusively — and perhaps not even principally — developing States.[33] As regards resources other than fish, in the case of offshore oil and gas the introduction of the EEZ effects no redistribution. Where the EEZ covers areas of sea bed that are continental shelf, any oil or gas there already belongs to the coastal State under the continental shelf doctrine. In areas of the EEZ where the sea bed is too deep to be continental shelf under the pre-LOSC regime, it is highly unlikely that there is any oil or gas. In the case of manganese nodules, the establishment of the EEZ means that about ten per cent of the nodules are now under national jurisdiction rather than in the International Sea Bed Area. This represents a redistribution in favour of those States whose EEZs contain manganese nodules, such as Mexico, from the international community as a whole. Overall, therefore, it is likely that the introduction of the EEZ concept has not and will not produce as much material gain for the developing countries as its original proponents suggested. Nevertheless, as a symbol of the control exercised by a State over its natural resources the introduction and acceptance of the EEZ may be a considerable psychological gain for developing countries.

Notes

1 See, for example, the Conclusions in the General Report of the African States Regional Seminar on the Law of the Sea, held in Yaoundé, June 1972. *UN Leg. Ser.* B/16, p. 601; *ND* I, p. 250.

2 Declaration of Santo Domingo, June 1972. *UN Leg. Ser.* B/16, p. 599; *ND* I, p. 247. Although this declaration is the first Latin American declaration to refer to the patrimonial sea, it is the culmination of a series of earlier Latin American proclamations moving towards this concept, in particular the Montevideo Declaration on the Law of the Sea, 1970, and the Lima Declaration on the Law of the Sea, 1970. *UN Leg. Ser.* B/16, pp. 586 and 587; *ND* I, pp. 235 and 237. For the differences between the Latin-American and African positions, see G. Pontecorvo (ed.), *The New Order of the Oceans*, New York, 1986, chapters 6 and 7, especially at p. 140.

3   Law regulating the Eighth Paragraph of Article 27 of the Constitution, relating
    to the Exclusive Economic Zone, 10 February 1976, art. 3. *UN Leg Ser.* B/19,
    p. 233; *ND* V, p. 292; subsequently replaced by Federal Act relating to the
    Sea, 1985, arts. 51 and 63. 7 *LOSB* 53 (1986); XXV *ILM* 889 (1986).

4   Decrees Nos. 78–143, 78–144, 78–146, and 78–147 (relating to French
    Polynesia; French Southern and Antarctic Territories; the islands of the
    Mozambique Channel; and Clipperton Island, respectively). *Journal Officiel*,
    11 February 1978, pp. 683–7; *Smith*, p. 154 *et seq.*

5   *Limits in the Seas* No. 101 (1984).

6   C. R. Symmons, *The Maritime Zones of Islands in International Law*, The
    Hague, 1979, pp. 125–6.

7   *Ibid.*, 'The Rockall dispute deepens: an analysis of recent Danish and
    Icelandic actions', 35 *ICLQ* 344–73 (1986).

8   Tokelau (Territorial Sea and Exclusive Economic Zone) Act, 1977. *ND* VII,
    p. 468; *Smith*, p. 341.

9   In practice, the coastal State and the State which is the owner of the pipeline
    may agree on a regime of concurrent jurisdiction. For an actual example, see
    the Agreement between Norway and the United Kingdom relating to the Ex-
    ploitation of the Frigg Field Reservoir and the Transmission of Gas therefrom
    to the United Kingdom, 1976, arts. 13–21.

10 For fuller discussion of these problems, see the articles by Brown and Robert-
    son listed in 'Further reading' and W. T. Burke, 'Exclusive fisheries zones and
    freedom of navigation' 20 *San Diego Law Review* 595–623 (1983).

11 Law No. 32/76 of 5 December 1976, s. 1. *UN Leg. Ser.* B/19, p. 134; *ND* IX,
    p. 295; *Smith*, p. 278.

12 Act No. 33/77 of 28 May 1977, art. 3. *UN Leg. Ser.* B/19, p. 93; *ND* VIII, p. 1;
    Smith, p. 371. Article 3 is somewhat ambiguous on this point. It reads: 'Establ-
    ishment of the exclusive economic zone shall take into account the rules of in-
    ternational law, namely those concerning innocent passage and overflight'.

13 Law No. 78, 043 of 28 February 1978 establishing Code of Merchant Marine
    and Fisheries, art. 186(1). *ND* IX, p. 76; *Smith*, p. 281.

14 Maritime Boundaries Act, 1977, s. 18. *UN Leg. Ser.* B/19, p. 33; *Smith*, p. 193.

15 Territorial Waters, Continental Shelf, Exclusive Economic Zone and other
    Maritime Zones Act, 1976, s. 7(6). *UN Leg. Ser.* B/19, p. 47; *ND* V, p. 305;
    Smith, p. 213.

16 Maritime Zones Act. 1977. s. 9   *ND* VII, p. 414; *Smith*, p. 287.

17 Territorial Waters and Maritime Zones Act, 1976, s. 6(4). *UN Leg. Ser.* B/19,
    p. 85; *ND* VII, p. 478; *Smith*, p. 357.

18 Maritime Zones Act, 1977, s. 9. *UN Leg. Ser.* B/19, p. 102; *ND* VIII, p. 11;
    Smith, p. 407.

19 Guyana's Act, ss. 19 and 41; India's Act, ss. 7 and 15; Mauritius's Act, ss. 10
    and 15; Pakistan's Act, ss. 6(5) and 14(2); Seychelles Act, ss. 10 and 15.

20 Territorial Waters and Maritime Zones Act, 1974, s. 9. *UN Leg. Ser.* B/19,
    p. 4; *ND* V, p. 286; *Smith*, p. 69.

21 Marine Boundaries and Jurisdiction Act, 1978, s. 8. *ND* VII, p. 335; *Smith*, p.
    73.

22 Marine Boundaries Act, 1978, s. 8. *Smith*, p. 175.

23 Exclusive Economic Zone Act, 1977, s. 15. *ND* VIII, p. 38; *Smith*, p. 483.

24 Maritime Zones Law, 1976, s. 12.*UN Leg. Ser.* B/19, p. 120; *ND* V, p. 317;
    Smith, p. 427.

25 Maritime Zones Act, 1981, s. 14. *Smith*, p. 471. Under s. 13(g) the Minister is also empowered to make regulations to provide for 'such other matters as may be required for giving full effect to the sovereignty of Vanuatu in relation to' the EEZ.
26 Exclusive Economic Zone Decree, 1978, s. 3(2). *ND* VII, p. 474; *Smith*, p. 347.
27 Decree No. 38 of 8 April 1977, art. 7. *Smith*, p. 201.
28 Decree No. 1–81–179 of 8 April 1981, art. 5. *Smith*, p. 303.
29 Decree Law No. 31/76, 19 August 1976, art. 2. *ND* VII, p. 427; *Smith*, p. 307.
30 Ordonnance No. 24 du 16 août 1977 portant délimitation des eaux territoriales et création d'une zone maritime économique protégée, art. 3. *UN Leg. Ser.* B/19, p. 130; *ND* VIII, p. 28; *Smith*, p. 439.
31 For a much fuller discussion of national laws relating to the EEZ and their compatibility with the Convention, see Burke, Juda and Smith (pp. 32–40), *op. cit.*, in 'Further reading'.
32 [1985] ICJ Rep. 13, at 33. Note, too, that in the Franco-Canadian Fisheries arbitration the tribunal acknowledged that the EEZ was part of customary law, at least as far as fisheries jurisdiction was concerned (see para. 49).
33 One calculation is that about two-thirds of the redistribution will go to developed States. See P. M. Wijkman, 'UNCLOS and the redistribution of ocean wealth', 16 *Journal of World Trade Law* 27 (1982), at 31–2.
34 But note that Smith, *op. cit.*, in 'Further reading', pp. 13–16, gives slightly different figures for the areas of some States' EEZs.

Further reading

L. M. Alexander and R. D. Hodgson, 'The impact of the 200 mile economic zone on the law of the sea' 12 *San Diego Law Review* 569–99 (1975).

D. Attard, *The Exclusive Economic Zone in International Law*, Oxford, 1987.

E. D. Brown, 'The exclusive economic zone. Criteria and machinery for the resolution of international conflicts between different users of the EEZ', 4 *Maritime Policy and Management* 325–50 (1977).

W. T. Burke, 'National legislation on ocean authority zones and the contemporary law of the sea', 9 *ODIL* 289–322 (1981).

J. I. Charney, 'The exclusive economic zone and public international law' 15 *ODIL* 233–88 (1985).

T. A. Clingan (ed.), *Law of the Sea: State Practice in Zones of Special Jurisdiction*, Honolulu, Hawaii, 1982.

B. Conforti (ed.), *La Zona Economica Esclusiva*, Milan, 1983.

W. C. Extavour, *The Exclusive Economic Zone*, Geneva, 1979.

A. L. Hollick, 'The origins of 200 mile offshore zones', 71 *AJIL* 494–500 (1977).

L. Juda, 'The exclusive economic zone: compatibility of national claims and the UN Convention on the Law of the Sea,' 16 *ODIL* 1–58 (1986).

L. Juda, 'The exclusive economic zone and ocean management', 18 *ODIL* 305–31 (1987).

R. B. Krueger and M. H. Nordquist, 'The evolution of the 200 mile exclusive economic zone. State practice in the Pacific basin', in International Law Association, *Report of the 58th conference, Manila, 1978*, London, 1980, pp. 248–89. A revised version of this article appears in 19 *VJIL* 321–400 (1979).

F. Orrego Vicuña (ed.), *The Exclusive Economic Zone: A Latin American Perspective*, Boulder, Colorado, 1984.

H. B. Robertson, 'Navigation in the exclusive economic zone' 24 *VJIL* 865–915 (1984).

R. W. Smith, *Exclusive Economic Zone Claims. An Analysis and Primary Documents*, Dordrecht, 1986.

UN, *The Law of the Sea. National Legislation on the Exclusive Economic Zone and the Exclusive Fishery Zone*, New York, 1986.

CHAPTER TEN
Delimitation of maritime boundaries

Introduction

This chapter is concerned with the delimitation of maritime boundaries between opposite and adjacent States. Judicial determinations of boundaries, such as the *Anglo-French Continental Shelf* case (1977), have attached importance to the distinction between opposite and adjacent States, although the tribunal in the *Guinea/Guinea-Bissau* case (1985) regarded the distinction as flexible and dispensable. In theory, each maritime zone demands a separate delimitation, yielding boundaries for the territorial sea, the EEZ or exclusive fisheries zone (in which the contiguous zone is commonly subsumed) and the continental shelf.

In practice, there is an increasing tendency to parcel these delimitations together. Thus, in the *Gulf of Maine* case (1984) a single boundary was for the first time determined by judicial decision (by a chamber of the International Court) for the continental shelf and superjacent waters (a Canadian exclusive fishery zone and a United States EEZ). Similarly, the arbitral tribunal in the *Guinea/Guinea-Bissau* case was asked to draw a line delimiting both the territorial sea and the sea and seabed within the EEZs of the two States. In addition, an increasing number of bilateral agreements, particularly in Latin America and Asia, lay down a single maritime boundary without distinguishing between different zones. Nonetheless, although there is a growing tendency for the principles on the delimitation of the various maritime zones to come together, it is convenient to consider them separately.

It should be emphasised that it is extremely difficult to offer any precise account of the principles of delimitation, such as might be applied in future to disputed boundaries. Quite apart from the inherent vagueness of the principles, each delimitation involves a situation which has its own unique characteristics which will have to be taken into account: previous practice and decisions will at best point to the kind of factors to be considered and approach to be adopted, and will not permit the deduction of a precise boundary line which must be applied.

Territorial sea boundaries

In the case of delimitations between opposite States (i.e. two States facing each other) the normal practice has been to agree upon the median line, equidistant from the nearest points of the opposing States' shores, as the boundary. This was done, for example, in the 1932 Danish-Swedish Declaration concerning the Sound, for a large part of the boundary between the two States. Sometimes States have employed instead the centre line of the main deep-water channel passing between their shores: an instance of this is the 1928 Agreement between Great Britain and the Sultan of Johore concerning the Johore Strait.[1]

Practice in delimiting the territorial seas of adjacent States has been less consistent. Considerable use has been made of the equidistance principle, drawing a median line outwards from the boundary on the shore: the 1976 Colombia-Panama delimitation agreement is one of many examples. But other criteria have also been used. Thus the Permanent Court of Arbitration, in its award in the *Grisbadarna* case in 1909, favoured a line drawn perpendicular to the general direction of the coast. While that case turned in part upon use of the perpendicular in seventeenth-century practice, made relevant by a treaty of 1661 concerning the Norwegian-Swedish boundary, the perpendicular line is still occasionally referred to in delimitations, such as the 1958 Poland-USSR delimitation agreement and the 1972 Brazil–Uruguay Agreement on the Chuy River Bank and the Lateral Sea Limit. In addition, some maritime boundaries between adjacent States follow the line of latitude passing through the point where the land boundary meets the sea. This method was used, for example, in the 1975 delimitation agreement between Ecuador and Colombia.

In all cases it is possible that special circumstances, such as the presence of offshore islands or the general configuration of the coast, or claims to water areas based upon an historic title, will demand the adoption of some other boundary line by agreement between the States concerned: in the 1974 Agreement between India and Sri Lanka on the Boundary in Historic Waters between the two countries, for instance, a modified median line was used, to take account of 'historical' factors. Indeed, it is the common practice at present to set boundaries by reference to geographical coordinates for the sake of certainty and simplicity, and such determinations almost inevitably demand some departure from the exact median line or other criterion. The particularity of the circumstances of each case make generalisation upon these delimitations difficult, and since they are motivated primarily by expediency and a spirit of compromise it is probably wrong in any event to attempt to infer any rules of international law from the practice which they generate. Indeed, in the *Guinea/Guinea-Bissau* case the tribunal decided that all delimitations had to be measured against the single goal of producing an equitable solution in the circumstances of each case. Many examples of recent agreements have been collected and analysed in the series *Limits in the Seas*, published by the Geographer of the US Department of State.

The conventional rules concerning delimitation are consistent with the pattern of State practice described above. Following the recommendations of the International Law Commission, article 12 of the 1958 Territorial Sea Convention provides:

(1) Where the coasts of two States are opposite or adjacent to each other, neither of the two States is entitled, failing agreement between them to the contrary, to extend its territorial sea beyond the median line every point of which is equidistant from the nearest points on the baselines from which the breadth of the territorial seas of each of the two States is measured. The provisions of this paragraph shall not apply, however, where it is necessary by reason of historic title or other special circumstances to delimit the territorial seas of the two States in a way which is at variance with this provision.

A substantially identical provision appears as article 15 of the Law of the Sea Convention.

Continental shelf and EEZ boundaries

Early delimitations of the continental shelf evidenced the application of no clear principles. The agreed delimitation in the Gulf of Paria in 1942, for example, was said to have secured an 'equitable division' between the United Kingdom and Venezuela. Similarly, the Truman Proclamation in 1945 referred to the application of 'equitable principles' in determining boundaries.

In the 1950s more specific principles emerged. Arguments for the adoption of the equidistance principle, under which a line equidistant from the nearest points of the coastlines of the States concerned would form the boundary, were pressed strongly in the ILC during the 1950s. That solution had the advantages of simplicity and certainty. It was, however, evident from the outset that inflexible application of the equidistance principle was undesirable. For example, since islands could generate their own continental shelves, a single small offshore island could create massive distortions in the line of equidistance which would be produced by considering only the coast of the mainland. Again, the configuration of the mainland coast might render equidistance an inequitable principle. This was the source of the dispute litigated in the *North Sea Continental Shelf* case (1969), for under the equidistance principle the concavity of the coastline of the Federal Republic of Germany and the adjacent States, Denmark and the Netherlands, resulted in Germany being allotted an exceptionally small part of the North Sea shelf. There may be other special circumstances, such as the presence of traditional fisheries or navigation routes, which would justify divergences from the equidistance principle. For these reasons the equidistance principle was from the first coupled with a reservation allowing such special circumstances to be accommodated. Thus the 1958 Convention provides that the boundary of the continental shelf shall be determined by agreement between the States concerned. However:

> In the absence of agreement, and unless another boundary line is justified by special circumstances, the boundary shall be determined by application of the principle of equidistance ... [CSC, art. 6(2); cf., art. 6(1)]

This provision represents a rule of treaty law only, applying 'equidistance plus special circumstances' in the absence of agreement — and many continental shelf boundaries have been settled by agreement — in relations between States accepting that obligation under the Convention. Thus the provision was not applicable in the *North Sea Continental Shelf* cases because Germany had not ratified the Convention. Under customary international law the rules on delimitation are less precise. In the *North Sea Continental Shelf* cases the International Court stated that under customary international law:

> delimitation is to be effected by agreement in accordance with equitable principles, and taking account of all the relevant circumstances, in such a way as to leave as much as possible to each Party all those parts of the continental shelf that constitute a natural prolongation of its land territory into and under the sea, without encroachment on the natural prolongation of the land territory of the other.[2]

This was accordingly achieved through the negotiation of a series of treaties between the littoral States concerned, in such a way as to give Germany a larger share of the shelf than it would have enjoyed under a delimitation employing only the equidistance principle.

In fact the practical application of the conventional and customary rules on delimitation seems to lead to much the same effect, although 'special circumstances' under the 1958 Convention are apparently rather more limited in scope than the general test of equitable delimitation under customary law. The reason is clear. The Arbitral Tribunal in the *Anglo-French Continental Shelf* case in 1977, dealing with delimitation of the Western Approaches between France and the United Kingdom (both parties to the 1958 Convention), stated that:

> ... the equidistance-special circumstances rule and the rules of customary law have the same object — the delimitation of the boundary in accordance with equitable principles. In the view of this Court, therefore, the rules of customary law are a relevant and even essential means both for interpreting and completing the provisions of Article 6.[3]

Accordingly, in that case the award took account of the 'special circumstances' of the area and departed from the median line so as to achieve a more equitable divison of the shelf: for example, the Scilly Isles were given only 'half effect', pushing the boundary line only half as far south as a strict application of the equidistance principle would have required.

The *Anglo-French Continental Shelf* case was only the second judicial settlement of a shelf delimitation dispute, the International Court of Justice having decided in 1978 that it lacked jurisdiction to consider the merits of the Greco-Turkish dispute, in the *Aegean Sea Continental Shelf* case. A third settlement was made by the International Court in 1982, in the *Tunisia/Libya Continental Shelf* case, when it explained and 'clarified' the principles of delimitation so as to enable experts to delimit the Libyan-Tunisian boundary without difficulty — a task somewhere between the expositon of principles in the *North Sea Continental Shelf* cases and the decision on the actual course of the boundary in the *Anglo-French Continental Shelf* case. In the Libya-Tunisia case the Court stressed, as it was required to by the parties, the principles of equity and the principle that there should be a reasonable degree of proportionality between the area of shelf appertaining to a State and the length of its coastline; and in the course of applying these principles to the particular circumstances of the case the Court decided to adopt the 'half effect' solution for dealing with distortion caused by the presence of offshore islands (the Kerkennahs).

The 'equitable' approach was given further impetus by the decision on the continental shelf and EEZ boundary in the *Gulf of Maine* case, which stressed both the central importance of the duty to settle delimitations by agreement and the underlying principle that delimitations must be based on criteria that lead to an equitable solution. The case is also significant for the great prominence which it gave to geographical factors in determining the equity of a delimitation. While other factors, such as the ecology of the area and the economic dependency of coastal communities on marine resources, might in principle be relevant in some cases, such as delimitations of exclusive fishing zones, they were not regarded as relevant in this case: the neutrality of the geographical factors secured their predominance.

The *Guinea/Guinea Bissau* and *Libya/Malta* cases in 1985 marked a further progression along this road. Both emphasised that the overriding goal, to which the application of all methods and principles for delimitation were subject, was the production of an equitable result, although not in the sense of an attempt to redress inequalities flowing from geography, such as the possession of coastlines relatively short in relation to the land area of the State. The *Libya/Malta* case is also notable for its accommodation of the move at UNCLOS III away from natural prolongation, on which the Court in the *North Sea Continental Shelf* cases had placed great emphasis, as a factor in delimitations: the Court noted that States were entitled to claim a continental shelf of at least 200 miles from the baseline (LOSC, art. 76), and held that geological or geomorphological arguments, of the kind implicit in the natural prolongation principle, were no longer relevant in determining boundaries, although they would remain relevant in setting the seaward limit of the shelf if it extends beyond 200 miles.

This leaves the law unclear — perhaps necessarily so given the uniqueness of each delimitation. The congruence of the principles for continental shelf and EEZ boundaries means that the delimitation of the two zones can be approached as a single problem, although States remain free to adopt different boundaries for each, as was done in the 1978 Australia–Papua New Guinea treaty concerning the Torres Strait, in order to preserve traditional fishing rights in part of the area in question (see below). It is to be expected that in future delimitations, in areas such as the East China/Yellow Sea, where delimitation is complicated by disputes over the ownership of certain islands, continental shelf and EEZ (or exclusive fishery zone) boundaries will be dealt with together.

It can further be said that at least four principles are clearly accepted. First, rights to the continental shelf are inherent, and this must be recognised in delimitations: there is, in theory, no element of distributive justice involved. Second, delimitation by agreement remains the primary rule of international law. Third, any delimitation, whether agreed or determined by a third party, must result in an equitable solution. Fourth, there is in principle no limit to the factors relevant to the determination of equitableness. In practice, geographical considerations are coming to predominate, and the existence of a significant disproportion between the relative maritime areas attaching to the States and the relative lengths of their coastlines is likely to be taken as a sign of inequity. Other factors, such as economic, ecological, security and geomorphological factors, are given less weight. Furthermore, features such as offshore islands which would produce an inequitable solution if given full effect in the application of the equidistance principle will be given a reduced effect or even ignored in order to achieve equity.

One word of caution should be entered. Of the seventy or more States which have legislated on the EEZ, well over one third include in their legislation reference to the equidistance principle, commonly as an interim solution pending the settlement of boundaries by agreement.[4] While this practice is, in view of the divergent practice of other States, probably insufficient to establish a rule of law of general application, the principles of opposability (see chapter one) are likely to secure the utilisation of the equidistance principle as a starting point for delimitations in several areas, such as the Pacific and the Arabian Gulf. In such contexts equidistance might be presented as an application of, rather than a departure from, the 'equitable' approach.

The uncertainty of the 'equitable' approach, at least compared with the equidistance rule, has led some jurists to question whether there is any longer any law on this matter; and it must be conceded that, given the uniqueness of each delimitation, the view that delimitation is entirely a matter of discretion in the circumstances of each case is a plausible one. However, the approach adopted in the more recent cases, based on customary law, is in accordance with the approach adopted in the 1982 Convention.

UNCLOS III had great difficulty in finding acceptable provisions concerning the delimitation of the continental shelf and EEZ. Article 83(1) of the Law of the Sea Convention provides simply:

The delimitation of the continental shelf between States with opposite or adjacent coasts shall be effected by agreement on the basis of international law, as referred to in Article 38 of the Statute of the International Court of Justice, in order to achieve an equitable solution.

The Convention adopts the same approach in relation to the delimitation of the EEZ: indeed, article 74 of the Convention, which deals with the matter, follows exactly, *mutatis mutandis*, the wording of article 83. If agreement on the boundary is not possible 'within a reasonable period of time', the matter is to be referred to the dispute settlement procedure set out in Part XV of the Convention (LOSC, arts. 74(2), 83(2)), unless there is a special treaty in force between the States concerned which covers the matter, in which case the dispute is to be resolved according to the provisions of such treaty (LOSC, arts, 74(4), 83(4)). Pending settlement of the dispute, the States concerned are to make every effort to enter into provisional arrangements of a practical nature (LOSC, arts. 74(3), 83(3)). Examples of such arrangements might include the 1985 France–Tuvalu agreement, under which the equidistance line is to be used as a temporary boundary pending agreement upon a permanent boundary, the 1977 Denmark–Sweden agreement, which provided that until a permanent boundary was agreed (as it was in 1984) the exclusive fishing zones in the area of the Kattegat lying beyond twelve miles from the coasts should be placed under joint Danish–Swedish fisheries jurisdiction, and the Japan–South Korea agreement of 1974, under which concessionaires exploit the resources of a disputed area of seabed on behalf of both States.

Articles 74 and 83 contain no reference to equidistance, which may now be applied only in so far as it leads to an equitable solution. Equity of result is the sole criterion. Innocuous as this vague approach might appear, it was unacceptable to some States, such as Venezuela, which voted against the adoption of the Convention, and Thailand, which abstained.

Although the provisions governing continental shelf and EEZ delimitation are the same, their wording is sufficiently imprecise for the provisions to be capable of application in more than one way, and thus for the continental shelf and EEZ boundaries to differ — a situation fraught with the potential for conflict: for example, if one State wanted to exploit its continental shelf underlying an area of another State's EEZ rich in fish stocks. In practice, in the case of the thirty-five or so EEZ boundaries that have already been agreed, the EEZ boundary is the same as the continental shelf boundary in all but one case, that being the Australia-Papua New Guinea Maritime Boundaries Treaty of 1978. This treaty provides for a divergence between the fisheries jurisdiction and the sea-bed jurisdiction boundaries in the Torres Strait, partly in order to recognise the importance of fishing to the inhabitants of certain Australian islands close to Papua New Guinea, and partly to avoid establishing Australian-inhabited enclaves north of a general maritime boundary between the two States.[5] Although it is generally desirable that EEZ and continental shelf boundaries should coincide, the fact that article 74 of the Law of the Sea convention stipulates that such boundaries should represent an 'equitable solution' will in many cases make it more difficult to agree on a common boundary: a boundary that might be equitable for EEZ purposes may not be equitable for continental shelf purposes because of the different considerations that are relevant to achieving an equitable solution in each case — for example, the location of fish stocks in the case of the EEZ, the geological characteristics of the sea bed and the location of sea bed mineral deposits in the case of continental shelf. The approach of the International Court in the *Gulf of Maine* case was to sidestep this problem by concentrating upon the equity of the delimitation from the geographical point of view, paying scant attention to the equity of the resulting division of the economic resources of the area. That is not, however, to say that such economic factors will not figure more prominently in negotiated settlements of boundary lines.

Treaty practice on delimitation

The principles described above will be applied, unless excluded or modified by the agreement of the parties, in judicial and arbitral determinations of maritime boundaries, and will also have a considerable influence on negotiated settlements. Many maritime boundaries have been settled by agreement — over one hundred such agreements exist, out of an estimated 400 boundaries.[6] In the case of territorial sea and continental shelf agreements, the equidistance principle, modified to take account of special circumstances, has tended to predominate as the basis of the delimitation. Territorial sea agreements have already been noted. The delimitation of the continental shelf between States such as Norway and the United Kingdom (1965, 1978), for example, also illustrate the use of the equidistance principle. Of the EEZ boundaries that have so far been agreed, the majority are based on the equidistance principle, sometimes with minor modifications to take account of special circumstances (e.g. the India-Sri Lanka Maritime Boundary Agreement of 1976, the Colombia-Haiti Maritime

Limits Agreement of 1978 and the France-Tonga Convention of 1980). A few agreements (e.g. the Colombia-Costa Rica Maritime Delimitation Treaty of 1977) appear to be based on equitable principles, while in two cases (the Colombia-Ecuador Marine Delimitation Agreement of 1975 and the Gambia-Senegal Maritime Boundaries Agreement of 1975) the boundary has been chosen, presumably for reasons of simplicity, as the line of latitude extending seawards from the terminus of the land boundary.

Cross-boundary resources

It may be that once the shelf has been divided between littoral States there is, for example, an oil deposit which straddles the boundary line. Such resources may, of course, in some circumstances constitute a 'special circumstance', so that the boundary line may be shifted so as to give one State full enjoyment of the resource. But the presence of such resources does not, in the absence of other factors such as historic rights of exploitation, automatically demand modification of the boundary, and shared deposits are generally to be considered, as the International Court of Justice put it in the *North Sea Continental Shelf* cases, as no more than 'a factual element which it is reasonable to take into consideration in the course of the negotiations for a delimitation'.[7] Where the boundary line does divide a shared deposit, the exigencies of economic exploitation will generally require the States concerned to negotiate an agreement on joint exploitation of the resources. Several such agreements exist, for example, that between Norway and the UK concerning the Frigg gas field in the North Sea (1976), under which production from the cross-boundary reservoir is apportioned between the two States and arrangements for coordinated administration of the field are established. The system adopted is in such cross-boundary agreements entirely a matter for the agreement of the parties. International customary law does not yet seem to yield any precise rules applicable in the absence of such agreement, although some writers have advanced general solutions based on a mixture of basic principles of law, previous treaty practice and robust expediency. Similar effects can be achieved in the case of cross-boundary fisheries by means of bilateral agreements giving access to EEZ or exclusive fishery zone stocks. Many such treaties exist: they are discussed in chapter fourteen.

Notes

1 See the *Straits Settlement and Johore Territorial Waters (Agreement) Act, 1928*, 18 and 19 Geo. 5, c. 23. This is, strictly, a colonial rather than international delimitation.
2 [1969] ICJ Rep. 3, at 54.
3 *ND* VIII, p. 283, at p. 323.
4 See *Smith, passim*. Barbados, Fiji, Iceland, India, Indonesia, Morocco,

Mozambique, New Zealand, Nigeria, Oman, Qatar, Spain, Tonga and Western Samoa are among the States concerned.

5 See Burmester, *op. cit*, in 'Further reading', at pp. 333–4. In relation to matters other than the sea bed and fisheries in the area of divergence, the treaty provides that a party may not exercise jurisdiction without the concurrence of the other (art. 4(3)).

6 See E. D. Brown, *op. cit.*, in 'Further reading', vol. III, pp. III. 4. 19–33, for a recent list.

7 [1969] ICJ Rep. 3, at 53.

Further reading

S. H. Amin, 'Law of continental shelf delimitation: the Gulf example', XXVII *Netherlands International Law Review* 335–46 (1980).

G. Blake (ed.), *Maritime Boundaries and Ocean Resources*, London, 1987.

M. D. Blecher, 'Equitable delimitation of continental shelf', 73 *AJIL* 60–88 (1979).

E. D. Brown, *Sea-Bed Energy and Mineral Resources and the Law of the Sea*, vols. 1 and 3, London, 1984, 1986

H. Burmester, 'The Torres Strait Treaty', 76 *AJIL* 321–49 (1982).

L. Caflisch, 'Les zones maritimes sous juridiction nationale, leurs limites et leur délimitation', 84 *RGDIP* 68–119 (1980) (and see D. Bardonnet and M. Virally (eds.), *Le Nouveau Droit International de la Mer*, Paris, 1983, for a later version).

J. I. Charney, 'Ocean boundaries between nations: a theory for progress', 78 *AJIL* 582–606 (1984).

R. R. Churchill, 'Delimitation in the Jan Mayen area', 9 *Marine Policy* 16–38 (1985).

D. A. Colson, 'The United Kingdom–France continental shelf arbitration', 72 *AJIL* 95–112 (1978), and 73 *AJIL* 112–20 (1979).

B. Conforti and G. Francalanci (eds.), *Atlas of the Seabed Boundaries*, Milan, 1979.

W. Friedmann, 'The North Sea continental shelf cases–a critique', 64 *AJIL* 229–40 (1970).

L. Gross, 'The dispute between Greece and Turkey concerning the continental shelf in the Aegean', 71 *AJIL* 31–59 (1977).

D. N. Hutchinson, 'The concept of natural prolongation in the jurisprudence concerning delimitation of continental shelf areas', 55 *BYIL* 133–87 (1984).

M. B. Feldman, 'The Tunisia–Libya continental shelf case: geographic justice or judicial compromise?', 77 *AJIL* 219–38 (1983).

L. L. Herman, 'The court giveth and the court taketh away: an analysis of the *Tunisia–Libya Continental Shelf* Case', 33 *ICLQ* 825–58 (1984).

S. P. Jagota, *Maritime Boundary*, Dordrecht, 1985.

D. E. Karl, 'Islands and the delimitation of the continental shelf: a framework for analysis', 71 *AJIL* 642–73 (1977).

R. Lagoni, 'Interim measures pending maritime delimitation agreements', 78 *AJIL* 345–68 (1984).

L. H. Legault and B. Hankey, 'From sea to seabed: the single maritime boundary in the Gulf of Maine', 79 *AJIL* 961–91 (1985).

Y–J. Ma, *Legal Problems of Seabed Boundary Delimitation in the East China Sea*, Baltimore, 1984.

T. L. McDorman *et al.*, *Maritime Boundary Delimitation: An Annotated Bibliography*, Lexington, 1983.

W. T. Onorato, 'Apportionment of an international common petroleum deposit', 17 *ICLQ* 85–102 (1968), and 26 *ICLQ* 324–37 (1977).

C. H. Park, 'Oil under troubled waters: the Northeast Asia seabed controversy', 14 *Harvard International Law Journal* 212–60 (1973).

J. R. V. Prescott, *The Maritime Political Boundaries of the World*, London, 1985.

S-M. Rhee, 'Seabed boundary delimitation between States before World War II', 76 *AJIL* 555–88 (1982).

F. Rigaldies, 'L'affaire de la délimitation du plateau continental entre la République Française et le Royaume-Uni de Grande Bretagne et d'Irlande du Nord', 106 *JDI* 506–31 (1979).

D. R. Robinson, D. A. Colson, and B. C. Rashkow, 'Some perspectives on adjudicating before the world court: the Gulf of Maine case', 79 *AJIL* 578–97 (1985).

J. Schneider, 'The Gulf of Maine Case: the nature of an equitable result', 79 *AJIL* 539–77 (1985).

C. R. Symmons, 'British off-shore continental shelf and fishery limit boundaries: an analysis of overlapping zones', 28 *ICLQ* 703–33 (1979).

—, *The Maritime Zones of Islands in International Law*, The Hague, 1979, chapter IV.

J. C. Woodliffe, 'International unitisation of an offshore gas field', 26 *ICLQ* 338–85 (1977).

R. Young, 'Equitable solutions for offshore boundaries: the 1968 Saudi Arabia–Iran Agreement', 64 *AJIL* 152–57 (1970).

And see further the bibliography in Brown (1986), vol. III, above.

CHAPTER ELEVEN
High seas

Introduction

The list of examples set out in the 1958 Convention has been extended in article 87 of the Law of the Sea Convention so as to include the freedom provisions. Many are concerned with general questions of jurisdiction and the freedoms of the seas; but others concern specific problems which, since 1958, have received close attention and have generated a considerable body of legal material of their own. Accordingly, we have reserved for treatment in later chapters some of these specific problems, such as the 'flag of convenience' question (see chapter thirteen) and the problem of marine pollution (see chapter fifteen). Here we discuss only the general regime of the high seas.

Definition

Traditionally, the high seas were defined as 'all parts of the sea not included in the territorial sea or in the internal waters of a state' (HSC, art. 1). With the advent of the EEZ and of the concept of archipelagic waters (see above, chapters nine and six), this definition has now to be modified. Article 86 of the Law of the Sea Convention states that the high-seas rules in the Convention apply to:

... all parts of the sea that are not included in the exclusive economic zone, in the territorial sea or in the internal waters of a State, or in the archipelagic waters of an archipelagic State.

Although some States, such as the United Kingdom, at one stage regarded the EEZ as a zone of high seas subject to special rights of coastal jurisdiction (this position has since been abandoned), and although, as we saw in chapter nine, high seas freedoms are preserved to a certain extent in the EEZ, the revised definition is more satisfactory; however, for States claiming an exclusive fishery zone rather than an EEZ the high seas will continue to include that zone (but, of course, the high seas freedom of fishing will not apply in the zone). The presumption of the exclusiveness of flag-State jurisdiction, which is the dominant principle on the high seas, is excluded in the case of the EEZ (see chapter nine), and reversed in the case of archipelagic waters by their subjection to the sovereignty of the coastal State (LOSC, art. 49). Accordingly, this chapter considers only the rules governing the area defined in article 86 of the Law of the Sea Convention. The legal concept of the high seas also extends to the superjacent air space, and formerly it extended to the sea bed and subsoil as well. However, the emergence of special legal regimes for the continental shelf and the sea bed beyond national jurisdiction has eroded this wider definition of the high seas, and we have accordingly consigned detailed discussion of the legal status of the sea bed to chapters eight and twelve.

The legal status of the high seas

The high seas are open to all States, and no State may validly purport to subject any part of them to its sovereignty (HSC, art. 2; LOSC, arts. 87, 89). This rule of customary law, codified in the conventions prepared by UNCLOS I and UNCLOS III, is a corner-stone of international law. But it has not always been so. In the fifteenth century there were many claims to sovereignty over extensive areas of the oceans: by Sweden and Denmark in the Baltic and Norwegian Sea; by Venice in the Adriatic and Genoa and Pisa in the Ligurian Sea; and by Britain in the ill-defined 'British seas' around its coasts. Though sometimes cited as extreme examples of such claims, the divisions of the Atlantic Ocean between Spain and Portugal by Pope Alexander VI in 1493, confirmed in the Treaty of Tordesillas in 1494, were really no more than delimitations of spheres of influence in the new territories then being colonised. Nonetheless, other claims did involve claims to levy tolls as a condition of passage, to license fishermen, and to demand salutes from foreign ships to the warships of the coastal State.

It was inevitable that during the great period of maritime exploration which began in the early seventeenth century opposition to the notion of closed seas would mount. The doctrinal battle was fought in the seventeenth century, in the first decade of which Grotius published his *Mare Liberum*, and was eventually won by the advocates of the open seas, as the importance of free navigation in the service of overseas and colonial trade came to overshadow national interests in coastal fisheries, and as the development of real naval power displaced notional claims to sovereignty over the seas. Most of the extravagant claims to maritime sovereignty were abandoned during the eighteenth century. By the first half of the nineteenth the conception of the high seas as an area juridically distinct from national waters and not susceptible to appropriation by any State had become clearly established. Nevertheless a few exceptional cases of claims to historic bays, and more recently to archipelagic waters, have been admitted in derogation of this principle (see chapters two and six), and the *laissez-faire* principles upon which the regime of the high seas is built have given rise to increasing criticism that the regime is incapable of dealing with the problems of controlling pollution and overfishing — a criticism which has produced a major derogation from the high seas in the form of the EEZ.

From the rule that no State can subject areas of the high seas to its sovereignty, or indeed to its jurisdiction, it follows that no State has the right to prevent ships of other States from using the high seas for any 'lawful purpose'. As is customary, we examine the idea of 'lawful purposes' under the heading of 'freedom of the high seas', in the next section. A second corollary of the status of the high seas is that apart from a few special cases, mostly created by treaty, no State has jurisdiction over foreign ships on the high seas: this aspect we consider in the final section below.

Freedom of the high seas

Precisely because States cannot in principle control foreign shipping on the high seas, so that users of the seas remain at liberty to do as they please apart from a few restrictive rules, and because new ocean technology is constantly developing, the freedoms of the high seas cannot be exhaustively listed. This was recognised in the 1958 Convention, which claimed to be 'generally declaratory of established principles of international law': article 2 listed the freedoms of navigation, fishing, laying of submarine cables and pipelines (the 'right of immersion', which, unlike the other listed freedoms, involves use of the bed of the high seas) and overflight, as examples of high seas freedoms, stating that:

These freedoms, and others which are recognised by the general principles of international law, shall be exercised by all States with reasonable regard to the interests of other States in their exercise of the freedom of the high seas. [HSC, art. 2]

All states, whether coastal or not, have the right to exercise high-seas freedoms. The requirement of 'reasonable regard' would seem to require that where there is a potential conflict between two freedoms (uses) of the high seas, there should be a weighing of the interests involved to determine which use is the more reasonable in the circumstances. For example, the stringing out of long lines of fishing nets across busy shipping lanes would not be permissible. Arguably, there is a presumption in favour of an established use as against a new use. Such a weighing of interests will normally occur through negotiations between the States concerned, though exceptionally third party dispute settlement might be possible — a possibililiy which will be increased for States parties to the Law of the Sea Convention when the Convention enters into force (see chapter nineteen). What has been said so far is perhaps more a description of the ideal than of what actually happens: in practice stronger States are often able to insist upon their own uses of the high seas notwithstanding that such uses may appear unreasonable to other States — witness, for example, the nuclear testing carried out in the Pacific by the United Kingdom and the United States in the 1950s. The exercise of high-seas freedoms is also, of course, subject to general rules of international law, such as those governing the use of force.

to construct artificial islands and other installations permitted under international law and freedom of scientific research. But the greater detail of the Law of the Sea Convention has also led to the subjection of some of these freedoms to conditions in addition to the 'reasonable regard' requirement (now termed 'due regard'), which is itself amended to protect not only the interests of others exercising the freedom of the high seas but also 'the rights under this Convention with respect to activities in the Area'— that is, the deep sea bed (LOSC, art. 87(2); see chapter twelve). Thus the right of immersion is subject to the rights of States to regulate the laying of cables and pipelines across their continental shelves (LOSC,art. 79; cf. HSC, art. 26, and chapter eight). Here the freedom of immersion exists, even on the shelf, but its exercise may be regulated. Coastal States may similarly regulate exercises of the freedom to establish non-economic installations (for example, installations for detecting the passage of submarines) on the shelf, to the extent necessary for safeguarding coastal rights of exploration and exploitation on the shelf (LOSC, arts. 80, 60). But artificial islands, and any other installations which may interfere with the exercise of the rights of the coastal State on the continental shelf, can, under the Law of the Sea Convention, be constructed only with the consent of the coastal State, and to this extent the freedom is abrogated in the ten per cent or so of the high seas which overlie those parts of the continental shelf protruding beyond the 200 mile EEZ. Similarly, freedom of research is limited by the rights of coastal States on their continental shelves, and of the International Sea Bed Authority in respect of the rest of the sea bed (see chapters eight, twelve and sixteen). Freedom of fishing is subjected to a general duty to negotiate fishing agreements and to enact national legislation in order to protect high-seas fisheries, and to limited derogations in favour of the 'home' States of anadromous and catadromous species (LOSC, arts. 116–20; see chapter fourteen).

The fact that the 1958 High Seas Convention and the 1982 Law of the Sea Convention purport only to give non-exhaustive lists of examples of high-seas freedoms, each of which is limited by the 'reasonable regard' ('due regard') requirement, leaves room for controversies. Thus there are high-seas activities alleged by some States to constitute freedoms, but denied this status by other States. The principle on which such disputes should be resolved is that any use compatible with the status of the high seas — that is, a use which involves no claim to appropriation of parts of the high seas and which involves no unreasonable interference with the rights of others — should be admitted as a freedom unless it is excluded by some specific rule of law. For example, it is generally accepted that some naval manoeuvres and conventional weapon testing may be conducted on the high seas.[1] Mariners are notified of the areas and times at which these take place, and although usually they are not actually forbidden to enter and care is taken to avoid busy areas of the sea, there is a clear expectation that foreign vessels should keep out of these areas. While this practice is often acquiesced in, when France (which is not a party to the 1963 Treaty banning Nuclear Weapon Tests in the Atmosphere, in Outer Space and under Water, which now prohibits such testing anywhere in the atmosphere or in territorial waters or high seas) declared a vast area of the Pacific closed to foreign shipping in 1974, and used force to prevent the entry into the zone of a vessel protesting against the French atmospheric nuclear tests therein, strong protests were made. Australia and New Zealand took the matter to the International Court, arguing that 'the interference with ships and aircraft on the high seas and in the superjacent air space, and the pollution of the high seas by radioactive fall-out, constitute infringements of the freedom of the high seas'. However, the *Nuclear Tests* cases (1974) ended without a judgment on the merits of this contention, the Court holding that French announcements of a termination of atmospheric testing had effectively brought an end to the dispute. Nonetheless, it is clear that in such cases the main criterion which the Court would use to determine whether or not the use fell within the freedom of the high seas would be that of reasonableness.

Jurisdiction on the high seas

In general, the flag State, that is, the State which has granted to a ship the right to sail under its flag (see further, chapter thirteen), has the exclusive right to exercise legislative and enforcement jurisdiction over its ships on the high seas (HSC, art. 6; LOSC, art. 92). Thus compliance with international duties concerning safety at sea and the rendering of assistance to ships in distress is sought by imposing on flag States the duty to adopt and enforce legislation dealing with such matters (HSC, arts. 10, 11; LOSC, arts. 94, 98; see chapter thirteen). Again, States must provide compensation for damage to pipelines and cables under the high seas by ships under their jurisdiction (HSC, arts, 27–8; LOSC, arts. 113, 114), although as a complement to this duty they must also ensure that compensation is available from pipeline and cable owners for ships which are obliged to sacrifice anchors or fishing gear in order to avoid damaging a cable or pipeline (HSC, art. 29; LOSC, art. 115).[2]

Collisions may involve two States, each of which considers the collision and those responsible for it to be within its jurisdiction. The existence of such concurrent jurisdiction was upheld by the Permanent Court of International Justice in the case of the French ship *Lotus* (1927), which had collided with a Turkish vessel, causing loss of life. The narrow, and best, ground of the decision was that the collision had 'taken place' on the Turkish ship and that the officer responsible could therefore be prosecuted by Turkey as well as by France. The *Lotus* decision was much criticised, and the rule which it adopted was reversed by the 1952 Brussels Convention for the Unification of Certain Rules relating to Penal Jurisdiction. The Brussels rule was adopted in the 1958 High Seas Convention and in the Law of the Sea Convention, both of which reserve penal and disciplinary proceedings in cases of collision or other navigational incidents to the authorities of the State in whose ship the defendant served or (if that be different) the State of which he is a national (HSC, art. 11; LOSC, art. 97). The latter alternative underlines the fact that a State retains jurisdiction over its nationals wherever they may be, whether on foreign ships or anywhere else; but the expectation is that in this case of concurrent jurisdiction it is the flag State whose jurisdiction has primacy (see, e.g., LOSC, art. 94).

The exclusiveness of the flag State's jurisdiction is not absolute. It admits of several exceptions, in which third States share legislative or enforcement jurisdiction, or both, with the flag State; and it is to these exceptions that we now turn.

Piracy

The first exception is the long-established right — and, indeed, duty (HSC, art. 14; LOSC, art. 100) — of every State to act against piracy. This exception arose from the common interest of the European powers in protecting the fleets which were the lifelines of their colonial empires. Piracy remains a serious problem, notably off parts of Africa and southeast Asia. Piracy includes any illegal act of violence, detention or depradation committed for private ends by the crew or passengers of a private ship (or aircraft) against another ship (or aircraft), or persons or property on board it, on (or over) the high seas (HSC, art. 15; LOSC, art. 101); and if a ship or aircraft is intended to be or has been used for such purpose by the persons in dominant control, it is a pirate ship or aircraft (HSC, art. 17; LOSC, art. 103). Acts of piracy by warships or government ships and aircraft are assimilated to those committed by private ships if the crew have mutinied and taken control: otherwise, the 'official' nature of actions by such ships precludes their classification as piracy, as does the fact that such actions are not committed for private ends (HSC, art. 16; LOSC, art. 102). In fact all recent cases of piracy have involved non-government ships. The requirement that two vessels — pirate and victim — be involved distinguishes piracy from hi-jacking, and explains why attempts by passengers to gain control of ships, as happened on the Portuguese vessel *Santa Maria* in 1961, and on the Italian liner *Achille Lauro* in 1985, are not acts of piracy. Unless the law of the flag State provides otherwise a ship retains its nationality even when it becomes a pirate ship (HSC, art. 18; LOSC, art. 104).

Article 22 of the High Seas Convention, which purports to codify the customary law concerning the high seas, and article 110 of the Law of the Sea Convention, allow the visiting and boarding of any ship, of whatever flag, reasonably suspected of being engaged in piracy. If, however, the suspicions prove unfounded, and the ship had done nothing to justify them, it must be compensated for any loss or damage which it sustained (HSC, art. 22; LOSC, art. 110). Pirate ships on the high seas may be seized (HSC, art. 19; LOSC, art. 105), though only by warships (or aircraft) or other authorised vessels in government service (HSC, art. 21; LOSC, art. 107). Where the seizure is wrongfully effected without adequate grounds the ship's flag State is entitled to compensation for any loss or damage caused from the State of the warship (HSC, art. 20; LOSC, art. 106). Similarly, those on board a pirate vessel may be arrested (HSC, art. 19; LOSC, art. 105). Pirates may be tried by any State before whose courts they are brought, and that State may determine by its laws the penalties to be imposed (HSC, art. 19; LOSC, art. 105).

Concerned at the continuing recurrence of acts of piracy and of other unlawful acts threatening the safety of navigation, the IMO established an *ad hoc* committee in 1986 to consider a draft convention on the suppression of unlawful acts against the safety of maritime navigation. The draft convention, which is likely to be put before a diplomatic conference in 1988, would require a State in which an alleged offender was present either to prosecute or extradite him.[3]

Unauthorised broadcasting

The second exception concerns unauthorised broadcasting on the high seas. In the early 1960s a number of ships anchored in the North Sea and began broadcasting, for profit, without a licence from the States where the transmissions were received. Since these 'pirate' radio stations were based on foreign ships on the high seas, the view was taken that coastal States had no jurisdiction over them. Under the European Agreement for the Prevention of Broadcasting transmitted from Stations outside National Territories, signed in 1965, several European States agreed to punish their nationals engaged in or assisting unauthorised broadcasting, as well as anyone, of whatever nationality, on ships flying their flag from which unauthorised broadcasts were being made. This forced most stations to close down. Thus far, action against pirate broadcasting had not exceeded the general principle of exclusive flag State jurisdiction. But the Law of the Sea Convention has gone further, allowing States where unauthorised transmissions either are received or result in interference with authorised radio communication to exercise jurisdiction over unauthorised broadcasters; flag States and national States of broadcasters retain a concurrent jurisdiction (LOSC, art. 109).

Rights of visiting and boarding, and of seizing ships, and arresting and prosecuting persons on board, are vested in those States which have jurisdiction over unauthorised broadcasting, and are exercised under the conditions described above in relation to piracy (LOSC, art. 110).

In the case of piracy and unauthorised broadcasting, States other than the flag State are given under the Convention both legislative jurisdiction and enforcement jurisdiction over ships on the high seas (which exist anyway as a matter of customary international law in the case of piracy). In a number of other cases States enjoy extended enforcement jurisdiction over foreign ships on the high seas, unaccompanied by a right to prescribe rules which such ships are obliged to obey there. These cases we consider next.

Slave and drug trafficking

Where a ship is reasonably suspected of being engaged in the slave trade, it may be visited and boarded. However, despite a British proposal in 1956 to make it so, slave trading is not in international law analogous to piracy (although it is in English municipal law), and only the flag State may actually proceed to seize the ship or arrest those on board if the suspicion is well founded: other States may only report their findings to the flag State, which is, however, obliged to adopt effective measures for the repression of slave trading by its ships (HSC, art. 13; LOSC, art. 99). If any slave succeeds in escaping and taking refuge on board any ship, of whatever flag, he becomes, *ipso facto*, free (*ibid.*). Several international agreements, such as the 1890 General Act for the Suppression of the Slave Trade, include provisions for international co-operation in action against slave traders, and some provide for reciprocal rights of visit and search over vessels in parts of the high seas; no such rights of visit and search were expressly included in the 1926 International Slavery Convention or the 1956 Supplementary Slavery Convention, although those rights (subject to the normal conditions concerning unwarranted action) persist, of course, under the High Seas Convention and 1982 Convention, which are generally regarded as codifying customary international law in this respect (HSC, art. 22; LOSC, art. 110)

Few powers exist in the case of ships suspected of illicitly trafficking in narcotic and psychotropic drugs, despite the obligation on States to co-operate in suppressing that trade: all that is allowed is that States with reasonable grounds for suspecting that their own ships are engaged in the trade may request the co-operation of other States in suppressing the traffic, although presumably there is an implication that other States should normally accede to such a request (LOSC, art. 108).

Ships of uncertain nationality

States may visit and enforce their laws against their own ships on the high seas. Consequently where a ship, though flying a foreign flag, is reasonably suspected of being of the same nationality as a warship which encounters it on the high seas, the warship may visit and board it, checking its documents and proceeding to a further examination on board if necessary, in order to verify its right to fly its flag. As before, if the suspicions are unfounded and unjustified by the conduct of the ship visited, the ship is to be compensated for any loss or damage sustained (HSC, art. 22; LOSC, art. 110).

Ships without nationality are in a curious position. Their 'statelessness' will not, of itself, entitle each and every State to assert jurisdiction over them, for there is not in every case any recognised basis, such as nationality or territoriality, upon which jurisdiction could be asserted over them while they are on the high seas. On the other hand it has been held, for example in the case of *Molvan* v. *A. G. for Palestine* (UK, 1948), that such ships enjoy the protection of no State, the implication being that if jurisdiction *were* asserted no State would be competent to complain. Widely accepted as this view is, it ignores the possibility of protection being exercised by the national State of the individuals on such stateless ships. No right to visit and board such ships was given under the High Seas Convention; such a right is, however, given by article 110 of the Law of the Sea Convention. Ships which sail under two or more flags, using them according to convenience, are assimilated to ships without nationality (HSC, art. 6(2); LOSC, art. 92).

Hot pursuit and constructive presence

The right of hot pursuit, recognised under customary law in cases such as the *I'm alone* (1935), allows a warship or military aircraft of a State to pursue a foreign ship which has violated that State's laws within its internal waters or territorial sea and to arrest it on the high seas. Pursuit must be begun while the ship or one of its boats is within the territorial sea (or, in the case of customs, fiscal, immigration or sanitary laws, within the contiguous zone), by the giving within range of the ship of a visual or auditory signal to stop, although the signalling ship need not be within the territorial sea or contiguous zone at the time. Pursuit must be hot and continuous; and the right of pursuit ceases as soon as the ship enters the territorial sea of its own or a third State, because to continue it therein would be to violate the sovereignty of the other State. Although it is provided that a ship or aircraft may take over pursuit from an aircraft which began it, there is no express provision allowing one ship to take over from another subsequently. It would, however, seem reasonable to allow this. The pursuing vessel may use any necessary and reasonable force to effect the arrest, even if this results in the unavoidable sinking of the ship: compensation is payable for loss or damage resulting from unjustified pursuit or for the exercise of unjustified force (HSC, art. 23; LOSC, art. 111). The Law of the Sea Convention extends the right to include pursuit from archipelagic waters, and also pursuit from the EEZ or the waters above the continental shelf in cases where a violation of the laws which the coastal State is entitled to make in respect of the zone or shelf has occurred. There is no reason why the right of pursuit should cease when the vessel pursued enters the EEZ of its own or a third State. It may be noted in passing that the right to enforce laws respecting the continental shelf will itself involve a right to exercise both legislative and enforcement jurisdiction over foreign ships on the high seas in cases where the shelf extends beyond the 200 mile zone.

There is also a right to arrest foreign ships which use their boats to commit offences within the territorial sea (and, perhaps, now the EEZ) while themselves remaining on the high seas. This is the doctrine of contructive presence, impliedly recognised in the provisions of the High Seas and Law of the Sea conventions relating to hot pursuit, and which we considered in chapter seven.

Major pollution incidents

A further exception to the exclusiveness of flag State jurisdiction is often said to exist in favour of States whose coastline is threatened with serious pollution from a foreign shipping casualty on the high seas. This right, which gained rapid recognition after the British action against the *Torrey Canyon* in 1967, was the subject of the 1969 'Intervention' Convention, and is included in the Law of the Sea Convention as article 221. It is also widely suggested that such a right exists in customary international law. This matter is discussed more fully in chapter fifteen.

Exceptional measures

States have sometimes justified interference with foreign ships on the high seas on the grounds self-defence or necessity. The classic incident, the *Virginius*, arose in 1873: there Spain seized on the high seas an American ship carrying American and British nationals and many weapons which they intended to use in the Cuban insurrection against Spain. Great Britain, but not America, accepted that the arrest of the ship was justified on the grounds of self-defence. More recently France asserted a right to visit and search on the high seas ships suspected of carrying arms to Algeria during the emergency of 1956–62. The Ministry of Defence argued in the case of the *Duizar* (1966) that this was justified by France's right of self-defence, but the French action was vigorously opposed by many of the States whose ships were affected. The explanation of the distinction between the responses to the *Virginius* and the Algerian incidents probably lies partly in the emergence during the intervening period of rules limiting the use of force generally, and notably article 51 of the UN Charter, which arguably limits the right of self-defence to cases of armed attack, and partly in the scale of the French operation — 4,775 ships were searched in the first year alone.

The most notorious example of interference with foreign shipping on the high seas is the Cuban 'quarantine' of 1962. Warships of the United States, and later Argentina, Dominican Republic and Venezuela, inspected ships bound for Cuba to determine whether they were carrying 'offensive military equipment' to the island. The primary basis of the quarantine was not the right of self-defence but the decision of the Organisation of American States, purportedly acting under Chapter VIII of the UN Charter (which it clearly was not), to institute the measure. The question of the legality of the quarantine, which is controversial, is closely bound up with questions of the competence of international organisations (also involved in the British-operated blockade of the port of Beira, authorised by the United Nations during the Rhodesian crisis) and of the scope of self-defence in general, which are beyond the range of this book (but see chapter seventeen). And if the intention to create a precedent for future behaviour is a desirable quality in State practice called in evidence to support the existence of a rule of customary law, then the incident is perhaps best forgotten. But it, and other cases, demonstrate that even in peacetime States do take exceptional measures of enforcement jurisdiction on the high seas, any opposition from other States being insufficient to deter them.

Perhaps the most notable claim to exceptional jurisdiction over foreign ships on the high seas will come to be seen in the development exemplified by the case of *US* v. *Gonzalez*, referred to in chapter seven. It will be recalled that in that case jurisdiction over a foreign ship engaged in attempts to smuggle drugs into the United States was based on the protective principle of jurisdiction in international law which, in the view of the court, justified the seizure and prosecution of ships and persons on the high seas 'to such an extent and to so great a distance as is reasonable and necessary to protect itself and its citizens from injury'. While the court went on to speak of the requirement that the conduct punished should be 'generally recognized as a crime under the laws of States that have reasonably developed legal systems', the absence of any other limiting criterion *ratione loci* or *ratione materiae* makes this principle one of enormous potential scope, capable of subsuming and considerably extending not only the rules on the contiguous zone, but also the rules on visit and search on the high seas. The manner in which such claims are received by other States will determine whether or not they are recognised as legitimate in customary law, but for the moment their legality must remain highly controversial.

Rights under treaty

With the exceptions outlined above, and with the further exception of rights in contiguous zones, which are discussed in chapter seven, the exclusiveness of flag State jurisdiction on the high seas remains, in principle, intact. But the principle can be varied by specific agreement, and is indeed departed from in a wide variety of treaties. Some, such as the 1967 Convention on the Conduct of Fishing Operations in the North Atlantic, grant only rights to visit and search or, like the 1884 Convention for the Protection of Submarine Cables, merely the right to approach, but not to board, suspected miscreants in order to determine their nationality. In these cases only enforcement jurisdiction is extended, the capacity to prescribe rules, and also to punish violations of them, resting with the flag State, to which third States' inspecting vessels would report. In a few cases, both enforcement and legislative jurisdiction is extended, notable examples being the agreements subjecting vessels calling at the deep-water port facility of Louisiana to the jurisdiction of the United States. United States legislation adopted in 1974 provided that foreign vessels might not use the facility unless their flag State had concluded such an agreement with the United States, which at that time regarded the operation of deep-water ports as an exercise of the freedom of the high seas;[4] however, the Louisiana facility is within 200 miles of the coast, and therefore now within United States jurisdiction by virtue of the EEZ which it has claimed since 1983.

More recently, the United Kingdom and United States concluded an agreement in 1981 to facilitate the interdiction by the United States of British vessels in defined areas of the Caribbean and Gulf of Mexico and up to 150 miles off the eastern seaboard of the United States suspected of trafficking in drugs. The agreement provides for the visit, search and seizure of such vessels on the high seas, and is comparable with the 'liquor treaties' of the 1920s discussed in chapter seven.

Notes

1 The provision that the high seas 'be reserved for peaceful purposes' (LOSC, art. 88; cf. art. 301) is widely regarded as prohibiting only acts of aggression on the high seas, and will certainly be interpreted in that way by naval powers (see further, chapter seventeen). On weapons testing, see the anonymous note and the articles by Margolis, McDougal and Schlei, and Swan, listed in 'Further reading', below.
2 See also the 1884 Convention for the Protection of Submarine Cables.
3 *IMO News*, 1987 No. 2, p. 1. The IMO Maritime Safety Committee has recommended a series of measures to improve port and on-board security: *ibid.*
4 See, for example, the UK–USA Exchange of Notes concerning the Use of the Louisiana Offshore Oil Port, 14/25 May 1979. Cf., *DUSPIL 1974*, pp. 356–60, where the provisions of the US Deepwater Port Act of 1974 are noted.

Further reading

C. H. Alexandrowicz, 'Freitas versus Grotius', 35 *BYIL* 162–82 (1959).

Anon., 'Exclusion of ships from nonterritorial weapons testing zones', 99 *Harvard Law Review* 1040–58 (1986).

B. H. Dubner, *The Law of International Sea Piracy*, The Hague, 1979.

A. De Smet, 'Policing on the high seas; with special reference to the North Sea', *ND* III, pp. 193–205.

N. M. Hunnings, 'Pirate broadcasting in European waters', 14 *ICLQ* 410–36 (1965).

E. Margolis, 'The hydrogen bomb experiments and international law', 64 *Yale Law Journal* 629–48 (1955).

M. S. McDougal and N. A. Schlei, 'Hydrogen bomb tests in perspective: lawful measures for security', 64 *Yale Law Journal* 648–710 (1955).

J. P. Pancracio, 'L'affaire de l'*Achille Lauro* et le droit international', 31 *AFDI* 221–36 (1985).

N. M. Poulantzas, *The Right of Hot Pursuit in International Law*, Leyden, 1969.

J. Siddle, 'Anglo-American cooperation in the suppression of drug smuggling', 31 *ICLQ* 726–47 (1982).

E. S. Sisco, 'Hot pursuit from a contiguous fishery zone', 14 *San Diego Law Review* 656–79 (1977).

G. Starkle, 'Les épaves de navires en haute mer et le droit international: le cas du *Mont Louis*', 18 *Revue belge de droit international* 496–528 (1984–85).

J. W. L. Swan, 'An explosive issue in international law: the French nuclear tests', 9 *Melbourne University Law Review* 296–306 (1973–74).

Y. van der Mensbrugghe, 'Le pouvoir de police et des états en haute mer', 11 *Revue belge de droit international* 58–102 (1975).

A. van Swanenberg, 'Interference with ships on the high seas', 10 *ICLQ* 785–817 (1961).

J. C. Woodliffe, 'The demise of unauthorised broadcasting from ships in international waters', 1 *International Journal of Estuarine and Coastal Law* 402–6 (1986).

CHAPTER TWELVE
The international sea bed area

Introduction

Over a century ago the *Challenger* expedition discovered the presence of potato-sized nodules scattered across large areas of the sea bed, mainly beyond the geological continental shelf at depths of around 3,500 metres. These manganese nodules, as they are known, are composed of high-grade metal ores. Their precise composition varies from site to site, but for those in the sites of main commercial interest, which lie around the Clarion-Clipperton fracture zones in the north central Pacific, it is typically about twenty-six per cent manganese, seven per cent iron, 1·3 per cent nickel, 1·1 per cent copper and 0·27 per cent cobalt. Nodule deposits, which form by ill-understood processes of accretion, are estimated to be of the order of many thousands of millions of tons, although much of this is composed of deposits which, because of their low grade or the configuration of the sea bed on which they lie, are not commercially attractive. Nonetheless, there are sufficient recoverable deposits to offer a high level of self-sufficiency in the main minerals derived from them to States capable of exploiting them, with the consequent benefits to the balance of payments of those States, and the strategic advantages of lessening dependence upon foreign land-based deposits.

The economic advantages to sea-bed mining States have corresponding disadvantages for land-based exporters of the minerals in question, especially those which are developing States. For example, Zaire produces about forty-two per cent of world cobalt supplies, and expects a substantial fall in export revenues when sea-bed mining gets under way. Similarly Gabon, which derives fifteen to twenty per cent of its export income from manganese, expects adverse economic effects. Nickel production, however, is dominated by Canada, the USSR, France (through its possession of New Caledonia) and Australia, and consequently the effects on existing producers will be less serious.

Sea-bed mining is an expensive industry. The recovery of nodules from such great depths presents formidable technical problems. Present plans envisage automated dredge-heads moving slowly across the sea bed, collecting nodules, which are then piped up to the mother ship. Control of the dredge-head is crucial, both in order to avoid submarine obstacles and to ensure that the collection path neither misses nodule deposits nor overlaps with previously harvested areas. Anticipating world shortages of copper, nickel and manganese in the 1990s and later, industries began developing the necessary technology. With investment costs for mining vessels alone of the order of $150–200 million, rising to $0·8–1·5 billion for a full system covering all stages from prospecting to processing and marketing of minerals, companies have come together in consortia in order to pool funds and expertise. At present there are about half a dozen such consortia; most have a substantial participation by United States companies but British, French, Canadian, Japanese, Belgian, German, Dutch, and Italian companies are also involved. There appears to have been no substantial development of deep sea-bed mining capabilities by the communist bloc or by third world States, although the Soviet Union has laid claim to a mine site in the Pacific and India has claimed a site in the Indian Ocean.

The background to the Law of the Sea Convention provisions

Since it was realised that sea-bed mining was a commercial possibility, over twenty years ago, it has been recognised that, as international law stood, the main benefit of mining would accrue to a handful of developed States. Three different interpretations of the law led to this conclusion. First, as technology for the exploitation of the sea bed improved, so, under the 'exploitability' criterion for the outer limit of the continental shelf (CSC, art. 1; see chapter eight), it was arguable that the seaward limit of States' continental shelves moved into deeper and deeper waters. It was foreseeable that eventually the whole ocean floor would be divided up among coastal States; and, as accidents of geography and colonial history would have it, if the equidistance principle were to be used in delimitation in such circumstances a handful of rich developed States would end up with the lion's share. In the case of the United Kingdom, for instance, possession of Rockall and the Falkland Islands would generate entitlement to vast areas of the bed of the north and south Atlantic.

Or, if continental shelf claims were not pushed out so far but limited to areas corresponding roughly with the geological shelf, the abyssal plains of the ocean beds would, in the absence of any special rules, be regarded as subject to the freedoms of the high seas. Manganese nodules could therefore be taken by any State able and wishing to do so. This interpretation derived some support from the preparatory work on the 1958 High Seas Convention. The ILC noted in its final report in 1956 that it had made no specific provision for the regulation of exploration and exploitation of the bed of the high seas, considering the question to have insufficient practical importance. It seems, however, that the Commission regarded these activities as subject to the general principle of the freedom of the seas and that, in so far as the question was considered at all, this view was widely accepted at the 1958 Geneva Conference itself. The practical result of this interpretation was not greatly different from that of the first: here, too, the developed States of the West, which were best placed to muster the necessary investment and technology, would be the main beneficiaries of sea-bed mining. The same is true of the third possible interpretation, under which title could be gained to areas of the sea bed by their occupation through use, so that mining States would become owners of parcels of the ocean floor and not, as under the previous interpretation, simply of the resources recovered from them (see chapter eight).

Although the first of these possibilities was considered in the abstract, resulting in a rather fanciful map of the oceans' beds entirely divided among coastal States which was drawn up by the Geographer of the United States Department of State, it is the second interpretation which was regarded by Western States as the correct one. In 1974 the American company, Deep Sea Ventures Inc, filed a 'Notice of Discovery and Claim of Exclusive Mining Rights, and Request for Diplomatic Protection and Protection of Investment' with the US Department of State.[1] The company sought a promise of diplomatic protection against any attempt to interfere with the exclusive mining rights it claimed in respect of a specified nodule deposit in the Clarion fracture zone of the Pacific. The State Department replied that it did not grant or recognise exclusive mining rights to the mineral resources of an area of the sea bed beyond the limits of national jurisdiction, but that pending the outcome of UNCLOS III such mining could proceed as a freedom of the high seas under existing international law.[2] The governments of Canada, the United Kingdom and Australia stated that they did not recognise the claim to exclusive rights, or to priority in rights of exploitation of the deposit as a result of publication of Deep Sea Ventures' claim.[3] However, these and other Western States have repeatedly affirmed that they regard the actual mining of the sea bed as a permissible exercise of the freedom of the high seas.

While most Western States held, and still do hold, this view, it is not the view to which the majority of States subscribe. The history of the sea bed question in the United Nations makes this apparent. The issue was first brought before the General Assembly in 1967 by the Maltese ambassador, Dr Arvid Pardo, who proposed that there should be drawn up a 'Declaration and Treaty concerning the reservation exclusively for peaceful purposes of the seabed and ocean floor underlying the seas beyond the present limits of national jurisdiction, and the use of their resources in the interests of mankind'. As the title suggests, this proposal was motivated by the desire to secure both the demilitarisation of the sea bed (on which see chapter seventeen) and the prevention of a 'land grab' for sea-bed minerals. Significantly, the proposal was referred to the General Assembly's First (Political) rather than Sixth (Legal) Committee, and its first result was the establishment of a thirty-five-State *ad hoc* committee, replaced in 1968 by the larger and 'permanent' Committee on the Peaceful Uses of the Sea-bed and Ocean Floor beyond the Limits of National Jurisdiction.

From the outset it was clear that most industrialised States, both capitalist and communist, wanted the committee's work to move at a different pace and in a different direction to that sought by most developing States. The former, wishing to build upon the 1958 Conventions, which they considered broadly satisfactory, favoured a cautious approach to the question with a view to the eventual enunciation of agreed principles concerning the exploitation of the sea bed: the latter preferred more rapid progress towards the establishment not only of agreed principles but of an international organisation with wide powers to regulate sea-bed mining. The developing States had a sufficient majority to secure the passing, during the 1969 debate on the Sea Bed Committee's report, of General Assembly Resolution 2574,[4] the so-called 'Moratorium Resolution', which declared that:

pending the establishment of [an international regime including appropriate machinery]
(a) States and persons, physical or juridical, are bound to refrain from all activities of exploitation of the resources of the area of the sea-bed and ocean floor, and the subsoil thereof, beyond the limits of national jurisdiction.
(b) No claim to any part of that area or its resources shall be recognized.

Some, especially the Islamic States, have asserted that this resolution is binding upon all States in international law. Western States vigorously deny this, and voted against the resolution, which was passed by sixty-two votes to twenty-eight, with twenty-eight abstentions.

Even if unanimous resolutions are regarded as having some quasi-legislative effect there is no good argument for holding that a resolution passed, as here, by a modest majority vote is binding upon those who voted against it or abstained; but it might be argued that States voting for the resolution in the belief that they were establishing or declaring a rule of law — that is, States possessing the *opinio juris* necessary for the creation of a rule of customary international law — had bound themselves by the resolution.

Despite continuing disagreement over the kind of regime envisaged for the sea bed, it was possible to produce, in 1970, a 'Declaration of Principles Governing the Sea Bed and Ocean Floor, and the Subsoil Thereof, beyond the Limits of National Jurisdiction', by 108 votes to nil, with fourteen abstentions, as General Assembly Resolution 2749.[5] The main reason for its general acceptability was its delphic construction. It solemnly declared, *inter alia*, that:

(1) The sea-bed and ocean floor, and the subsoil thereof, beyond the limits of national jurisdiction (hereinafter referred to as the Area), as well as the resources of the Area, are the common heritage of mankind.
(2) The Area shall not be subject to appropriation by any means by States or persons, natural or juridical, and no State shall claim or exercise sovereignty or sovereign rights over any part thereof.
(3) No State or person, natural or juridical, shall claim, exercise or acquire rights with respect to the Area or its resources incompatible with the international regime to be established and the principles of this Declaration.
(4) All activities regarding the exploration and exploitation of the resources of the Area and other related activities shall be governed by the international regime to be established.

The Group of 77 developing States (which in fact includes around 120 States) has consistently regarded this resolution as a binding statement of law rendering unilateral sea-bed mining unlawful. Western States, in accordance with their sound, and equally consistent, opinion that voting for United Nations resolutions does not of itself create legal obligations, regard the resolution as merely a statement of political principle and intent. In any event, Resolution 2749 admits of a wide range of interpretations, from that supporting open access, at present, to seabed resources under the freedom of the high seas, to that supporting a moratorium on unilateral development of sea-bed resources pending the establishment of an international organisation to govern the Area. The resolution bought acceptability at the cost of certainty.

Throughout the proceedings of the Sea Bed Committee and, from 1973 onwards, of Committee I of UNCLOS III, to which the sea-bed question was allocated, the divergence between the views of developed and developing States was evident. The Group of 77 sought an international sea-bed authority having the power to engage in sea-bed mining itself, and to control mining by other licensees, who would pay it royalties which, along with its own profits, would be distributed among all States as the 'common heritage of mankind'. The developed States, in contrast, proposed initially that the authority should be little more than a registry of national claims to sea-bed mining sites, having few, if any, powers to interfere with the exploitation of the Area by their companies. There were divisions within both camps. The group of landlocked and other geographically disadvantaged States (see, further, chapter eighteen), for example, included both developed and developing States, and pressed hard for guarantees concerning their representation in the authority and their share in the benefits of seabed mining. Similarly those States, from both north and south, which had wide continental shelves opposed the efforts of the geographically disadvantaged States, among others, to establish narrow limits to national sea-bed jurisdiction in order to maximise the area constituting the common heritage of mankind.

These proceedings have inspired a vast and detailed literature, rendering further discussion here otiose. Suffice it to say that there was a steady movement away from the position of the Western States and towards that of the Group of 77. Fears that an international authority having extensive regulatory powers would interfere for purely political reasons in mining operations were largely assuaged by provisions confining such discretion as was left to the authority within closely defined limits, and by an elaborate system of decision-making. The result, Part XI of the Law of the Sea Convention and the associated annexes, is an extraordinarily complicated legal regime which we can explain only in outline.

Principles of the Law of the Sea Convention regime

The regime governs all activities connected with exploration and exploitation of mineral resources in the Area (LOSC, art. 134(2)). The latter is defined as the 'sea bed and ocean floor and subsoil thereof beyond national jurisdiction' (LOSC, art. 1). This last phrase was discussed in chapter eight, where it was shown the 'national jurisdiction' for these purposes extends to the outer edge of the continental margin, or to a distance of 200 miles from the baseline where the margin does not extend up to that distance. The Area, which comprises about sixty per cent of the whole sea bed, and its resources (limited by article 133 to mineral resources) are the 'common heritage of mankind'. As such they are not susceptible of unilateral national appropriation: rights in the Area can be obtained only in accordance with the provisions of the Convention, which is to say, only with the authorisation of the International Sea Bed Authority (LOSC, arts. 136, 137). All activities in the Area, which may be conducted both by the Authority itself through its mining arm, the 'Enterprise', and by commercial operators, are to be carried out for the benefit of mankind as a whole, taking into particular consideration the interests of developing States and peoples who have not attained self-governing status (LOSC, art. 140). Furthermore, since the superjacent waters and air space remain high seas, reasonable regard must be had to other legitimate uses of those waters and of the Area itself (LOSC, art. 147). These, and other general principles (LOSC, arts. 138–49), are elaborated upon in the Convention, but the delicate compromise between the developed and developing States which the Convention represents rests to a considerable extent upon the institutional arrangements, and these will be considered first.

The International Sea Bed Authority

It would be wrong to say that the Area is intended to be governed by the Authority, since many uses of the Area itself, such as pipeline and cable laying and scientific research unconnected with the exploitation of sea-bed resources may be carried out without the need for the Authority's permission (LOSC, arts. 112, 143, 256). But the Authority is the body through which States parties are to organise and control all resource-oriented uses of the sea bed beyond national jurisdiction (LOSC, arts. 156, 157).

The Authority has three principal organs: the plenary Assembly, the thirty-six-State Council, and the Secretariat (LOSC, art. 158). The Council is served by two specialised bodies, the Economic Planning Commission and the Legal and Technical Commission (LOSC, art. 163). In addition, there is the Authority's mining arm, the Enterprise, which has its own Governing Board, Director General and staff. These will be considered in turn.

The Assembly

All States parties to the Convention are *ipso facto* members of the Authority and so, too, of the Assembly, wherein each State has one vote (LOSC, arts. 156(2), 159). The Assembly, as 'the supreme organ of the Authority to which the other principal organs shall be accountable', has the power to lay down general policies for the Authority which must, however, be consistent with the specific provisions set out in the Convention. In addition, the Assembly is allotted certain specific tasks. These include the election of the Council and Secretary General of the Authority, and of the Governing Board and Director General of the Enterprise; approval of the budget of the Authority and of the rules governing the distribution of financial and other economic benefits from exploitation of the resources of the Area and the continental margin beyond the 200 mile limit; approval of the rules governing the exploration and exploitation of the area and the internal management of the Authority; the establishment of a system of compensation for developing State land-based mineral producers whose economies suffer as a result of sea-bed mineral production; and the suspension of members (LOSC, art. 160). With the exception of the election of Council members, all the other listed powers (which will be considered further below) are to be exercised on the basis of recommendations from the Council. The Assembly is also to approve the rules governing the transfer of funds from the Enterprise to the Authority, in this case upon the recommendation of the Governing Board of the Enterprise.

Decisions of the Assembly on procedural questions require only a simple majority, but questions of substance require a two-thirds majority, and questions are presumed to be questions of substance unless a two-thirds majority resolves otherwise. These unexceptional provisions are supplemented by two other devices which afford some protection against steamrollering by a large bloc vote. First, when any matter of substance is first raised, the President of the Assembly may on his own initiative defer a vote on the question for up to five days, and must do so if requested by one-fifth of the members of the Assembly. This allows a 'cooling off' period, during which a compromise may be sought on divisive issues. The second allows one-quarter of the members of the Authority to require the deferral of a vote pending the receipt of an advisory opinion from the Sea Bed Disputes Chamber on the conformity of any action proposed before the Assembly with the provisions of the Convention. The intention here is to offer a means of testing the constitutionality of *proposed* action, rather than challenging an exercise of the Authority's powers after the fact, by which time the challenge may be too late to be effective (LOSC, art. 159(7)–(10)).

The Council

The Council, which is responsible for the implementation of the Convention regime within the limits set by the Convention and the policies established by the Assembly, will have thirty-six members. Members are to be elected by the Assembly, in the following order:

(*a*) four members from among those States Parties which, during the last five years for which statistics are available, have either consumed more than 2 per cent of total world consumption or have had net imports of more than 2 per cent of total world imports of the commodities produced from the categories of minerals to be derived from the Area, and in any case one State from the Eastern European (Socialist) region, as well as the largest consumer;

(*b*) four members from among the eight States Parties which have the largest investments in preparation for and in the conduct of activities in the Area, either directly or through their nationals, including at least one State from the Eastern European (Socialist) region;

(*c*) four members from among States Parties which on the basis of production in areas under their jurisdiction are major net exporters of the categories of minerals to be derived from the Area, including at least two developing States whose exports of such minerals have a substantial bearing upon their economies;

(*d*) six members from among developing States Parties, representing special interests. The special interests to be represented shall include those of States with large populations, States which are land-locked or geographically disadvantaged, States which are major importers of the categories of minerals to be derived from the Area, States which are potential producers of such minerals, and least developed States;

(*e*) eighteen members elected according to the principle of ensuring an equitable geographical distribution of seats in the Council as a whole, provided that each geographical region shall have at least one member elected under this subparagraph. For this purpose, the geographical regions shall be Africa, Asia, Eastern European (Socialist), Latin America and Western European and Others. [LOSC, art. 161(1)].

It is further provided that the numbers of landlocked and geographically disadvantaged States, and of coastal (especially developing) States, on the Council should be reasonably proportionate to their representation in the

Assembly; and that each of the listed groups of States is to be represented on the Council by the members, if any, nominated by that group (LOSC, art. 161(1)–(2)).

The Council is a powerful body, and while careful control of its composition would go some way towards safeguarding the various interests of States, it has also been seen as necessary to define its powers closely, and to establish a complex decision-making procedure. Some substantive decisions must be taken by consensus. These include the adoption, on the recommendation of the Economic Planning Commission, of measures (such as participation in international commodity agreements) to protect the economies of developing countries from adverse effects of sea-bed mining; recommendations to the Assembly on the sharing of the benefits of sea-bed mining; and the adoption of amendments to this Part of the Convention. 'Consensus' here means the absence of any formal objection, which effectively gives each State a veto, and accordingly a 'conciliation procedure' has been built in to facilitate progress. Within fourteen days of the submission of a proposal to the Council, the President of the Council is to determine whether or not any objection will be raised, and if so he has three days within which to establish a nine-man conciliation committee, which he chairs. That committee has fourteen days within which to recommend a proposal which will be adopted by consensus or, if it cannot, to set out in its report to the Council the grounds on which the proposal is being opposed. This procedure should minimise opposition based upon misunderstandings of proposed actions (LOSC, art. 161(8)).

Decisions on other questions of substance require either a three-quarters or two-thirds majority in the Council. The more important matters — such as the establishment of specific policies for the Authority; selection of applicants for mining licences; the institution of proceedings before the Sea Bed Chamber for non-compliance with the Authority's rules (see chapter nineteen); the exercise of control over activities in the Area; the election of the Legal and Technical, and Economic Planning Commissions; and arrangements concerning the funding of the Authority and the Enterprise — require a three-quarters majority of members present and voting. The remaining decisions — on questions such as reports to the Assembly; the issue of specific directives to the Enterprise, within the framework of the Convention and policies laid down by the Assembly and Council; the recommendation to the Assembly, on the basis of advice from the Economic Planning Commission, of a system of compensation to cushion developing land-based mineral-producing States against adverse economic effects of sea-bed mining; and the requesting of advisory opinions from the Sea Bed Chamber — require a two-thirds majority (LOSC, art. 161(8)).

Two points call for comment. First, by no means all the most sensitive questions require adoption by consensus; indeed, most of them require only a three-quarters majority vote. Consensus decisions seem to have been limited to general issues of principle upon which consensus might reasonably be expected, and not for decisions upon particular licences, for instance. Second, where a three-quarters majority is required, any group of ten members can block Council action. While the Group of 77 would possess such voting strength, and the industrialised West almost certainly would not, the significance of this point should not be overrated. As Ambassador Engo, chairman of the First Committee at UNCLOS III, has observed, 'neither group is without diversity of concrete interests given the factor of uneven development within each. We should bear in mind the manifold, the divergent interests, and abandon the false assumption of a bipolarized situation'.[6] Furthermore, the Convention's provisions are so detailed that opportunities for the exercise of voting power are much reduced.

The Commissions

The Economic Planning Commission and the Legal and Technical Commission are both organs of the Council (LOSC, art. 163). The former is to advise the Council on economic matters, and in particular to review trends of and factors affecting supply, demand and prices of raw materials which may be obtained from the Area; to recommend measures for the protection of developing countries' economies from adverse effects of sea-bed mining; and to propose to the Council, for submission to the Assembly, a system of compensation for such developing countries and recommend its application in particular cases (LOSC, art. 164). The Legal and Technical Commission has a wider competence, including the supervision of activities in the area; the making of recommendations to the Council on such matters as the acceptance of applications for sea-bed mining, environmental protection, the establishment of an inspectorate for day-to-day supervision of sea-bed mining; the institution of cases before the Sea Bed Disputes Chamber, and measures to enforce decisions of the Chamber. In addition, this Commission drafts the rules and regulations of the Authority (LOSC, art. 165). Both Commissions are composed of persons with appropriate qualifications such as economists, mineral resource managers, oceanographers, mining engineers, environmentalists and, of course, lawyers. However, while the Council is to endeavour to ensure that the Commissions include all necessary skills, it is also required that due regard be paid to the need for equitable geographical distribution and representation of special interests when electing members.

The Enterprise

The Enterprise is constituted as a separate organ of the Authority, and is to engage in prospecting and mining the Area, and in the transportation, processing and marketing of the minerals recovered. The fifteen members of the Governing Board are to be persons having appropriate qualifications, elected by the Assembly with due regard to the principles of equitable geographical representation, upon the recommendation of the Council. Unlike the Commissions, there is no express obligation to seek representation of special interests, and it is expressly provided that Board members serve in their personal capacities. All decisions are taken by a simple majority vote. Day-to-day control is in the hands of the Director General, appointed by the Assembly and responsible to, but not a member of, the Board. Subject to obligations to comply with the Assembly's general policies and the Council's directives and to report to the Authority, the Enterprise is an autonomous organisation, and so it stands in much the same relationship to the Authority as do commercial operators. Thus mining by the Enterprise is dependent upon authorisation by the Authority, following applications made by the Governing Board. As will be seen, the Enterprise will gain the necessary mining technology by buying it from commercial operators, or entering into joint ventures with them. Its 'profits' are to be distributed, as part of the 'common heritage of mankind', by the Authority (LOSC, art. 170 and Annex IV).

Financing the Authority

In its early years the Authority will be financed by contributions from its members. The Secretary General will submit a draft annual budget to the Council, which will pass it on, together with any recommendations thereon, to the Assembly for approval. Contributions are then to be raised from member States in accordance with a scale based on that used for the regular UN budget: given universal membership of the Authority, this would result in the EEC and the USA each providing about a quarter of the total contributions. These contributions may be supplemented by borrowing, and by voluntary contibutions. As sea-bed mining gets under way the Authority should move steadily towards being self-financing. Income will come from the fees and production charges paid by commercial operators and, after a period of up to ten years from the commencement of commercial production during which it makes no contributions, from the fees and production charges paid by the Enterprise (LOSC, arts. 160(2), 162(2), 171, 172, 174, and Annex IV).

Financing the Enterprise

The financing of the Enterprise is quite distinct from that of the Authority. Funds required for the development of one mine site, through all stages from exploration to processsing and marketing recovered minerals, are to be assessed by a preparatory Commission. States parties are to contribute half this amount in the form of long-term interest-free loans, in accordance with a scale based on the UN budgetary scale, within sixty days of the entry into force of the Convention. The other half is to be borrowed by the Enterprise, in capital markets or from international institutions such as the development banks, the loans being guaranteed by the parties in accordance with the same scale. If non-participation in the Convention results in a shortfall in this initial funding, the Assembly is to adopt necessary remedial measures by consensus. In addition, the Enterprise may gain income from voluntary contributions, or by exercising its borrowing powers. Later on, the Enterprise will generate its own funds from its mining activities: any 'net income' remaining once its operating costs have been met is to be divided between the Authority and the reserves of the Enterprise, by the Assembly acting upon the recommendation of the Governing Board. In order to make the Enterprise self-supporting, the whole of the net income is to remain in its reserves for a period of up to ten years from the commencement of commercial production by the Enterprise. The Authority is also empowered to transfer to the Enterprise any funds, apart from the assessed contributions of States, which remain once its administrative expenses have been met: thus surpluses attributable to fees, production charges, Authority borrowing and voluntary contributions may be so transferred (LOSC, Annex IV, and art. 173(2)).

The system of exploitation

Attention can now be turned from the institutions to the substantive provisions which are the most complicated part of the sea-bed regime. They are based on the 'parallel system', under which the Area will be exploited both by the Enterprise and by commercial operators.

Prospecting is the first stage of exploitation under this system. Although the term is not defined, it seems to connote general searches for sea-bed resources, rather than the detailed pre-production surveying, which appears to be covered by the term 'exploration'. Prospecting is essentially free, requiring only notification to the Authority of the broad areas where it is being carried out and a written undertaking to observe the Convention rules on environmental protection and co-operation in programmes for training personnel from developing States. No exclusive rights arise from such notification. It is probable that all, or most, of the prospecting necessary for mining in the foreseeable future will have been completed before the Convention enters into force (LOSC, Annex III, art. 2).

Exploration and exploitation, in contrast, require specific authorisation by the Authority, which carries with it exclusive rights. Qualified applicants may submit plans of work for the approval of the Authority.

Applicants are 'qualified' if they are entities possessing the nationality of States parties and effectively controlled by them or by their nationals; if control lies elsewhere, the controlling State or national State of the controllers must co-sponsor the application. In the case of multinational consortia, the national (and controlling) States of all the members must be parties. The applicants must also be sponsored by those States, and meet the qualification standards set out by the Authority. These standards 'shall relate to the financial and technical capabilities of the applicant and his performance under any previous contracts with the Authority', so permitting the disqualification of applicants who have broken the terms of previous contracts. Applicants are also obliged to undertake to comply with the Convention and rules made under it, to accept the control of the Authority over activities in the Area, to give a written assurance of good faith in fulfilling contractual obligations, and, most significantly, to comply with the provisions on transfer of technology (LOSC, Annex III, art. 4).

Agreement on technology transfer long eluded the conference. The LOSC contains detailed provisions on the matter, which provide, in short, that the applicant must undertake to make available to the Enterprise, on fair and reasonable commercial terms and conditions, any technology which it uses in sea-bed activities which it is legally entitled to transfer, when the Enterprise cannot obtain such technology or equally efficient and useful technology on reasonable commercial terms on the open maket. If the applicant is not entitled to transfer the technology, it is to get a similar undertaking from the owner of the technology, and if this undertaking is not obtained the applicant must not use the technology in question. Thus the Enterprise should have access to all the technology employed in activities under LOSC licences in the Area. The possibility of developing States wishing to begin sea-bed mining before the Enterprise is covered by requiring transfer of technology to such States in the manner described above, where the technology has not already been requested by the Enterprise. All these undertakings must be included in all contracts until ten years after the beginning of commercial production by the Enterprise, by which time the Enterprise should be developing technology of its own (LOSC, Annex III, art. 5).

This is clearly a fertile area for disputes. States are responsible for ensuring, under their national laws, that the entities they sponsor comply with them, as well as all other contractual terms and conventional rules. But disputes may arise over the scope of contractual terms. Hence it is provided that disputes over the fairness and reasonableness of the terms on which transfer is offered may be referred by either party to binding commercial arbitration under UNCITRAL rules or other rules laid down by the Authority and that other disputes be subject to the compulsory jurisdiction of the Sea Bed Disputes Chamber (LOSC, Annex III, arts. 4,5; and arts. 187, 188(2); see also chapter nineteen below).

The plans of work submitted by qualified applicants (not by the Enterprise) must specify two sites of equal estimated commercial value, which may or may not be contiguous, each large enough to support a mining operation. Data concerning both sites and their resources must also be submitted. The Authority may then approve a plan of work relating to one of the two sites, and enter into a contract, with the applicant incorporating that plan. If it does so, it must designate the other site as a 'reserved site'. Reserved sites are available only for development by the Authority, acting through the Enterprise or in association with developing States. The Enterprise may choose to exploit such a site at any time, but must decide within a reasonable time whether it wishes to proceed if a developing State announces that it intends to submit a plan of work in respect of that site. Thus plans of work may be submitted by the Enterprise or developing States (or their nationals or companies) for any reserved site, and by any applicant for unreserved sites (LOSC, Annex III, arts. 8, 9).

Applications are to be dealt with by the Authority in order of receipt. To preclude any possibility of the Authority unreasonably impeding development of the sea bed, it is provided that approval of plans can be refused only in certain specified circumstances. These are, first, that all or part of the proposed site falls in a plan already approved, or awaiting final decision, by the Authority; second, that all or part of the proposed area is disapproved by the Authority because substantial evidence indicates the risk of serious harm to the marine environment from activities therein. The third ground is the 'anti-monopoly clause', allowing disapproval where the plan is sponsored by a State which either already holds approved plans for sites which, together with either site in the proposed plan, would amount to more than thirty per cent of the area of a circle of 400,000 square kilometres surrounding the centre of either of those sites, or alternatively has had plans approved for sites whose area exceeds two per cent of the Area, excluding reserved sites and areas disallowed on environmental grounds. Where proposals are submitted by consortia sponsored by several States, areas are computed on a *pro rata* basis. Even where the anti-monopoly criteria are met, the Authority may still approve the plan if it determines that approval would not in fact permit the State party or its sponsored entities to monopolise activities in the Area (LOSC, Annex III, art. 6).

In all cases it is the Legal and Technical Commission which first reviews the proposed plan. If it recommends approval, the plan is deemed to be approved unless a Council member objects in writing, specifying an alleged violation of the foregoing rules. Such an objection is to be followed by the conciliation procedure, and if the objection is maintained, the plan is nonetheless deemed to be approved unless the Council disapproves it by consensus among its members, excluding any State making or sponsoring the application in question. If the Commission recommends disapproval or makes no recommendation, the Council may approve the plan by a three-fourths majority of members present and voting (LOSC, art. 162(2)). There is, therefore, a strong bias in favour of the approval of plans of work. Approval of a plan gives an exclusive right to the unreserved site, but commercial production needs separate authorisation.

The Authority is obliged to issue production authorisations — to States, commercial operators or the Enterprise — if all applications in each four-monthly round can be approved without hitting the production ceiling (LOSC, Annex III, art. 7). This ceiling, designed to protect land-based producers, is based on the growth of world nickel consumption. Applicants would be authorised to recover a fixed amount of nickel each year from sea-bed nodules, (plus other metals such as copper, cobalt and manganese in the amounts found in the same quantity of nodules) so as to satisfy only increases in world demand (LOSC, art. 151(2)–(7)).

The ceiling is defined as the whole of the increase in world nickel consumption during a five-year period ending in the year before the earliest commercial production under the Convention regime, plus sixty per cent of the increase during the period between the year before the earliest commercial production and the year for which authorisation is sought (LOSC, art. 151(4)). For example, the first operator, planning the necessary capital investment, might apply in 1995 for authorisation to produce in 2000 onwards. The Authority would calculate the trend-line values for nickel consumption on the basis of the most recent available data covering a fifteen-year period — probably 1979-93 here — using a regression line (the 'original trend line') derived from that data. The 2000 ceiling would then be the whole of the 1994–99 increase, plus sixty per cent of the 1999–2000 increase in those values. If a second operator sought authorisation for production to commence in 2002 the ceiling would be the whole of the 1994–99 increase, plue sixty per cent of the 1999–2002 increase, although part of that ceiling would have been allocated under the previous authorisation.

It is also provided that if the annual rate of increase in the original trend line is less than three per cent, the ceiling is to be calculated on the basis of a trend line passing through the original trend-line value for the first of the fifteen years whose data is used, and increasing at three per cent annually. However, the ceiling so calculated must not exceed the difference between the values for the first year of the five-year 'pre-production period' and that for the year for which authorisation is sought, on the original trend line. For example, if the first authorisation sought were for production in 2000 onwards, and this provision applies, the ceiling would be the 1994–99 increase, plus sixty per cent of the 1999–2000 increase using the values on the 'deemed three per cent line', but that ceiling must not exceed the 1994–99 increase plus the whole (rather then merely sixty per cent) of the 1999–2000 increase, using the values on the original trend line.

The Authority must reserve 38,000 tons of nickel from the ceiling for the initial use of the Enterprise, which may apply in the normal way for further authorisations. No single authorisation may exceed 46,500 tons of nickel per year, although there is some flexibility allowing a degree of overproduction in some years to be compensated for by underproduction in other years to which the authorisation relates.

It might happen that the authorisations sought in a round of applications could not be accommodated within the ceiling. In such a case the Authority would choose between applicants, giving priority to applications to develop reserved sites (which could come only from the Enterprise or developing States) whenever fewer reserved than unreserved sites were under exploitation. Otherwise, priority would be given to applicants refused in previous rounds, to those offering better assurances of performance or earlier prospective benefits to the Authority, and to those who had already invested most resources and effort in prospecting or exploration (LOSC, Annex III, art. 7).

The financial terms of contracts concluded pursuant to approved plans of work and production authorisations are more complicated still. Having paid the fixed fees of $500,000 for processing the application and $1 million annually for the duration of the contract, the operator must choose between two systems. The first, designed mainly for operators from socialist States, involves only a production charge, being five per cent of the market value of processed metals extracted from the nodules for each of the first ten years of production, and twelve per cent of that value each year thereafter. The second system is designed for capitalist operators, and may be outlined as follows. Two periods of production are distinguished, the first ending and the second beginning in the year when the operator's development costs with interest on the unrecovered portion thereof are fully recovered by his cash surplus. During the first period a production charge of two per cent of recovered metal market value is payable, together with a share of attributable net proceeds which varies according to the profitability of the mining venture – rising from thirty-five per cent of net proceeds, representing a return on investment of less than ten per cent, through forty-two and a half per cent of returns between ten and twenty per cent, to fifty per cent of that portion of net proceeds representing a return of twenty per cent or more. During the second period the production charge rises to four per cent, except in years when the return on investment would fall below fifteen per cent as a result of the payment of the four per cent charge, in which years it remains at two per cent. Shares of attributable net proceeds in the second period rise to forty, fifty and seventy per cent of the three bands of profitability. 'Attributable net proceeds' are the product of actual net proceeds and the ratio of development costs in the mining sector generally to the contractor's development costs, subject to certain limitations on the ratio (LOSC, Annex III, art. 13).

It is difficult to estimate the resultant income to the Authority, since much depends upon movements in metal prices, interest rates and other imponderables. But estimates made in 1978, based on similar systems proposed in the past, suggested that an average operation, having development costs of about $559 million, annual operating costs of about $100 million, and annual gross proceeds of about $258 million, might yield sums of the order of $200 or $300 million during the estimated twenty-year life of a mine site. At the end of UNCLOS III it was being suggested that there could be a dozen mine sites by the end of the century. It was also thought that the Enterprise could be operating by then, although its ten-year 'tax holiday', during which it makes no payments to the Authority, might well have extended up to that date (LOSC, Annex IV, art. 10). However, the slump in world metal prices has led to fundamental revisions of such estimates, and it has been suggested by one authoritative commentator that there will be no investment in commercial mining this century.[7] That is not necessarily to say that some States (Japan, acting as a 'pioneer investor', is perhaps the most likely), or the Enterprise, will not engage in mining operations which would be uneconomic by the criteria of Western capitalist economies.

Throughout the contract period the Authority will supervise operations, and may require operators to transfer to it any data necessary for the performance of its functions. Thus compliance with the terms of plans of work and production authorisations, to which operators will be contractually bound, can be checked, as can compliance with other regulations concerning, for example, environmental matters or the obligation of operators to establish training schemes for personnel from the Authority or developing States. The Authority may impose monetary penalities, and, in serious cases, suspend or terminate the contract, although in all cases the contractor has the right to take the matter through the dispute settlement procedure (LOSC, arts. 186–91, and Annex III, arts. 14–19; see also chapter nineteen).

That procedure ensures that rights and duties provided for in the Convention are enforced. Neither the Authority nor the contractor has the right to modify the terms of a contract without the other's consent, although if circumstances arise in which the contract becomes inequitable, or the achievement of objectives in the contract or Convention becomes impracticable or impossible, there is a duty to negotiate an adjustment.

The common heritage

The Enterprise may engage in mining on its own, using its rights to require transfer of technology. It may enter into joint ventures with commercial operators, so enabling them to turn their expertise to good account, to have access to reserved areas, and to collect the accompanying political kudos and financial benefits of such collaboration. Through such activities of the Enterprise, know-how and technology would be acquired which would be passed onto the nationals of developing States via the training programmes which the Authority, with the co-operation of sea-bed mining operators, would promote. This is one way in which the 'common heritage' would be exploited for the benefit of 'mankind as a whole', and not simply the industrialised States. The other means of realising the 'common heritage' is the collection and distribution among States–in particular, developing States and peoples — of the Authority's share of profits earned by the Enterprise and commercial operators. But it seems clear that the financial benefits of the sea-bed exploitation are likely to be relatively modest: one common guess during UNCLOS III was that by the end of this century the monies would amount to about fifty cents *per capita* if distributed among the forty poorest States and substantially less if other States such as India and China were to be included in the share-out, and the general view now is that no significant profits are likely by then.

The Convention does not stipulate the precise manner in which the financial benefits are to be shared out; only that the sharing should be 'equitable' (LOSC, art. 140). Precise rules would be decided upon by the Authority. In fact some States will, in effect, have a preferential claim on the monies anyway. These are the developing States who suffer adverse effects on their export earnings or economies as a result of falls in mineral prices caused by sea-bed mining, for whose benefit the Convention requires the Authority to establish a compensation system (LOSC, art. 151(10)).

Preparatory investment protection

One of the major obstacles to the acceptance of these provisions by the United States was the lack of protection said to exist for investments which had already taken place in sea-bed mining. Accordingly, in a final effort to find a compromise acceptable to all, the spring 1982 session of UNCLOS III prepared special rules for 'pioneer investors', which amount to an almost complete rewriting of the Convention's rules on sea-bed mining in their favour. These rules are contained in two resolutions appended to the Final Act of UNCLOS III. Resolution I provides for the establishment of a Preparatory Commission (known as PrepCom), composed of representatives of States which have signed the Convention, to convene within three months of signature by the fiftieth State (see further p. 16, above). The Commission is to prepare for the establishment of the International Sea Bed Authority, drafting its rules and procedures, and also to undertake studies of the economic problems arising from sea-bed mining. In addition, it is responsible for the administration of the preparatory investment protection provisions.

Resolution II contains the rules designed to accommodate the demands of the six consortia which had, by 1982, invested heavily in deep sea-bed mining. The nationalities of consortia members, though subject to occasional variation, are broadly as follows: Association Française pour l'étude et la recherche des nodules (AFERNOD) (France); Deep Ocean Resources Development Company (DORD) (Japan); the Kennecott Consortium (USA, UK, Canada, Japan); Ocean Mining Associates (OMA) (USA, Belgium, Italy); Ocean Management Inc (OMI) (Canada, USA, Federal Republic of Germany, Japan); and Ocean Minerals Company (OMC) (USA, Netherlands). The resolution allows for eight 'pioneer investors', four from France, Japan, India and the USSR (including AFERNOD and DORD), and four from Belgium, Canada, the Federal Republic of Germany, Italy, Japan, the Netherlands, the UK and the USA (being Kennecott, OMA, OMI and OMC), and possibly others from developing States, to be given 'pioneer status'. Each investor must be certified by its sponsoring State to have invested at least $30 million in preparation for sea-bed mining, of which at least ten per cent must be invested in a specific site.

Certifying States must detail two sites, each of up to 150,000 square kilometres, having resolved between themselves any competing or overlapping claims. One site is to be allocated by the Preparatory Commission to the pioneer, and the other banked for eventual use by the International Sea Bed Authority. In their sites, pioneers are to have immediate and exclusive rights to conduct exploratory activities short of commercial production. Pioneers must submit plans of work to the Authority, which will approve them, as soon as the Convention enters into force. The national States of all companies involved in the pioneer consortia must have become parties to the Convention by this stage: if they have not, the companies concerned must either change their nationality (which raises complex questions of municipal law, and is unlikely to be a practical proposition) or lose their pioneer status. Pioneers must also apply for production authorisation, which means that no actual commercial mining can take place until the Convention is in force. They are to apply for authorisations in respect of not more than half their allotted site (less if the area of exploitation sites allowed under the Authority's rules is under half the area of the original 'pioneer' site), the other half being relinquished in stages over an eight-year period, and reverting to the international sea bed area. Pioneers have priority, within the production ceiling described above, over all other applicants, apart from the Enterprise, which is entitled to authorisation for two of its sites. If the level of production for which they seek authorisation cannot be accommodated within the ceiling, they may agree among themselves upon the sharing of the available quota. But no other miners are to be given production authorisations until the pioneers have, perhaps only after several years during which the production ceiling will have risen, had all their demands for authorisation met.

In return for this preferential treatment, pioneers must pay an initial fee of $250,000 and an annual fixed fee of $1 million (and the production levy when they begin production), and maintain investment in their site at levels to be prescribed by the Preparatory Commission. They must also undertake, prior to the entry into force of the Convention, to perform the obligations therein concerning technology transfer. And in order to advance the progress of the Authority's involvement in sea-bed mining, each pioneer must, at the Authority's request, explore that one of the two sites detailed in the original application and reserved to the Authority, on a cost plus ten per cent basis, and also train designated personnel. Certifying States must, in addition, ensure that the Enterprise is provided with the funds necessary to begin operations when the Convention enters into force. Of course, the main consideration for this privileged treatment of pioneer investors was intended to be the adherence of the Western mining States to the Law of the Sea Convention regime, but it seems that some of those States are not willing to pay the price.

PrepCom is currently drawing up more detailed rules on the implementation of Resolution II. While it is not clear what authority PrepCom has to do so, those rules have effected some significant changes in the regime set out in the Convention and Resolution II, notably in the Understanding on new procedures and mechanisms, of September 1986. That Understanding was based on the Arusha Understanding concluded by the four pioneer investor States, which dealt with overlaps between the French, Japanese and Soviet claims in the Pacific (there is no overlap with the Indian claim in the Indian Ocean). For example, the time limit within which the $30 million investment had to be made in order to qualify as a pioneer investor, originally 1 January 1983 for the consortia and 1 January 1985 for developing States, has been extended by the September 1986 Understanding in the case of developing States (and, in addition, for the Eastern European States, who may apply for one pioneer area) up to the date of entry into force of the Convention; and the provisions concerning the nomination of two sites to the Authority, one of which would be licensed and the other 'banked', have been modified so as to allow pioneer investors to specify a part of the seabed 'that shall form part of the total area to be allocated to it'. The Understanding also provides that the four pioneer investors will assist PrepCom and the Authority in exploring a mine site for the first operation of the Enterprise.[8] It is possible that these and similar accommodations to the exigencies of commercial life might yet achieve the original purpose of the pioneer investor regime by producing a sea-bed mining regime sufficiently attractive to induce the Federal Republic of Germany, the United Kingdom and the United States to accede to the Convention. Certainly, without their economic and technical participation the operation of the Convention regime, long heralded as a symbol of the 'New International Economic Order', will be seriously hampered, even if a rise in world metal prices makes sea-bed mining commercially viable. For the present, however, those three States are proceeding along a different path, under the so-called Reciprocating States Regime.

The Reciprocating States Regime

Multilateral agreements commonly take five or ten years to attract enough ratifications to enter into force. Faced with this possible delay, during which domestic industries which had already invested hundreds of millions of dollars in preparations for sea-bed mining could get no direct return on their investments, a number of Western States decided to set up an interim regime to permit and regulate mining before the Convention enters into force. No doubt dissatisfaction with some aspects of the Law of the Sea Convention, which would weigh against ratification by these States at any time, also made it desirable that a separate regime for mining be set up. These 'Like-minded States' have established a 'Reciprocating States Regime' (or 'mini-treaty') under which each State adopts similar national laws which interlock so as to provide for comprehensive regulation of sea-bed mining. The United States led the way with its Deep Sea Bed Hard Mineral Resources Act of 1980, followed by the Federal Republic of Germany's Act on the Interim Regulation of Deep Sea Bed Mining in the same year. In 1981 Britain, with its Deep Sea Mining (Temporary Provisions) Act, and France, followed suit, as did Japan in 1982 and Italy in 1985. Belgium, the Netherlands, and perhaps some other States, are also expected to adopt such laws. The Soviet Union also adopted, in 1982, legislation very similar in many respects to that of the Western States, but it is not expected to become a party to the 'Reciprocating States Regime'.[9]

The Reciprocating States Regime is sometimes known as the 'mini-treaty', and although there was originally no published treaty underlying it,

an Agreement concerning Interim Arrangements relating to Polymetallic
Nodules of the Deep Sea Bed, made between France, the Federal Republic of Germany, the United Kingdom and the United States, was published in September 1982. That agreement provides for consultations in
order to avoid overlapping claims under the national laws of the parties,
including provision for arbitration in case of disputes, and for consultation
between the parties before any of them enters into any other international
arrangements with respect to deep sea-bed operations. However, the
agreement is not concerned with the substantive rules governing sea-bed
exploitation. In this respect, the Reciprocating States Regime depends
entirely upon the provisions of the national laws, all of which follow the

same basic pattern. In each, citizens of, and companies incorporated in,
the State concerned are prohibited from engaging in exploration or exploitation of deep sea-bed resources unless they are licensed by that State or by
one of the reciprocating States. Equally, such citizens and companies are
prohibited from interfering with the licensed operations of others. Detailed regulations and licence terms govern the conduct of activities in the
area, and deal with matters such as the prevention of pollution, the safety
of employees, and the orderly development of the nodule 'mine'. Licensees
are obliged to pay a levy, equivalent to 3·75 per cent of the value of the
nodules recovered or, if that value cannot be determined, 0·75 per cent
of the value of the metals derived from them, which is roughly the same.
Licensing States will transfer the monies derived from their levies to the
International Sea Bed Authority if and when the Law of the Sea Convention enters into force for them: otherwise the funds will be distributed as
the State sees fit, although the German law requires their use for development aid purposes.

These laws differ from the Law of the Sea Convention regime in important respects. The levy is only about half that envisaged in the Convention, and no provision is made for the 'banking' of reserved sites for
eventual use by the Enterprise or developing States. Nor is there any
requirement concerning the transfer of technology. The reciprocating
States emphasise, however, that this legislation is interim, and will apply
only pending the entry into force for them of the Law of the Sea Convention; and each law allows the modification of licence terms so as to bring
them into line with that treaty. However, the reciprocating States may not
ratify until some time after the Convention enters into force for other
States, if they ratify at all. There is, therefore, a fear that this interim
regime may become permanent, supplanting for all practical purposes the
Law of the Sea Convention regime.

As has been mentioned, the Reciprocating States Regime was faced
with the problem of overlaps between the sites claimed by the consortia.
Efforts to resolve this problem were the subject of lengthy and complex

negotiations, following on from the 1982 Interim Arrangements and resulting in the conclusion in August 1983 of a Draft Memorandum of Understanding on the Settlement of Conflicting Claims with Respect to Seabed Areas, and in August 1984 of a Provisional Understanding Regarding Deep Seabed Matters (the cautious terminology reflects the insistence of the parties that the Regime is a purely interim scheme) to which Belgium, France, the Federal Republic of Germany, Italy, Japan, the Netherlands, the United Kingdom and the United States are parties. The 1984 Provisional Understanding lays down procedures for avoiding overlapping licences (some of which have already been issued by the United States, the United Kingdom and the Federal Republic of Germany), the consortia having entered in 1983 into voluntary agreements for resolving overlapping claims; it also provides a framework for the harmonisation of national laws and procedures regulating sea bed mining.[10]

The reciprocating States regard their legislation as an exercise of the undoubted right of States to regulate the activities of their nationals on the high seas. Between these States, and their nationals, the legislation will be effective in awarding and protecting exclusive rights of exploration and exploitation of deep sea-bed sites. But, while the reciprocating States would claim that sea-bed miners were entitled to 'reasonable regard' from other users of the high seas of any nationality (see chapter eleven — for example, there should be no wilful interference with mining vessels) their laws do not — and, in so far as they are based on the freedom of the high seas, cannot — create exclusive rights over sea-bed sites enforceable against other States outside the Reciprocating States Regime. There is nothing to stop any other State, or the Authority, issuing licences overlapping with those issued by the reciprocating States, nor could nationals of other States be prevented from exploiting parts of licensed sites, as long as they did not unreasonably interfere with mining by the licensee or any other operators. In short, third States would retain much the same rights to exploit the sea bed, licensed areas included, as they would to share in the exploitation of unregulated high seas fisheries.

This is not how the Group of 77 see the position. They have repeatedly stated that unilateral legislation and mining under it contravene customary international law as evidenced in the Declaration of Principles governing the Sea Bed and other United Nations resolutions. These, and other declarations made over the past decade at various meetings of Third World States, are seen as having constituted a rule establishing that the deep sea bed is not subject to the legal regime of the high seas and prohibiting its appropriation and the exploitation of its resources except under the regime contained in the Law of the Sea Convention. PrepCom has endorsed this view. It has criticised the Reciprocating States Regime strongly, and in its view the recognition under that regime of non-

Convention licences is tantamount to a recognition of dispositions of parts of the Area, incompatible with article 137 of the Convention and customary law. A PrepCom resolution of 30 August 1985 affirmed that the Convention regime is 'the only regime' for sea-bed mining, and rejected all other claims, agreements and actions regarding the Area and its resources as incompatible with the Convention and its related resolutions and as 'wholly illegal'.[11]

This view has some force. Although customary international law is usually created by State practice coupled with *opinio juris*, it is difficult to see what 'practice' there could be in the case of a prohibitive rule. Since customary law is quite clearly capable of including prohibitive rules, such as that alleged to prohibit unilateral sea-bed mining, abstract declarations of the law must be sufficient to generate such rules. There seems no good reason for denying that the series of resolutions, inside and outside the United Nations, which purport to declare the unlawfulness of unilateral legislation could have this effect. But even if a rule has been established in this way, it would not necessarily follow that it is binding upon all States. Those who have persistently objected to such a rule throughout the period of its emergence are not bound by it — as we saw, for example, when the application of the alleged 'ten-mile rule' on baselines to Norway was discussed in chapter one. The reciprocating States have persistently objected to the view that international law prohibits unilateral mining, and so could not be bound by any such rule. To meet this objection, the Group of 77 argue that the rule in question is a rule of *jus cogens*, a peremptory norm of international law which is universally binding and does not permit 'opting out'. The reciprocating States, for their part, would not accept that the sea-bed rules belong to that highly controversial category.

Even if a rule were shown to be binding upon the reciprocating States, they would argue that their legislation does not violate it. It is arguable that the Declaration of Principles could be read so as to permit unilateral mining pending the entry into force of the Law of the Sea Convention, although the Group of 77 regard licensing as tantamount to an assertion of sovereignty over the Area incompatible with the principle of the 'common heritage'. The unilateral legislation does not, however, seem capable of reconciliation with the terms of some of the other declarations.

This legal dispute seems intractable, both positions being defensible, and both sincerely and tenaciously held. The Group of 77 have suggested that the matter be referred to the International Court of Justice, which could give an advisory opinion at the request of the United Nations General Assembly. The outcome of such a reference is unpredictable, but much would depend upon the exact questions posed. Asked if the unilateral legislation is consistent with the various declarations on the deep sea bed, the Court would probably have to say, no. But asked if those declarations bound, in law, the reciprocating States not to enact and operate such legislation, the Court would probably have again to answer, no.

Concluding remarks

We have seen that, to the extent that any sea-bed mining occurs in the near future, it is likely to occur under either the preparatory investment provisions of the Convention or under the Reciprocating States Regime. The 1986 PrepCom Understanding seeks to provide for the resolution of conflicts between claims under the Convention and those of 'potential applicants', i.e., the consortia presently operating under the Recipro-cating States Regime. This move will doubtless please States such as Japan which have, perhaps surprisingly, been allowed by PrepCom to keep a foot in both camps, by resolving conflicts both with other pioneers proceeding within Prepcom and with the consortia proceeding within the Reciprocating States Regime.

Only non-pioneer operators whose national States were parties to the Convention would mine under the Convention regime from the outset, and they would not be able to proceed to production until any requests from pioneers for production authorisation had been met. In the longer term it is provided that a Review Conference be convened, to undertake a fundamental review of the Convention regime, fifteen years after the earliest commercial production under the Convention (LOSC, art. 155). Decisions of this conference would ideally be taken by consensus, in the absence of which they may, after five years, be taken by a three-quarters majority of States parties, whereupon they would bind all parties. Thus, even if the Convention were to come into force and sea-bed mining to be organised under it, between the short-term provisions and the long-term revisions it is probable that the actual Convention regime itself would be of much less practical importance than might have been expected. There is no doubt that the critical factor in determining the shape of the sea-bed mining, both within and without the Convention, is PrepCom. It, rather than the Convention and Resolution II, is proving the major determinant of the detailed rules on sea bed mining, and the progress of its work merits the closest attention.

Notes

1 *ND* V, p. 376.
2 *Ibid.*, p. 390.
3 *Ibid.*, p. 391.
4 *ND* II, p. 737.
5 *Ibid.*, p. 740.
6 UNCLOS III, Official Records, Vol. VII, Doc. A/Conf. 62/C.I/L.20.

7   M. A. Dubs, 'Minerals of the Deep Sea: myth and reality', in G. Pontecorvo, *The New Order of the Oceans: The Advent of a Managed Environment*, New York, 1986, 85–121.
8   8 *LOSB* 38–52 (1986).
9   The legislation has been reproduced as follows: Federal Republic of Germany, XX *ILM* 393 (1981), XXI *ILM* 832 (1982); France, XXI *ILM* 808 (1982); UK, XX *ILM* 1219 (1981); USA, XIX *ILM* 1003 (1980), XX *ILM* 1228 (1981), XXI *ILM* 867 (1982); USSR, XXI *ILM* 551 (1982); Japan XXII *ILM* 102 (1983); Italy XXIV *ILM* 983 (1985).
10 For full details and texts see E. D. Brown, *op. cit.*, in 'Further reading'. It was reported that all overlapping claims were resolved by September 1987.
11 See 6 *LOSB* 85–6 (1985).

Further reading

The further reading suggested in chapters eight, eleven and nineteen is also relevant to this chapter. A fuller bibliography appears in volume 3 of the definitive study by Brown, cited below.

R. P. Anand, *Legal Regime of the Sea Bed and Developing Countries*, Leyden, 1976.

M. Bennoua, 'Les droits d'exploitation des ressources minérales des océans', 84 *RGDIP* 120–43 (1980).

R. L. Brooke, 'The current status of Deep Seabed Mining', 24 *VJIL* 359–417 (1984).

E. D. Brown, *Sea-Bed Energy and Mineral Resources and the Law of the Sea*, vol. 2, *The Area Beyond the Limits of National Jurisdiction*, London, 1986, and *ibid.*, vol. 3, *Tables and Bibliography*, London, 1986.

B. Buzan, *Seabed Politics*, New York, 1976.

C. J. Joyner, 'Legal implications of the common heritage of mankind', 35 *ICLQ* 190–9 (1986).

T. G. Kronmiller, *The Lawfulness of Deep Seabed Mining*, 2 vols., New York, 1980.

P. V. McDade, 'The interim obligation between signature and ratification of a treaty', 32 *Netherlands International Law Review* 5–47 (1985).

F. H. Paolillo, 'The international arrangements for the international sea-bed', 188 *Receuil des Cours* 135–338 (1984, vol. 4).

A. M. Post, *Deepsea Mining and the Law of the Sea*, The Hague, 1983.

J. K. Sebenius, *Negotiating the Law of the Sea*, Cambridge, Mass., 1984.

T. Treves (ed.), *Lo Sfruttamento dei Fondi Marini Internazionali*, Milan, 1982.

R. Young, 'The legal regime of the deep sea floor', 62 *AJIL* 641–53 (1968).

CHAPTER THIRTEEN

Navigation

Introduction

Along with fishing, navigation is the oldest use of the sea, and it remains one of the most important. While aircraft may have replaced ships as the prime means of conveying people across the oceans, ships are still the most important means of transporting goods on such routes: ninety-five per cent, by weight, of all international trade is seaborne. On the military side, the uneasy balance of terror between the two superpowers is heavily dependent upon the strategic qualities of nuclear submarines. While almost all coastal States and some landlocked ones have a merchant navy of some description, one of the remarkable features of the international shipping industry is the degree to which ships are concentrated under the flags of a very few States — although this does not necessarily indicate a similar distribution of ownership, since the beneficial owners of the ships[1] may not be nationals of or resident in the flag States concerned. Table 2 shows the distribution of ships between the major flag States in 1986. It will be seen that the ten leading flag States accounted for 65·6 per cent of world merchant shipping tonnage, and the next ten States for a further 15·8 per cent. Although ships are concentrated under the flags of very few States, in recent years the distribution of ships has become slightly less uneven. Thus, in 1978, when the total world merchant shipping fleet was almost exactly the same size as in 1986, the leading ten States accounted for no less than 72·9 per cent of all shipping and the leading twenty States for 88·2 per cent (compared with 81·4 per cent in 1986). Moreover, the number of States possessing fleets totalling in excess of one million tons has gone up from forty-one in 1978 to forty-four in 1986. Looking at the division of the world fleet among different categories of States, in 1986 the flags of developed market economy States accounted for 42·8 per cent (54·1 per cent in 1978); flags of convenience (a term explained below) for 28·8 per cent (27·3 per cent in 1978); developing States 19·1 per cent (10·6 per cent in 1978); and developed State-trading States 9·3 per cent (8·0 per cent in 1978). Thus the change in the distribution of flag State ownership between 1978 and 1986 has been largely from developed market economy States to developing States.

From the end of the Second World War the world merchant shipping fleet increased steadily and reached a zenith of nearly 425 million tons in 1982. Since then, as a result of the severe recession in the shipping industry that began in the late 1970s, there has been a steady decline to the present world total of nearly 405 million tons. For some traditional shipping nations, the decline has been much more severe. This has notably been the case for France, Norway, Sweden and the United Kingdom (excluding its dependent territories), each of which has seen the size of its merchant shipping fleet more than halved since 1978. Liberia has also suffered a steep decline in its fleet, from eighty million tons in 1978 to fifty-two million tons in 1986.

In the rest of this chapter we look at the different rights of navigation enjoyed by ships on the high seas and in the various maritime zones subject to the jurisdiction of the coastal State, and then at the network of international conventions imposing safety standards and regulations, which has arisen in order to ensure that these navigational rights are exercised in an orderly and safe manner. The need for such standards and regulations has become particularly apparent in recent years as a result of a number of factors. First, there has been a tremendous increase in the number of ships (total world tonnage increased fivefold between 1948 and 1978), creating serious traffic problems in the busiest waterways. Secondly, the size of ships has increased enormously, with consequent reductions in manoeuvr-

Table 2. *Distribution of world merchant shipping tonnage in 1986: leading twenty States ('000 gross registered tons)*

Liberia	52,649	South Korea	7,184
Panama	41,305	Philippines	6,922
Japan	38,488	India	6,540
Greece	28,391	Singapore	6,268
USSR	24,961	Brazil	6,212
UK	23,986[a]	Bahamas	5,985
USA	19,901[b]	France	5,936
China	15,840[c]	West Germany	5,565
Cyprus	10,617	Spain	5,422
Norway	9,295	Other States	75,546
Italy	7,897	*Total, all States*	404,910

Notes

a. Includes 8·180 million GRT registered in Hong Kong and 4·239 million GRT registered in other UK dependent territories.

b. Includes (i) USA reserve fleet, estimated at 2·6 million GRT; (ii) 1·5 million GRT used for service on the Great Lakes.

c. Includes 4·272 million GRT registered in Taiwan.

Source: Lloyd's Register of Shipping Statistical Tables, 1986, pp. 3–5.

ability: for example, a supertanker travelling at full speed takes several miles to stop. Thirdly, ships are now carrying more dangerous cargoes, such as oil, liquefied natural gas, toxic chemicals and radioactive matter, thus making the consequences of any accident more serious.

Before we turn to look at navigation rights and safety obligations, we must first consider the question of the nationality of ships. This is necessary because these various rights and obligations, being imposed by international law, cannot be enjoyed by or imposed on ships as such, since ships are not subjects of international law. Instead, ships derive their rights and obligations from the State whose flag they fly and whose nationality they accordingly bear.

Nationality of ships

The ascription of nationality to ships is one of the most important means by which public order is maintained at sea. As well as indicating what rights a ship enjoys and to what obligations it is subject, the nationality of a vessel indicates which State is to exercise flag State jurisdiction over the vessel. Nationality also indicates which State is responsible in international law for the vessel in cases where an act or omission of the vessel is attributable to the State, and which State is entitled to exercise diplomatic protection on behalf of the vessel.

States usually grant their nationality to vessels by means of registration and by authorising vessels to fly their flag. Thus expressions such as 'the State of registration' or the 'flag State' are synonyms for the State whose nationality the vessels bears.[2] In view of the importance of nationality, it is desirable to know whether international law lays down any rules which govern the circumstances in which a State may grant its nationality to a vessel. Originally it seems that States had complete discretion in this matter. In the *Muscat Dhows* case (1905), where France had permitted subjects of the Sultan of Muscat to fly the French flag, the Permanent Court of Arbitration said that 'Generally speaking it belongs to every sovereign to decide to whom he will accord the right to fly his flag and to prescribe the rules covering such grants.'[3] This approach appears at first sight to have been followed in the 1958 Convention on the High Seas. Article 5 begins by providing that 'Each State shall fix the conditions for the grant of its nationality to ships, for the registration of ships in its territory, and for the right to fly its flag.' However, the article goes on to limit the discretion enjoyed by States by providing that:

There must exist a genuine link between the State and the ship; in particular, the State must effectively exercise its jurisdiction and control in administrative, technical and social matters over ships flying its flag.

In adding this requirement of a 'genuine link', the draftsmen of the Convention (principally the ILC) were strongly influenced by the then recent judgment of the International Court of Justice in the *Nottebohm* case (1955). In that case the Court required that where a State claimed to exercise diplomatic protection in respect of one of its nationals in the circumstances there in question, nationality should be the legal reflection of a factual link — a 'genuine link' — between the individual and the State. The introduction of the requirement of a 'genuine link' as far as the nationality of ships is concerned gives rise to the difficulty of knowing what exactly comprises such a link. In its 1955 draft the ILC laid down objective criteria for determining the existence of a genuine link, but in its final draft the Commission felt that it was not practicable to suggest specific criteria. The position therefore remains unclear. Equally, it is uncertain what consequences follow when there is no genuine link between a vessel and the State whose nationality it purports to bear.

In spite of the fact that the Preamble to the High Seas Convention speaks of its provisions as being 'generally declaratory' of established principles of international law, it seems unlikely, in the light of the background to article 5 described above, that the requirement in that article of a 'genuine link' between the vessel and the State purporting to confer nationality represents customary international law. This helps to explain why the requirement of a genuine link has not been widely observed in practice. While a number of States (e.g. Portugal, Norway, France) do require a genuine link with the ship, usually expressed in the requirement that all or a fixed proportion of the ship's owners and/or crew must have the nationality of the State concerned, other States require very little or virtually no link. This latter group of States, none of which is party to the High Seas Convention, are generally known as 'flag of convenience' or 'open registry' States. These expressions are generally taken to refer to States that permit foreign shipowners having no real connection with those States (in practice such shipowners come mainly from the USA, Greece, Hong Kong and Japan) to register their ships under the flags of those States. The low fees and taxation levied by such States, together with lower crew costs (which result from low wages and manning levels), and in some cases savings from not having to comply with international safety standards, reduce the shipowner's operating costs and therefore often give him a significant competitive advantage over shipowners whose vessels are not registered under flags of convenience. Flags of convenience include Liberia, which has the largest merchant fleet in the world under its flag, Panama, Singapore, Cyprus and Somalia. These States are often said to be lax in the qualifications required of the crews of their ships, and to be unwilling or unable to exercise effective jurisdiction over their ships in matters of pollution control and shipping safety. Their past record certainly gives support to this point of view,[4] although at least in the case of Liberia recent changes in policy suggest that a more vigorous enforcement of flag State jurisdiction is occurring.[5] It must, however, be stressed that substandard ships can be found under most, if not all, flags: they are by no means peculiar to flags of convenience. In fact, the establishment of a genuine link in the case of ships owned by companies, which can be freely incorporated in States other than the State where the majority of shareholders are resident, is difficult to determine: a British ship, for instance, may be owned by a British company, itself a subsidiary of other British companies, members of a corporate group whose ultimate holding company may be registered in another State and whose shareholders are resident in a third State. The distinction between 'convenience' and other flags, based on the existence of a genuine link prior to registration, is by no means clear-cut, and is perhaps of less practical importance than the question of the vigour with which the flag State exercises its jurisdiction and control over ships after registration.

A novel development similar to the use of flags of convenience arose in 1987, when Kuwait, alarmed at the increasing attacks on third country shipping by the protagonists in the Iran–Iraq war, inquired of both the USSR and USA the possibility of re-registering its tankers under the flags of those two States. Its motive was to obtain the diplomatic (and probably military) protection of the two superpowers for its shipping. Several Kuwaiti tankers were re-registered under the US flag. With the USSR Kuwait arranged to charter a number of Soviet tankers for the transport of its oil. In addition, some Kuwaiti vessels have been re-registered under other flags, including the British (Gibraltar) flag.

An opportunity to give the requirement of a genuine link more substance was offered to the International Court of Justice in 1960 in the *Constitution of the Maritime Safety Committee of IMCO* case. There the Court was asked the meaning of the phrase 'the largest ship-owning nations' in article 28(a) of the Convention of IMCO (the Intergovernmental Maritime Consultative Organisation, as the IMO was then known), which at that time required that the eight 'largest ship-owning nations' be elected to the Maritime Safety Committee. The Court held that the concept of the genuine link was irrelevant for determining the meaning of this phrase and that the nations with the largest registered tonnage fell within the terms of the phrase, whether or not they were flags of convenience. That the Court refused this opportunity of giving its support to the requirement of a genuine link is perhaps understandable in view of the controversy over flags of convenience both within and outside IMCO.

In spite of the fact that the 'genuine link' requirement appears to have had little influence on State practice since the High Seas Convention came into force, the requirement is repeated in the Law of the Sea Convention (art. 91), although the requirement is not linked to the effective exercise of jurisdiction by the flag State, as it is in article 5 of the High Seas Convention. (The effective exercise of flag State jurisdiction is dealt with by article 94, discussed below.) There seems little reason for supposing that article 91 will have any more influence on State practice than article 5 of the High Seas Convention. The direct attack mounted on flags of convenience in the past few years by UNCTAD may prove more effective. Following a number of reports by the UNCTAD Secretariat, and the work of various working groups UNCTAD sponsored a diplomatic conference which met from 1984–86 and which adopted the United Nations Convention on Conditions for Registration of Ships, 1986. The Convention aims to strengthen the genuine link between ship and flag State, and to ensure that States effectively exercise jurisdiction and control over their ships, not only in relation to administrative, technical, economic and social matters, but also with regard to the identification and accountability of shipowners and operators who, in the past, have sometimes hidden behind a complex and artificial veil of interconnecting companies. The Convention requires the adoption of laws requiring a clear link with the State, in the form of an appropriate level of participation (a matter on which each State is left with considerable discretion) by its nationals in the ownership or crewing of the ship (arts. 8, 9). It further requires the maintenance of a detailed register from which the owners and operators, and a resident agent of the owner, can be readily identified, and the adoption of measures to ensure that the owner or operator can meet financial obligations to third parties (arts. 6, 10, 11). In addition, the Convention requires States to maintain a competent and effective maritime administration, to secure compliance with national and international shipping standards. The Convention should secure a tightening of flag State control over ships, but because its implementation will require substantial changes in the conditions of registration and the administrative organisation of some States, it is likely to be some time before it enters into force.

So far we have discussed only the right of States to confer their nationality and flag upon ships. The question arises whether ships can sail under the flag of subjects of international law other than States, notably international organisations. In preparing the draft articles which eventually became the High Seas Convention, the ILC rejected the idea of including a provision recognising the right of the UN, and possibly other international organisations, to sail ships exclusively under their own flag, on the ground that since the legal system of the flag State applied to a ship authorised to fly its flag, the flag of the UN could not be assimilated to the flag of a State. Notwithstanding the negative approach of the ILC, the 1958 Geneva Conference inserted an article dealing with the question. Article 7 of the High Seas Convention states that the provisions of the Convention 'do not prejudice the question of ships employed on the official service of an intergovernmental organisation flying the flag of the organisation'. The exact meaning of this provision is not really clear, but it would seem to leave the question open. In practice, ships have on a few occasions sailed under the flag of the UN, e.g. some of the vessels used in the UN Emergency Force in Egypt in 1956–57.[6] The Law of the Sea Convention contains a provision very similar to article 7 of the High Seas Convention (LOSC, art. 93), except that it limits intergovernmental organisations to the UN, its specialised agencies and the IAEA. It seems difficult to see why the article should be limited in its application to just these intergovernmental organisations, when there are other, more developed organisations such as the EEC which, since they have embryonic legal systems of their own, would pose fewer legal problems were their flags flown by vessels, and which, furthermore, can become parties to the Law of the Sea Convention.

Finally, it should be noted that a vessel flying two or more flags is regarded as having no nationality (HSC, art. 6; LOSC, art. 92; and see chapter eleven).

Rights of navigation

We have mentioned in earlier chapters the different navigational rights enjoyed by the ships of foreign States in the various zones of coastal States and on the high seas, and here we therefore do no more than briefly recapitulate them. In internal waters foreign vessels normally enjoy no rights of navigation, in the absence of a right given by treaty — for example, a treaty of friendship, commerce and navigation which might confer a right of access to ports, as was explained in chapter three. The major exception to this rule is that in those internal waters which, before their enclosure by straight baselines drawn under article 4 of the Territorial Sea Convention or article 7 of the Law of the Sea Convention, were part of the territorial sea or high seas, the right of innocent passage for foreign vessels is preserved (TSC, art. 5(2); LOSC, art. 8(2)). In the territorial sea itself foreign vessels enjoy the right of innocent passage, the meaning and scope of which were discussed in chapter four, although the coastal State may temporarily suspend that right in limited areas where necessary for its security. In straits consisting of territorial sea, this right of innocent passage may not, under the Territorial Sea Convention, be suspended (TSC, art. 16(4)). As we saw in chapter five, some of the existing special treaty regimes for particular straits (e.g. the 1936 Montreux Convention) give foreign vessels greater navigational rights, and the Law of the Sea Convention provides a general regime of transit passage for many straits (LOSC, arts. 37–44). In archipelagic waters, foreign vessels will, under the Law of the Sea Convention, enjoy the right of innocent passage: they will also enjoy a more extensive right of archipelagic sea lanes passage in sea lanes designated by the archipelagic State in its archipelagic waters and territorial sea (LOSC, arts. 52 and 53; and see chapter six).

Beyond the territorial sea all vessels enjoy, in principle, freedom of navigation under the exclusive jurisdiction of their flag State. This freedom is, however, subject to a number of limitations. In a coastal State's contiguous zone it is subject to the right of the coastal State to exercise the control necessary to prevent and punish infringements of its customs, fiscal, immigration or sanitary regulations committed within its territory or territorial sea (TSC, art. 24; LOSC, art. 33, and see chapter seven). In the exclusive economic zone, freedom of navigation is subject to the coastal State's jurisdiction relating to pollution and resource control (see chapter nine); and in both the exclusive economic zone and in waters over the continental shelf it is subject to the obligation to 'respect' safety zones around artificial islands and installations. However, the coastal State is under a duty not to erect artificial islands and installations 'where interference may be caused to the use of recognised sea lanes essential to international navigation' (CSC, art. 5(3) and (6); LOSC, arts. 60(6) and (7), 80). On the high seas the freedom of navigation is subject to the general obligation to have 'reasonable regard' ('due regard' in the Law of the Sea Convention) 'to the interests of other States in their exercise of the freedom of the high seas' (HSC, art. 2; LOSC, art. 87(2)).

Finally, wherever a vessel may be, whether in one of a coastal State's zones or on the high seas, it will be subject to any relevant international obligations which have been undertaken by its flag State; for example, in relation to pollution control or shipping safety. The question of pollution is dealt with separately (see chapter fifteen): here we now turn to consider the scope of such obligations in relation to the safety of shipping.

Safety of shipping

It is obviously in the interests of shipowners, seafarers and the community at large that the transportation of people and goods by ships should be made as safe as possible, and that accidents such as foundering, stranding or collision should be kept to a minimum. Recognising this, article 10 of the High Seas Convention provides that every State shall take such measures for its vessels as are necessary to ensure safety at sea with regard to communications, the prevention of collisions, crew conditions and the construction, equipment and seaworthiness of ships, in conformity with 'generally accepted international standards'. The Law of the Sea Convention adopts the same basic approach, but sets out in more detail the duties of the flag State — including, for example, the duty to maintain regular checks upon the seaworthiness of ships, to ensure that crews are properly qualified and to hold inquiries into shipping casualties (LOSC, art. 94).

The emphasis upon internationally accepted standards in article 10 of the High Seas Convention and article 94 of the Law of the Sea Convention is dictated by practical necessity. While each State remains free in theory to apply its own legal standards relating to such matters as seaworthiness and crew qualifications to ships flying its flag and, to a more limited extent, to foreign ships entering its ports or territorial sea, there would be chaos if these standards varied widely or were incompatible. Furthermore, because improved safety measures usually involve extra costs for shipowners, and because shipping is a very competitive industry, most States are reluctant to impose stricter safety legislation on their shipowners unless other States do the same. For these reasons, therefore, the international community has developed a set of uniform international standards to promote the safety of shipping. These standards are contained in a number of international conventions, most of which are the work of IMO. The shipping safety standards dealt with by these conventions can be considered under four main headings: seaworthiness of ships, collision avoidance and ships' routeing, crewing standards, and the establishment of navigational aids.

Seaworthiness of ships

The main convention dealing with the seaworthiness of ships is the 1974 International Convention for the Safety of Life at Sea (SOLAS Convention), the latest in a succession of SOLAS Conventions, the first of which was inspired by the sinking of the *Titanic*. The Convention contains a large number of complex regulations laying down standards relating to the construction of ships, fire-safety measures, life-saving appliances, the carriage of navigational equipment and other aspects of the safety of navigation, the carriage of dangerous goods and special rules for nuclear ships. These standards are to be prescribed by contracting States for their vessels. Enforcement lies largely with the flag State, but port States have a limited degree of control. They are entitled to see that ships of other contracting parties in their ports have on board valid certificates of the kind required by the Convention. Where 'there are clear grounds for believing that the condition of the ship or of its equipment does not correspond substantially with the particulars of any of the certificates', or where a certificate has expired or where the ship and its equipment do not comply with the provisions of Regulation 11 of Chapter I of the 1974 Convention (which requires the condition of a ship and its equipment to be maintained after a survey), the authorities of the port State 'shall take steps to ensure that the ship shall not sail until it can proceed to sea or leave the port for the purpose of proceeding to the appropriate repair yard without danger to the ship or persons on board' (Chapter I, Regulation 19, as amended).

In 1978, at an IMO Conference on Tanker Safety and Pollution Prevention, a Protocol to the SOLAS Convention was adopted which makes the use of inert gas systems, additional radar and emergency steering gear mandatory on all ships above a certain size, and improves procedures for the inspection and certification of ships. The Protocol came into force in 1981. In addition, various amendments were made to the regulations contained in the Convention in 1981 and 1983. Further amendments to the Convention are due to be considered at a conference in 1988.

As well as the SOLAS Convention, there are three other IMO conventions which are concerned with the seaworthiness of ships. The International Convention on Load Lines of 1966 deals with the problem of overloading, often the cause of casualties to ships, by prescribing the minimum freeboard (or the minimum draught) to which the ship is permitted to be loaded. Enforcement of the Convention is very similar to that of the SOLAS Convention, including the power of port States to detain ships which lack an appropriate and valid certificate. The 1971 Agreement on Special Trade Passenger Ships, together with its Protocol of 1973, deals with the safety of ships carrying large numbers of unberthed passengers in special trades, such as the pilgrim trade, while the 1977 International Convention for the Safety of Fishing Vessels (which is not yet in force) lays down regulations governing the construction and equipment of fishing vessels.

In addition to conventions, the IMO (largely through its Assembly) has adopted numerous recommendations, guidelines and codes relating to the seaworthiness of ships. Such measures, being usually in the form of resolutions of the Assembly, are not as such legally binding. Nevertheless, some of these measures, especially the codes, do make a transition from 'soft' to 'hard' law. For example, the Code for the Construction and Equipment of Ships carrying Dangerous Chemicals in Bulk, originally adopted by the IMO Assembly in 1971 as a non-binding resolution,[7] was subsequently incorporated in the legislation of at least a dozen States (and thus legally binding on the municipal level in those States), and finally was incorporated in the SOLAS Convention by the 1983 amendments to the Convention, thus becoming legally binding on the international plane.

Collision avoidance and ships' routeing

Like the SOLAS Conventions, there has been a series of regulations for preventing collisions at sea. The current regulations are annexed to the Convention on the International Regulations for Preventing Collisions at Sea of 1972. The Regulations are principally concerned with a vessel's conduct and movements in relation to other vessels, particularly when visibility is poor, for the purposes of collision avoidance, and with the establishment of common standards in relation to sound and light signals. While the 1972 Convention is less than precise about the legal effects of these Regulations in so far as the relationship between breach of the Regulations and civil liability for collisions is concerned (breach does not necessarily result in

civil liability, it seems: cf. Warbrick, *op. cit.*, in 'Further reading', p. 138),
breach is commonly made an offence under the criminal law of the flag
State party to the Convention, but prosecutions are rare because in many
cases substantial discretion rests with the master. Under the Law of the Sea
Convention ships exercising their right of innocent passage through the
territorial sea or their right of transit passage through straits must observe
the Regulations, regardless of whether the flag State or the coastal State is
a party to the 1972 Convention (LOSC, arts. 21(4), 39(2)).

An important means of reducing the risk of collisions between ships is
the use of traffic separation schemes to separate shipping in congested areas
into one-way-only lanes. Early examples of such schemes can be found in
the voluntary agreements on routeing made by shipowners trading on certain routes (for example, in the China Sea) in the nineteenth century. They
are now prescribed by the IMO, which began recommending such schemes
in 1967: there are now over ninety routeing schemes laid down. At first
compliance with IMO-recommended schemes was voluntary: flag States
were not obliged to order their ships to follow them. But since the entry
into force of the Collisions Regulations Convention in 1977 their observance
has been mandatory for the ships of all parties to that Convention (Rule
10). The introduction of traffic separation schemes is thought to be responsible for the general decrease in the number of collisions at sea: for example,
in north-west European waters, where there are many separation schemes,
the number of collisions dropped from 156 in the period 1956–61 to only
forty-five between 1976 and 1981.[8]

While the IMO is recognised as the only international body competent
to prescribe traffic separation schemes (SOLAS Convention, Chapter V,
Regulation 8(b)), coastal States also have some competence in this area.
Thus article 17 of the Territorial Sea Convention provides that in its territorial sea a coastal State may enact regulations relating to the navigation of
foreign vessels exercising their right of innocent passage. The Law of the
Sea Convention contains a similar provision (LOSC, art. 21), but adds that
a coastal State prescribing a traffic separation scheme in its territorial sea
must take into account any IMO recommendations and such factors as the
special characteristics of particular ships and the density of traffic (LOSC,
art. 22). The IMO itself recommends coastal States wishing to establish
routeing systems in their territorial sea to 'design them in accordance with
IMO criteria for such schemes and submit them to IMO for adoption'.[9]
Coastal States can exercise enforcement jurisdiction against foreign vessels
infringing prescribed schemes (TSC, art. 19; LOSC, art. 27). In practice
enforcement is usually limited to requesting vessels to rejoin the separation
scheme or, in more serious cases, reporting the infringement to the authorities of the flag State; although if an offending vessel put into one of the
coastal State's ports it could be prosecuted. In straits subject to the regime

of transit passage, the Law of the Sea Convention provides that the coastal State's competence is more limited. While the coastal State may still prescribe traffic separation schemes, proposed schemes must 'conform to generally accepted international regulations' and must be referred to the IMO 'with a view to their adoption' before being prescribed by the coastal State (LOSC, art. 41). The controversial question as to what enforcement jurisdiction coastal States have in straits subject to transit passage is discussed in chapter five. Finally, the limited competence which States enjoy to prescribe anti-pollution regulations in their EEZ includes the competence to prescribe regulations relating to 'navigational practices' (LOSC, art. 211, discussed in chapter fifteen).

As well as traffic separation schemes, the IMO also recommends deep water routes, areas to be avoided (which are areas in which either navigation is particularly hazardous or it is exceptionally important to avoid casualties), and other routeing measures.

In future it seems likely that the management of marine traffic will go beyond traffic separation and other routeing schemes and become more comprehensive, though it seems unlikely that it will ever reach the precision or sophistication of air traffic control. Already the IMO has taken some action in this regard: for example in both the Baltic Straits and the Straits of Malacca it has recommended such measures as speed restrictions, the reporting by vessels of their position and the use of pilots.[10] The IMO is also at present considering the feasibility of making it mandatory for ships to report their positions to the appropriate authorities of local coastal States where they are in difficulties which are likely to result in pollution.[11] In addition to such international measures, there are many national schemes, mainly in the form of Vessel Traffic Services in the approaches to ports and harbours.[12] The IMO has recommended 'Guidelines for Vessel Traffic Services', which national authorities are urged to follow 'in the interests of international harmonisation and improving maritime safety'.[13]

Crewing standards

Inadequately trained or qualified crews are a major factor in the cause of shipping accidents. It should therefore follow that an improvement in the quality of crews would lead to a reduction of accidents. The 1974 SOLAS Convention requires that all ships shall be 'sufficiently and efficiently manned' (Chapter V, Regulation 13), while under ILO Convention No. 147 of 1976 concerning Minimum Standards in Merchant Ships each contracting State must 'ensure that seafarers employed on ships registered in its territory are properly qualified or trained for the duties for which they are engaged' (art. 2(e)). Similarly, article 94(4) of the Law of the Sea Convention provides that flag States must ensure that each of their ships 'is in the charge of a master and officers who possess appropriate qualifications

... and that the crew is appropriate in qualification and numbers for the type, size, machinery and equipment of the ship'. More precise content is given to these rather vague and general obligations by the International Convention on Standards of Training, Certification and Watchkeeping for Seafarers, (the 'STCW' Convention), adopted under the IMO's auspices in 1978. This convention lays down mandatory minimum requirements for the certification of masters and other officers and prescribes basic principles for keeping navigational and engineering watches. Enforcement of the STCW Convention's provisions rests essentially with the flag State, although port States have certain powers of control for the purpose of verifying that seafarers required by the Convention to be certificated are so certificated (art. X). The entry into force of the Convention in 1984 should lead in future to a significant improvement in the standards of crews and, as a probable result, a reduction in the number of shipping accidents.

The working conditions of crews have been the subject of a large number of ILO conventions, which make up the International Seafarers' Code. The most important of these conventions include: Convention concerning Wages, Hours of Work on Board Ship and Manning (No. 109 (1958), revising earlier conventions), Convention concerning Crew Accommodation on Board Ship (No. 92 (1949), supplemented by No. 133 (1970)), and Convention concerning Continuity of Employment of Seafarers (No. 145 (1976)). The ILO has also adopted a number of non-binding recommendations on the working conditions of seafarers, notably the Social Conditions and Safety (Seafarers) Recommendation, 1958 (No. 108). In addition, ILO Convention No. 147 (referred to above) requires States parties to it to prescribe for their ships and effectively enforce safety standards, social security measures and shipboard conditions of employment equivalent to the provisions of various ILO conventions listed in the annex to the Convention.

Finally, it should be noted that article 9 of the 1986 UN Convention on Conditions for Registration of Ships requires flag States to promote, in cooperation with shipowners, the education and training of seamen, and to ensure that manning levels and competence and working conditions on board its ships conform to international rules and standards.

Establishment of navigational aids

Of obvious importance to the safety of shipping is the establishment of navigational aids such as lighthouses, lightships, buoys and radar beacons. An obligation is laid down by the SOLAS Convention on States parties to it to:

arrange for the establishment and maintenance of such aids to navigation, including radio beacons and electronic aids, as, in their opinion, the volume of traffic justifies and the degree of risk requires, and to arrange for information relating to these aids to be made available to all concerned. [Chapter V, Regulation 14]

It may also be noted that under the Territorial Sea and Law of the Sea Conventions there is an obligation on every coastal State to 'give appropriate publicity to any dangers to navigation, of which it has knowledge, within its territorial sea' (TSC, art. 15(2); LOSC, art. 24(2)). Similar obligations arise under customary law (see chapter four, pp. 67, 84). The cost of installing and maintaining navigational aids is one that is normally borne solely by the coastal State, and it is not entitled to demand a contribution from ships sailing through its territorial sea (TSC, art. 18; LOSC, art. 26). However, there are one or two instances where States have entered into an agreement to share the cost of navigational aids, e.g. the 1962 International Agreement regarding the Maintenance of Certain Lights in the Red Sea. Under article 43 of the Law of the Sea Convention States bordering a strait subject to transit passage and user States are to co-operate 'in the establishment and maintenance in [the] strait of necessary navigational and safety aids', although nothing is said about how the costs of this are to be borne. Presumably local agreements or arrangements will allocate the sharing of costs.

Miscellaneous safety measures

Finally there are a number of miscellaneous initiatives taken by the IMO that bear on maritime safety and which are worthy of brief mention. First, the Convention on the International Maritime Satellite Organisation (INMARSAT) of 1976 provides for a world-wide maritime communications satellite system, which, since it began operations in February 1982, has led, for the several thousand ships now connected to the system, to a significant increase in the speed, reliability and quality of maritime communications, thus making for increased efficiency of navigation and safety at sea. Secondly, in November 1977 the IMO Assembly adopted a Plan for the Establishment of a World-wide Navigational Warning Service.[14] The plan provides for shipping to be given information required for safe navigation and meteorological warnings through a number of regional authorities responsible for broadcasting such information. Lastly, in April 1979 an International Convention on Maritime Search and Rescue was adopted at a conference held under the IMO's auspices. The main purpose of the Convention is to facilitate international co-operation in search and rescue operations at sea by establishing an international search and rescue plan.

Evaluation of IMO conventions

In general, it must be said that the IMO has performed a very useful service in drafting the above conventions. While the criticism may be made that the conventions are rather slow to enter into force and are not always widely ratified, this is scarcely the fault of the IMO, since ratification of conventions is entirely a matter within the discretion of its member States, and not the Organisation. Furthermore, it should be pointed out that the most important conventions — SOLAS, the Collision Regulations and Load Lines — have been ratified by virtually all the major shipping nations (see table 3). As far as speed of entry into force is concerned, the use of the tacit amendment procedure for the technical annexes of all IMO Conventions concluded since 1972, whereby amendments enter into force unless objected to, rather than — as formerly — requiring positive approval by a certain number of States, should mean that in future it will be easier and quicker to amend the annexes of IMO Conventions in order to keep them abreast of technical developments.

A basic defect of these IMO conventions is that, for the most part, enforcement lies in the hands of the flag State. Thus, if that State is unable or unwilling to enforce these standards — and this is alleged usually to be the case with flags to convenience (except perhaps now Liberia), although flags of convienence States are not the only flag States culpable in this regard — then, however admirable the standards may be in theory, they will in practice be ineffective in dealing with the problems at which they are aimed. The position may improve if the UN Convention on Conditions for Registration of Ships comes into force and is widely ratified, since article 5 of the Convention requires flag States to implement, and ensure compliance by its vessels with, international rules and standards concerning safety of shipping.

In the meantime the current drawbacks of flag State enforcement are to some extent overcome by the powers of control given to the port State by some of the IMO Conventions, as has been seen (and see chapter fifteen for the use of port State jurisdiction in controlling pollution). A similar, but more comprehensive, approach is found in ILO Convention No. 147 of 1976 concerning Minimum Standards in Merchant Ships. Under this convention, a State which believes that a foreign vessel in one of its ports does not conform to certain specified safety standards may inform the flag State and 'may take measures necessary to rectify any conditions on board which are clearly hazardous to safety or health', provided that it does not 'unnecessarily detain or delay the ship' (art. 4). It would seem that under customary international law port States have — and in practice exercise — the competence to inspect foreign vessels in their ports and detain them if unsafe, so that the ILO and IMO Conventions essentially do no more than consolidate and clarify existing law and encourage port States to use their powers. Going somewhat further than the Conventions, but still in accordance with customary international law, the maritime authorities of fourteen West European States signed a Memorandum of Understanding on Port State Control on 26 January 1982.[15] Under this memorandum, each author-

Table 3. *Ratification of maritime safety conventions*

Convention	Date of signature	Date of entry into force	Number of ratifications	Fleets of ratifying States as percentage (to nearest whole number) of world merchant shipping fleet[a]
1. *IMO conventions*				
SOLAS 1974	1.11.1974	25.5.1980	96	98
SOLAS Protocol	1.6.1978	1.5.1981	61	92
Loadlines	5.4.1966	21.7.1968	108	99
Collision Regulations	20.10.1972	15.7.1977	95	96
Special trade passenger ships	6.10.1971	2.1.1974	13	22
Protocol	13.7.1973	2.6.1977	11	22
Fishing vessels	1.10.1977	Not in force (fifteen ratifications required representing 50% of total number of fishing vessels)	15	18[b]
Seafarers certification, etc.	1.12.1978	28.4.1984	55	73
2. *ILO conventions*				
No. 92	18.6.1949	29.1.1953	31	59
No. 109	14.5.1958	Not in force (nine ratifications required plus certain tonnage requirements)	11	11
No. 133	30.10.1970	Not in force (twelve ratifications required plus certain tonnage requirements)	17	36
No. 145	28.10.1976	3.5.1979	16	11
No. 147	29.10.1976	28.11.1981	19	49

Notes
a. These figures are based on the size (in GRT) of merchant shipping fleets in 1986.
b. This figure is the percentage of the total world fishing fleet (by numbers of vessels) that ratifying States' fishing fleets represent.
IMO Conventions: information correct as at 31 January 1987; ILO Conventions: information correct as at 1 January 1987.

ity undertakes to maintain an effective system of port State control to ensure that vessels visiting its ports comply with the main IMO safety conventions discussed above, ILO Convention No. 147 and the International Convention for the Prevention of Pollution from Ships, 1973, as modified by a Protocol of 1978, to the extent that such conventions are in force and the port State is a party — but regardless of whether the flag State of the ship concerned is a party. Each authority must inspect a minimum of twenty-five per cent of the ships using its ports. Guidelines for inspection are set out in Annex 1. Where an inspection reveals deficiencies that are clearly hazardous to safety, health or the environment, the hazard must be removed before the ship is allowed to proceed to sea. Arrangements are made for a regular exchange of information relating to inspections between the authorities parties to the memorandum. During the first four years of operation of the memorandum, 38,000 inspections took place. In about four per cent of cases ships were found to have deficiencies serious enough to result in their being delayed or detained.[16] The third annual report of the memorandum warns, however, that its 'impact so far has not been spectacular. The number of deficiencies and of sub-standard ships has not yet declined significantly, which justifies the conclusion that the aims of the [memorandum] can be achieved only gradually.'[17] Since 1984 Japan has applied the same port controls as the memorandum.

Finally, going much less far than any of the provisions mentioned above, but similarly motivated, article 94(6) of the Law of the Sea Convention provides that a State which has clear grounds for believing that a flag State has not exercised proper jurisdiction and control over one of its ships may report the facts to the flag State, and that 'upon receiving such a report, the flag State shall investigate the matter and, if appropriate, take any action necessary to remedy the situation'.

It should be noted that neither under the Conventions nor under the memorandum are port States given the right to prosecute foreign vessels for failure to comply with the required standards, although they have this competence already under customary international law where a breach of a standard is committed in the port which is a violation of local law (see chapter three).

Other IMO conventions

Most of the conventions adopted under the auspices of the IMO are concerned with maritime safety (discussed above) or marine pollution (discussed in chapter fifteen). There are, however, a few IMO conventions which deal with neither of these topics, and it may be appropriate to make brief mention of them here. First, the Convention on Facilitation of International Maritime Traffic of 1965 reduces and simplifies government formalities, documentary requirements and procedures connected with the arrival, stay and departure of ships engaged in international voyages. Secondly, the 1969 International Convention on Tonnage Measurement of Ships establishes a unified system of tonnage measurement. Such a system had not existed prior to the entry into force of the Convention in 1982. The system laid down by the Convention, in comparison with previous tonnage measurement regulations, greatly simplifies the calculation of tonnages. Thirdly, the International Convention for Safe Containers of 1972 facilitates the international inter-modal transport of containers, while seeking to maintain a high level of safety in their handling. Fourthly, there are two conventions concerned with questions of liability: the 1976 Convention on Limitation of Liability for Maritime Claims (which, on its entry into force in 1986, replaced, as between parties to the Convention, the 1957 International Convention relating to the Limitation of the Liability of Owners of Sea-going Ships (which allowed a shipowner to limit his liability in relation to a variety of possible claims), in particular increasing the limits of shipowners' liability and making clear the circumstances in which a shipowner is not entitled to limit his liability), and the 1974 Convention relating to the Carriage of Passengers and their Luggage by Sea (which lays down uniform rules governing the liability of maritime carriers for death or injury of passengers and for damage or loss of luggage: in general liability is strict but limited). Finally, the IMO's Legal Committee has prepared a draft salvage convention (to replace the 1910 Convention on Salvage and Assistance at Sea) which is to be considered at a diplomatic conference in 1988 or 1989.

It should not be forgotten that there are also many non-IMO international conventions relating to shipping, the majority of which are concerned with private law aspects and thus are beyond the scope of this book. Many of these private law conventions have been adopted under the auspices of the International Maritime Committee.

Notes

1   The beneficial owner of a ship is defined by UNCTAD as the person or company which gains the pecuniary benefits from the operation of the ship. See UNCTAD, *Review of Maritime Transport, 1978*, New York, 1981, p. 11.
2   Not all writers accept that the three terms are synonymous: see, for example, D. H. N. Johnson, *op. cit.*, in 'Further reading'. Other writers have gone further and argued that the concept of nationality is inapplicable to ships and creates unnecessary difficulties: see, for example, R. Pinto, 87 *Journal du Droit International* 344–69 (1960). *O'Connell* goes in the same direction, arguing that it is difficult to attribute a coherent meaning to the expression 'nationality of a ship': see Vol. II, pp. 750–69, especially at 751–5. On the other hand, the High Seas Convention (art. 5(1)), the Law of the Sea Convention (art. 91) and the UN Convention on Conditions for Registration of Ships (discussed below)

(art. 4(2)) treat the flag State and State of nationality as synonymous, and the last-mentioned convention treats the flag State and State of registration as generally being identical (see, in particular, arts. 4 and 11).

3   2 *AJIL* 921 (1908) at 924.

4   For example, in the period 1980–83 the four largest flags of convenience accounted for twenty-seven per cent of the world shipping fleet but for 37 per cent of lost tonnage, while in 1985 1·9 and 0·7 per cent of the tonnage of Panama and Cyprus, respectively, was involved in serious incidents, compared with less than 0·1 per cent for Japan, the USSR and the United Kingdom. See *The Guardian*, 5 January 1987.

5   For details of the Liberian action, see D. W. Abecassis, *The Law and Practice relating to Oil Pollution from Ships*, 1st edition, London, 1978, pp. 56–7.

6   For details of this and other examples, see UNCLOS I, *Official Records*, Vol. IV, p. 138. It is also of interest to note that in December 1983 the UN Secretary-General sought the views of the Security Council on his intention to authorise the flying of the UN flag by ships evacuating members of the Palestine Liberation Organisation from Tripoli. See 3 *LOSB* 43 (1984).

7   Resolution A.212 (VII).

8   *IMCO News*, 1981, No. 4, p. 3.

9   IMO Assembly Resolution A.572 (XIV), Annex, para. 3.12.

10 IMO Assembly Resolutions A.339 (IX) (1975), A.480 (XII) (1981) and A.579 (XIV) (1985) on the Baltic; and A.375 (X) (1977) and A.476 (XII) (1981) on the Straits of Malacca.

11 Note also EEC Council Directive 79/116/EEC of December 1978 (*Official Journal of the European Communities (OJEC)*, 1979, L33/33), which obliges EEC Member States to ensure that all oil, gas and chemical tankers of 1,600 GRT or over using their ports give advance notification of certain information and make use of pilots where required. Also of interest is a French decree of 24 March 1978 which requires the captain of any oil tanker intending to enter France's territorial sea, or involved within fifty miles of the French coast in any accident likely to cause serious oil pollution, to notify the French authorities. A circular of the same date requires oil tankers to keep more than seven miles from the French coast unless using traffic separation or similar schemes or the approaches to ports approved for such vessels. See *Journal Officiel*, 26 March 1978, pp. 1338–9, reproduced in 82 *RGDIP* 744–46 (1978).

12 For examples, see Abecassis and Jarashow, *op. cit.*, in 'Further reading', pp. 446–7; and E. Gold and D. M. Johnston, 'Ship-generated pollution: the creator of regulated navigation' in T. A. Clingan (ed.), *Law of the Sea: State Practice in Zones of Special Jurisdiction*, Honolulu, Hawaii, 1982, p. 156 at 169–74.

13 IMO Assembly Resolution A.578 (XIV) (1985).

14 IMO Assembly Resolution A.381 (X). Subsequently replaced by IMO Assembly Resolution A.419 (XI) (1979).

15 XXI *ILM* 1 (1982). This memorandum replaces an earlier and less comprehensive memorandum of understanding signed at The Hague in March 1978 (text in Second Report from the Expenditure Committee, *op. cit.*, in 'Further reading', Vol. III, pp. 91–100) and appears to render obsolete an EEC draft directive on port State inspection (*OJEC*, 1980, C192/8). See A. V. Lowe, 6 *Marine Policy* 326–30 (1982).

16 *ACOPS Yearbook 1986–87*, p. 34.

17 Quoted in *IMO News*, 1986, No. 1, p. 16.

Further reading

General

E. Gold, *Maritime Transport*, Lexington, 1981.

C. Warbrick, 'The regulation of navigation', *ND* III, pp. 137–54.

Nationality of ships

B.A. Boczek, *Flags of Convenience. An International Legal Study*, Cambridge, Mass., 1962.

D. H. N. Johnson, 'The nationality of ships', 8 *Indian Yearbook of International Affairs* 3–15 (1959).

G. Marston, 'The UN Convention on the Registration of Ships', 20 *Journal of World Trade Law* 575–80 (1986).

H. Meyers, *The Nationality of Ships*, The Hague, 1967.

OECD, 'Study on flags of convenience', 4 *JMLC* 231–54 (1972).

E. Osieke, 'Flags of convenience vessels. Recent developments', 73 *AJIL* 604–27 (1979).

UN, *Laws concerning the Nationality of Ships*, UN Leg. Ser. B/5 (1956), and *Supplement*, UN Leg. Ser. B/8 (1959).

Rights of navigation

E. D. Brown, *Passage through the Territorial Sea, Straits used for International Navigation and Archipelagos*, London, 1973.

W. T. Burke, *Contemporary Law of the Sea. Transportation, Communication and Flight*, Law of the Sea Institute, University of Rhode Island, Occasional Paper No. 28, 1975.

R. J. Dupuy and D. Vignes (eds.), *Traité du Nouveau Droit de la Mer*, Paris, 1985, chapter 15.

W. Riphagen, 'La navigation dans le nouveau droit de la mer', in D. Bardonnet and M. Virally (eds.), *Le Nouveau Droit International de la Mer*, Paris, 1983, pp. 141–76.

I. A. Shearer, 'Problems of jurisdiction and law enforcement against delinquent vessels', 35 *ICLQ* 320–43 (1986).

Safety of shipping

D. W. Abecassis and R. L. Jarashow, *Oil Pollution from Ships*, 2nd ed., London, 1985, chapter 4.

A. Cockcroft and J. F. Lameijer, *A Guide to the Collision Avoidance Rules*, 3rd ed., London, 1982.

S. Mankabady, *The International Maritime Organisation*, 2nd ed., London, 1986.

E. Osieke, 'The International Labour Organisation and the control of sub-standard merchant vessels', 30 *ICLQ* 497–512 (1981).

Second Report from the Expenditure Committee, *Measures to Prevent Collisions and Strandings of Noxious Cargo Carriers in Waters around the United Kingdom*, House of Commons Paper (1978–79) 105 (especially the memorandum by Mrs P. W. Birnie, 'The legal regime for prevention of collisions and strandings of vessels carrying noxious or hazardous cargoes', Vol. I, pp. lix–xciv).

CHAPTER FOURTEEN
Fishing

Background to the international law of fisheries

In the period 1981–83 the total world marine fish catch averaged 66·4 million metric tonnes a year. A further 8·6 million metric tonnes were caught in inland waters. In the period 1948–52 the annual total world marine catch averaged 19·4 million tonnes, from 1958–62 34·0 and from 1968–72 57·5 million tonnes, so that since the Second World War there has been a steady increase. This increase is mainly due to two factors: technical improvements, such as sophisticated electronic fish-finding equipment, and greater investment in the fisheries of developing countries. While the rate of increase in the world catch has slowed down in recent years, mainly because most commercially exploitable fish stocks are now fully exploited, it has been estimated by FAO that with proper management the total catch could be increased to about 100 million tonnes a year, and if less familiar species such as krill become commercially exploitable the figure could be even higher.

The twenty leading fishing States by weight of catch, in the period 1981–83, are shown in table 4. The catches in the period 1973–75, the last three years before the general expansion to 200 mile fishing limits, are also shown by way of comparison. It is important to realise, however, that the monetary value of a catch is not necessarily proportionate to its weight. As with most areas of economic activity, fishing shows marked inequalities between States. The leading twenty States account for about eighty-two per cent of the total world catch, whereas the remaining eighteen per cent is shared between about 120 coastal States. Among the twenty leading States, developed States are less dominant than in, for example, shipping. As developing countries increase their investment in fisheries and improve their technology their share of the world catch will rise, while the catches of distant-water fishing States (i.e. those that fish predominantly off the coasts of other States, rather than their own coasts), which are mainly developed, are likely to decrease as the States off whose coasts they fish gain greater control over the fish stocks by means of 200 mile exclusive fishing zones

(EFZs) or EEZs. Nevertheless, for basic geographical and biological reasons, there will always remain substantial differences between the fish catches of States. First, the offshore zones of States, such as EFZs and EEZs, are of varying sizes. Secondly, fish are found in greatest abundance in the areas where there is most zooplankton, on which many species feed, directly or indirectly: these areas are the sub-tropical western coasts of America and Africa, along the Equator, temperate and sub-Arctic waters and shallow continental shelf waters.

One of the most important characteristics of fish is their migratory nature. Most fish stocks migrate often considerable distances during the course of their life cycle. This has important implications as far as jurisdictional boundaries in the sea are concerned. Furthermore, few, if any, fish stocks exist in isolation: most stocks are interrelated, either in the sense that one stock feeds on another (as seals do upon cod), or in that they inhabit the same area, so that fishermen intending to fish for one species will often take other species as by-catches. Thus regulations designed to deal with one particular stock may well have consequences for other stocks.

The principal and most obvious use of fish is as food for human consumption. Fish is an important source of animal protein, accounting for about twenty per cent of the total world supply, and contains important vitamins and minerals. Not all fish goes to human consumption, however. About twenty-eight per cent is converted into fishmeal or oil and used as fertiliser or animal feed. This is particularly the case with small species such as sand eels, capelin and Peruvian anchoveta, which are not easily processed for human consumption.

Before looking at the international law of fisheries it is necessary to examine a basic characteristic of marine fisheries which has profoundly influenced their regulation, both at the national and international level. Fisheries are a common property natural resource. In other words, free-swimming fish in the sea are not owned by anyone: property rights only arise when the fish are caught and reduced into the possession of an individual fisherman. It therefore follows that anyone can, in principle, fish in the sea. From the common property nature of marine fish, there follow four consequences of particular note as far as the regulation of marine fisheries is concerned — a tendency for fish stocks to be fished above biologically optimum levels; a tendency for more fishermen to engage in a fishery than is economically justified: a likelihood of competition and conflict between different groups of fishermen: and the necessity for any regulation of marine fisheries to have a substantial international component. Each of these consequences needs to be examined in a little more detail.

Because fish are a common property resource, anyone can enter a particular fishery. It obviously follows that as more fishermen enter the fishery, more and more fish will — initially at least — be caught. If the quantity of

Table 4. *Catches of the twenty leading fishing States*

	Average annual catch 1981–83 inclusive ('000 metric tonnes)	Average annual catch 1973–75 inclusive ('000 metric tonnes)
1. Japan	10,679·2	9,844·0
2. USSR	8,950·8	8,422·9
3. USA	3,894·6	2,746·4
4. Chile	3,678·6	898·3
5. China	3,246·9	3,020·5
6. Norway	2,607·6	2,656·7
7. Peru	2,551·1	3,300·8
8. South Korea	2,305·3	1,674·4
9. Denmark (including Faroes and Greenland)	2,238·4	1,981·5
10. Thailand	1,970·3	1,429·2
11. Indonesia	1,490·7	939·1
12. India	1,482·4	1,388·2
13. North Korea	1,465·0	931·7
14. Canada	1,333·0	984·6
15. Mexico	1,292·4	423·5
16. Spain	1,266·5	1,512·0
17. Philippines	1,248·3	1,161·9
18. Iceland	1,022·8	946·7
19. United Kingdom	874·1	1,058·0
20. France	770·5	790·3
Total, all States	66,352·7	57,144·5

Source: G. Pontecorvo, 'The impact of the Law of the Sea Treaty on the organisation of world fisheries: some preliminary observations', in E. D. Brown and R. R. Churchill (eds.), *The UN Convention on the Law of the Sea: Impact and Implementation*, Honolulu, Hawaii, 1987, pp. 143–4.

fish caught, together with fish lost through natural mortality, exceeds the amount of fish being added to the stock through reproduction, then the size of the stock will start to decrease: in extreme cases the stock may even collapse, as has happened with the Antarctic whales and the California sardine. This phenomenon is known as overfishing. Moreover, in the absence of any regulation, an individual fisherman has no incentive to restrain his activities in order to prevent overfishing because there is no guarantee that other fishermen will follow his example: indeed, the opposite is more likely to occur, for with one competitor removed there is more fish for those that remain. Thus, just as common land was over-grazed before the enclosure movement, so an unregulated fishery will normally lead to overfishing.

Thus to prevent overfishing it is usually necessary to regulate the amount of fish to be caught. To do this, it is necessary to know how much fish can be caught without overfishing resulting. As the result of research done by fisheries biologists, it is known that the growth of a particular fish stock is limited by environmental factors, such as the availability of food and the presence of natural predators, and that the stock will thus reach a particular size that cannot be exceeded. A stock which is not fished at all will tend to remain at this maximum size, and natural mortality and reproduction will balance out. Once the stock begins to be fished, however, its size will decrease. To recover its losses, the stock then starts growing at a rapid rate in an attempt to reach its original level. This rate of increase is greatest when a stock has been reduced to a particular size (which varies from stock to stock). It is at this level, which is known as the maximum sustainable yield (MSY), that the greatest quantity of fish can be caught year after year without the total size of the stock being adversely affected (assuming that environmental factors do not upset the balance).

Until thirty or so years ago MSY was frequently suggested as the principal objective of fisheries management, but over the past three decades its limitations have been increasingly revealed. First, ascertaining the MSY for a particular stock is by no means an easy task, even where the data exists (which is not always the case). Secondly, because of the inter-relationship of stocks (as explained above), it makes little sense to determine the MSY for each stock in isolation: if one stock is fished at the level of MSY, it may be impossible to achieve the level of MSY for a related stock. Thus it is desirable to establish fishing levels for inter-related stocks as a single exercise.

A second consequence of the common property nature of fish is that it leads to economic inefficiency. Typically a fishery will begin with few entrants, each of whom will make a profit. Other fishermen, seeing these profits, will be attracted to the fishery. As the number of fishermen participating in the fishery increases, so the size of catch — and hence economic return — per vessel will decrease. Thus, in the absence of any limitation on the number of fishermen entering a fishery, the economic return for each vessel will be below the optimum (or Maximum Economic Yield (MEY), as it is known) and indeed in the long term total revenue from the fishery will tend to equal the total cost of fishing. In other words, the same quantity of fish is caught as could be caught with substantially fewer vessels than those actually employed. This phenomenon is known as overcapacity (or over-capitalisation) and is found in most of the world's fisheries.

The third notable consequence of the fact that marine fish are a common property resource is the likelihood of competition and conflict between different groups of fishermen. It follows from the open access nature of fisheries that competition between fishermen is inevitable. Nor is such competition in itself necessarily harmful. Where it raises problems and may produce conflict is where competition is at such a level as to lead to overfishing and economic inefficiency. More directly, conflict may also arise between fishermen using different types of gear, notably where trawlers seek to fish in areas where there is stationary gear such as standing nets. Conflict may also arise between fishing and other uses of the sea, such as the offshore oil and gas industry and dredging for sand and gravel.

Finally, because much fishing takes place outside what has traditionally been regarded as the territory of States it follows that the problems discussed above must be regulated — in part at least — on the international level through co-operation between States and through the medium of international law. The international law regulating marine fisheries falls into two very distinct phases. The first is the period up to the middle 1970s, which was characterised by generally narrow coastal State maritime zones and a considerable amount of international co-operation in fisheries management through a score of international fishery commissions. The second phase is the period since the mid-1970s when broad coastal State zones in the form of 200 mile EFZs and EEZs, inspired by the work of UNCLOS III and embracing most commercially exploitable fish stocks, have become the norm, while the role of international fishery commissions has been significantly reduced.

We will examine each of these phases in turn, the first briefly, the second in more detail.

International fisheries law prior to the mid-1970s

International fisheries law in this period was concerned mainly with three questions — access to resources, conservation and the avoidance of conflicts between different types of fishing gear.

Access to resources

The way in which international law regulated access to fishery resources during this period is best understood by considering, first, the various jurisdictional zones of coastal States and, secondly, the regime of the high seas.

Internal waters and territorial sea. As we saw in chapters three and four, internal waters and the territorial sea form part of a State's territory and the only right which other States enjoy under general international law in these waters is a right of innocent passage in the territorial sea and, in very limited circumstances, in internal waters. It therefore follows that a State enjoys exclusive access to the fish stocks in its internal waters and territorial sea, unless a foreign State is accorded access by agreement (as under the EEC's Common Fisheries Policy): this, however, is most unusual in practice.

The exclusive fishery zone.   The exclusive fishery zone (EFZ) is a concept of relatively recent origin in the international law of the sea. While there had been a few claims to EFZs before 1958, notably the claims made in the late 1940s and early 1950s by some of the Pacific coast Latin American States to 200 mile zones, the EFZ is essentially a product of the failure of UNCLOS I and II to agree on the breadth of the territorial sea or to accord coastal States any special rights of access to fish stocks beyond the territorial sea. This failure led to a wave of unilateral claims by coastal States to twelve-mile EFZs (and some zones of greater breadth), a number of bilateral agreements recognising these claims, and at a regional level in Western Europe the Fisheries Convention of 1964. The development of this practice was such that, in the 1974 *Fisheries Jurisdiction* cases, the International Court of Justice had no hesitation in pronouncing that the twelve-mile EFZ had become established as a rule of customary international law. Within the EFZ the coastal State had exclusive or priority access to the resources of the zone, although in most cases States whose vessels had traditionally fished in the waters embraced by the new zones were given a period of time in which to phase out their activities and in some cases indefinite, though limited, continued access.

The continental shelf.   Articles 1–3 of the Convention on the Continental Shelf, which the International Court of Justice in the *North Sea Continental Shelf* cases (1969) said also represent customary international law, give the coastal State exclusive access to the natural resources of its continental shelf. These include 'living organisms belonging to sedentary species, that is to say, organisms which, at the harvestable stage, either are immobile on or under the seabed or are unable to move except in constant physical contact with the seabed or the subsoil' (CSC, art. 2(4)). While these sedentary species clearly include such things as oysters, clams and mussels, there has been considerable controversy as to whether they include creatures such as crabs and lobsters. Reference was made in chapter eight to some of the disputes that have arisen in this area.

High seas.   As we saw in chapter eleven, the high seas are not susceptible to appropriation and are open to use by all States. Thus the vessels of all States have access to the fish stocks of the high seas. However, this freedom of access is clearly of most benefit to those States that have the capital and technology to take advantage of it, that is, in the main, developed distant-water fishing nations. While access to the fishery resources of the high seas is in principle free and unrestricted, in practice many States have agreed, through arrangements regulating high-seas fisheries, to limit their access. These arrangements will be considered in the next section. A common consequence of freedom of fishing on the high seas, particularly where access is not limited through agreement, is that more vessels engage in fishing then is economically justifiable, i.e. fishing is often at a level considerably above the MEY.

In the *Fisheries Jurisdiction* cases, where the International Court of Justice was faced with determining the validity of Iceland's extension of its fishing limits in 1972 from twelve to fifty miles, the Court held that under customary international law a coastal State particularly dependent on fishing for its economic livelihood in certain circumstances enjoyed preferential rights of access to the high-seas fishery resources in the waters adjacent to its coasts. This finding by the International Court has been criticised because of the lack of evidence for and the imprecision of the alleged rule, and in practice no coastal State, either before or since the Court's judgment, has sought to rely on it.

Conservation

A regards conservation (i.e. the prevention of overfishing), the concern of international law was originally largely limited to allocating the competence to adopt conservation measures, but later international law became directly and increasingly concerned with substantive rules of conservation through the establishment of international fishery commissions and a number of *ad hoc* agreements regulating fishing.

As far as the competence to adopt conservation measures was concerned, this was distributed between coastal States, flag States and international fishery commissions. By virtue of the fact that internal waters and the territorial sea form part of its territory, a State has the competence to prescribe regulations governing fishing in those waters by vessels of whatever nationality and the competence to enforce such regulations. The coastal State has a similar competence in its EFZ and in respect of the sedentary species of its continental shelf. A flag State has the competence to prescribe fishery regulations for vessels flying its flag, wherever they may be. The flag State may take action to enforce such regulations, however, only on the high seas or in its own internal waters, territorial sea or EFZ. It thus follows that the only way in which regulations may be prescribed and enforced in respect of vessels fishing on the high seas is through flag States.

This division of jurisdictional competence between coastal States and flag States did not provide an adequate framework for effective conservation. Since in most areas of the world territorial seas and EFZs formed a rather narrow band of waters, coastal States had in practice control only over a comparatively small area containing rather limited fish stocks: furthermore, in many cases fish stocks which were found within their areas of control migrated outside those areas at certain times of the year. As far as flag States were concerned, while they alone could regulate fishing on the high seas, there was in practice little incentive for them to take conservation measures. If a flag State took measures to conserve a particular fish stock, those measures would not have any beneficial effect unless other flag States fishing the same stock took similar measures; but there was no way in which other flag States could be compelled to do so. The fact that article 2 of the High Seas Convention provides that the freedom of fishing on the high seas 'shall be exercised by all States with reasonable regard to the interests of other States in their exercise of the freedom of the high seas' appears in practice not to have been a factor encouraging flag States to take conservation measures, either singly or in concert, or restraining them from excessive fishing.

In order to try to overcome some of the drawbacks of flag State juris-diction and narrow coastal State jurisdiction — although, it must be em-phasised, without attempting to change the basic nature of the jurisdiction enjoyed by coastal and flag States or the distribution of jurisdiction between them — some twenty or more international fishery commissions were es-tablished, the vast majority since 1945. These commissions were either set up to regulate particular species (e.g. whales, seals, tuna) or to regulate fisheries in particular regions (e.g. the North Atlantic, the North Pacific, the Baltic, Mediterranean, etc.). The functions and powers of these com-missions varied considerably, but they all tended to have the same short-comings: the inability to agree on conservation measures recommended by scientists as essential; the possibility of opting out of any conservation mea-sures adopted; and poor enforcement of such measures. The last two tend to be self-perpetuating in the sense that if one State sees another not accept-ing a recommendation, or not properly enforcing it, there is no incentive for it to adhere to its obligations, since this will put its fishermen at a dis-advantage compared with the fishermen of the defaulting State. Finally, an international fishery commission cannot control the fishing activities of those States which are unwilling to become members of it.

Apart from international fishery commissions, there were a number of international agreements, largely of an *ad hoc* character, which attempted to conserve fisheries on the high seas. Most of these agreements were bi-lateral or regional, as well as often being short-term, in character, but there was one general multilateral agreement — the 1958 Convention on Fishing and Conservation of the Living Resources of the High Seas, adopted at UNCLOS I. This convention required States parties to it to agree upon measures to conserve the fishery resources of the high seas: in certain very limited circumstances it gave a coastal State the right unilaterally to adopt conservation measures for areas of the high seas adjacent to its territorial sea. However, the Convention largely proved to be a dead letter. Many major fishing nations did not ratify it, since it did not correspond to the interests of coastal States, and since in many regions international fishery commissions had already been set up to take conservation measures.

Avoidance of gear conflicts ✓ v.b.ried

The avoidance and resolution of conflicts arising out of fishing activities, particularly conflicts between different types of gear, such as the interference and damage trawling may cause to standing nets, have been the subject of a number of bilateral treaties and one regional agreement. The latter is the 1967 Convention on Conduct of Fishing Operations in the North Atlantic, which is aimed at preventing collisions between vessels while fishing and conflicts between trawling and the users of fixed gear, and at facilitating the resolution of disputes arising out of such collisions and conflicts. Of the bilateral agreements, one of the most important in practice and most sophisticated in the institutional machinery it provides for conflict resolution is the 1973 Agreement between the USSR and USA relating to the Consideration of Claims resulting from Damage to Fishing Vessels or Gear and Measures to Prevent Fishing Conflicts. These kinds of agreement are still important, although as the trend in the reduction of foreign fishing in the 200 mile zones of coastal States increases their practical application will decrease.

Developments since the mid-1970s

In spite of the considerable body of international fisheries law which had evolved by the early 1970s, there was much dissatisfaction with the regime for fisheries which this law had established. Most developing coastal States were resentful of the fact that the vessels of distant developed States, equipped with the latest technology, were catching fish a comparatively short distance from their coasts. Even if these States did not have adequate vessels of their own to fish their offshore waters, they wished at least to be able to control the activities of foreign operators and to be able to obtain some revenue through licence fees and to gain access to technological know-how. At the same time some developed coastal States were not happy with the existing legal regime, either because they wanted greater access to or more control over their offshore fishery resources, or because they were sceptical of the ability of international fishery commissions effectively to regulate fishing in the face of the increasing pressure on stocks resulting from ever more intensive methods of fishing. Many coastal States therefore seized the opportunity presented by the decision to convene UNCLOS III to press for a radical revision of the international legal regime governing fisheries.

The Sea Bed Committee and the earlier stages of UNCLOS III revealed three broad approaches to the question of fisheries. First, the developing countries, supported later by some developed countries such as Australia, Canada, New Zealand and Norway, advocated broad coastal State jurisdiction for fisheries, an idea which was subsequently developed and incorporated in proposals concerning the EEZ. The USA, and initially Canada, proposed an approach to fisheries management based on the migratory characteristics of different species. This proposal categorised fish into sedentary, coastal (i.e. non-sedentary species which inhabit nutrient-rich areas adjacent to the coast), anadromous and wide-ranging species: access to and management of the first three of these would vest exclusively or primarily in the coastal State, but wide-ranging species would be regulated by international fishery organisations. Finally, the two greatest traditional distant-water fishing nations, Japan and the USSR, wanted as little change in the *status quo* as possible, and proposed that only developing coastal States should enjoy preferential rights in the waters adjacent to their coasts.

The Law of the Sea Convention's provisions on fisheries generally reflect the first of these approaches, though elements of the species approach can also be seen. By 1976 the fisheries provisions of the UNCLOS negotiating texts had received very wide support, and before the conference ended had inspired a large amount of State practice in the form of claims to 200 mile EEZs and EFZs and bilateral and regional agreements. Thus although the Law of the Sea Convention is not yet in force, its provisions concerning fisheries have already had an enormous impact on State practice.

The core of the fisheries provisions of the Law of the Sea Convention is to be found in the articles dealing with the EEZ. The universal establishment of 200 mile EEZs and EFZs would embrace an area where over ninety per cent of commercial fishing currently takes place. Thus the regime for this area is obviously crucial to the proper management of marine fisheries.

The coastal State's rights and duties

Within the EEZ the coastal State has 'sovereign rights for the purpose of exploring and exploiting, conserving and managing' the fish stocks of the zone (LOSC, art. 56(1)). These rights are subject to a number of duties. The coastal State must take such conservation and management measures as will ensure that fish stocks in its EEZ are not endangered by over-exploitation, and that such stocks are maintained at or restored to 'levels which can produce the maximum sustainable yield, as qualified by relevant environmental and economic factors, ... and taking into account fishing patterns, the interdependence of stocks and any generally recommended' subregional, regional or global minimum standards (LOSC, art. 61 (3)). Subject to this, the coastal States is required to promote the objective of optimum utilisation of the living resources of its EEZ (LOSC, art. 62(1)). Finally, the coastal State is to establish the allowable catch (often referred to as the total allowable catch: TAC) for each fish stock within its EEZ (LOSC, art. 61(1)).

It can be seen that these duties are formulated in very broad and general terms and that the coastal State is given a very broad discretion, particularly in relation to setting the allowable catch, where the management objective of MSY is so heavily qualified that a coastal State could legitimately set practically any size of allowable catch, as long as it did not lead to over-exploitation which endangered fish stocks. This, and the fact that the coastal State's management duties are exempted from the provisions of the Convention dealing with compulsory settlement of disputes (except for compulsory conciliation in certain cases, see p. 338), has significant implications for the access of foreign fishermen, as will shortly be seen.

By 1987 some seventy-two States had claimed a 200 mile EEZ and a further fifteen States a 200 mile EFZ (as well as some claims to lesser breadths, and twelve 200 mile territorial sea claims: see Appendix). This practice, coupled with the absence of protest, suggests that there is now in customary international law a right to claim a 200 mile EEZ or EFZ (and see chapter nine, p. 146). What is much less certain is whether the coastal State's fishery management duties set out in articles 61 and 62 have become part of customary law. Relatively few States' national legislation refers to these duties. This may be, not because the duties are not accepted, but because these duties are not considered as an appropriate matter for legislation, since they relate to administrative practices. On the other hand, the duties may be too vague and insufficiently of a 'norm-creating character' to pass into customary law. In any case, even if the duties are customary rules, their vagueness, coupled with the possibility of factual disputes over such matters as the state of fish stocks, means that it is very difficult, if not impossible, to tell whether in any particular case the duties have been observed.

Access of foreign States to the EEZ

Article 62(2) provides that where its fishermen are not capable of taking the whole of the allowable catch, the coastal State is to permit the fishermen of other States to fish for the balance between what its fishermen take and the allowable catch. This obligation supports the objective of optimum utilisation mentioned above. The coastal State is given a broad discretion in deciding which other States' fishermen shall be given access to this surplus. Article 62(3) provides that in giving access,

the coastal State shall take into account all relevant factors, including *inter alia*, the significance of the living resources of the area to the economy of the coastal State concerned and its other national interests, the provisions of articles 69 and 70, the requirements of developing States in the subregion or region in harvesting part of the surplus and the need to minimise economic dislocation in States whose nationals have habitually fished in the Zone or which have made substantial efforts in research and identification of stocks.

Articles 69 and 70, which deal with landlocked and geographically disadvantaged States and are discussed in detail in chapter eighteen, in general give a guaranteed access for such States to a portion of any surplus, but other States are completely subject to the coastal State's discretion (which again is exempted from compulsory dispute settlement), particularly since by having the latitude described above in determining the allowable catch, the coastal State can also determine the size of any surplus (if any). Where the fishermen of third States are given access to any surplus, the coastal State can prescribe and enforce conditions to govern such fishing. These conditions may include, for example, requiring foreign fishermen to have licences, to observe the coastal State's conservation measures, to carry out research programmes, to land part or all of their catches in the coastal State, and to train coastal State personnel (LOSC, arts. 62(4), 73).

State practice concerning the access of foreign fishermen to the EEZ, found not only in the legislation of States claiming an EEZ but also in over 300 bilateral agreements, displays considerable diversity and some divergence from the Convention's provisions. In some cases foreign vessels are given access even where there is no surplus: thus, for example, the EEC (which in relation to fisheries agreements has replaced its Member States) and Norway give each other reciprocal access to their waters in order that previous fishing patterns should not be disrupted too severely by the introduction of 200 mile limits. Some States make access contingent upon being granted trade concessions (as Canada does with the EEC, and the USA does with a number of States); or upon the payment of financial compensation in addition to licence fees (as several African States do with the EEC); or upon the establishment of joint ventures with coastal State companies or other forms of economic co-operation (as some Latin American and African States do). In many of these cases the agreements concerned make no reference to the existence of any surplus. While there may be a rule of customary international law that coastal States must give foreign vessels access where there is a surplus (academic opinion is divided on this question), the diversity of practice is such that it is unlikely that there is any customary rule requiring coastal States to give access to any particular category of State (which, indeed, is also the position under the Convention).

The management of shared and straddling stocks

The Law of the Sea Convention conveys the impression that most fish stocks confine themselves to the EEZ of a single coastal State. In fact in some areas, such as the North-East and East Central Atlantic, this is very far from being the case; many stocks migrate between the EEZs of two or more States (usually known as shared or joint stocks) and/or the waters beyond (straddling stocks). The Convention contains one brief provision dealing with this situation. Article 63 exhorts the States concerned (which in the case of straddling stocks include States fishing on the high seas for such stocks) to agree upon the measures necessary for the conservation of such stocks. Nothing further is said, for example, about management objectives or allocation of the catch among interested States. Instead it has been left to States to work out arrangements for the management of shared and straddling stocks. A number of agreements on this question now exist, particularly in the North Atlantic. Examples of the management of shared stocks are the series of annual arrangements agreed by the EEC and Norway under their 1980 Fisheries Agreement, whereby they set a total allowable catch based on the recommendations of the International Council for the Exploration of the Sea for their shared stocks in the North Sea and allocate this on the basis of the proportion of the stock of catchable size found in each party's zone; and the annual arrangements agreed by Norway and the USSR under their 1976 Fisheries Agreement for shared stocks in the Barents Sea, where again a total allowable catch is set, although the criterion for allocation is different, being in fixed percentages, the figures varying from one species to another. An example of an agreement providing for the management of straddling stocks is the Convention on Future Multilateral Co-operation in the North West Atlantic Fisheries (1978), which provides that the Commission established by the Convention and the coastal States of the north-west Atlantic are to coordinate management measures in regard to migrating stocks.

The regulation of fishing beyond the 200 mile zone

While the overwhelming majority of the world's fish stocks are to be found within 200 miles of land, the Law of the Sea Convention also contains provisions governing fishing on the high seas. Here fishing is in principle open to all States, apart from the restrictions arising out of the rules relating to particular species mentioned below (arts. 87 and 116). Nevertheless, articles 117–120 lay down a duty on interested States to co-operate in the management and conservation of high seas fishery resources, making use, where appropriate, of international fishery commissions. The aim of such management should be to 'maintain or restore populations of harvested species at levels which can produce the maximum sustainable yield, as qualified by relevant environmental and economic factors, including the special requirements of developing States, and taking into account fishing patterns, the interdependence of stocks and any generally recommended international minimum standards' (art. 119 (1)). Any conservation measures adopted should not discriminate in form or in fact against the fishermen of any State.

In the past few years many fishery commissions responsible for managing high seas fisheries have had their functions adapted to take into account the developments in fisheries law resulting from UNCLOS. This has been done either by amending the convention establishing the commission e.g. the

Protocol of 1978 amending the International Convention for the High Seas
Fisheries of the North Pacific Ocean 1952, which established the Inter-
national North Pacific Fisheries Commission; or by establishing a new
Commission to replace an existing body, e.g. the Convention on Future
Multilateral Co-Operation in the Northwest Atlantic Fisheries (1978),
which set up the Northwest Atlantic Fisheries Organisation (NAFO) to
replace the International Commission for the Northwest Atlantic Fisheries;
and the Convention on Future Multilateral Co-Operation in the North-
East Atlantic Fisheries (1980), which set up a new North-East Atlantic
Fisheries Commission to replace the original Commission of this name. Of
these new or amended international fishery commissions, the role and
functions of NAFO are typical. Its main functions are to manage the fishery
resources of the Northwest Atlantic found beyond 200 mile limits, to co-
operate with coastal States over the management of stocks that migrate
between their 200 mile zones and the high seas, and co-ordinate scientific
research. To this end NAFO has adopted quotas, conservation measures
such as minimum mesh sizes and by-catch levels, and, more unusually, a
scheme of joint international enforcement.

Rules for particular species

The rules of the Law of the Sea Convention so far expounded are considerably modified in the case of anadromous, catadromous, sedentary and
highly migratory species and marine mammals. In the case of *anadromous
species*, i.e. species such as salmon which spawn in fresh water but spend
most of their life in the sea, the State in whose rivers such fish spawn (the
State of origin) is primarily responsible for their management. This State
can establish total allowable catches and admit foreign States to its EEZ to
fish for any surplus there may be, but it is not obliged to do so. Furthermore, fishing for anadromous species beyond 200 mile limits is forbidden
except where this would result in 'economic dislocation' for a State other
than the State of origin. Where high seas fishing is permitted, the States
concerned are to agree on the terms and conditions of such fishing (art.
66). These provisions are the result of proposals put forward by two of the
main States of origin — Canada and the USA. They argued that since the
State of origin may be required to expend money to ensure the continued
propagation of salmon, e.g. by reducing pollution in rivers or by providing
salmon ladders, it should be entitled to the whole or at least the greater
part of the fruits of its expenditure. The Convention's provisions on anadromous species have been implemented in the 1982 Convention for the Conservation of Salmon in the North Atlantic Ocean, which prohibits fishing
for salmon on the high seas, and even within 200 mile zones prohibits fishing
in most areas beyond twelve miles. It establishes a North Atlantic Salmon

Conservation Organisation through which co-operation over the conservation and management of North Atlantic salmon is to take place. In relation to the North Pacific Canada and the USA signed a Treaty concerning Pacific Salmon in 1985. The aims of this Treaty are to 'prevent overfishing and provide for optimum production' and to 'provide for each Party to receive benefits equivalent to the production of salmon originating in its waters'. To assist in realising these aims the Treaty establishes a Pacific Salmon Commission.

In the case of *catadromous species*, i.e. species such as eels which spawn at sea but spend most of their lives in fresh water, the general rules governing fishing in the EEZ apply, but are supplemented by an obligation on coastal States through whose EEZs catadromous species migrate to co-operate over management (including harvesting) of these species with the State in whose waters the species spend the greater part of their life cycle: the latter State has overall management responsibility for these species. Fishing for catadromous species on the high seas is prohibited (art. 67). In practice the management of catadromous species appears to have raised few problems.

In relation to *sedentary species*, which, as we have seen earlier, are considered to be part of the natural resources of a coastal State's continental shelf, the coastal State is under no obligation to take any management or conservation measures, nor to accommodate foreign fishermen (art. 68).

In the case of *highly migratory species*, such as tuna, which are listed in Annex 1 of the Convention, the coastal State's normal fishery management functions are supplemented by an obligation to co-operate with other interested States in conservation and to promote the objective of optimum utilisation both within and beyond the EEZ, either directly or through arrangements such as regional fishery commissions, which are either already in existence (such as the Atlantic and Inter-American Tuna Commissions), or are to be specially created (art. 64). The application of these provisions has given rise to particular problems in the Pacific. The USA has, since the enactment of its Fisheries Conservation and Management Act in 1976, maintained, contrary to the Convention, that the coastal State has no jurisdiction over tuna (although the USA accepts that the coastal State has jurisdiction over highly migratory species other than tuna), and its fishermen have fished for tuna without permission in the 200 mile zones of many of the small Pacific island States, for which tuna is a major resource. This has led to seizures of US vessels and the imposition of economic embargoes by the USA in retaliation. This dispute appears at last to have been settled with the signature in April 1987 of a Treaty on Fisheries by the USA and twelve Pacific Island States. On entry into force the Treaty will permit US vessels to fish under licence for tuna in an area of some ten million square miles in the South Pacific. A similar dispute with various Eastern Pacific

States will be resolved if and when the Eastern Pacific Ocean Tuna Fishing Agreement, signed in March 1983, comes into force. Under that Agreement tuna fishermen would buy an annual licence permitting them to fish in the area covered by the Agreement (which includes 200 mile zones).

Finally, in the case of *marine mammals* (whales, seals, sirenians), the coastal State is entitled to limit or prohibit the exploitation of such species rather than establishing an allowable catch and promoting the objective of optimum utilisation (art. 65). In accordance with this provision, some States, such as Australia, the United Kingdom and the USA, have prohibited whaling in their 200 mile zones. International organisations may also limit or prohibit exploitation of marine mammals, both within and beyond the EEZ (arts. 65 and 120). States are to co-operate in the conservation of marine mammals, and in the case of cetaceans are to work through the appropriate international organisations, principally the International Whaling Commission (IWC), for their conservation, management and study. The IWC has had a rather chequered history. Set up in 1948, it failed during the first twenty-five years of its existence to prevent the overfishing and near extinction of many whale species, largely because quotas were set too high, were set in standard units (blue whale units) rather than for individual species, and were not allocated among interested States. In 1974 a new management policy was adopted which led to rather better management: in particular, catching of all but the five most populous species was prohibited. Since 1980 many small non-whaling States have joined the IWC, and as a result of this development and pressure from environmental groups, the IWC in 1982 adopted a prohibition on all commercial whaling from 1986. This measure was objected to, and therefore under the IWC Convention not binding on, Japan, Norway and the USSR. However, each of these States has subsequently announced that it will cease commercial whaling after 1988. Some other States, such as Iceland, have sought to get round the ban by engaging in relatively large-scale whaling under the spurious pretext of scientific research, catches for which are exempt from the ban. A further circumvention of the ban occurs through the use of vessels registered in flag of convenience States which are not parties to the IWC. The effectiveness of the ban is to be reviewed by the IWC in 1990.

Conclusions

The result of the changes in international fisheries law that have occurred since the mid- or late 1970s due to UNCLOS III and State practice is that fishing has moved from an era of limited international regulation to an era where it is regulated largely by coastal States. It is too soon to say whether this new pattern of regulation will lead to a more effective management of fishery resources than under the old regime. It certainly has the potential to do so. It avoids the shortcomings of the former law, but much will depend on the measures and attitudes taken by coastal States, not only in adopting and enforcing effective management programmes for their waters but also in co-operating with their neighbours. The need for such co-operation is particularly important in areas such as the north-east and east central Atlantic, where numerous fish stocks migrate during their life cycle through the waters of several different States. Furthermore, many developing States require help in building up the necessary expertise to manage their fisheries, as well as the necessary investment and technology to exploit them fully. In this area considerable assistance is being provided under FAO's EEZ Programme. Joint ventures may also prove useful, as well as alleviating the problems of distant-water fishing States.

The new fisheries regime is leading, as pointed out at the end of chapter nine, to a redistribution in fish catches from traditional distant-water fishing States to coastal States. By changing the status of those areas of high seas richest in fish to EEZ, the new regime makes possible a move from a free-for-all where much destructive and uneconomic fishing took place to a situation where greater regulation allows the coastal State, if it wishes, to introduce a greater economic rationality into fishing operations. Few States, however, are likely to make the maximum economic yield the goal of their fisheries management: in most cases economic rationalism will be tempered by the needs of local communities dependent on fishing and nutritional requirements. As ever, proper fisheries management depends on adequate scientific research. It is very much to be hoped that the new controls on scientific research introduced by the Law of the Sea Convention, which are discussed in chapter sixteen, will not hamper the research essential to good fisheries management.

Further reading

The regime prior to the mid-1970s
F. T. Christy and A. Scott, *The Common Wealth in Ocean Fisheries*, Baltimore, Md., 1965.

D. J. Driscoll and N. McKellar, 'The changing regime of North Sea fisheries', in C. M. Mason (ed.), *The Effective Management of Resources*, London, 1979, pp. 126–167.

J. A. Gulland, *The Management of Marine Fisheries*, Bristol, 1974.

D. M. Johnston, *The International Law of Fisheries*, New Haven, Conn., 1965.

H. G. Knight, *Managing the Sea's Living Resources*, Lexington, Ky., 1977.

A. W. Koers, *International Regulation of Marine Fisheries*, London. 1973.

The new regime
D. Attard, *The Exclusive Economic Zone in International Law*, Oxford, 1987, chapters five and six.

P. Birnie, *International Regulation of Whaling*, New York, 1985.

W. T. Burke, 'The Law of the Sea Convention and fishing practices of non-signatories, with special reference to the United States', in J. M. Van Dyke (ed.), *Consensus and Confrontation: The United States and the Law of the Sea Convention*, Honolulu, Hawaii, 1985, pp. 314–37.

W. T. Burke, 'Highly migratory species in the new law of the sea', 14 *ODIL* 273–314 (1984).

J. E. Carroz, 'Institutional aspects of fishery management under the new regime of the oceans', 21 *San Diego Law Review* 513–40 (1984).

J. E. Carroz, 'Les problèmes de la pêche à la Conférence sur le droit de la mer et dans la pratique des Etats', 84 *RGDIP* 705–51 (1980). Revised version in D. Bardonnet and M. Virally (eds.), *Le nouveau droit international de la mer*, Paris, 1983, pp. 177–229.

J. E. Carroz and M. J. Savini, 'The new international law of fisheries emerging from bilateral agreements', 3 *Marine Policy* 79–98 (1979).

P. Copes, 'The impact of UNCLOS III on management of the world's fisheries', 5 *Marine Policy* 217–28 (1981).

M. Dahmani, *The Fisheries Regime of the Exclusive Economic Zone*, Dordrecht, 1987.

W. R. Edeson and J-F. Pulvenis, *The Legal Regime of Fisheries in the Caribbean Region*, Berlin, 1983.

FAO, *Legislation on Coastal State Requirements for Foreign Fishing*, FAO Legislative Study No. 21, 2nd revision, Rome, 1986.

FAO, *Report of the Expert Consultation on the Conditions of Access to the Fish Resources of the Exclusive Economic Zones*, FAO Fisheries Report No. 293, Rome, 1983.

D. M. Johnston (ed.), *The Environmental Law of the Sea*, Berlin, 1981, especially chapter two.

J. L. Meseguer, 'Le régime juridique de l'exploitation des stocks conjoints de poissons au-delà de 200 milles', 28 *AFDI* 885–99 (1982).

G. Moore, 'National legislation for the management of fisheries under extended coastal State jurisdiction', 11 *JMLC* 153–82 (1980).

OECD, *Experiences in the Management of National Fishing Zones*, Paris, 1984.

J-P. Troadec, *Introduction to Fisheries Management*, FAO Fisheries Technical Paper No. 224, Rome, 1983.

G. Ulfstein, '200 mile zones and fisheries management', 52 *Nordisk Tidsskrift for International Ret* 3–33 (1983).

CHAPTER FIFTEEN
Marine pollution

Introduction

In March 1967 the *Torrey Canyon*, a 118,000 ton oil tanker registered in Liberia, ran aground on the Seven Stones Reef, a few miles from Land's End, and broke up, spilling about 100,000 tons of crude oil into the sea. Eleven years later the *Amoco Cadiz*, another and much larger Liberian tanker, drifted on to the coast of Brittany following the breakdown of her steering gear, and discharged 210,000 tons of crude oil into the sea. Oil pollution comes not only from ships. In April 1977 a blow-out occurred in an oil well in the Ekofisk field in the Norwegian sector of the North Sea. It took eight days to stop the blow-out and bring it under control, by which time about 30,000 tons of crude oil and $1\cdot7$ Nm^3 of gas had escaped. A similar, but much worse, blow-out occurred two years later in the Ixtoc I well on the Mexican continental shelf off the Yucatan peninsula: this time it was over nine months before the blowout was finally brought under control, and about 400,000 tons of oil were lost.

Oil is not the only serious marine pollutant. From time to time the United Kingdom and some other Western European States have disposed of some of the radioactive waste matter from their nuclear power stations by putting it into special containers and dumping the containers in the Atlantic: whether these containers will last as long as their contents remain radioactive is still to be seen. Another pollutant is DDT, which has for many years been used as a pesticide by farmers. Some of the DDT finds its way to the sea, either via rivers or rainfall, where it is absorbed by marine life such as shellfish, fish and sea birds: even penguins in the Antarctic have been found to contain DDT.

These, and many more, instances have in recent years alerted policy-makers, legislators and the public generally to the growing problem of marine pollution. In this chapter we examine the response of international law to this problem. As the above examples show, marine pollution originates from a number of different sources, marine pollutants are many and varied in their effects, and pollution may be both accidental and deliberate. Before we consider the detailed rules of international law relating to marine pollution, we shall say something about the different sources of this pollution, the principal kinds of marine pollutants and the general framework of international law in this area. At the outset, however, it is desirable to try to state more precisely what is meant by marine pollution. This term has been defined by UNESCO's Inter-governmental Oceanographic Commission and the UN's Group of Experts on the Scientific Aspects of Marine Pollution as:

Introduction by man, directly or indirectly, of substances or energy into the marine environment (including estuaries) resulting in such deleterious effects as harm to living resources, hazard to human health, hindrance to marine activities including fishing, impairment of quality for use of sea water and reduction of amenities.[1]

A very similar definition is found in the Law of the Sea Convention (art. 1) and a number of other conventions concerned with marine pollution. As this definition suggests, it is not the aim of international law to prevent all substances being added to the sea — many substances are harmless or are rapidly rendered so by the sea — but only those which have deleterious effects. For this very reason, the definition has sometimes been criticised for not taking sufficient account of the need to prevent changes in the marine environment as such, and apart from any immediately identifiable deleterious effects.

Sources of marine pollution

Shipping. There are four main sources of marine pollution: shipping, dumping, sea-bed activities and land activities. As far as shipping is concerned, some pollution results from the operation of ships. Ships which are driven by oil-burning diesel engines (the vast majority) may discharge some oil with their bilge water; and the fumes discharged through their funnels into the atmosphere will eventually return to the sea. Some ships other than oil tankers also use their fuel tanks for ballast water and subsequently may discharge this oily ballast water into the sea. The few nuclear-powered ships (mainly submarines) may also cause some pollution. All ships, however propelled, will pollute the sea if they throw their garbage overboard or discharge their sewage directly into the sea. By far the greatest amount of pollution from ships, however, comes from their cargoes. Oil, the commodity which is transported most extensively by sea, is often deliberately discharged at sea, notably when seawater which has been pumped into an empty oil tanker to clean out the tanks or serve as ballast is later pumped out again. This practice is gradually declining as more tankers come to use the 'load on top' system (see below). Some oil, as well as other noxious cargoes like chemicals, liquid gas and radioactive matter, enter the sea as a result of accidents, such as collisions, strandings and explosions, as happened in the case of the *Torrey Canyon* and *Amoco Cadiz*. The growing number of ships, which we noted in chapter thirteen, has increased the risk of such accidents, and the trend to larger ships makes the result of any accident more serious.

Dumping. In the 1950s and 1960s dumping at sea became an increasingly popular way of disposing of waste resulting from land-based activities. This was partly because of its relative cheapness and ease, and partly as a reaction to the tightening up of pollution controls on land. The main kinds of waste dumped include radioactive matter, military materials (including obsolete weapons and explosives), dredge spoils, sewage sludge and industrial waste, which contains a variety of different pollutants, many of them highly toxic. Although waste is dumped from ships, international conventions treat dumping as a source of pollution separate from shipping. This is partly because dumping, unlike other pollution from ships, is always deliberate and usually the *raison d'être* of a particular voyage, and partly because dumping is an extension of pollution from land (although it has to be considered separately from land-based sources because the areas where dumping takes place are obviously juridically different from land).

Sea-bed activities. As far as installations for exploring and exploiting oil and gas from the sea bed are concerned, little deliberate pollution results from such structures, except for the disposal into the sea of domestic refuse, industrial debris and small amounts of oily and chemical wastes. Accidental pollution may result from blow-outs (as in the case of the Ekofisk and Ixtoc wells mentioned above); from collisions between ships and installations; or from the breaking of pipelines, either through natural wear and tear or through being fouled by a trawl. Some pollution may result from the mining of manganese nodules in the international sea bed area, but until commercial production begins it is difficult to assess what the impact of this will be.

Land-based and atmospheric pollution. The last source — but far and away the most important, accounting for about three-quarters of all marine pollution — is the polluting matter entering the sea from land. This includes sewage and industrial wastes discharged into rivers or directly into the sea; chemicals used as fertilisers and pesticides in agriculture running off from the land into rivers; warm water from power stations (some of them nuclear) built on coasts and estuaries; and discharges into the atmosphere of vehicle exhaust, fumes from chimneys (domestic and factory) and sprayed agricultural chemicals, all of which may eventually be precipitated into the sea.

The primary approach of administrators and legislators has generally been to tackle the problems of marine pollution according to the source of such pollution, rather than dealing with the problems according to the nature of particular pollutants. The differing jurisdictional natures of land and sea make such an approach readily understandable. At the same time, however, whatever the particular source of marine pollution, attention has concentrated on tackling the more noxious and the more visible — which is not always the same — pollutants. It is therefore necessary to say a few words about some of the more serious of the many marine pollutants.

Marine pollutants

Although oil is the marine pollutant which has received most attention from legislators and attracted most public concern (perhaps because it is the most frequently obvious and visible pollutant), it is not the most noxious of marine pollutants, partly because it is eventually broken down by marine bacteria. Before it is so broken down, however, oil can cause great damage, fouling beaches and killing sea birds, fish and other marine life. Even if they are not killed by the oil, fish can suffer damage in other ways — for example, skin cancer or disequilibrium — and shellfish are rendered inedible. Oil spills can to some extent be dealt with, either by keeping the oil together by means of booms and skimming it off the surface of the sea, or by dispersing it with chemicals. The former method can never be more than partially successful and can be used only when the sea is comparatively calm, while in the latter case the chemicals employed are sometimes as toxic as the oil they disperse.

Unlike oil, chlorinated hydrocarbons (such as DDT and polychlorinated biphenyls (PCBs)), heavy metals (such as lead, mercury and cadmium) and radioactive wastes are not biodegradable, nor is there any possibility of removing them from the sea once they have entered it. These substances vary in their effect, but in general they are absorbed by marine organisms, often becoming concentrated as they move up the food chain, and affecting the growth, reproduction and mortality of marine life. In some cases it is unsafe for humans to eat fish containing these substances: for example, in the 1950s in Minamata Bay in Japan forty-three people died and many more suffered blindness, muscular weakness and brain damage after eating mercury-contaminated fish.

Sewage in small amounts is broken down by the sea and rendered innocuous, but large amounts lead to overfertilisation, followed by de-composition and de-oxygenation of the water. This effect is particularly marked in enclosed seas such as the Baltic. When water is de-oxygenated, the eggs of fish will not hatch, fish larvae are unable to develop and adult fish move to more richly oxygenated waters. Sewage can also cause tides of toxic phytoplankton (which may kill or damage marine life), and contaminate seawater used for swimming and other recreational uses with micro-organisms dangerous to man.

The framework of international law relating to marine pollution

Custom. Customary international law contains few rules relevant to the question of marine pollution. In the *Corfu Channel* case (1949) the International Court of Justice said that each State was under an obligation 'not to allow knowingly its territory to be used for acts contrary to the rights of other States';[2] and in the *Trail Smelter arbitration* (1938–41), a case involving damage to property in the USA caused by noxious fumes emitted by a smelter in Canada, the arbitral tribunal held that 'no State has the right to use or permit the use of its territory in such a manner as to cause injury by fumes in or to the territory of another' State.[3] Article 2 of the High Seas Convention, which is stated to be declaratory of customary international law, provides that States must exercise the freedoms of the high seas 'with reasonable regard to the interests of other States in their exercise of the freedom of the high seas'. It could be argued that, taking the principles enunciated in Article 2 and in the *Corfu Channel* case together and extending the principle in the *Trail Smelter* case by analogy, there is a general rule of customary international law that States must not permit their nationals to discharge into the sea matter that could cause harm to the nationals of other States. However, this rule appears to be too vague to be very effective, and certainly would seem incapable of being developed, given the nature of customary international law, into the detailed emission standards or liability regimes that are required.

Customary international law also defines the extent of States' legislative and enforcement jurisdiction, a question which, as we shall see, is particularly important as far as marine pollution is concerned. However, the customary rules on jurisdiction have been considered by many States to be both inadequate and incapable of sufficiently speedy or extensive development to sustain effective action against pollution. One State taking this view is Canada. In 1970 the Canadian Parliament, alarmed at the possible harm to the delicate Arctic environment which might result from the passage of oil tankers through Arctic waters, passed the Arctic Waters Pollution Prevention Act, which prohibits all pollution and regulates shipping within 100 miles of Canada's Arctic coasts. The USA protested that the Act was an infringement of the freedoms of the high seas.[4]

Treaties. Given these deficiencies of customary international law, it is not surprising to find that the international law relating to marine pollution is contained almost wholly in treaties, of which there is now a considerable number. The first of these treaties was adopted in 1954 — although a draft treaty dealing with oil pollution from ships was drawn up in 1926 but was never opened for signature. Little attention was paid to pollution at UNCLOS I, apart from the general obligations imposed on States to prevent marine pollution by oil and radioactive waste, in articles 24 and 25 of the High Seas Convention; but since 1969, in response to growing international concern over pollution of the marine environment, a steady stream of treaties has been concluded.

Marine pollution treaties can be divided into four categories: general multilateral treaties, regional treaties, bilateral treaties and the Law of the Sea Convention. Of the general multilateral treaties, there are some half a dozen concerned with pollution from ships (details of which are given in the next section) and one concerned with dumping. There are no general multilateral treaties dealing with marine pollution from land-based sources or sea-bed activities. The treaties concerned with pollution from ships were all adopted under the auspices of the IMO and the IMO exercises certain supervisory functions in the relation to them.

At the regional level there are a number of treaties dealing with all the sources of marine pollution within a single framework treaty. Such treaties have been adopted for the Baltic,[5] Mediterranean,[6] Arabian/Persian Gulf and Gulf of Oman,[7] West Africa,[8] South-East Pacific,[9] Red Sea and Gulf of Aden,[10] Caribbean,[11] East Africa[12] and South Pacific:[13] many of these areas are suffering particularly badly from the effects of marine pollution. With the exception of the Baltic Convention, the initiative for these agreements has largely come from, and much of the preparatory work has been done by, the United Nations Environment Programme (UNEP), as part of its Regional Seas Programme, and to a rather more limited extent the IMO. Each of the agreements is accompanied by an Action Plan. Such Plans have also been adopted for the East Asian and South Asian Seas, although there are not (as yet) any legal instruments accompanying them. In the north-east Atlantic and North Sea there is no equivalent single framework convention, but a number of *ad hoc* agreements have been adopted, dealing with co-operation in oil pollution emergencies,[14] dumping,[15] land-based sources[16] and liability for pollution resulting from sea-bed activities.[17] On a smaller scale, the four Nordic States (Denmark, Finland, Norway and Sweden) have concluded two agreements dealing with marine pollution,[18] while France, Italy and Monaco in 1976 signed an Agreement relating to the Protection of the Waters of the Mediterranean Coast.

In a number of cases States have also found it desirable to conclude bilateral agreements to deal with more specific or local questions of marine pollution. Thus, for example, Italy and Yugoslavia have signed an Agreement on Co-operation for the Protection of the Waters of the

Adriatic Sea and Coastal Zones from Pollution (1974); Denmark and Sweden an Agreement concerning Protection of the Sound from Pollution (1974); Canada and the USA an Agreement relating to the Establishment of Joint Pollution Contingency Plans for Spills of Oil and other Noxious Substances (1974); and Canada and Denmark an Agreement for Co-operation relating to the Marine Environment (1983).

In view of this extensive treaty action, it was not necessary for UNCLOS III to consider detailed standards relating to marine pollution, nor perhaps would the conference have been well suited to the elaboration of such technically complex matters. Instead, having for the first time laid down a general duty to protect and preserve the marine environment (LOSC, art. 192, *et seq.*) from pollution from all sources (LOSC, arts. 207–12), the conference concentrated on defining the jurisdictional rights and obligations, both legislative and enforcement, of flag, coastal and port States. Provisions on these matters are now found in articles 207–34 and 236 of the Law of the Sea Convention. The remainder of the articles in Part XII (Protection and Preservation of the Marine Environment) deal with general principles (arts. 192–6), global and regional co-operation (arts. 197–201), technical assistance (arts. 202–3), monitoring and environmental assessment (arts. 204–6) and responsibility and liability (art. 235).

The achievement in negotiating all the treaties mentioned above and bringing most of them into force should not be underestimated, for the conclusion of marine pollution treaties raises many economic, technical and political difficulties. The adoption of stricter anti-pollution standards usually means increased costs for industry and shipowners. States are therefore reluctant to accept stricter anti-pollution standards unless other States do the same, lest their shipping and other industries lose their competitive edge. More broadly, developing States are reluctant to accept strict anti-pollution standards which they consider may hinder their industrial development, when in their view — and rightly — it is the developed States which are responsible for most marine pollution. As far as technical difficulties are concerned, there is little point in setting emission standards with which present-day technology cannot ensure compliance: on the other hand, emission standards ought to be set at the level of the most technologically advanced industry. Furthermore, the prohibition or limitation of one particular type of marine pollution should not lead to that pollution being diverted elsewhere so as to cause as great or greater harm to the environment, a problem recognised by the Law of the Sea Convention (see art. 195).

It is encouraging to see that in some areas the problems of marine pollution have led to States which can agree on little else agreeing on regional conventions to prevent marine pollution. Thus both Israel and its Arab neighbours, as well as Greece and Turkey, are parties to the

Mediterranean Convention; and both Iran and the Arab States of the Gulf have signed the Kuwait Convention. Nevertheless, there is no room for complacency. In the case of most marine pollutants there is a considerable lapse of time between the action being taken to control pollution and that action having any significant effect.

Having looked at the general framework of international law relating to marine pollution, we must now consider its provisions in more detail, looking in turn at each of the different sources of pollution.

Pollution from ships

Pollution from shipping raises a number of questions: standards to reduce or eliminate pollution; the prescription and enforcement of such standards; measures to avoid accidental pollution; action taken by coastal States against pollution casualties; co-operation in dealing with emergencies; and liability for pollution damage. We shall consider each of these points in turn.

Standards to reduce or eliminate intentional pollution
The 1954 Oil Pollution Convention. The first pollutant for which international control standards were set was oil. When an oil tanker has discharged its cargo of oil a certain amount of the oil remains clinging to the tanks. This oil has to be disposed of before a new cargo can be taken on board.[19] One way of doing this is for tankers to wash out their empty tanks at sea. In addition, empty tankers also use sea water as ballast, and this water, containing residues of oil, has of course to be pumped out before a new cargo can be taken on board. Other ships also use sea water as ballast in their empty fuel tanks, and this too is eventually pumped out. Ships which use heavy oils as fuel accumulate oily sludges which eventually have to be disposed of. In each of these different ways oil may enter the sea. It was to deal with these forms of marine pollution that the International Convention for the Prevention of Pollution of the Sea by Oil was drawn up in 1954. In its original form the Convention prohibited the discharge of oil and any oily mixture having an oil content of more than 100 parts per million within fifty miles of land and in certain special areas such as the North Sea, Baltic and Black Sea (art. III and Annex A), although in the case of ships other than tankers this prohibition did not apply if the ship was making for a port not equipped with reception facilities for oily residues (art. III(2)). These discharge standards were tightened up by amendments to the Convention adopted in 1962, but they remained relatively ineffective, partly because of the difficulty of detecting violations of the standards and partly because of the reluctance of many flag States to prosecute the masters of their vessels where violations were detected.

The failure of the 1954 Convention and its 1962 amendments to prevent oil discharges at sea prompted the search for alternative ways of disposing of unwanted oil. The result was the development in the 1960s of the 'load on top' system. This system separates the oil from the oily water on board: the almost oil-free water is returned to the sea, and the oil residues are retained on board. The next cargo can, in most cases, then be loaded on top of the residues. In 1969 further amendments to the 1954 Convention were adopted, requiring tankers to discharge oil en route at sea, and only to the extent that this occurs through use of the load-on-top system, the discharge rate not exceeding sixty litres per mile and the total quantity of oil discharged not exceeding one-fifteen-thousandth of the total cargo-carrying capacity. The effect of the 1969 amendments is that tankers must either operate the load-on-top system or retain all oily residues on board for eventual disposal ashore. Ships other than tankers must discharge oily water through a suitable separator, and retain sludges from heavy fuel oils on board. There is no doubt that the development of the load-on-top system and the 1969 amendments to the 1954 Convention have made a significant contribution to the reduction of deliberate pollution of the sea by oil. A report published by the IMO in September 1981 concluded that this form of pollution had decreased by about thirty per cent over the decade 1971–80, in spite of the fact that over the same period the amount of oil transported by sea increased by about seventeen per cent.[20] Nevertheless, the 1969 amendments are not wholly effective. This is partly because of the fact that the load-on-top system cannot always be used (for example, on short-haul voyages or where successive oil cargoes are incompatible), and partly because many ports still do not have adequate reception facilities for oily wastes, despite the obligation on parties to the 1954 Convention to provide such facilities (art. VIII). As we shall see, the International Convention for the Prevention of Pollution from Ships, 1973 (hereafter referred to as the MARPOL Convention) has attempted to remedy these deficiencies. Before discussing the MARPOL Convention it should be pointed out that a further set of amendments to the 1954 Convention was adopted in 1971. These amendments, which are not yet in force, are concerned not with operational discharges, but with accidents. Their object is to limit the oil pollution resulting from the stranding or collision of an oil tanker by setting limits on the size of the individual tanks in which the oil is carried.

The MARPOL Convention. The MARPOL Convention was adopted in 1973 and is intended to deal with all forms of intentional pollution of the sea from ships, other than dumping. Detailed pollution standards are set out in five annexes. These are concerned with oil (Annex I), noxious liquid substances in bulk (Annex II), harmful substances carried by sea in packaged forms (Annex III), sewage (Annex IV) and garbage (Annex V).

The acceptance of Annexes I and II is obligatory for all contracting parties, but acceptance of the remaining annexes is optional. By 1978 the Convention was still a long way from receiving the necessary number of ratifications to enter into force, mainly because of the considerable economic cost and technical difficulties of complying with its provisions. In an effort to speed up ratification, a Protocol to the Convention was adopted at the IMO's Conference on Tanker Safety and Pollution Prevention, held in February 1978. The effect of the Protocol was to provide that a State could become a party to the MARPOL Convention initially by accepting only Annex I. Annex II would not become binding until three years after the entry into force of the Protocol or such longer period as might be decided by the parties to the Protocol. In this modified form the Convention and Annex I came into force in October 1983 and Annex II in April 1987. As between the parties to it, the MARPOL Convention supersedes the 1954 Convention.

The detailed regulations dealing with oil pollution contained in Annex I (as amended by the 1978 Protocol and further amendments adopted in 1984) are similar to those described above in the 1954 Convention as amended, but with some significant additions. The most important of these are: the reintroduction of special areas (the Mediterranean, Baltic, Black and Red Seas, and the Arabian Gulf. The areas are not the same as those which had been done away with by the 1969 amendments to the 1954 Convention) where no discharges at all are permitted, even by tankers operating the load-on-top system; the requirement for ships other than tankers to be fitted with oily water separating or filtering equipment and adequate sludge tanks; the requirement for most tankers to be fitted with segregated ballast tanks[21] and for crude oil washing,[22] and for new non-tankers over 4,000 GRT to be fitted with segregated ballast tanks; and, finally, making the obligation on parties to provide reception facilities more effective.

The provisions of the remaining annexes to the MARPOL Convention (of which only Annex II is yet in force) are extremely complex, and can be only briefly summarised here. Under Annex II (which was substantially amended in 1985) the discharge of residues containing noxious liquid substances must be made to a reception facility, unless they are adequately diluted, in which case they may be discharged into the sea in accordance with detailed regulations. The annex also contains provisions for minimising pollution in the event of an accident. This last is the chief concern of Annex III, which seeks to prevent or minimise pollution from harmful substances carried in packaged forms by laying down regulations concerning packaging, marking, labelling, documentation, stowage and quantity limitations. Annex IV prohibits the discharge of sewage within four miles of land unless a ship has in operation an approved treatment plant.

Between four and twelve miles from land, sewage must be comminuted and disinfected before discharge. Finally, Annex V sets specified minimum distances from land for the disposal of all the principal kinds of garbage, and prohibits the disposal of all plastics. For the substances covered by Annexes II, IV and V contracting States are obliged to provide adequate reception facilities in their ports.

Other treaties. The 1954 Convention as amended and the MARPOL Convention are the main multilateral instruments regulating pollution from ships, but there are some other, less important, instruments which should be briefly mentioned. The International Convention for the Safety of Life at Sea, 1974 (SOLAS Convention) (Chapter VII) and the IMO's International Maritime Dangerous Goods Code, adopted in 1966, both contain provisions relating to the packing, marking, labelling, documentation and stowage of dangerous goods, which have the objective *inter alia* of reducing the risk of pollution resulting from the carriage of such goods by ships. Chapter VIII of the SOLAS Convention lays down regulations governing non-military nuclear-powered ships. These regulations, and the Code of Safety for Nuclear Merchant Ships, which the IMO adopted in November 1981,[23] should help to reduce the risk of accidental or deliberate pollution arising out of the operation of such ships. This question has also been dealt with by a number of bilateral agreements, e.g. USA–UK Agreement relating to the Use of United Kingdom Ports and Territorial Waters by the N.S. *Savannah*, 1964.

The various regional conventions deal with pollution from ships in a very general way, simply referring their parties to the general multilateral provisions discussed above. Thus article 6 of the 1976 Mediterranean Convention provides that its parties:

shall take all measures in conformity with international law to prevent, abate and combat pollution of the Mediterranean Sea Area caused by discharges from ships and to ensure the effective implementation in that Area of the rules which are generally recognised at the international level relating to the control of this type of pollution.

The other regional conventions are in similar vein. The one exception is the Baltic Convention, Annex IV of which contains detailed regulations dealing with pollution from oil, noxious liquid substances in bulk, harmful substances in packaged forms, sewage and garbage. These regulations are broadly similar to, but in most cases rather stricter than, the equivalent regulations of the MARPOL Convention.

Although international law, particularly in the 1954 and MARPOL Conventions, has now built up an imposing body of standards to reduce or eliminate pollution from ships, this law has not escaped criticism. First, it is said that the various conventions are slow to enter into force. This cannot be denied: for example, the 1969 amendments to the 1954 Convention took eight years to enter into force and the MARPOL Convention of 1973, even in its modified form, took ten years to enter into force. On the other hand, once a convention has been adopted, most new ships are built in accordance with its requirements even though the convention might not have come into force, in order to avoid any reconversion that might be necessary when the convention came into force. Furthermore, now that the MARPOL Convention is in force, it will be possible to amend the detailed pollution regulations contained in its annexes much more quickly than the 1954 Convention, because such amendments will be subject to the tacit amendment procedure. Secondly, it is said that even where the conventions have entered into force, they have not been widely ratified. At first sight there appears to be some force in this criticism. For example, the MARPOL Convention has been ratified by forty-three States, only about one quarter of the world's total number of States. However, this relatively low number is somewhat misleading, because these forty-three States collectively own about eighty per cent of the total world shipping tonnage. A third criticism is that the conventions are oriented in their pollution standards too much in favour of the shipping industry. However, there is little point in a convention laying down standards for the implementation of which the necessary technology does not exist or is regarded as unduly costly, for such a convention will simply not be ratified and brought into force. The fact that some of the standards laid down in the MARPOL Convention were for some years at the limits of current technology helps to explain why that convention was so slow to attract ratifications. A final criticism is that while the pollution standards of the various conventions look fine on paper, in practice they are not properly implemented and enforced. This is a question which we must now consider in some detail.

The prescription and enforcement of pollution standards

In discussing this question it is essential to keep constantly in mind certain distinctions. First, it is necessary to distinguish between a State's competence to *prescribe* legislation for individuals or ships (legislative jurisdiction), and its competence to *enforce* legislation thus prescribed (enforcement jurisdiction). It is convenient here to subdivide enforcement jurisdiction into the competence to *arrest* (arrest jurisdiction) and the competence of *courts* to deal with alleged breaches of the law (judicial jurisdiction). Secondly, the legislative or enforcement jurisdiction that a State has in respect of a particular vessel varies depending on whether it is a flag, coastal or port State. A *flag State* is the State whose nationality a particular vessel has. A *coastal State* is the State in one of whose maritime zones a particular vessel is. A *port State* is the State in one of whose ports a particular vessel is. Finally, it is necessary to distinguish between the pre-UNCLOS III rules (both customary and conventional) on the one hand, and the provisions of the Law of the Sea Convention on the other. When looking at both the pre-UNCLOS and the Law of the Sea Convention rules, the general framework of the discussion will be to consider States' legislative jurisdiction first, followed by enforcement jurisdiction. Within each type of jurisdiction, the competence of flag, coastal and port States will be examined successively.

Rules adopted prior to UNCLOS III. As far as legislative jurisdiction is concerned, under customary international law a *flag State* can prescribe anti-pollution rules applicable to its vessels, wherever in the world they might be. Both the 1954 Convention (arts. III and IV) and the MARPOL Convention (arts. 3 and 4) oblige flag States so to apply their pollution standards. Under the Territorial Sea Convention and under customary international law a *coastal State* may prescribe any legislation relating to pollution that it wishes for foreign vessels in its territorial sea, provided that such legislation does not have the effect of hampering innocent passage (see chapter four). Parties to the MARPOL Convention are obliged to prescribe its provisions for all vessels in their territorial sea[24] (art. 4(2)). There is no corresponding obligation in the 1954 Convention, although article XI makes it clear that coastal States may certainly prescribe its provisions for their territorial sea if they so wish. Finally, as regards *port States*, under customary international law a State can adopt anti-pollution legislation for foreign vessels in its ports and even make the observance of such legislation or particular international conventions a condition of entry to its ports, although usually, under bilateral treaties of friendship, commerce and navigation, it will have to ensure that such legislation and conditions are not discriminatory.

As far as enforcement jurisdiction is concerned, under customary international law a *flag State* can exercise judicial jurisdiction in respect of violations committed anywhere by its vessels. The flag State can arrest its vessels when they are on the high seas or in its territorial sea or ports: where the vessel is in the territorial sea or port of another State, the flag State may not arrest it, but may nevertheless institute criminal proceedings against it before its own courts provided the shipowner is within, or the vessel returns to, the flag State. Under the MARPOL Convention (arts. 4(1) and 6(4)) a flag State is obliged to institute criminal proceedings against any of its vessels suspected of having violated the Convention. A similar obligation is implied under the 1954 Convention (see art. X(2)). Article 19 of the Territorial Sea Convention, and customary international law, permit a *coastal State* to enforce violations of its pollution legislation committed in its territorial sea by foreign ships by arresting suspected vessels and instituting legal proceedings against them. Under the MARPOL Convention a coastal State party to the Convention, which is obliged, as we have already seen, to prescribe the Convention's provisions for foreign ships in its territorial sea, is under the further obligation either to take legal proceedings itself against a ship which has violated the Convention's provisions in its territorial sea or to forward to the authorities of the flag State such information and evidence as it has that a violation has occurred: where they have sufficient evidence, the flag State authorities must bring legal proceedings against the vessel concerned as soon as possible (arts. 4(2), 6(3) and (4)). There are no corresponding obligations in the 1954 Convention, but equally there is nothing to prevent a coastal State, in the exercise of its rights under customary international law or the Territorial Sea Convention, from taking enforcement action against foreign vessels violating the Convention in its territorial sea. A *port State* can exercise enforcement jurisdiction (in both its forms) against a foreign vessel violating its anti-pollution legislation in one of its ports or territorial sea, but it cannot take any action in respect of violations committed before the ship enters its territorial sea. However, both the 1954 Convention and the MARPOL Convention give port States some role in law enforcement. Under the former, the authorities of the port State may inspect the oil record book of a foreign vessel in one of its ports. If this inspection, or other factors, give the port State reason to think that the vessel has violated the Convention, it must forward its evidence of a violation to the flag State authorities, and the latter shall, if there is sufficient evidence, take legal proceedings against the vessel (arts. IX(5) and X). Under the MARPOL Convention the port authorities may inspect a foreign vessel, and where the condition of the vessel warrants it, they may detain the vessel until it can proceed to sea without presenting an unreasonable threat of harm to the marine environment.[25] Furthermore, where the inspection indicates a violation of the MARPOL Convention, the authorities of the flag State shall be informed and again must take legal proceedings if there is sufficient evidence (arts. 5(2), 6, 7). Under both the 1954 Convention (arts. X(2), XII) and the MARPOL Convention (arts. 4(3), 6(4), 11), flag States must inform the IMO of the enforcement action they take against their vessels, whether acting on their own initiative or as the result of information provided by other States.

This framework for the prescription and enforcement of pollution standards is less than satisfactory for a number of reasons. First, many flag States — especially flags of convenience — have been lax in enforcing the provisions of conventions to which they are parties. The procedure for reporting enforcement action taken under the 1954 Convention to the IMO, which in theory might have secured better enforcement of the Convention, in practice does not seem to have been properly observed, and the IMO appears to have been reluctant to press those States which did not report properly to do so. Had this been done, the IMO might then have spotted at least some of the failures to enforce the Convention properly and applied political and diplomatic pressure to the States concerned to take their enforcement responsibilities more seriously. The failures of flag States to take proper enforcement action have been compounded by the fact that these States are the only States which can take enforcement action against a vessel polluting the waters beyond the territorial sea, which is where most pollution from vessels occurs. Secondly, under both customary law and the Territorial Sea Convention there are no limits on the type of pollution regulations a coastal State can prescribe for its territorial sea. The result may be widely differing and conflicting regulations which, particularly if they relate to design and construction standards, may make it impossible for a vessel to comply with all the laws to which it might become subject during the course of its voyage.

The Law of the Sea Convention. These dissatisfactions with the traditional legal framework led to two main strands of change at UNCLOS. On the one hand, the more environmentally conscious and many non-maritime States sought to extend the enforcement powers of coastal and port States in order to compensate for the shortcomings of flag State enforcement. On the other hand, the maritime States tried to limit the legislative discretion of coastal States in order that there should be a degree of uniformity in coastal States' regulations. The maritime States also sought safeguards to accompany the proposed increase in the enforcement powers of coastal and port States for the purpose of preventing undue delay to — and hence increased operating costs for — their vessels. Both groups were relatively successful in seeing their concerns met in the Law of the Sea Convention, which reflects a carefully balanced compromise between them.

As far as the prescription of pollution standards is concerned, the Law of the Sea Convention makes no change in the traditional competence of *flag States* to prescribe their legislation for their vessels wherever they may be: it does, however, go further, by placing an obligation on flag States to adopt pollution regulations for their vessels which 'at least have the same effect as that of generally accepted international rules and standards established through the competent international organization or general diplomatic conference' (LOSC, art. 211(2)). There is no definition of 'generally accepted international rules ...', although article 211(7) provides that they include *inter alia* those relating to notification of accidents likely to cause marine pollution (these rules are discussed below). Presumably 'generally accepted international rules' include the 1954 convention. But do they include the MARPOL Convention, which is not widely ratified? And if so, do they include the provisions of all five annexes, or only those of the compulsory first two? 'The competent international organization' is usually taken as meaning the IMO. Do the 'standards' established by the IMO include only those found in conventions or do they include those contained in non-binding IMO Assembly resolutions? Whatever the precise scope of 'generally accepted international rules . . .' — and it is regrettable that no guidance as to what they comprise is given — the effect of article 211(2) may be in some cases to oblige flag States to prescribe for their vessels the provisions of conventions to which they are not parties.[26] While the intention behind article 211(2) is laudable, it may discourage ratification of both the Law of the Sea Convention (so that the obligation of article 211(2) may be avoided) and of the marine pollution conventions themselves (because it may be felt that ratification is no longer necessary with the existence of article 211(2)). Furthermore, the lack of clarity as to the meaning of 'generally accepted international rules . . .' may give rise to disputes as to whether the obligation of article 211(2) has been complied with.

The legislative competence of *coastal States* has been reduced by the Law of the Sea Convention in respect of the kind of pollution regulations which may be adopted, but increased in respect of the geographical area to which such regulations may be applied. In the territorial sea the coastal State may prescribe pollution regulations for foreign vessels in innocent passage, provided such regulations do not 'apply to the design, construction, manning or equipment of foreign ships unless they are giving effect to generally accepted international rules or standards' (LOSC, art. 21 (2)). Furthermore, such regulations must be duly publicised, must be non-discriminatory and must not hamper the innocent passage of foreign vessels (LOSC, arts. 21(3), 24, 211(4)). Where the territorial sea consists of straits subject to the regime of transit passage, the coastal State's legislative competence is even more restricted. Here pollution regulations may be adopted only if they give 'effect to applicable international regulations regarding the discharge of oil, oily wastes and other noxious substances in the strait' (LOSC, art. 42(1)). Such regulations must be non-discriminatory, must not hamper transit passage and must be duly publicised by the strait State (LOSC, art. 42(2), (3)). While the Law of the Sea Convention has restricted the scope of coastal States' legislative competence in their territorial sea, it has increased the geographical scope of their legislative competence by giving them certain powers to legislate for marine pollution from foreign vessels in their EEZ. Under article 211(5) a coastal State may adopt pollution legislation for its EEZ which conforms and gives effect to 'generally accepted international rules and standards established through the competent international organization or general diplomatic conference'. Where the latter rules are considered inadequate to provide sufficient ecological protection for certain areas of the EEZ, the coastal State may adopt regulations implementing international rules and standards or navigational practices which the IMO has made applicable to special areas, or it may adopt additional regulations of its own, provided that these do not impose design, construction, manning or equipment standards on foreign vessels other than generally accepted international rules and standards. In each case, special procedures are required: these include consultation with the IMO and obtaining its approval, and giving at least fifteen months' notice of the entry into force of the coastal State's regulations (LOSC, art. 211(6)). Finally, article 234 provides that for ice-covered areas, lying 'within the limits' of the EEZ (which would seem to include the territorial sea as well as the EEZ), the coastal State may adopt non-discriminatory pollution regulations: here there is no requirement that design, construction, etc., standards must conform to generally accepted international rules, although the coastal State's regulations must have 'due regard to navigation'.

The Law of the Sea Convention makes no changes to the legislative competence of *port States* (except to the extent necessary to accommodate their enlarged enforcement jurisdiction: see below, p. 259), but article 211(3) does provide that States which make observance of particular standards a condition for the entry of foreign vessels to their ports must give due publicity to such conditions and notify the IMO of them.

Turning now to enforcement jurisdiction, article 217 of the Law of the Sea Convention provides that *flag States* not only *may* enforce (in the sense of judicial jurisdiction) violations of pollution laws applying to their ships wherever committed, but *must* do so. In particular, flag States must lay down penalties adequate in severity to discourage violations; prohibit their vessels from proceeding to sea unless they comply with the requirements of international rules and standards; ensure that their vessels carry the certificates required by such rules; periodically inspect their vessels; and investigate alleged violations of the rules by their vessels. Where allegations are made by another State, that State and the IMO must be informed by the flag State of the action taken by it in response to the allegation. One largely theoretical question which the Law of the Sea Convention does not deal with directly is whether a flag State can arrest one of its vessels in the EEZ of another State. The answer would seem to be that it can. Article 92 of the Convention gives the flag State exclusive jurisdiction over its vessels on the high seas. By virtue of article 58(2), article 92 applies in the EEZ to the extent that it is not incompatible with the coastal State's rights. Since, as we shall shortly see, the coastal State has no general right to arrest foreign vessels in its EEZ for breach of anti-pollution regulations, it would seem that there is no coastal State right with which article 92 is incompatible, that therefore article 92 does apply, and thus that a flag State can arrest one of its vessels in the EEZ of another State.

Enforcement by *coastal States* is governed largely by article 220. Where a foreign vessel is suspected of having violated during its passage through the territorial sea the coastal State's anti-pollution legislation or applicable international rules relating to pollution from ships, the coastal State may, without prejudice to its general enforcement competence in the territorial sea as set out in section 3 of Part II of the Law of the Sea Convention, undertake physical inspection of the vessel and, where the evidence so warrants, institute legal proceedings (LOSC, art. 220(2)). The coastal State will have a power of arrest under section 3 of Part II. Where the pollution from the foreign vessel is 'wilful and serious', then the passage of that vessel is no longer innocent (see chapter four), and so the coastal State has unrestricted enforcement jurisdiction. However, where the alleged violation of the coastal State's legislation is committed by a vessel during the exercise of its right of transit passage through a strait, the coastal State may arrest the vessel only if the violation causes or threatens 'major damage to the marine environment of the straits' (LOSC, art. 233). Where an alleged violation takes place in the EEZ the coastal State may, either in its territorial sea or EEZ, require the offending vessel to give information regarding its identity and port of registry, its last and next port of call and other information required to establish whether a violation has occurred. Where the alleged violation in the EEZ has resulted 'in a substantial discharge causing or threatening significant pollution of the marine environment' the coastal State may undertake physical inspection of the vessel in the EEZ or territorial sea if the vessel has refused to give the necessary information or has given manifestly incorrect information. But only where the alleged violation has resulted 'in a discharge causing major damage or threat of major damage to the coastline or related interests of the coastal State, or to any resources of its territorial sea or exclusive economic zone' may the coastal State arrest the vessel (LOSC, art. 220(3)– (8)). Whether the distinction between a 'substantial discharge ...' and a 'discharge causing major damage ...' will be clear-cut in practice seems doubtful: it is likely that coastal States will tend to assume that any significant discharge will fall into the latter category, thus endowing themselves with the greater enforcement competence. The coastal State may exercise its enforcement powers in its territorial sea or EEZ in respect of violations not only of its own pollution rules, but also of 'applicable international rules and standards'. The effect may be that some coastal States take action to enforce the provisions of conventions to which they, and possibly also the flag State of the offending vessel, are not parties, unless 'applicable' is taken to refer to rules which are contained in a convention to which the coastal State is a party or are part of customary international law. Finally, where a coastal State has prescribed anti-pollution regulations for ice-covered areas in its territorial sea or EEZ, or both, it may enforce such regulations: no limitations or qualifications are attached to this enforcement competence (art. 234).

The most radical innovations made to the enforcement of marine pollution standards by the Law of the Sea Convention concern the powers given to *port States*. Article 220(1) follows customary international law — though supplementing it as a result of the introduction of the EEZ — by providing that a State may arrest and prosecute a vessel in one of its ports which is alleged to have violated that State's pollution laws or applicable international rules in its territorial sea or EEZ. However, article 218 is truly innovatory because it provides that a port State can also take legal proceedings where a vessel is alleged to have discharged polluting matter *outside* that State's territorial sea or EEZ 'in violation of applicable international rules and standards established through the competent international organization or general diplomatic conference'. The port State must not take legal proceedings where the discharge occurred in the internal waters, territorial sea or EEZ of another State unless that State or the flag State so requests. Additionally, under article 219, where a port State has ascertained that a vessel in one of its ports is 'in violation of applicable international rules and standards relating to seaworthiness of vessels and thereby threatens damage to the marine environment', it shall take administrative measures to prevent the vessel from sailing until the causes of the violation have been removed or unless the vessel is going to the nearest repair yard.

Where either a port State or a coastal State arrests and proceeds against a foreign vessel for alleged violation of pollution regulations in the situations referred to above, its actions are subject to a number of safeguards set out in articles 223–32. These provide *inter alia* that arrests may be made only by government officials and State-owned ships and aircraft, and must be done in such a way as not to endanger navigation or the marine environment; foreign vessels may not be detained longer than necessary; legal proceedings must normally be suspended when the flag State takes proceedings in respect of the same incident; the penalties imposed for a violation must normally be limited to monetary ones; and flag States must be promptly notified of proceedings taken against their vessels. Curiously, and possibly the result of an oversight in drafting, not all these safeguards apply to enforcement action taken by a coastal State in ice-covered areas. The requirement that the port or coastal State must normally suspend legal proceedings if the flag State institutes proceedings, while having the desirable effect of acting as a safeguard against double jeopardy, might at first sight seem to undermine the Law of the Sea Convention's attempts to remedy the deficiencies of flag State jurisdiction by strengthening coastal and port State enforcement jurisdiction. It must be noted, however, that there is no obligation to suspend proceedings where the pollution offence was committed in the territorial sea or caused 'major damage to the coastal

State', or where the flag State has not instituted proceedings within six months of the coastal or port State taking action, or where the flag State has repeatedly disregarded its duty to enforce effectively violations of international rules committed by its vessels. Furthermore, article 228 appears to suggest that if the flag State begins legal proceedings but does not bring them to a conclusion, the port or coastal State may lift the suspension on its own proceedings and continue with the case.

The provisions of the Law of the Sea Convention should lead to much more effective enforcement of international pollution standards. Where a flag State is lax in taking enforcement action, port and coastal States can now step in. In practice, given the difficulties of arresting a vessel in passage which is unwilling to comply, port State jurisdiction will probably be more frequently exercised and more effective than the jurisdiction of coastal States (although there may be some doubt as to how far port States will wish to bother prosecuting vessels which have committed offences far from that State's waters or territory). The shift in recent international pollution conventions — particularly in the MARPOL Convention — away from discharge standards to construction standards which have to be certificated will facilitate the exercise of port State jurisdiction, in as much as the difficulties of proving violations of discharge standards will be avoided. At the same time the existence of port State jurisdiction may persuade flag States which have hitherto been lax in enforcing standards to take a more effective line in future — if only for reasons of national pride.

The Law of the Sea Convention's provisions governing the prescription and enforcement of pollution standards do not apply to warships or other State-owned ships used only on government non-commercial service (LOSC, art. 236). This reflects the general international legal rules relating to sovereign immunity, and similar provisions are found in both the 1954 Oil Pollution Convention (art. II) and the MARPOL Convention (art. 3(3)). Like the provisions of those conventions, however, article 236 of the Law of the Sea Convention provides that 'each State shall ensure, by the adoption of appropriate measures not impairing operations or operational capabilities of such vessels or aircaft owned or operated by it, that such vessels or aircraft act in a manner consistent, so far as is reasonable and practicable, with this Convention'.

As regards the impact of the Convention's provisions on pollution jurisdiction before its entry into force, although most of the seventy-four States which have so far claimed an EEZ have included in their legislation a broad claim to jurisdiction over pollution in that zone, very few of these States appear to have any specific legislation governing pollution in the EEZ. Fewer States still have provided for port State jurisdiction in their legislation.

Measures to avoid accidental pollution

A certain amount of pollution coming from ships is the result of accidents, such as hull failure, collisions and strandings, which lead to oil and other noxious cargoes entering the sea. Earlier we saw that there are provisions, such as the limitation on the size of tanks in an oil tanker, which are designed to reduce the scale of marine pollution when an accident occurs. Rules of international law have also been adopted to try and reduce the risk of an accident occurring in the first place. These rules are concerned with such matters as improving the seaworthiness of ships and the qualifications of crews, and regulating marine traffic in crowded waters. We examined these rules in some detail in chapter thirteen.

Action by coastal States in respect of pollution casualties

The Intervention Convention. If an accident does occur, the question arises as to what measures a State can take to prevent or reduce pollution from a stricken vessel in the vicinity of its coasts. If the vessel is in the territorial sea, the coastal State can take any measures it considers appropriate (subject to the principle of proportionality). This is because the vessel, being no longer 'in passage', will have ceased to enjoy a right of innocent passage, and will thus be subject to the unfettered sovereignty of the coastal State. If the vessel is beyond the territorial sea, however, the position is different. The question of what powers the coastal State has in this situation was posed in the case of the *Torrey Canyon*, which, although on the high seas, was bombed by the United Kingdom authorities in the hope of reducing pollution from the vessel by setting its cargo of oil on fire. Doubts about the legality of its action led the United Kingdom government to refer the question to the IMO. The result was the adoption in 1969 of the International Convention relating to Intervention on the High Seas in Cases of Oil Pollution Casualties (hereafter referred to as the Intervention Convention). Under article I of the Intervention Convention, States parties:

> may take such measures on the high seas as may be necessary to prevent, mitigate or eliminate grave and imminent danger to their coastline or related interests from pollution or threat of pollution of the sea by oil, following upon a maritime casualty or acts related to such a casualty, which may reasonably be expected to result in major harmful consequences.

'Maritime casualty' is defined as a collision, stranding or other incident of navigation or occurrence resulting in actual or threatened material damage to a ship or its cargo (art. II). The measures taken under article I, which are not available for use against warships or other State-owned ships used for non-commercial purposes, must be proportionate to the actual or threatened damage (arts. I and V). Excessive measures causing damage require the payment of compensation to the flag State (art. VI). Before taking measures under article I the State concerned must, except in cases of extreme urgency, consult the flag State and other States affected by the casualty and notify anyone likely to be affected by the proposed measures. In any case, after the measures have been taken, such States and persons, as well as the IMO, must be notified (art. III).

The Intervention Convention applies only to measures of intervention against casualties causing or threatening pollution by oil. In 1973 a Protocol to the Convention was adopted, extending coastal States' powers of intervention to casualties causing or threatening pollution by substances other than oil.

Both the Intervention Convention and its Protocol apply only to measures taken 'on the high seas'. Taken literally, this would mean that the coastal State could not rely on the powers given by the Convention and its Protocol to take action in its EEZ. Since no other convention gives powers of intervention in the EEZ, and unless such powers derive from customary international law (a question we shall consider in a moment), this would mean that a coastal State would have greater powers of intervention on the high seas than in its EEZ, which is plainly absurd. Since the EEZ concept did not exist at the time the Intervention Convention and its Protocol were drafted, it would seem not unreasonable to consider that the phrase 'high seas' should be read to mean 'beyond the territorial sea'.

The Law of the Sea Convention.　　The Law of the Sea Convention contains no provision directly giving coastal States the right to take action against pollution casualties. Article 221, however, does provide that the Convention is not to 'prejudice the right of States, pursuant to international law, both customary and conventional' to intervene in the manner described above 'beyond the territorial sea'.

Custom.　　Whether a coastal State possesses powers of intervention on the high seas under customary international law, as article 221 assumes, is perhaps controversial. At least, there must have been some doubt about this question, for otherwise it would not seem necessary to have concluded the Intervention Convention. On the other hand, it can be argued that the United Kingdom's action against the *Torrey Canyon* in 1967, coupled with its ready acceptance by other States, constituted an emerging rule of customary international law which the Intervention Convention simply crystallised and clarified.

Co-operation in taking action to deal with pollution emergencies
Global conventions.　　Where large-scale pollution occurs, usually because of an accident to a ship, it will often be desirable that States co-operate, for

example by the State which first becomes aware of the pollution warning other States which are likely to be affected, or by States assisting each other with equipment and know-how for dealing directly with a pollution emergency. Provision for such co-operation is made, on the global level, but to a limited extent, in the MARPOL Convention. Under article 8 and Protocol 1 a ship involved in a pollution incident must report the details to the authorities of a State party (though exactly which State or States is not made clear), which in turn must relay the report to the flag State and any other State likely to be affected. In similar vein, article 198 of the Law of the Sea Convention provides that 'when a State becomes aware of cases in which the marine environment is in imminent danger of being damaged or has been damaged by pollution, it shall immediately notify other States it deems likely to be affected by such damage, as well as the competent international organizations'. Article 199 goes on to provide that affected States shall co-operate 'in eliminating the effects of pollution and preventing or minimising the damage'. To this end, States are to develop joint contingency plans for responding to pollution incidents.

Regional conventions. Such co-operation has already been extensively developed through many of the regional pollution conventions and some bilateral agreements. The Mediterranean Convention provides, in article 9, that its parties are to co-operate in taking the necessary measures for dealing with pollution emergencies. Any party aware of an emergency must immediately notify UNEP, the Regional Oil Combating Centre for the Mediterranean (established at Malta), and other parties likely to be affected: during the first ten years of its existence the Centre was notified of over 100 alerts and accident reports.[27] The general obligation to co-operate referred to in article 9 is given more concrete detail in the Protocol concerning Co-operation in Combating Pollution of the Mediterranean Sea by Oil and other Harmful Substances in Cases of Emergency (1976). Under this Protocol the parties must maintain, individually or jointly, contingency plans (art. 3) and monitor for emergencies (art. 4) Under article 10 of the Protocol any party requiring assistance in combating a pollution emergency may call for assistance from other parties. Such assistance may include expert advice and the supply of anti-pollution equipment. The other regional conventions are broadly similar to the Mediterranean Convention and its Protocol, although only the Red Sea and Kuwait Conventions establish a regional emergency centre.

More modest than these regional conventions is the Agreement for Co-operation in dealing with Pollution of the North Sea by Oil, 1969. Under this agreement, which applies not only to the North Sea but also to the English Channel, the ships and aircraft of the parties are requested to report to their flag State all large oil slicks they observe and all casualties causing or likely to cause oil pollution. The flag State in turn must notify other States which may be affected (art. 5). For the purposes of the agreement, the North Sea is divided into zones of responsibility. A State party in whose zone a slick or casualty occurs must make an assessment of the situation and keep the slick under observation (art. 6). A party requiring help to dispose of oil may request assistance from other parties (art. 7). The agreement is serviced by the same secretariat as services the Paris and Oslo Commissions (see below, p. 279). In 1983 a new agreement was signed which, when it enters into force, will replace the 1969 agreement. The new agreement is similar to the 1969 agreement, except that it covers all harmful substances and not just oil, and also contains provisions concerning reimbursement by one party to another for assistance given pursuant to the agreement. Similar to the North Sea Agreement, but limited to co-operation in pollution emergencies involving only oil, is the Agreement between Denmark, Finland, Norway and Sweden concerning Co-operation in taking measures against Pollution of the Sea by Oil, 1971. However, this Nordic Agreement goes further in that its parties undertake to provide themselves with equipment for dealing with any significant oil slicks at sea, and to collaborate with each other so as to achieve the greatest possible efficacy in the use of this equipment (art. 4). On the other hand, unlike the North Sea Agreement, the Nordic Agreement does not create zones of responsibility.

Bilateral treaties.   Finally, the question of co-operation in combating pollution has been the subject of some bilateral agreements. For example, the USA has concluded agreements with Canada[28] and Mexico[29] which establish joint contingency plans for dealing with serious pollution threats in waters of mutual interest, and Canada has concluded a similar agreement with Denmark.[30]

Liability for pollution damage

While the primary aim of the international law relating to marine pollution should be to prevent such pollution, a subsidiary aim should be to facilitate the bringing of compensation claims by those who have suffered damage where pollution has occurred. Indeed, the existence of liability schemes favouring the victims of pollution damage may well encourage shipowners to take more care in observing the standards which are designed to prevent pollution. A person who has suffered damage from pollution — even if he can identify the vessel which has caused the pollution and can show a causal link between this pollution and the damage he had suffered (and this will often not be easy) — may face further difficulties in bringing an action for compensation against the shipowner. First, he may find it difficult to prove fault on the part of the shipowner — and most legal systems require proof of fault in most kinds of claims for compensation for damage caused by one person to another. Secondly, he may find it difficult to bring an action before the courts of his own State when the shipowner is a foreign national, because the courts may be reluctant to assume jurisdiction; and even if he succeeds, it may be difficult to enforce the judgment. Thirdly, the compensation awarded to the victim of pollution damage may exceed the financial resources of the shipowner.

The Civil Liability and Fund Conventions. The International Convention on Civil Liability for Oil Pollution Damage of 1969 (hereafter referred to as the Civil Lability Convention) and the International Convention on the Establishment of an International Fund for Compensation for Oil Pollution Damage of 1971 (hereafter referred to as the Fund Convention) attempt to overcome the difficulties which may be faced by the victims of oil pollution. The Civil Liability Convention provides that where oil escapes or is discharged from a ship and causes damage on the territory, including the territorial sea, of a contracting State, the shipowner, subject to three exceptions, is strictly liable for such damage and the cost of any preventive measures taken. The three exceptions are where the damage (1) results from war or acts of God; (2) is wholly caused by an act or omission done by a third party with intent to cause damage; (3) is wholly caused by the negligence or other wrongful act of any government or other authority responsible for the maintenance of lights or other navigational aids. In these three cases the shipowner is not liable at all (art. II and III). Where the shipowner is liable, however, his liability is limited. Originally the Civil Liability Convention expressed the limits of liability in terms of Poincaré francs, but under a 1976 Protocol the limits of liability are now expressed in terms of Special Drawing Rights (SDRs; in August 1987 one SDR was worth about £0·80 or $1·26). Under article V, as amended by the Protocol, the limits of liability are 133 SDRs for each ton of the ship's tonnage, subject to an overall limit of fourteen million SDRs. However, the shipowner's liability is unlimited if the pollution is 'the result of the actual fault or privity' of the shipowner (art. V(2)).

The above provisions are supplemented by the Fund Convention. First, the Convention provides that where the shipowner is not liable at all under the Civil Liability Convention by reason of an act of God or the second or third of the three exceptions or, in cases where the shipowner is liable, but is financially incapable of meeting his obligations in full or if the pollution damage exceeds the limits of his liability, compensation will be paid to the victim from the International Oil Pollution Compensation Fund (which is established by the Convention), up to a limit of 675 million Poincaré francs (increased in 1979 from the original limit of 450 million francs) (art. 4). Under a Protocol to the Convention, adopted in 1976 but not yet in force, the original limit is converted to thirty million SDRs: presumably the new limit will at some stage be expressed in SDRs. Secondly, the Fund Convention provides that the Fund is to relieve shipowners of some of the financial burden placed on them by the Civil Liability Convention by paying that part of the shipowner's liability which is in excess of 1,500 Poincaré francs per ton or 125 million francs, whichever is the less (under the 1976 Protocol, 100 and 8·333 million SDRs respectively). However, the Fund will not relieve the shipowner in this way if the pollution results from the 'wilful misconduct' of the owner, or where it results from his failure to observe the provisions of certain conventions concerned with the safety of shipping or oil pollution, where such failure is the cause of the damage (art. 5). The idea behind the Fund Convention, realised by raising the Fund's income by a levy on oil imports, is that the owners of the cargo which causes the pollution (oil companies) should also bear a share of the liability, and not merely the shipowner. During the first six years of its existence the Fund paid out about $42 million on sixteen claims.

The owner of a ship registered in a State party to the Civil Liability Convention and carrying more than 2,000 tons of oil as cargo must maintain insurance or other financial security sufficient to cover his maximum liability for pollution damage under the Convention (art. VII(1)). The ship is to be issued with a certificate by the authorities of the flag State to this effect (art. VII(2)). Such a certificate must be carried on board the ship, and the ship shall not be permitted 'to trade' unless it has been issued with a certificate (art. VII(4), (10)). Parties to the Convention must ensure that every ship carrying more than 2,000 tons of oil as cargo and using its ports is insured as required by article VII(1), whether the flag State of the ship is a party to the Convention or not (art. VII(11)).

As far as procedure is concerned, the Civil Liability Convention provides that the victim of oil pollution damage may bring an action for compensation only in the courts of the contracting State in whose territory the damage occurred (art. IX(1)). An action must be brought within three years of the the date on which the damage occurred (art. VIII). Where an action is brought, the shipowner shall constitute a fund for the total sum representing the limit of his liability with the court or other competent authority of the State in which the claim is brought (art. V(3)). The fund is to be distributed by the court among the claimants in proportion to the amounts of their established claims (arts. V(4), IX(3)). The judgement of the court in which the action is brought is to be recognised and enforceable in all States parties to the Civil Liability Convention (art. X). Similar procedural provisions apply where a claim for compensation is brought against the International Oil Pollution Compensation Fund (arts. 6–8 of the Fund Convention).

In 1984 two Protocols to amend the Civil Liability and Fund Conventions were adopted: neither Protocol is yet in force. The first Protocol increases the maximum limits of liability under the Civil Liability Convention to three million SDRs for ships under 5,000 tons: for larger ships liability increases by 420 SDRs per ton above 5,000 tons to a maximum of 59·7 million SDRs. The Protocol also extends the geographical scope of the Convention to cover damage caused in the EEZ and the cost of preventive measures wherever taken, and clarifies the kinds of environmental damage which are covered by the Convention. The Protocol to the Fund Convention raises the maximum limit of liability under that Convention to 135 million SDRs, to be increased to 200 million SDRs when certain conditions are fulfilled.

Industry liability schemes.   The world's leading tanker and oil companies have established two private schemes, the Tanker Owners' Voluntary Agreement concerning Liability for Oil Pollution (TOVALOP — in force since October 1969) and the Contract regarding an Interim Supplement to Tanker Liability for Oil Pollution (CRISTAL — in force since April 1971), which broadly mirror the provisions of the Civil Liability and Fund Conventions. These schemes were particularly important before the Conventions came into force (in June 1975 and October 1978 respectively), and still remain of great benefit to the victims of oil pollution damage in the approximately eighty coastal States which are not parties to the Civil Liability Convention, especially since TOVALOP covers over ninety per cent of the world's oil tankers. A further benefit is that CRISTAL can operate quite happily in conjunction with the Civil Liability Convention in cases where the Fund Convention is not applicable, thus providing additional compensation and relieving the shipowner of part of his liability. This is particularly useful, since at present only about two-thirds of the States parties to the Civil Liability Convention are parties to the Fund Convention. By the end of 1986 CRISTAL had paid out some $60 million in compensation. In 1986 TOVALOP and CRISTAL were substantially amended: in particular, the maximum amount of compensation was increased fourfold.[31]

Other liability treaties.   Special liability regimes have also been elaborated for pollution damage caused by radioactive matter. Such pollution may result either from an accident to a ship carrying radioactive matter, or from the operation of or an accident to a nuclear-powered ship. In the case of the former, the Paris Convention on Third Party Liability in the Field of Nuclear Energy of 1960 and the Vienna Convention on Civil Liability for Nuclear Damage of 1963 each provide that the operator of a nuclear installation is the person exclusively liable for damage caused by a nuclear incident occurring in the course of the maritime carriage of nuclear material. In each case the operator's liability is strict but limited. The Convention

relating to Civil Liability in the Field of Maritime Carriage of Nuclear
Material of 1971 reaffirms the exclusive liability of the operator of the nuclear installation, and makes it clear that the shipowner is never liable for
damage caused by the carriage of nuclear material unless he committed or
omitted to do an act with intent to cause damage.

As far as pollution damage resulting from nuclear-powered ships is concerned, the Brussels Convention on the Liability of Operators of Nuclear
Ships of 1962 provides that the operator of a nuclear ship is to be strictly
liable for damage caused by a nuclear accident up to a maximum of 1,500
million Poincaré francs. However, this convention has not yet come into
force, and is apparently unlikely to do so. In the absence of the application
of the Convention, the position is as follows. Most nuclear-powered ships
are naval vessels, and therefore if faced with an action before the court of a
foreign State would be able to raise the defence of sovereign immunity.
The liability of the handful of civilian nuclear-powered ships is generally
governed by bilateral agreements. Thus the United States has entered into
agreements[32] with those States whose territorial waters or ports have been
visited by N. S. *Savannah* whereby the USA has assumed strict liability for
all damage arising out of a nuclear incident involving the *Savannah* up to a
limit of $500 million. The Federal Republic of Germany has entered into
similar agreements[33] in respect of N. S. *Otto Hahn*: here the maximum
limit of liability is DM 400 million.

In 1984 the same IMO conference which adopted the protocols to the
Civil Liability and Fund Conventions also considered a Draft Convention
on Liability and Compensation in Connexion with the Carriage of Noxious
and Hazardous Substances by Sea.[34] However, the Conference revealed
widespread disagreement on the Draft Convention, and referred the matter
back to the IMO with a request that a new draft be prepared. Until such
time as a new draft has been adopted and come into force, a shipowner,
faced with a claim for compensation for pollution damage caused by substances other than oil or radioactive matter, will often be able to limit his
liability under the 1957 or 1976 conventions on the limitation of shipowners'
liability, which were discussed briefly in chapter thirteen (see p. 220).

Dumping

The London Convention.   International action to control the dumping of
wastes at sea began in the early 1970s (although before that the High Seas
Convention had required States to take measures to prevent marine pollution from the dumping of radioactive waste: HSC, art. 25(1)). So far this
action has resulted in one convention that is world-wide in scope and several
regional agreements. The global convention is the Convention on the Prevention of Marine Pollution by Dumping of Wastes and Other Matter,

1972 (hereafter referred to as the London Convention). This Convention defines dumping as the deliberate disposal of waste from ships and aircraft, but excluding the disposal of waste incidental to the normal operation of ships and aircraft (art. III (1)). Wastes are divided into three categories. The first category consists of the substances listed in Annex I (the 'black list'). These include organohalogen compounds, mercury, cadmium, oil, plastics and high-level radioactive wastes defined by the International Atomic Energy Agency (IAEA) as unsuitable for dumping. The dumping of substances on the black list is prohibited (art. IV(1)). The second category of wastes comprises the somewhat less noxious substances listed in Annex II (the 'grey list'). These include arsenic, lead, copper, zinc, organosilicon compounds, cyanides, fluorides, pesticides, scrap metal and radioactive matter not included in Annex I. The dumping of such substances is permitted only if a prior special permit (issued by the national authorities of a contracting party) has been obtained (art. IV (1)). In issuing a permit for the dumping of radioactive waste the parties must take full account of the recommendations of the IAEA. The third category comprises all wastes not on the black or grey lists: such wastes may nevertheless be dumped only if a prior general permit has been obtained (art. IV(1)). Annex III sets out a number of factors which are to be taken into account by the national authorities of contracting parties when issuing special and general permits. These factors include the characteristics and composition of the matter, the characteristics of the dumping site, the method of deposit and the possible effects of the dumping. In 1978 the parties to the London Convention adopted amendments to the annexes dealing with the incineration of wastes at sea.[35] A special permit is required for the incineration of wastes listed in Annexes I and II, and such incineration must comply with the regulations set out in the revised annexes. In emergencies the above provisions may be waived: such situations are limited to cases where there is a danger to human life or the safety of a ship or aircraft is threatened, and if 'dumping appears to be the only way of averting the threat and if there is every probability that the damage consequent upon such dumping will be less than otherwise would occur' (art. V). Special procedures are to be followed where black list wastes are concerned.

Each party to the London Convention must take legislative action to prescribe the above system of regulating dumping for (*a*) vessels and aircraft registered in its territory or flying its flag; (*b*) vessels and aircraft loading in its territory or territorial sea matter which is to be dumped; and (*c*) vessels and aircraft 'under its jurisdiction'[36] believed to be engaged in dumping (art. VII). The Convention is rather imprecise about enforcement, but it would seem that this is governed by the general rules of customary law, i.e. a coastal State can take enforcement action against any ship illegally dumping waste in its territorial sea and against any ship about to leave one of its ports for the purposes of dumping without having the necessary permit: on the high seas enforcement will lie solely with flag States. It should be noted that under article XIII of the London Convention the parties agree to meet after UNCLOS III 'with a view to defining the nature and extent of the right and responsibility of a coastal State to apply the Convention in a zone adjacent to its coast' and that under article VII(3) the parties agree to 'co-operate in the development of procedures for the effective application of [the] Convention particularly on the high seas'. No meeting under article XIII has yet been held.

Parties to the London Convention must keep a record of all dumping they permit and monitor the condition of the sea for the purposes of dumping (art. VI(1)). Under article X they 'undertake to develop procedures for the assessment of liability' for damage caused by dumping: no such 'procedures' have yet been developed. Under article IX the parties are to promote support for those parties requiring assistance in the training of scientific and technical personnel, the supply of research and monitoring equipment and facilities, and in waste disposal and treatment. The parties are also to co-operate in promoting the codification of signals to be used by vessels engaged in dumping (art. XII).

Parties to the London Convention must meet not less than once every two years. These meetings may *inter alia* consider amendments to the Convention and its annexes, consider national reports on the implementation of the Convention, and develop further guidelines for dumping in emergency situations (art. XIV). Secretariat duties in respect of these meetings and other aspects of the Convention are performed by the IMO.

The practical operation of the London Convention has given rise to two particularly controversial matters. The first is the dumping of radioactive waste. In 1983 the parties to the Convention adopted a resolution calling for a two-year moratorium on the dumping of radioactive waste pending the results of a scientific review of the harm caused by such dumping. Following such a review (which was not entirely conclusive in its findings), a further resolution was adopted in 1985 calling for a continuation of the moratorium pending further studies.[37] Although the resolutions are not legally binging, they appear so far to have been observed. The other matter is whether the Convention covers the sub-sea-bed disposal of waste (considered by some States to be a suitable means for disposing of radioactive wastes). No agreement has yet been reached on this question, but the parties to the Convention have agreed that no such disposal should take place until it is proved to be technically feasible and environmentally acceptable.

Regional treaties. Three of the regional conventions dealing with dumping adopt a very similar approach to the London Convention. These are the Convention for the Prevention of Marine Pollution by Dumping from

Ships and Aircraft, 1972 (hereafter referred to as the Oslo Convention), which applies to the north-east Atlantic and North Sea, the Protocol to the Mediterranean Convention and the Protocol to the South Pacific Convention. Apart from their geographical scope, the differences between the London Convention and these other instruments are relatively minor. Thus, for example, there are small variations in the contents of the black and grey lists, and the institutional arrangements differ in each case. The Oslo Convention is the only regional agreement so far to deal with the incineration of wastes at sea (see its Protocol of 1983), while the South Pacific Convention goes further than either of the other agreements in its treatment of radioactive waste, article 10 of the Convention (not the Protocol) prohibiting the dumping (including sub-seabed disposal) of all such waste. (A similar prohibition is also found in article 7 of the 1985 Treaty of Raratonga). The South Pacific Protocol also goes further in its jurisdictional provisions, reflecting the Law of the Sea Convention (discussed below).

The Baltic Convention takes a rather different and much stricter approach to dumping than the agreements mentioned above. Article 9 prohibits all dumping, except of dredged spoils, and even this is prohibited if the wastes contain significant quantities of certain listed noxious substances. Where such dumping is permitted, a special prior permit must be obtained. Like the above conventions, however, the Baltic Convention permits dumping if it appears to be the only way of averting a threat to the safety of life or of a vessel.

The other regional conventions are much more general, and simply call on contracting parties to take all appropriate measures to prevent and reduce pollution caused by dumping and ensure effective compliance with the internationally agreed rules on dumping. It may be that in time, if dumping is perceived as being a particular problem in the areas to which those conventions apply, detailed protocols will be elaborated.

Outside the regional framework conventions on marine pollution, the Council of the Organisation for Economic Co-operation and Development (OECD) in 1977 adopted a Decision establishing a Multilateral Consultation and Surveillance Mechanism for Sea Dumping of Radioactive Waste.[38] This Mechanism involves the establishment of guidelines and recommendations to be applied to the dumping of radioactive waste by OECD Member States; procedures for notification and consultation concerning proposed dumping; international surveillance of dumping; and recording and reporting on actual dumping.

The Law of the Sea Convention. Both the London and all the regional conventions except the South Pacific Protocol adopt a traditional jurisdictional approach as far as the prescription and enforcement of dumping regulations are concerned, although the London Convention recognises that a more radical approach may be possible following the conclusion of UNCLOS. This is indeed the case. Articles 210(5) and 216 of the Law of the Sea Convention give a coastal State the right to make and enforce regulations — which must be at least as effective as global rules — to control dumping, not only in its territorial sea but also in its exclusive economic zone and over its continental shelf. The language of article 210 suggests that there is not merely a right, but a duty, to do so. In addition, article 210 obliges a State to adopt legislation to make dumping by all vessels in its maritime zones and by its own vessels anywhere, subject to a system of permits. Such legislation must be not less effective than global rules and standards. As with its provisions concerning the prescription of pollution standards by flag States for their vessels (discussed earlier), the Law of the Sea Convention is here imposing by reference obligations contained in international conventions on States which may not be parties to those conventions, with the same uncertainty as to exactly what international rules are meant and with the same possibly undesirable effects on ratification of the Law of the Sea Convention and international dumping conventions.

As far as the practical effect of the various dumping agreements is concerned, the only information which appears to be available relates to the Oslo Convention. The annual reports of the Oslo Commission show that the quantities of industrial waste and sewage sludge which are dumped have steadily declined (by about thirty per cent between 1980 and 1983), though the amount of dredged spoils remains about the same. While the total quantities of waste say nothing about their toxicity, the quantity of most trace metals found in these wastes has also declined. In 1986 a British Parliamentary Committee concluded that there was little scientific evidence of pollution damage attributable to present dumping practices, and that any such damage was largely short-lived or locally confined.[39]

Pollution from sea-bed activities

In considering pollution from sea-bed activities, it is necessary to distinguish between operations in the territorial sea and on the continental shelf (mainly the exploration and exploitation of oil and gas) on the one hand, and mining in the international sea bed area on the other.

Territorial sea and continental shelf

Neither exploratory drilling for nor production of oil and gas in the territorial sea or on the continental shelf will cause any significant pollution if properly conducted. Furthermore, any escape of oil or gas is contrary to the commercial interests of the operator, for such an escape represents lost production and may give rise to claims for compensation. In is thus not surprising that little effort has been spent on negotiating international agreements dealing with deliberate pollution from continental shelf installations. Instead, States have hitherto concentrated on co-operation over measures to reduce the risks of accidental pollution through blow-outs or pipeline fractures, and on agreeing on liability regimes (which may act as an incentive to operators to take particular care).

Both the Geneva and Law of the Sea Conventions address general exhortations to States to take measures to avoid both deliberate and accidental sea-bed pollution. Thus article 24 of the High Seas Convention provides that every State shall draw up regulations to prevent pollution from pipelines or from exploration or exploitation of the sea bed (articles 208(1) and 214 of the Law of the Sea Convention contain a similar obligation), and article 5(7) of the Continental Shelf Convention provides that States are obliged to take in the safety zones round continental shelf installations 'all appropriate means for the protection of the living resources of the sea from harmful agents'. Furthermore, article 208(5) of the Law of the Sea Convention calls on States to 'establish global and regional rules, standards and recommended practices and procedures to prevent, reduce and control pollution' from sea-bed activities under their jurisdiction.

Prevention of accidental pollution.   International co-operation to reduce the risks of accidental pollution has so far been at the regional level. The differences between various regions are such that detailed co-operation on a global scale would seem to be impracticable and unnecessary, although it should be noted that the IMO has produced a recommended Code for the Construction and Equipment of Mobile Offshore Drilling Units[40]. The most extensive cooperation has been between the States of north-west Europe. Since 1973 they have met several times in an informal Diplomatic Conference on Safety and Pollution Safeguards in the Development of North West European Offshore Mineral Resources. This conference has studied the safety of installations and personnel and pollution safeguards, but is still undecided whether to produce a treaty or a code of conduct on these matters. It may also be noted that under various bilateral agreements Norway and the United Kingdom co-operate over safety standards for certain North Sea installations and pipelines.[41] Outside north-west Europe, the various regional framework conventions are general and imprecise. Article 10 of the Baltic Convention provides that 'each contracting party shall take all appropriate measures in order to prevent' pollution from sea-bed activities, and 'shall also ensure that adequate equipment is at hand to start an immediate abatement of pollution'. A similar general obligation is contained in the other regional conventions, although protocols to the Mediterranean and Kuwait Conventions are currently under elaboration to lay down more more detailed provisions. It may also be noted that under the Canada–Denmark agreement of 1983 the parties undertake to take measures to ensure that offshore installations are 'designed, constructed, placed, equipped, marked, operated and maintained in such a manner that the risk of pollution of the marine environment is minimised' (art. V). The parties must also notify each other, and if necessary consult, over the initiation of offshore operations which may create a significant risk of pollution.

As regards the question of avoiding accidental pollution resulting from collisions between ships and installations, there are some general rules of international law which are relevant. In chapters eight and nine it was pointed out that sea-bed installations must not be placed where interference may be caused to the use of recognised sea lanes essential to international navigation, and must be properly marked and lit. In addition, the IMO has recommended that fairways or routeing systems for shipping should be established through offshore exploration areas where the proliferation of oil installations or traffic patterns warrant it.[42] Such fairways have been established in the Gulf of Mexico (done in fact before the IMO recommendation) and elsewhere. Compliance by ships with fairways may be enforced by the coastal State in its territorial sea, but beyond that limit enforcement lies solely with the flag States (cf. chapter thirteen, p. 213). The IMO has also recommended that ships not involved with the offshore oil industry should avoid certain areas, such as the Gulf of Campeche, because of the degree of offshore oil and gas activitiy in such areas.[43]

Where large-scale accidental pollution has occurred, for example as the result of a blow-out, the various conventions dealing with co-operation in pollution emergencies, referred to earlier when discussing pollution from shipping, apply. In addition,the offshore oil industry in many areas has its own schemes for dealing with accidents: for example, since 1978 North Sea operators have been grouped into six 'Sector Clubs', within each of which plans have been developed for operators to assist each other in the event of an emergency with fire-fighting vessels and other emergency equipment.[44]

Liability.   Special rules concerning liability for damage caused by sea-bed pollution at present exist only for north-west European waters, although all the regional conventions and the Law of the Sea Convention (art. 235) contain a general provision committing their parties to develop special liability regimes for this, as well as for other forms of marine pollution. In north-west Europe the Convention on Civil Liability for Oil Pollution Damage resulting from Exploration for and Exploitation of Seabed Mineral Resources was signed in 1977, although it is not yet in force and appears unlikely ever to enter into force. The 1977 Convention is modelled on the 1969 Civil Liability Convention (discussed above) and thus is based, with some exceptions, on the principle of strict, but limited, liability. The operator of a continental shelf installation causing pollution damage is automatically liable for that damage and any remedial measures taken unless he can prove that the damage resulted from war or an act of God or from an abandoned well more than five years after it was abandoned, or from an intentional or negligent act done by the person suffering pollution damage (art. 3). As a *quid pro quo* for this strict liability, the operator's liability is limited to forty million SDRs (art. 6), although it is open to a State party, if it so wishes, to provide that the liability of the operators of installations on its continental shelf shall be higher or even unlimited in respect of pollution damage caused in that State (art.15). In any case, an operator's liability is unlimited if the pollution damage 'occurred as a result of an act or omission by the operator himself, done deliberately with actual knowledge that pollution damage would result' (art. 6(4)). The rest of the 1977 Convention deals, in a manner broadly similar to the 1969 Convention, with compulsory insurance (which must provide cover of not less than thirty-five million SDRs) (art. 8); the procedure for bringing claims (the limitation period is shorter than in the 1969 Convention, but there is a wider choice of forum) (arts. 10 and 11); and the recognition of judgments (art. 12).

Even though the 1977 Convention is not yet in force, the advantages which it would bring for both operators and the victims of pollution damage are already provided for in north-west European waters by an industry scheme — the Offshore Pollution Liability Agreement (OPOL)[45] — which has been in existence since 1975. OPOL, whose parties are oil companies operating in north-west European waters, broadly parallels the Convention, rather as the industry schemes of TOVALOP and CRISTAL parallel the 1969 Civil Liability and 1971 Fund Conventions in respect of pollution from shipping. Unlike the Convention, the limits of liability in OPOL are expressed in US dollars and not SDRs. The upper limit of liability is US $60 million (raised from the initial limit of $25 million). According to the Eighth Report of the Royal Commission on Environmental Pollution,[46] by 1981 only £150 had been paid out under OPOL as far as incidents on the United Kingdom continental shelf are concerned — a reflection of the high safety standards at present prevailing on the British continental shelf.

Miscellaneous sea-bed pollution. Miscellaneous deliberate, but relatively minor, pollution from sea-bed installations may occur in a number of ways — the discharge of drilling muds and cuttings, production water and displacement water,[47] which contain oil and chemicals; the dumping of debris; and the discharge of sewage and garbage. Such pollution is governed by a number of conventions. The 1973 MARPOL Convention, referred to earlier, applies to pollution from continental shelf installations, other than the 'release of harmful substances directly arising from the exploration, exploitation and associated offshore processing of seabed mineral resources' (art. 2). Annex I regulates the amount of oil which can be discharged in offshore operations, while Annexes IV and V (when they enter into force) will regulate the discharge of sewage and garbage. The London, Oslo and Mediterranean Conventions apply to dumping from continental shelf installations, but they do not cover the disposal of wastes incidental to or derived from the normal operation of installations. The London Convention also contains the same proviso as article 2 of the MARPOL Convention. Finally, the Paris Convention (discussed below under 'Landbased sources') applies to continental shelf installations. In this regard there would appear to be some overlap between the Paris and Oslo Conventions, but so far this does not appear to have given rise to any practical difficulties, perhaps because the Paris and Oslo Commissions hold joint, as well as separate, meetings using as far as possible the same commissioners, and are serviced by the same secretariat.

The international sea bed area

Article 145 of the Law of the Sea Convention provides that the International Sea Bed Authority is to adopt rules to prevent pollution from deep-sea mining, particular attention being paid to the consequences of 'such activities as drilling, dredging, excavation, disposal of waste, construction and operation or maintenance of installations, pipelines and other devices related to such activities'. Assuming such rules fall within the category of 'rules, regulations and procedures [relating to] prospecting, exploration and exploitation in the Area (and article 17 of Annex III strongly suggests this is the case), pollution rules are to be approved by the Assembly after having been provisionally adopted by the Council, which in turn is to receive recommendations from the Legal and Technical Commission (LOSC, arts. 160(2)(f), 162(2)(o), 165(2)(e)). In addition to pollution regulations adopted by the Authority, article 209 requires States to adopt national legislation which is no less effective than the Authority's regulations.

As far as the enforcement of pollution regulations in the Area is concerned, article 215 states that enforcement shall be governed by the provisions of Part XI. In fact this part contains no provisions specifically dealing with enforcement. Article 139 of the Law of the Sea Convention suggests that in respect of activities by companies, whether private or State-owned, enforcement will be by the State whose nationality the company has; and in respect of activities by the Enterprise enforcement will be by the Enterprise and the Authority. It should be noted, however, that even in respect of non-Enterprise operations the Authority appears to have residual enforcement powers. Under article 153 the Authority is to 'exercise such control over activities in the Area as is necessary for the purpose of securing compliance with' its regulations, and every applicant for sea-bed mining undertakes to accept such control (LOSC, Annex III, art. 4(6)(b)). Furthermore, under article 162(2) the Council can 'issue emergency orders, which may include orders for the suspension or adjustment of operations, to prevent serious harm to the marine environment arising out of activities in the Area' (sub-paragrah w) and 'establish appropriate mechanisms for directing and supervising a staff of inspectors who shall inspect activities in the Area to determine' whether the Authority's regulations are being complied with (sub-paragraph z). In addition, the Legal and Technical Commission, at the request of the Council, is to supervise activities in the Area (LOSC, art. 165(2)(c)).

The Basic Conditions of Prospecting, Exploration and Exploitation, set out in Annex III, will also help to secure compliance with the Authority's pollution regulations. Prospecting is to be conducted only after the Authority has received a satisfactory written undertaking that the proposed prospector will comply with the Authority's pollution regulations and will accept verification by the Authority of compliance (LOSC, Annex III, art. 2(1)(b)). Exploration and exploitation are to take place only in accordance with a contract between the operator and the Authority: one of the conditions of such contracts is that the Authority's pollution regulations are strictly observed (LOSC, Annex III, arts. 3, 4). Failure to do so will lead to the contract being suspended or terminated, and monetary penalities being imposed on the contractor (LOSC, Annex III, art. 18). Furthermore, the Council is not to allow exploration and exploitation in areas 'where substantial evidence indicates the risk of serious harm to the marine environment' (LOSC, art. 162(2)(x)).

For sea-bed mining which begins before the Law of the Sea Convention comes into force or which take place outside the framework of the Convention — an increasingly likely possibility (see chapter twelve) — at present little international law is applicable. The MARPOL and London Dumping Conventions would to some extent apply (and most reciprocating States are parties to both conventions). In time the reciprocating States may feel it necessary to conclude a special agreement on the topic, or at least harmonise their legislation which at present is very diverse in this respect.

Land-based sources of marine pollution

Although pollution from land is the most important source of marine pollution, it is the source in respect of which least international legislative action has so far been taken. No general multilateral convention on the subject has yet been negotiated, although the Law of the Sea Convention requires States to adopt legislation to reduce marine pollution from land-based sources (LOSC, art. 194, 207):[48] however, this obligation is so imprecisely and broadly formulated that it is unlikely to have much practical effect. Regional conventions, which are better suited to tackle the problems of land-based marine pollution, have dealt with it less extensively and more slowly than the other sources of marine pollution. This is not surprising. Land-based pollution is the most 'national' source of marine pollution. It emanates from an area that is under the sovereignty of a State and in which other States enjoy no rights (unlike the position in relation to other forms of marine pollution). There is only one State (the territorial State) that can legislate for such pollution and enforce that legislation (unlike shipping or dumping). Furthermore, different national traditions of legislation and policy make it difficult for countries to agree on a uniform approach: see, for example, the differences between the United Kingdom and its EEC partners over the question of whether EEC directives should be based on uniform emission standards or water quality standards. Proponents of the former view argue that such standards make the cost of taking anti-pollution measures the same for all industries, while proponents of the latter view (such as the United Kingdom) argue that the capacity of some water areas to break down pollutants more quickly should be recognised. Added to these difficulties is the fact that there are so many different pollutants produced by a wide variety of activities and that there are various ways for them to enter the sea from land (rivers, the atmosphere or direct). Furthermore, much of this pollution is difficult to monitor.

The Paris Convention.   The first regional convention to tackle land-based marine pollution in detail was the Convention for the Prevention of Marine Pollution from Land-based Sources, 1974 (hereafter referred to as the Paris Convention), which applies to the north-east Atlantic and North Sea and covers all pollution emanating from land (arts. 2, 3). The Convention regulates land-based pollution by dividing pollutants into four categories. The first category (the 'black list') consists of the most noxious pollutants, and includes organohalogen compounds, mercury, cadmium, persistent synthetic materials and oil (Part I of Annex A). Parties to the Paris Convention have undertaken to 'eliminate' pollution by such substances (art. (art. 4(1)). The second category (the 'grey list') consists of rather less noxious pollutants, including organic compounds of phosphorous, silicon and tin, phosphorous, non-persistent oils, arsenic and heavy metals (Part II of Annex A). Pollution by these substances must be strictly limited, and each contracting party has had to introduce a system of permits to regulate the discharge of such pollutants (art. 4). Radioactive substances come into a special category because, as we have seen earlier, they are already the subject of research and recommendations by various international organisations: in respect of these substances contracting parties have undertaken to 'adopt measures to forestall and, as appropriate, eliminate pollution' (art. 5). The final category consists of all other pollutants. No special measures are required of contracting parties in the case of such pollutants, but they have to try to reduce pollution by such substances, taking into account relevant circumstances such as the nature and quantity of the pollutants in question, the state of the waters which may be affected, and so on (art. 6). Where pollution (other than from substances falling into the first category) from the territory of one State is likely to prejudice the interests of another State, the States concerned are to consult together with the object of negotiating a co-operation agreement (art. 9). No such agreements appear yet to have been concluded.

Implementation and enforcement of the Paris Convention's provisions are carried out by the national authorities of the parties (art. 12), but the Convention has also established a Commission, the functions of which include overall supervision of the implementation of the Convention; reviewing the state of the seas in the Convention area; assessing the effectiveness of control measures and, where appropriate, recommending additional measures; reviewing and distributing information from contracting parties on the state of the seas in the Convention area and measures taken to reduce pollution; and recommending amendments to the different lists of pollutants (art. 16). Recommendations of the Commission, which must be adopted by a majority of not less than three-quarters of the parties, are binding on all the parties unless objected to (art. 18). The Commission shares a secretariat with the Oslo Dumping Commission, and the two commissions are composed, as far as possible, of the same representatives and usually meet at the same time, both separately and jointly.

Since it came into being, the Commission has studied the sources of the more noxious pollutants — an essential preliminary before taking any regulatory measures. In relation to the latter there has been an intense — and so far unresolved — debate over whether to use uniform emission standards (UES) or water quality objectives (WQO). As a result, for the substances for which it has so far adopted discharge standards — mercury, hydrocarbons, cadmium and organohalogen compounds — the Commission has set both UESs and WQOs.

The Mediterranean Protocol.   The 1980 Protocol to the Mediterranean Convention is in many ways similar to the Paris Convention. The Protocol covers all pollution emanating from land except that discharged into the atmosphere, which is to be the subject of a subsequent annex to the Protocol (art. 4). The parties to the Protocol are to 'eliminate' pollution by the substances listed in Annex I (which is similar to the Paris Convention's 'black list') (art. 5) and 'strictly limit' pollution by the substances listed in Annex II (which is much more extensive than the Paris Convention's 'grey list') by means of permits (and more guidance is given than in the Paris Convention as to when such permits may be issued — see Annex III) (art. 6). In order to fulfil these obligations, the parties shall agree on timetables and measures such as common emission standards, and also adopt common guidelines and criteria relating to pipelines used for coastal outfalls; effluents requiring separate treatment; the quality of sea water; and the control and progressive replacement of products and processes causing significant marine pollution (art. 7).

The parties must inform each other through UNEP of the measures they have taken, the results achieved and difficulties encountered in applying the Protocol (art. 13). Meetings shall be held every two years for the purposes *inter alia* of keeping implementation of the Protocol under review; amending the annexes to the Protocol; and adopting the timetables, measures, guidelines and criteria referred to above (art. 14). In implementation of the Protocol the parties have adopted measures concerning the quality of bathing water and shellfish water, the quality of shellfish for human consumption, and mercury in marine products.

Other treaties. The Baltic Convention adopts a not dissimilar approach from the Paris Convention and the Mediterranean Protocol. Article 6(1) lays down a general obligation on States parties to 'take all appropriate measures to control and minimise land-based pollution'. Certain noxious pollutants listed in Annex II, such as heavy metals, hydrocarbon compounds, radioactive materials, oil and acids, may be discharged only if a permit has been issued by a State party. The parties are to co-operate in the development of common criteria for the issue of such permits. Under article 5 the parties undertake to 'counteract the introduction' into the marine environment of DDT and its derivatives and PCBs from any source. They shall control and minimise pollution from other pollutants by aiming at attaining the goals and applying the criteria enumerated in Annex III: these are concerned with the treatment of sewage, industrial wastes and the discharge of cooling water. The Commission which has been set up by the Convention is to define these goals and criteria more precisely. This the Commission has so far done for pollutants used in agriculture, the treatment of sewage, waste water from industrial plants and the treatment of stormwater.

The Protocol to the South-East Pacific Convention is fairly similar to the Mediterranean Protocol. The other regional conventions, however, are much less detailed, simply providing that States parties are to take all appropriate measures to prevent, reduce and control marine pollution from land-based sources. It may be that in time protocols to give detailed effect to this general obligation will be elaborated, as has happened with the Mediterranean Convention, and indeed a protocol to the Kuwait Convention is currently being elaborated.

The EEC has also adopted a number of measures which are concerned with reducing land-based marine pollution, but lack of space prevents any discussion of their details.[49] Finally, in considering agreements concerned with pollution from land-based sources, mention should be made of agreements whose aim is to control and reduce the pollution of rivers (which of course will in turn help to reduce pollution of the sea). There are a number of such agreements, the most important of which in practice are perhaps two agreements of 1976 relating to the Rhine. The first agreement is aimed at reducing the discharge of chlorides into the Rhine, while the aim of the second is to eliminate the discharge of the most noxious chemical pollutants, and control the discharge of less noxious chemicals by means of a system of permits.

Liability. Unlike the case with shipping or sea-bed activities, there are no international agreements to facilitate the bringing of claims for compensation by a national of one State who has suffered damage from pollution emanating from another State. The one — and geographically limited — exception is the Nordic Convention on the Protection of the Environment, article 3 of which provides that a national of one Nordic State may bring an action before the court of another Nordic State to prevent a particular pollution from continuing or to claim compensation for damage suffered. If an individual is unwilling or unable to proceed, his role in instituting proceedings may be taken over by the Supervisory Authority which each State Party has established for this purpose. The lack of other agreements is not surprising. With land-based pollution it is often difficult to identify the source of the pollution, and to establish a causal link between that source and the damage suffered. It is likely, therefore, that only in exceptional cases will an action for compensation have any chance of success. On the other hand, it might be desirable to introduce provisions similar to the Nordic Convention in other regions in order to facilitate the bringing of actions by litigants before foreign courts.

Atmospheric pollution

Although pollution from the atmosphere is essentially a form of land-based pollution, the Law of the Sea Convention treats it as a separate source of marine pollution. Articles 212 and 222 provide that States shall prescribe and enforce legislation to prevent marine pollution from the atmosphere, applicable to the air space under their sovereignty and to their vessels and aircraft. Article 212(3) calls on States to establish global and regional rules to prevent atmospheric pollution. The most significant attempt so far to develop international rules dealing with atmospheric pollution is the UN Economic Commission for Europe's Convention on Long-range Trans-boundary Air Pollution, 1979. Under that convention, which was particularly inspired by the problems of 'acid rain', contracting parties are obliged gradually to reduce and prevent air pollution. While the Convention is notable for the absence of any precise details as to how or when this shall be done, a protocol to the Convention, adopted in 1985, provides that States parties to it are to reduce sulphur dioxide emissions by thirty per cent of 1980 levels by 1993.

There are also a number of other agreements concerned with atmospheric pollution. As already mentioned, the Oslo and London Dumping Conventions regulate the incineration of wastes at sea. In 1986 a protocol to the Paris Convention was adopted (though it is not yet in force) which extends the scope of the Convention to atmospheric pollution. Finally, one of the consequences of the 1963 Nuclear Test Ban Treaty (discussed in chapter seventeen) is the end of pollution of the sea by radioactive fallout from nuclear weapons testing in the atmosphere.

Conclusion

As this chapter shows, a vast amount of international law dealing with marine pollution has been adopted in recent years. With the exception of UNEP's Regional Seas Programme, where some work still remains to be done, the time has now come for a period of consolidation. The international community should concentrate on three matters. First, it should seek to bring into force those conventions that are not yet in force and to increase the number of ratifications of all conventions. Secondly, it should aim to improve the observance and enforcement of existing international rules. Finally, there needs to be greatly increased monitoring of the effects of existing rules on marine pollution, with the aim of seeing what deficiencies there are in the rules and whether further international legislative action is desirable.

Notes

1 Quoted in M. Hardy, 'Definition and forms of marine pollution', in *ND* III, p. 73.
2 [1949] ICJ Rep. 3, at 22.
3 III *RIAA* 1905, at 1965.
4 The correspondence between Canada and the USA on this question is reproduced in IX *ILM* 605–15 and *ND* I, pp. 211–21.
5 Convention on the Protection of the Marine Environment of the Baltic Sea

Area, 1974 (hereafter referred to as the Baltic Convention).

6 Convention for the Protection of the Mediterranean Sea against Pollution, 1976 (hereafter referred to as the Mediterranean Convention), together with its protocols on dumping (1976), co-operation in emergencies (1976), land-based sources (1980) and specially protected areas (1982).

7 Kuwait Regional Convention for Co-operation on the Protection of the Marine Environment from Pollution, 1978 (hereafter referred to as the Kuwait Convention), together with its protocol on co-operation in emergencies (1978).

8 Convention for Co-operation in the Protection and Development of the Marine and Coastal Environment of the West and Central African Region, 1981 (hereafter referred to as the West African Convention), together with its protocol on co-operation in emergencies (1981).

9 Convention for the Protection of the Marine Environment and Coastal Area of the South-East Pacific, 1981 (hereafter referred to as the South-East Pacific Convention), together with its agreement and supplementary protocol on co-operation in emergencies (1981 and 1983) and protocol on land-based sources (1983).

10 Regional Convention for the Conservation of the Red Sea and Gulf of Aden Environment, 1982 (hereafter referred to as the Red Sea Convention), together with its protocol on co-operation in emergencies (1982).

11 Convention for the Protection and Development of the Marine Environment of the Wider Caribbean Region, 1983 (hereafter referred to as the Caribbean Convention), together with its protocol on co-operation in emergencies (1983).

12 Convention for the Protection, Management and Development of the Marine and Coastal Environment of the Eastern African Region, 1985 (hereafter referred to as the East African Convention), together with its protocols on protected areas (1985) and co-operation in emergencies (1985).

13 Convention for the Protection of the Natural Resources and Environment of the South Pacific Region, 1986 (hereafter referred to as the South Pacific Convention), together with its protocols on co-operation in emergencies (1986) and dumping (1986).

14 Agreement for Co-Operation in Dealing with Pollution of the North Sea by Oil 1969; Agreement for Co-Operation in Dealing with Pollution of the North Sea by Oil and Other Harmful Substances, 1983.

15 Convention for the Prevention of Marine Pollution by Dumping from Ships and Aircraft, 1972, together with its protocol on incineration (1983).

16 Convention for the Prevention of Marine Pollution from Land-based Sources, 1974, together with its protocol on atmospheric pollution (1986).

17 International Convention on Civil Liability for Oil Pollution Damage resulting from Exploration for, or Exploitation of, Submarine Mineral Resources, 1977.

18 Agreement concerning Co-operation in Measures to deal with Pollution of the Sea by Oil, 1971 and Convention on the Protection of the Enviroment, 1974.

19 There are a number of reasons why this has to be done. If the oil remains, the risk of an explosion increases, drainage of the tanks may be impeded, the cargo capacity of the tank is decreased and the oily residue may be incompatible with the next cargo to be loaded.

20 *IMCO News*, 1981, No. 4, pp. 8–9.

21 I.e tanks used for ballast water must be kept separate from tanks carrying oil.

22 A method of cleaning cargo oil tanks by using crude oil instead of water.

23 IMO Assembly Resolution A. 491 (XII).

24 In fact the MARPOL Convention does not use the term 'territorial sea', but 'jurisdiction'. 'Jurisdiction' clearly includes the territorial sea, and may in time include the EEZ (see the discussion of the position under the Law of the Sea Convention at pp. 256–7 below). Cf. art. 9(3) of the MARPOL Convention, which states that the term 'jurisdiction' 'shall be construed in the light of international law in force at the time of application or interpretation' of the Convention.

25 It may be noted that the MARPOL Convention is one of the conventions for compliance with which ships are to be inspected under the Western European Memorandum of Understanding on Port State Control, discussed in chapter thirteen.

26 Some of the provisions of these conventions may represent customary international law, in which case the Law of the Sea Convention merely confirms obligations which exist already. For a much fuller discussion of this whole topic, see W. Van Reenen, 'Rules of reference in the new Convention on the Law of the Sea, in particular in connection with the pollution of the sea by oil from tankers', XII *NYIL* 3–44 (1981).

27 *IMO News*, 1986 No. 3, p. 14.

28 Agreement relating to the Establishment of Joint Pollution Contingency Plans for Spills of Oil and other Noxious Substances, 1974.

29 Agreement of Co-operation regarding Pollution of the Marine Environment by Discharges of Hydrocarbons and other Hazardous Substances, 1980.

30 Agreement for Co-Operation relating to the Marine Environment, 1983.

31 *ACOPS Yearbook 1986–87*, pp. 62 and 67.

32 E.g. UK–USA Agreement relating to the Use of United Kingom Ports and Territorial Waters by the N. S. *Savannah*, 1964. For a list of other agreements of this type, see *ND* VI, pp. 770–2.

33 E.g. Federal Republic of Germany–Liberia Treaty on the Use of Liberian Waters and Ports by N. S. *Otto Hahn*, 1970. For a list of other agreements of this type, see *ND* VI, p. 772.

34 Text in XXIII *ILM* 150 (1984).

35 XVIII *ILM* 510–16 (1979).

36 A term which is probably deliberately vague, but which includes the territorial sea, and under art. 210 of the Law of the Sea Convention (see below) will in time include the EEZ and continental shelf.

37 The text of the resolution is reproduced in 1 *International Journal of Estuarine and Coastal Law* 209–11 (1986).

38 XVII *ILM* 445–52 (1978).

39 House of Lords Select Committee on the European Communities, *op. cit.*, in 'Further reading', p. 21.

40 IMO Assembly Resolution A. 414 (XI) of 1979.

41 See, for example, the Agreement relating to the Transmission of Petroleum by Pipeline from the Ekofisk Field and Neighbouring Areas to the United Kingdom, 1973, art. 8; and the Agreement relating to the Exploitation of the Frigg Field Reservoir and the Transmission of Gas therefrom to the United Kingdom, 1976, arts. 7, 8, 17 and 18.

42 IMO Assembly Resolution A. 379 (X) of 1977.

43 IMO Assembly Resolution A. 527 (XIII) of 1983.

44 Royal Commission on Environmental Pollution, *op. cit.*, in 'Further reading', p. 120.

45 *ND* VI, p. 507.
46 *Op. cit.*, in 'Further reading', p. 76.
47 I.e. water displaced from containers which some production platforms have for storing oil.
48 Furthermore, art. 207(4) provides that States 'shall endeavour to establish global and regional rules, standards and recommended practices and procedures to prevent, reduce and control pollution of the marine environment from land-based sources'. Once such international rules and standards have been adopted, they should be implemented by States (LOSC, art. 213). It should also be noted that in 1985 UNEP adopted a set of 'Guidelines for the Protection of the Marine Environment against Pollution from Land-Based Sources' which it has recommended States and international organisations should take into account when developing national legislation and international agreements on land-based pollution. The Guidelines are intended to be a checklist of basic provisions rather than a model agreement. The text of the Guidelines is reproduced in 14 *Environmental Policy and Law* 77–83 (1985).
49 As to which see *ACOPS Yearbooks* and N. Haigh, *EEC Environmental Policy and Britain: An Essay and a Handbook*, London, 1984.

Further reading

General

A. E. Boyle, 'Marine pollution under the Law of the Sea Convention', 79 *AJIL* 347–72 (1985).

D. J. Cusine and J. P. Grant (eds.), *The Impact of Marine Pollution*, London, 1980.

E. Du Pontavice and P. Cordier, *La mer et le droit*, Paris, 1984, chap. 3.

K. Hakapää, *Marine Pollution in International Law*, Helsinki, 1981.

M. Hardy, 'International control of marine pollution', in J. E. S. Fawcett and R. Higgins (eds.), *International Organisation*, London, 1974, pp. 103–41.

J. L. Hargrove (ed.), *Who Protects the Ocean? Environment and the Development of the Law of the Sea*, St. Paul, Minn., 1975.

D. M. Johnston (ed.), *The Environmental Law of the Sea*, Berlin, 1981.

Royal Commission on Environmental Pollution, Eighth Report, *Oil Pollution of the Sea*, Cmnd. 8358, London, 1981.

G. J. Timagenis, *International Control of Marine Pollution*, Alphen aan den Rijn, 1980.

Pollution from ships

D. W. Abecassis and R. L. Jarashow, *Oil Pollution from Ships*, 2nd ed., London, 1985.

P. W. Birnie, 'The legal regime for prevention of collisions and stranding of vessels carrying noxious or hazardous cargoes', in Second Report from the Expenditure Committee, *Measures to Prevent Collisions and Strandings of Noxious Cargo Carriers in Waters around the United Kingdom*, House of Commons Paper (1978–79) 105, Vol. I, pp. lix-xciv.

E. D. Brown, 'The International Oil Pollution Compensation Fund: an analytical report on Fund practice', in W. E. Butler (ed.), *The Law of the Sea and International Shipping*, New York, 1985, pp. 275–313.

A. F. M. De Bièvre, 'Liability and compensation for damage in connection with the carriage of hazardous and noxious substances by sea', 17 *JMLC* 61–88 (1986).

E. Gold, *Handbook on Marine Pollution*, Arendal, 1985.

R. Kbaier and V. Sebek, 'New trends in compensation for oil pollution damage', 9 *Marine Policy* 269–79 (1985).

A. Kiss, 'L'affaire de l'*Amoco Cadiz*: responsibilité pour une catastrophe écologique', 112 *JDI* 575–601 (1985).

R. M. M'Gonigle and M. W. Zacher, *Pollution, Politics and International Law. Tankers at Sea*, Berkeley, Cal., 1979.

S. Z. Pritchard, *Oil Pollution Control*, London, 1987.

P. C. Szasz, 'The Convention on the Liability of Operators of Nuclear Ships', 2 *JMLC* 541–69 (1971).

Dumping

J. M. Bewers and C. J. R. Garrett, 'Analysis of the issues related to sea dumping of radioactive wastes', 11 *Marine Policy* 105–24 (1987).

S. Boehmer–Christiansen, 'An end to radioactive waste disposal at sea?', 10 *Marine Policy* 119–31 (1986).

C. E. Curtis, 'Legality of seabed disposal of high-level radioactive waste under the London Dumping Convention', 14 *ODIL* 383–415 (1985).

R. N. Duncan, 'The 1972 Convention on the Prevention of Marine Pollution by Dumping of Wastes at Sea', 5 *JMLC* 299–315 (1974).

House of Lords Select Committee on the European Communities, *Dumping of Waste at Sea*, HL Paper (1985–86) 219.

UN, *The Law of the Sea: Pollution by Dumping*, New York, 1985.

Pollution from sea-bed activities

E. D. Brown, *Sea-Bed Energy and Mineral Resources and the Law of the Sea*, London, Vol I (1984), chap. 12 and Vol. II (1986), chap. 9.

A. L. C. De Mestral, 'The prevention of pollution of the marine environment arising from offshore mining and drilling', 20 *Harvard International Law Journal* 469–518 (1979).

B. A. Dubais, 'The 1976 London Convention on Civil Liability for Oil Pollution Damage from Offshore Operations', 9 *JMLC* 61–78 (1977).

S. M. Evans, 'Control of marine pollution generated by offshore oil and gas exploration and exploitation', 10 *Marine Policy* 258–70 (1986).

Pollution from land-based sources

S. Burchi, 'International legal aspects of pollution of the sea from rivers', 3 *Italian Yearbook of International Law* 115–42 (1977).

J. I. Charney (ed.), *The New Nationalism and the Use of Common Spaces*, Totowa, N. J., 1982, chaps 2–4.

J. E. Hickey, 'Custom and land-based pollution of the high seas', 15 *San Diego Law Review* 409–75 (1978).

S. Kuwabara, *The Legal Regime of the Protection of the Mediterranean against Pollution from Land-Based Sources*, Dublin, 1984.

B. Kwiatkowska, 'Marine pollution from land-based sources: current problems and prospects', 14 *ODIL* 315–35 (1984).

J. G. Lammers, *Pollution of International Watercourses*, The Hague, 1984.

Regional pollution agreements

B. A. Boczek, 'International protection of the Baltic Sea environment against pollution. A study in marine regionalism', 72 *AJIL* 782–814 (1978).

S. Boehmer-Christiansen, 'Marine pollution control in Europe', 8 *Marine Policy* 44–55 (1984).

A. Boyle, 'Regional pollution agreements and the Law of the Sea Convention', in W. E. Butler (ed.), *op. cit. supra*, pp. 315–51.

J. A. De Yturriaga, 'Regional conventions on the protection of the marine environment', 162 *Recueil des Cours* 319–449 (1979).

P. Fotheringham and P. W. Birnie, 'Regulation of North Sea marine pollution', in C. M. Mason (ed.), *The Effective Management of Resources*, London, 1979, pp. 168–223.

P. Hayward. 'Environmental protection: regional approaches', 8 *Marine Policy* 106–19 (1984).

C. O. Okidi, *Regional Control of Ocean Pollution. Legal and Institutional Problems and Prospects*, Alphen aan den Rijn, 1978.

The Oslo and Paris Commissions, *The First Decade*, London, 1984.

L. J. Saliba, 'Protecting the Mediterranean — coordinating regional action', 2 *Marine Policy* 171–80 (1978).

CHAPTER SIXTEEN

Marine scientific research and the transfer of technology

Introduction

Marine scientific research serves a wide variety of purposes. Adequate and effective scientific research is a basic precondition for the rational exploitation of the sea's resources. For example, the harvesting of a particular stock of fish at levels which do not lead to overfishing can be achieved only if there is constant monitoring of the size of and recruitment to the stock. Exploitation of offshore oil is possible only where the necessary geological research has been carried out to locate oilfields. The study of waves, currents, the sea bed and weather helps to make navigation safer. Furthermore, the preservation of the marine environment is also dependent on scientific research — first, to discover what substances cause what kinds of harm to the sea and its living organisms, and, secondly, to find ways in which pollution can be abated or eliminated. Marine research may also be more or less directly linked to military uses of the sea: for example, by trying to improve the ability to detect submarines. Finally, marine scientific research may also help to tell us more about the earth generally: for example, it is study of the sea floor which has largely prompted the theory that the earth's crust consists of a number of large, moving plates.

This chapter begins by examining the scope of the competence to conduct marine scientific research. It then goes on to deal with the legal status of installations used in conducting research and with international co-operation in marine research. Finally, the chapter considers a question separate from, but related to marine scientific research, the transfer of marine technology.

Scope of the competence to conduct marine scientific research

Until the middle of the twentieth century no legal controls on the conduct of marine scientific research were perceived to be necessary, and indeed the law of the sea literature up to this time contains virtually no mention of scientific research. This may be explained partly by the generally prevailing attitude that scientific research should be free of governmental controls, and partly by the modest scale and limited practical application of marine scientific research. It is the great increase in marine research since the Second World War, together with a better appreciation of its practical application to resource and military purposes, that has led the international community to introduce controls on marine scientific research, first in the Geneva Conventions and latterly, and rather more extensively, in the Law of the Sea Convention.

The 1958 rules.   Under the Geneva regime marine research is generally regarded as being a freedom of the high seas, even though not mentioned in the list of freedoms in article 2 of the High Seas Convention. However, this list is expressly stated not to be exhaustive, and in its commentary on the draft article which eventually became article 2, the International Law Commissional specifically referred to marine research as an example of a freedom not mentioned in the article. Furthermore, scientific research has been conducted on the high seas by the vessels of many different States for the past century or more without giving rise to any recorded protest.

The restrictions on marine research laid down in the Geneva Conventions relate to research in the territorial sea and on the continental shelf. As regards the former, the territorial sea is subject to the sovereignty of the coastal State, and the only right which third States enjoy there is the right of innocent passage (see chapter four). It therefore follows that research in the territorial sea will be permissible only where the coastal State has given its consent, and subject to any conditions which the coastal State lays down. The one possible exception would be if, during the course of exercising its right of innocent passage through the territorial sea, a vessel engaged in research in such a way that this research was regarded as being incidental to the main purpose of the vessels' passage through the territorial sea. However, this question is controversial, and it may be that whatever the form of research it would always take the vessel outside the concept of 'passage'. Even if a vessel could engage in research while exercising the right of innocent passage, the coastal State would be able to prescribe conditions regulating such research (see TSC, art. 17). Although the Geneva Conventions say nothing about internal waters, it is clear from the legal status of such waters in customary international law (see chapter three) that research may be undertaken there only with the consent of the coastal State.

Research on the continental shelf is dealt with by article 5 of the Continental Shelf Convention. Article 5(1) begins by stating that the 'exploration of the continental shelf and the exploitation of its natural resources must not . . . result in any interference with fundamental oceanographic or other scientific research carried out with the intention of open publication'. This broad principle is, however, considerably qualified by article 5(8), which reads:

The consent of the coastal State shall be obtained in respect of any research concerning the continental shelf and undertaken there. Nevertheless, the coastal State shall not normally withhold its consent if the request is submitted by a qualified institution with a view to purely scientific research into the physical or biological characteristics of the continental shelf, subject to the proviso that the coastal State shall have the right, if it so desires, to participate or to be represented in the research, and that in any event the results shall be published.

The result is that both pure and applied research on the continental shelf require the consent of the coastal State, but in the case of the former consent shall not 'normally' be withheld if the various conditions as to participation, publication, etc., are complied with. While the broad intent of article 5(8) is reasonably obvious, the details of its drafting give rise to many difficulties. For instance, two interpretations are possible of the phrase 'research concerning the continental shelf and undertaken there'. One is that it means that consent is required only where the research both concerns the continental shelf and is physically undertaken on the shelf, i.e. on the sea bed: the other is that consent is required both for research concerning the continental shelf — whether conducted on the sea bed or in the superjacent waters — and for research conducted on the sea bed, whether it concerns the continental shelf or not. As to which interpretation is correct, the *travaux préparatoires* of the Continental Shelf Convention give little guidance, while the practice of parties to the Convention,[1] though not conclusive, appears to support the second interpretation. Whichever interpretation is right, it is clear that consent is not required for research in the superjacent waters which does not concern the continental shelf: such research comes under the high-seas freedom of research and is not subject to coastal State interference, as article 5(1) makes clear.

The second sentence of article 5(8) also raises a number of difficulties. The distinction it makes between pure and applied research may not be easy to apply in practice. What may begin and be intended as 'pure' research may, once the research has actually been undertaken and its results analysed, turn out to have significant practical implications. Then the article gives no guidance as to what may be 'normal' situations in which consent to pure research should be given. There are further problems. What is a 'qualified' institution? At what stages in a project should coastal State participation begin and end? The imprecision of the Continental Shelf Convention's definition of the outer limit of the continental shelf (see chapter eight) also adds to the uncertainties surrounding marine research on the continental shelf.

A further restriction on scientific research has arisen in customary international law since the adoption of the Geneva conventions with the development of the concept of the exclusive fishing zone (see chapter fourteen). The majority of States which have claimed an exclusive fishing zone have also claimed the competence to regulate fisheries research within this zone where such research involves the taking of fish. The lack of protests against such claims suggests that this limitation on marine research has become part of customary international law. On the other hand, no States prior to UNCLOS III appear to have claimed the competence to regulate fisheries research in their exclusive fishing zones where such research does not involve the taking of fish, although there has in the past been a certain amount of discussion amongst writers as to whether such a claim would be permissible.

The controls on research introduced by the exclusive fishing zone and article 5(8) of the Continental Shelf Convention — which is often thought also to represent customary international law — appear in practice to have led to a definite restriction of marine research. A study of requests made between 1972 and 1978 by US vessels to undertake research in areas under other States' jurisdiction shows that seven per cent of such requests were rejected by the coastal State concerned — in nearly half these cases no reason was given — and a further twenty-one per cent of the requests were subject to inordinate (and therefore costly) delays.[2]

The Law of the Sea Convention. UNCLOS III was faced with much stronger demands for controls over marine scientific research than the Geneva Conference had been. These demands came chiefly from the developing countries and were inspired by two principal factors. First, the developing countries felt that they would be unable to benefit fully from the right to exploit the resources off their coasts which the introduction of the 200 mile EEZ would give them unless they had control over the research in those waters that might have application to resource exploitation. The second factor was the suspicion among at least some developing countries that research vessels, particularly those of the major military powers, were often used for espionage: these suspicions had been fuelled by incidents like that in 1968 involving the *Pueblo*, where a US ship posing as a research vessel was found by North Korea, allegedly inside its twelve-mile territorial sea, engaged in spying. The demands for greater controls over marine scientific research were resisted first and foremost by the scientific community. They had found the existing controls, which had begun to be applied from the mid-1960s onwards with the entry into force of the Continental Shelf Convention and the development of the exclusive fishing zone, irksome, and feared that further controls would lead to proposed research projects being refused or being made subject to undesirable conditions or long bureaucratic delays. They argued that scientific research benefited all mankind, and that the unity of the ocean demanded that its study be restricted by the fewest man-made boundaries. These concerns of the scientists were taken up at UNCLOS by the developed States, which are responsible for the overwhelming proportion of marine research at present being conducted. Nevertheless, the demands of the developing countries for greater controls over marine scientific research have largely been met by the Law of the Sea Convention, although these controls are to some extent more precisely, and therefore more narrowly, formulated than those of the Geneva Conventions. The major areas subject to controls are the EEZ and continental shelf, but the Law of the Sea Convention also makes changes to the position adopted by the Geneva Conventions for other maritime zones.

As far as the high seas are concerned, marine research is now specifically mentioned as a freedom of the high seas (art. 87). In comparison with the Geneva regime, it must be borne in mind that under the Law of the Sea Convention the sea bed and subsoil of the high seas beyond the continental shelf are now the international sea bed area. All States have the right to engage in research in the area, provided that it is carried out 'exclusively for peaceful purposes and for the benefit of mankind as a whole' (LOSC, art. 143(1)). A further condition is that of article 143(3), which requires States to 'promote international co-operation in marine scientific research in the Area by ... effectively disseminating the results of research and analysis when available, through the [International Sea Bed] Authority or other international channels when appropriate'. Where 'research' moves on to the stage of 'prospecting' or 'exploring' it is no longer unrestricted, but becomes subject to the provisions of Annex III (see chapter twelve). The Convention contains no precise guidance as to how 'research', 'prospecting' or 'exploring' are to be distinguished.

The basic principle that research in the territorial sea may be conducted only with the consent of, and subject to the conditions laid down by, the coastal State is affirmed by the Law of the Sea Convenion (art. 245). Although not specifically stated in the Convention, the same principle applies to research in archipelagic waters: this follows from the legal status of such waters (see chapter six). Unlike the Geneva Convention, the Law of the Sea Convention makes it clear that research may not be undertaken while a ship is exercising a right of innocent passage: any research or survey activities render the passage non-innocent (LOSC, art. 19). Similarly, a vessel engaged in transit passage through straits or archipelagic sea lanes passage through archipelagic waters may not carry out any research or survey activity without the prior authorisation of the strait or archipelagic State (LOSC, arts. 40, 54).

The most important provisions of the Law of the Sea Convention dealing with controls over marine scientific research are those relating to research in the EEZ and on the continental shelf, contained in articles 246–55. These provision adopt the same basic approach as article 5(8) of the Continental Shelf Convention. Thus all research in the EEZ and on the continental shelf requires the consent of the coastal State (LOSC, art. 246(2)). Like the Continental Shelf Convention, the Law of the Sea Convention seeks to distinguish in essence between pure and applied research, although it must be stressed that nowhere does the Convention in fact use these terms. Unlike the Continental Shelf Convention, however, an attempt is made to define each of the two categories of research. What will be labelled for convenience as applied research is that which is of 'direct significance for the exploration and exploitation of natural resources'; or which involves drilling into the continental shelf, the use of explosives or the introduction of harmful substances into the marine environment; or which involves the construction, operation and use of artificial islands, installations and structures (LOSC, art. 246(5)). What will be labelled here as pure research is research which is carried out 'exclusively for peaceful purposes and in order to increase scientific knowledge of the marine environment for the benefit of all mankind' (LOSC, art. 246(3)). In the case of pure research, consent must 'in normal circumstances' be given. In view of the difficulties that have been faced by marine scientists in the past, it is important to note that coastal States 'shall establish rules and procedures ensuring that such consent will not be delayed or denied unreasonably' (LOSC, art. 246(3)). In the case of applied research, the coastal State has a complete discretion whether to give its consent or not. It also has the same discretion when the researcher has provided inaccurate advance information as to the nature and objectives of the project or if the researcher has outstanding obligations to the coastal State from a prior research project (LOSC, art. 246(5)). It is important to note that any dispute over whether a coastal State has improperly withheld consent is not subject to any form of compulsory third-party settlement except compulsory conciliation under Annex V of the Convention (for details see chapter nineteen): but even here the coastal State's discretion to withhold consent to applied research or for the other reasons listed in article 246(5) may not be called into question (LOSC, art. 297(2)). In certain circumstances — where the proposed research project is to be carried out by an international organisation of which the coastal State is a member or where the coastal State does not respond within four months of being furnished with the necessary advance information by the researching State — consent is implied (LOSC, arts. 247, 252).

Those wishing to undertake research in a foreign State's EEZ or on its continental shelf are subject to a number of obligations. First, they must provide the coastal State with specified information about the proposed project at least six months in advance (LOSC, art. 248). Secondly, they must allow the coastal State to participate or be represented in the project (LOSC, art. 249(1)(a)). Thirdly, they must provide coastal States with the results of the research and ensure that such results are made internationally available as well as assisting the coastal State, if requested, in assessing and interpreting the results and data of the research (LOSC, arts. 249(1) (b)–(e)). Failure to comply with these obligations entitles the coastal State to suspend the research or require its cessation (LOSC, art. 253). In the case of pure research, it would seem from the wording of articles 246(1) and 249(2) that the coastal State is not entitled to lay down any conditions other than those just mentioned: in the case of applied research, on the other hand, it appears from article 249(2) that the coastal State can do so. Finally, whether research be pure or applied, it must be so conducted that it does not unjustifiably interfere with the legitimate activities of the coastal State (LOSC, art. 246(8)).

Compared with the Continental Shelf Convention, the distinction between pure and applied research is much clearer, and should give rise to fewer difficulties as to the types of research projects for which consent should normally be given. The obligation on the coastal State not to delay unreasonably in giving consent and the provisions on implied consent are also an improvement on the Continental Shelf Convention, as are the provisions specifying the conditions to which pure research may be subject and the amount of notice required. On the other hand, what is meant by 'normal circumstances' is little clearer than the corresponding phrase in the Continental Shelf Convention, except that article 246(4) stipulates that 'normal circumstances' can exist in spite of the absence of diplomatic relations between the coastal State and the researching State. This perhaps suggests that circumstances are 'normal' except where there is hostility or serious tension between the coastal State and the researching State.

A further problem concerns research carried out in the water column above the continental shelf where the latter extends beyond 200 miles. It is not clear whether coastal State consent is required where the research is directed at the sea bed (cf. the similar problem raised by the Continental Shelf Convention, discussed above). Article 246(2) simply talks of coastal State consent for research '*on* the continental shelf' (emphasis added), which may suggest that consent is only required for research physically taking place on the sea floor. The problem is lessened by article 246(6), which provides that a coastal State may not withhold its consent for applied research 'on' its continental shelf beyond the 200 mile limit outside those areas it has designated as areas in which exploitation or detailed exploratory operations are to take place.

It will be recalled from chapter nine that even though the Law of the Sea

Convention has not entered into force some seventy-four States have unilaterally claimed an EEZ. These claims vary widely in how they deal with
marine scientific research. A few States claim no jurisdiction over research.
This is notably the case with the USA: however, it has said that it will recognise the claims of other States which are 'exercised reasonably in a
manner consistent with international law'.[3] Secondly, many States (probably the majority) claim simply 'jurisdiction' or 'exclusive jurisdiction' over
research, or 'exclusive jurisdiction to authorise, regulate and control scientific research', with no further elaboration. Thirdly, the legislation of a few
States (such as Honduras,[4] Indonesia,[5] Ivory Coast[6] and Morocco[7])
requires the consent of the coastal State to be given for research in the
EEZ, but contains no further details. Somewhat more detailed is the legislation of Iceland,[8] Roumania[9] and Venezuela,[10] which broadly reflects the
basic outline of the Convention regime. The only States which so far have
adopted legislation which deals fully with all the matters in the Convention
are Malaysia[11] and the USSR,[12] whose legislation follows very closely the
Convention's provisions for the most part. Finally, it may be of interest to
note that since the adoption of the Convention Italy has issued regulations
for research on its continental shelf (Italy does not claim an EEZ) which
are broadly in accordance with the Convention, except that there is no
provision for implied consent.[13]

The above practice supports the conclusion that the principle of coastal
State consent for research in the EEZ and on the continental shelf is now
part of customary international law. However, many of the details of the
Convention regime, such as the period of notice and implied consent, are
not, and are probably incapable of becoming, part of customary international law because of the paucity of State practice and because they would
not seem to have the fundamentally norm-creating character necessary for
custom. In addition, the question of opposability (see chapters one and
nine) will be crucial in determining the validity of individual claims.

In addition to these EEZ claims, most of the fifteen States claiming a
200 mile exclusive fishing zone claim the jurisdiction to control fisheries
research in the zone where it involves the taking of fish. Although the
validity of such claims will again turn on the issue of opposability, it is
likely that there is and will be little opposition to these claims, first because
of the lack of protest at 200 mile exclusive fishing zones, and secondly
because similar claims made in respect of twelve-mile exclusive fishing
zones were — as we have seen — generally accepted.

As regards the practical operation of the consent regime now established by most coastal States, a recent study concerning the experience of
the USA[14] shows that in the period 1979–84 inclusive the USA made a
total of 590 requests for consent for its scientists to carry out marine scientific research in the maritime zones of sixty-two States. In twenty-seven

cases the request was denied completely; in nineteen cases the request for clearance was granted but was so delayed that the project could not be carried out; in eleven cases no answer was received at all to the request and the project was therefore cancelled; and in five cases permission was granted but on unacceptable conditions. Thus a total of sixty-two requests (10·5 per cent) were in one way or another unsuccessful. This study suggests that the reasons for consent being denied or delayed are not always due to a conscious desire to restrict US research: denials or delays may be the result of bureaucratic problems (especially in developing countries not used to receiving requests for consent to carry out research), the general state of relations between the USA and some coastal States (such as Cuba and Nicaragua), and last-minute changes in research projects. However, the study also suggests that the figures for denials and delays are artificially low, because many US scientists, knowing the attitude of some coastal States such as Cuba, simply do not apply to carry out research in the waters of such States.

In connection with the practical operation of the consent regime it is also of interest to note that the International Council for the Exploration of the Sea (ICES) (further discussed at pp. 300–1 below) in 1984 adopted a resolution in which it noted that 'research has occasionally been impeded by bureaucratic procedures' and called on its Member States to 'simplify relevant procedures to the extent possible, for example by keeping the time required for advance notification to a minimum, and by considering the use of a standard clearance information form'.[15]

Wherever marine research be conducted — whether on the high seas or in one of the coastal State's jurisdictional zones — it must conform to certain broad principles laid down by the Law of the Sea Convention. First, under article 240, marine scientific research must be conducted 'exclusively for peaceful purposes'; with appropriate scientific methods and means compatible with the Convention; so as not unjustifiably to interfere with other legitimate uses of the sea; and in compliance with all relevant regulations adopted in conformity with the Convention. Only the first of these is likely to raise problems. It may suggest that research primarily intended to have military application is prohibited. If so, this would represent a significant curtailment of the research activities of the major military powers, in particular the USSR and USA. Similar phrasing in the Antarctic and Outer Space Treaties has given rise to similar problems and led some to argue that 'peaceful' really means 'non-aggressive' or 'peacetime':[16] such arguments will, no doubt, be employed in respect of article 240. A further general principle is that contained in article 241, which provides that 'marine scientific research activities shall not constitute the legal basis for any claim to any part of the marine environment or its resources'.

The Law of the Sea Convention, by adopting a twelve-mile territorial sea and the concept of archipelagic waters where research is entirely subject to coastal State consent, and by imposing coastal State controls on research in the EEZ and on the continental shelf, has, in comparison with the Geneva Conventions and previous customary international law, considerably increased the areas of sea where marine scientific research is restricted and controlled. These areas, moreover, are those which are of the greatest interest to marine scientists and where consequently most marine scientific research takes place. On the other hand, the coastal State's controls in the EEZ and on the continental shelf are somewhat more clearly formulated than those of the Continental Shelf Convention, but there may still be scope for a coastal State unreasonably to deny or delay foreign research. Whether coastal State controls will operate so as not unreasonably to restrict marine scientific research remains largely to be seen, although the US experience described above is not very encouraging. Certainly such controls will add to the work of marine scientists in terms of complying with notification procedures, providing access for coastal State scientists to projects and often instructing them as to the details and methodology of the project. These factors will almost certainly increase the cost of marine scientific research. Coastal State controls may also prove to be an inhibiting factor in carrying out the research necessary for co-operative marine management, notably as regards fish stocks which migrate between EEZs and/or between EEZs and the high seas and the protection of the marine environment from pollution.

To some extent the provisions of the Law of the Sea Convention may soon become obsolete. A significant proportion of marine scientific research is likely in the near future to be carried out by remote sensing from satellites. This is a form of research for which the Convention makes no provision, and it is not clear whether it is legally possible or in practice feasible for the coastal State to require consent for such research in its EEZ.

The legal status of research installations

Marine research often involves the emplacement of fixed structures, buoys and other floating objects in the sea. The legal status of such objects, often referred to as ocean data acquisition systems (ODAS), began to be studied by the Intergovernmental Oceanographic Commission (IOC) of UNESCO in collaboration with the IMO in the 1960s. In 1969 they published a report on 'Legal Problems associated with Ocean Data Acquisition Systems (ODAS)'.[17] A preliminary draft convention was produced in the following year[18] and discussed at a diplomatic conference held in 1972. The conference decided to defer finalisation and adoption of the draft until after the conclusion of UNCLOS III. In the event many of the matters relating to the legal status of ODAS dealt with by the draft convention are now covered by the Law of the Sea Convention.

The central provision of the Law of the Sea Convention is article 258. It reads:

The deployment and use of any type of scientific research installations or equipment in any area of the marine environment shall be subject to the same conditions as are prescribed in this Convention for the conduct of marine scientific research in any such area.

The effect of this provision would seem to be as follows. In the territorial sea and archipelagic waters the deployment and use of research installations and equipment will require the consent of the coastal State. It further follows from the legal nature of these waters that such installations and equipment will be subject to the jurisdiction of the coastal State. In the EEZ and on the continental shelf the consent of the coastal State will again be required. Since the definition of applied research in the EEZ and on the continental shelf includes research which involves the construction and operation of 'artificial islands, installations and structures', it would seem that the deployment and use of research installations and equipment which take the form of 'artificial islands', 'installations' or 'structures' will be subject to the discretionary consent a coastal States enjoys in respect of applied research, regardless of the kind of research which is to be carried out from such research installations and equipment. It further follows from articles 60 and 80 that a coastal State will have jurisdiction over such research installations and equipment. Where the research installations and equipment do not take the form of 'artificial islands', 'installations' or 'structures' — and floating buoys and other floating objects might well come into this category — but such objects are used for applied research, the coastal State will still have a discretion to refuse or permit deployment of such objects. Under article 249(2) the coastal State can impose such conditions on the deployment of these types of ODAS as it sees fit, and this provision may well be broad enough to give the coastal State jurisdiction over such objects. On the other hand, where floating research objects are used for pure research, the coastal State should not normally withhold its consent to the deployment and use of such objects. There would appear to be no provision giving the coastal State jurisdiction over such objects once consent has been given, and provided nothing is done which entitles the coastal State to exercise its rights under article 253 to suspend or order the cessation of research. On the other hand, the emplacing State, while it would presumably have legislative jurisdiction over the object on a quasi-territorial basis analogous to flag State legislative jurisdiction over ships, would have no enforcement jurisdiction in the coastal State's EEZ and on its continental shelf because there is no provision of the Law of the Sea Convention which gives it such jurisdiction in these areas. Since no State would therefore appear to have enforcement jurisdiction over the object (and such jurisdiction does not appear to be entirely theoretical: it would, for example, be required in order to take action against anyone unauthorisedly interfering with the object), to decide who should have jurisdiction it would seem necessary to have recourse to article 59 (the formula for resolving conflicts regarding the attribution of rights and jurisdiction in the EEZ — see chapter nine). On the high seas the researching State is free to deploy any research installation or equipment, whether to be used for research of the water column and superjacent air space or for research of the sea bed and subsoil (i.e. the international sea bed area). Such installations and equipment will be subject to the jurisdiction of the researching State.[19]

Further provisions relating to the deployment of research installations and equipment are set out in articles 259–62. Such objects do not have the status of islands, nor do they affect the delimitation of maritime zones (LOSC, art. 259). It is possible, however, to establish safety zones of up to 500 metres in radius around such objects, and flag States must ensure that their ships respect such zones (LOSC, art. 260). Deployment of research installations and equipment must not 'constitute an obstacle to established international shipping routes' (LOSC, art. 261), and such objects must bear identification marks indicating the State of registry or the international organisation to which they belong and have adequate internationally agreed warning signals to ensure safety at sea and safety of air navigation (LOSC, art. 262).

Now that UNCLOS III has finished, the IOC and IMO have decided to take up their work again on the draft convention on ODAS, though no timetable for this has yet been set. Although some provisions of the original draft convention, such as those covering the deployment of ODAS and certain jurisdictional matters, are probably now redundant in the light of the Law of the Sea Convention's provisions (unless it be thought desirable to repeat the latter in an ODAS Convention in order to cover the eventuality of the major researching States not becoming parties to the Law of the Sea Convention), there are a number of matters in the draft which are not dealt with by the Law of the Sea Convention. These include the recovery and return of ODAS found in maritime zones under the jurisdiction of a foreign State, liability for unauthorised interfence with ODAS, the registration of ODAS, and safety rules covering ODAS. The last two of these could usefully lead to a development of the provisions of article 262 of the Law of the Sea Convention.

International co-operation in marine research

Much marine research is carried out on a purely national basis, but international co-operation does take place, and indeed is encouraged by the

Law of the Sea Convention (see in particular arts. 143 and 242). Such co-operation may be on an *ad hoc* basis for specific projects: for example, the Joint North Sea Data Acquisition Project (JONSDAP), which involved twenty-one European and American oceanographic research vessels between May and June 1976 making observations and collecting data in the North Sea. Much international co-operation is institutionalised, in both non-governmental and intergovernmental international organisations. The former, which include the International Council of Scientific Unions and its subsidiary, the Scientific Committee on Oceanic Research, fall outside the ambit of international law and thus of this book. Within this ambit, however, are the considerable number of intergovernmental organisations concerned with marine scientific research.

At the global level, there are several UN bodies. Of the specialised agencies, the Food and Agriculture Organisation (FAO) undertakes a good deal of fisheries research; much of the work of the World Meteorological Organisation (WMO) is concerned with weather observation at sea; and in 1960 UNESCO established an Intergovernmental Oceanographic Commission (IOC) to 'promote scientific investigation with a view to learning more about the nature and resources of the ocean through the concerted action of its members'.[20] The IOC has subsequently organised and co-ordinated a number of co-operative investigations, particularly in the Indian Ocean, eastern central Atlantic, Mediterranean and Pacific. It has also studied the legal problems connected with ODAS and freedom of research, and established various ocean services such as the International Oceanographic Data Exchange programme. Apart from the UN's specialised agencies and the UN Environment Programme (UNEP), which supports the scientific work of other organisations, there are also bodies coordinating the activities of the various parts of the UN system concerned with marine scientific research: two such are the Group of Experts on the Scientific Aspects of Marine Pollution (GESAMP) and the Intersecretariat Committee on Scientific Programmes relating to Oceanography.[21] Outside the UN system but still on the global level is the International Hydrographic Organisation, established in 1970 as the successor to the International Hydrographic Bureau. Its functions are to co-ordinate the activities of national hydrographic offices, to bring about the greatest possible uniformity in nautical charts and documents, to adopt reliable and efficient methods of carrying out and exploiting hydrographic surveys, and developing hydrographical sciences and the techniques employed in descriptive oceanography.

Much research co-operation takes place at the regional level. The oldest and perhaps foremost regional organisation is the International Council for the Exploration of the Sea, founded as long ago as 1902. It promotes and coordinates research relating to fisheries, and more recently pollution, in the North Atlantic, North Sea and Baltic, and gives scientific advice to fisheries and pollution organisations and commissions. Originally performing a similar function for the Mediterranean was the International Commission for the Scientific Exploration of the Mediterranean, founded in 1919, but much of its work has now been taken over by the General Fisheries Council for the Mediterranean. A number of other regional fisheries organisations either conduct their own research (e.g. the International Pacific Halibut Commission, the Inter-American Tropical Tuna Commission) or co-ordinate the research of their member States (e.g. the North West Atlantic Fisheries Organisation, the North Pacific Fur Seal Commission). States may also co-operate in marine research at the bilateral level. Thus, for example, in 1971 Portugal and Spain concluded an Agreement concerning Oceanographic Co-operation whereby they undertake to co-operate in the oceanographical research essential to making an inventory of the marine resources in the areas of interest to them.

Greater use of international co-operation in research projects, involving developing countries and the coastal States of the region where the project is being carried out, may help to mitigate the drawbacks of the controls given by the Law of the Sea Convention to the coastal State in the EEZ and on the continental shelf, because in such cases coastal State consent is likely to be obtained more quickly.

The transfer of marine technology

Related to the question of marine scientific research is that of the transfer of marine technology. In general terms, of course, transfer of technology has a compass going far beyond the law of the sea. Developing countries have long felt that one of the more important reasons for their economic backwardness is that they lack much of the technology which developed countries enjoy, and that without a substantial transfer of technology their economies will not adequately develop. Whatever the level of technology it is that developing countries require — and the more radical development economists have suggested that it is generally intermediate, labour-intensive technology, rather than advanced high-capital technology — the developing countries have sought to make transfer of technology one of the central features of the New International Economic Order. Thus the Declaration on the Establishment of a New International Economic Order of 1974, noting that 'the benefits of technological progress are not shared equitably by all members of the international community', states that one of the principles of the New International Economic Order should be 'to give to the developing countries access to the achievements of modern science and technology, to promote the transfer of technology and the creation of indigenous technology for the benefit of the developing

countries'[22] The Programme of Action on the Establishment of a New
International Economic Order goes on to call for the formulation of an
international code of conduct for the transfer of technology, giving developing countries access on improved terms to modern technology and
adapting commercial practices governing the transfer of technology to the
requirements of developing countries.[23] In pursuance of this Programme of
Action, UNCTAD in 1978 produced a draft International Code of Conduct on the Transfer of Technology.[24] This draft, which seeks to facilitate
the transfer of technology as well as reduce its cost to developing countries,
has subsequently been discussed at several sessions of a diplomatic conference, but agreement has not yet been reached on all its provisions:
the main outstanding points of disagreement are the draft Code's provisions on restrictive practices and on applicable law and dispute settlement.
To deal with some of the difficult questions raised for the transfer of
technology by patents and other aspects of intellectual property law, the
World Intellectual Property Organisation (WIPO) — a UN specialised
agency — has undertaken a revision of the 1883 International Convention
for the Protection of Industrial Property. Although it has been discussed at
four sessions of a diplomatic conference since 1980, agreement has not yet
been reached on the proposed revision. The proposed code and revised
Convention are not specifically concerned with marine technology but are
of general application: it is therefore beyond the confines of this book to
say anything of the details of their present draft provisions. Such information can be found in the articles listed in 'Further reading' at the end of this
chapter.

While UNCTAD and WIPO have been engaged in work on the transfer
of technology in general terms, UNCLOS III has dealt with the transfer of
marine technology. This matter is referred to in the Law of the Sea Convention in two places — first, and more concretely, in the provisions on the
international sea bed regime, and secondly in Part XIV. As regards the
former, articles 4 and 5 of Annex III require anyone who applies to engage
in mining in the international sea bed area to undertake in certain circumstances to transfer sea-bed mining technology to the Enterprise and/or
developing countries. These provisions are discussed in further detail in
chapter twelve (pp. 189–90). In addition, articles 144 and 274 require the
International Sea Bed Authority to train nationals of developing countries,
to make technical documentation on sea-bed mining available to developing countries, and to assist such countries in the acquisition of sea-bed
mining technology. In carrying out these functions the Authority must act
subject to 'all legitimate interests including, *inter alia*, the rights and duties
of holders, suppliers and recipients of technology'.

The second part of the Law of the Sea Convention dealing with the transfer of technology, Part XIV, essentially takes the form of a number of *pacta de contrahendo*. Article 266 calls on States, directly or through international organisations, to co-operate in promoting the development and transfer of marine science and technology on fair and reasonable terms and conditions. To facilitate the transfer of marine technology, States are to promote the establishment of generally accepted guidelines, criteria and standards (LOSC, art. 271). The means envisaged for the development and transfer of marine technology include the establishment of programmes of technical co-operation, holding conferences and symposia on scientific and technological subjects, exchanges of scientists and technologists, undertaking joint ventures and the establishment of national and regional marine scientific and technological research centres (LOSC, arts. 269 and 275–77).

Clearly the effectiveness of these provisions will depend on what action is taken to implement them after the Convention enters into force, not least the action taken by international organisations, for whom the Convention envisages a significant role. In this respect it is noteworthy that already some international organisations are engaged in the transfer of marine technology: for example, the FAO has done considerable work in facilitating the transfer of fisheries technology to many developing States,[25] while the IMO provides technical assistance to developing States in the fields of shipping safety and pollution, as well as assisting in the training of maritime personnel; and UNESCO, mainly through the IOC, has assisted in the transfer of technology through its research, information exchange and training programmes. In addition, a number of regional, mainly UN-sponsored, centres of technology transfer have been set up in Asia, Africa, Latin America and the Middle East, though none of them is specially for marine technology.

Apart from transfer of technology through international organisations, a certain amount of technology is already being transferred through bilateral agreements for scientific and technological co-operation and, probably more extensively, by transnational corporations through investment in foreign subsidiaries, joint ventures, technical assistance agreements and licensing arrangements. The activities of transnational corporations are viewed as particularly controversial by developing countries since the transfer of proprietary technology is the virtual preserve of transnational corporations because of their control of patents, methods of manufacture, channels of distribution and industrial processes.[26] An improvement in this position is probably more likely to result if agreement is reached on the UNCTAD draft Code of Conduct and on revision of the 1883 Convention, rather than from the provisions of the Law of the Sea Convention, which in Boczek's view 'do not lay down clear legal obligations but only establish certain standards of conduct which to a large extent reflect the already existing practice ... and are not likely to have any immediate discernible legal effect upon the transfer of marine technology'.[27]

Notes

1   Discussed in Soons, *op. cit.*, in 'Further reading', pp. 66–82.
2   W. S. Wooster, 'Research in troubled waters. US research vessel clearance experience, 1972–1978', 9 *ODIL* 219–39 (1981).
3   Statement by the President of the USA, 10 March 1983. XXII ILM 464 (1983).
4   Decree No. 921 of 13 June 1980 on the Utilisation of Marine Natural Resources, art. 1(c). *National Legislation on the EEZ*, p. 139; *Smith*, p. 205.
5   Act No. 5 of 18 October 1983 on the Indonesian Exclusive Economic Zone, art. 7. *National Legislation on the EEZ*, p. 150; *Smith*, p. 227.
6   Law No. 77–926, art. 6. *National Legislation on the EEZ*, p. 71; *Smith*, p. 241.
7   Act No. 1–81, art. 5. *National Legislation on the EEZ*, p. 195; *Smith*, p. 303.
8   Law No. 41 of 1 June 1979, arts. 9 and 10. *National Legislation on the EEZ*, p. 142, *Smith*, p. 209.
9   Decree No. 142 of 25 April 1986, art. 10. 8 *LOSB* 17 (1986).
10   Act establishing an Exclusive Economic Zone along the Coasts of the Mainland and Islands of 26 July 1978, art. 9. *National Legislation on the EEZ*, p. 333; *Smith*, p. 477.
11   Exclusive Economic Zone Act 1984, ss. 16–20. The Bill on which the Act is based, which as regards marine scientific research is identical with the Act, is reproduced in *Smith*, p. 259.
12   Decree on the Economic Zone of 28 February 1984, arts. 8–11. *National Legislation on the EEZ*, p. 314; *Smith*, p. 417. Decree of 19 December 1985. 1 *International Journal of Estuarine and Coastal Law* 386 (1986). See also the accompanying article by E. Franckx, 'Marine scientific research and the new USSR legislation on the economic zone', in *ibid.*, pp. 367–83.
13   Regulations of 9 July 1984. Summarised in *Italy and the Law of the Sea Newsletter* No. 13 (January 1985), p. 10.
14   J. A. Knauss and M. H. Katsouros, 'The effect of the law of the sea on marine scientific research in the United States: recent trends', in E. D. Brown and R. R. Churchill (eds.) *The UN Convention on the Law of the Sea: Impact and Implementation*, Honolulu, Hawaii, 1987, pp. 373–82.
15   Text of the Resolution given in a letter of 15 July 1987 to the authors from the General Secretary of ICES.
16   For discussion of this question, see G. Gal, *Space Law*, Leyden, 1969, pp. 164–72, and S. Gorove, *Studies in Space Law. Its Challenges and Prospects*, Leyden, 1977, pp. 90–4.
17   IOC Technical Series No. 5 (1969).
18   Doc. SC/IOC. EG-1 (IV)/12, 17 September 1970, Annex III.
19   It should also be noted that under the pre-UNCLOS law the rules governing the deployment and use of ODAS in the territorial sea and high seas are the same as those of the Law of the Sea Convention.
20   Art. 1(2) of the Statutes of the IOC.
21   For further information on the work of the UN relating to marine research, see L. M. Alexander, 'Organisational responses to new ocean science and technology developments', 9 *ODIL* 241 (1981), at 249–56, and the UN Secretary

General, *Annotated Directory of Intergovernmental Organisations concerned with Ocean Affairs*, UN Doc. A/Conf. 62/L. 14 (1976), pp. 11–105.

22 UN General Assembly Resolution 3201 (S–VI), paras. 1 and 4 (p): reproduced in XIII *ILM* 715 (1975).

23 UN General Assembly Resolution 3202 (S–VI), para. N: reproduced in XIII *ILM* 720 (1974). Similar calls are made in art. 13 of the Charter of Economic Rights and Duties of States, UN General Assembly Resolution 3281 (XXIX), reproduced in XIV *ILM* 251 (1975).

24 UNCTAD Doc. TD/CODE TOT/1. A later version of the draft is reproduced in XIX *ILM* 773 (1980).

25 It should also be noted that under art. 62 of the Law of the Sea Convention the conditions which a State may impose on the vessels of other States wishing to fish in its EEZ include the requirement to train personnel and transfer fisheries technology. In practice such conditions are found in many bilateral agreements: see, for example, the EEC's Fisheries Agreements with Senegal (1979) and Guinea-Bissau (1980), and Spain's Fisheries Agreements with Angola (1980) and Cape Verde (1983). For further examples, see J. E. Carroz and M. J. Savini, 'The new international law of fisheries emerging from bilateral agreements' 3 *Marine Policy* 79 (1979), at pp. 88–91.

26 See Boczek, *op. cit.*, in 'Further reading', pp. 11–12.

27 *Ibid.*, pp. 33–4.

Further reading

Competence to conduct marine research
E. D. Brown, 'Freedom of scientific research and the legal regime of hydrospace', 9 *IJIL* 327–80 (1969).

W. T. Burke, *A Report of International Legal Problems of Scientific Research in the Oceans*, Springfield, Va., 1967.

R. J. Dupuy and D. Vignes (eds.), *Traité du Nouveau Droit de la Mer*, Paris, 1985, chap. 18.

O. Freymond, *Le Statut de la Recherche Scientifique Marine en Droit International*, Geneva, 1978.

W. S. Scholz, 'Oceanic research — international law and national legislation', 4 *Marine Policy* 91–127 (1980).

A. H. A. Soons, *Marine Scientific Research and the Law of the Sea*, The Hague, 1982.

T. Treves, 'Principe du consentement et nouveau régime juridique de la recherche scientifique marine', in D. Bardonnet and M. Virally (eds.), *Le Nouveau Droit International de la Mer*, Paris, 1983, pp. 269–85.

W. S. Wooster (ed.), *Freedom of Oceanic Research*, New York, 1973.

Legal status of research installations
N. Papadakis, *The International Legal Regime of Artificial Islands*, Leyden, 1977, chapters 6–9.

International co-operation
K. A. Bekiashev and V. V. Serebriakov, *International Marine Organisations*, The Hague, 1981.

H. Charnock, 'Marine science. Organising the study of the oceans', 8 *Marine Policy* 120–36 (1984).

E. Miles, 'IOC data and information exchange: implications of the Law of the Sea Convention', 7 *Marine Policy* 75–89 (1983).

W. Sullivan, 'Constituting the IOC as a more autonomous or independent body', 4 *Marine Policy* 290–308 (1980).

Transfer of technology

Anon., 'WIPO. Revision of the Paris Convention', 13 *Journal of World Trade Law* 564–77 (1979).

B. A. Boczek, *The Transfer of Marine Technology to Developing Nations in International Law*, Law of the Sea Institute Occasional Paper No. 32, Honolulu, Hawaii, 1982.

E. Gold, 'The international transfer and promotion of technology', in R. St J. Macdonald, D. M. Johnston and G. L. Morris (eds.), *The International Law and Policy of Human Welfare*, Alphen aan den Rijn, 1978, pp. 549–81.

D. Kay, 'International transfer of marine technology. The transfer process and international organisations', 2 *ODIL* 351–77 (1974).

P. Roffe, 'UNCTAD. Code of conduct for the transfer of technology', 14 *Journal World Trade Law* 160–72 (1980); and see updating notes by the same author in *ibid.*, Vol. 18 (1984), pp. 176–82 and Vol. 19 (1985), pp. 669–72.

D. Thompson, 'The UNCTAD code on transfer of technology', 16 *Journal of World Trade Law* 311–37 (1982).

T. Treves, 'Le transfert de technologie et la Conférence sur le droit de la mer', 104 *Journal du Droit International* 43–65 (1977).

CHAPTER SEVENTEEN
Military uses of the sea

Introduction

The 1958 and 1982 Conventions on the Law of the Sea were intended to regulate the uses of the seas in time of peace. The conferences on the Law of the Sea consciously avoided negotiation of the rules applicable to military operations on the seas. Consequently, the extent to which the conventions are modified or suspended in time of war is a highly controversial matter, compounded by the uncertainty of the Law of Treaties on this point, although that does not mean that all uses of the sea by naval vessels are equally controversial. Thus, routine law enforcement of, for instance, fishery limits, is plainly regulated by those Conventions, and certain other matters are regulated by other specific treaties. This chapter seeks to outline the limits of the controversy and to describe the main treaties governing military uses.

The law of the sea and laws of war

There is a well-defined body of Laws of War at Sea, deriving in part from conventions, notably those drafted by the Hague Peace Conference of 1907 and in part from customary law.[1] These laws recognised and regulated such traditional belligerent rights as the right to visit and search neutral merchant ships on the high seas in order to intercept contraband goods destined for the enemy, and the right to maintain a close and effective blockade of enemy ports, and also defined the rights and duties of neutrals to prevent the use of their territorial waters as bases of naval operations by belligerents (although innocent passage by belligerents was not regarded as a violation of neutrality). Those laws presupposed the existence of a legal state of war, as distinct from the normal state of peace. But since the outlawing of war by the Kellogg — Briand Pact (or Pact of Paris) in 1928, and the wider prohibition in article 2(4) of the United Nations Charter on the threat or use of force against the territorial integrity or political independence of a State, it is not clear if international law can now recognise a state of war so as to render the Laws of War applicable.[2]

One view, probably the most widely held, is that force may now be lawfully used only with the authorisation of the Security Council (or the General
Assembly, acting under the 'Uniting for Peace' resolution) or in exercise of
the inherent right of self-defence preserved by article 51 of the United
Nations Charter, and that all actions formerly referred to the Laws of War
must now seek their justification under one of these two headings. The
existence of the permanent members' (PR China, France, UK, USA,
USSR) power of veto in the Security Council means that for political reasons authorisation is rarely given, although in 1966 the United Kingdom
was authorised to blockade the (then Portuguese) port of Beira, through
which oil was being taken to support the Smith regime in Rhodesia. Two
Greek ships attempting to run the blockade, the *Joanna V* and the *Manuela*,
were boarded, and later shots were fired across the bows of the French
tanker *Artois*, in order to enforce the oil import ban. The United States did
not observe the requirement of Security Council consent before mounting
the Cuban 'quarantine' in 1962 in order to prevent the import of missile
parts to the island. The Organisation of American States approved the
exercise, but this approval was patently insufficient to establish its legality
(see art. 53 of the United Nations Charter); nor was the threat to the United
States sufficiently proximate to justify the use of force in self-defence.

Self-defence, permitting States threatened by an immediate armed attack
upon themselves or their ships or aircraft to use force proportionate to the
threat in order to avert the threat, is in practice the more important basis.
Indeed, the United Kingdom conducted the whole of the 1982 naval conflict over the Falkland Islands (Islas Malvinas) on the basis of its rights of
self-defence. After dispatching a naval task force to repossess the islands
after their occupation by Argentina, the United Kingdom established for
the protection of the task force a 200-mile 'maritime exclusion zone' (MEZ),
measured from a single point in the middle of the islands rather than from
baselines, which Argentinian warships and naval auxiliaries were forbidden
to enter. This zone was soon replaced by a 200-mile 'total exclusion zone'
(TEZ), which was stated to apply:

... not only to Argentine warships and Argentine naval auxiliaries but also to any
other ship, whether naval or merchant vessel, which is operating in support of the
illegal occupation of the Falkland Islands by Argentine forces.
The Exclusion Zone will also apply to any aircraft, whether military or civil,
which is operating in support of the illegal occupation. Any ship and any aircraft
whether military or civil which is found within this Zone without due authority from
the Ministry of Defence in London will be regarded as operating in support of the
illegal occupation and will therefore be regarded as hostile and will be liable to be
attacked by British Forces.

The establishment of the TEZ avoided the necessity for determining
whether any ship or aircraft in the area in fact presented an immediate

threat to the task force, in circumstances where the time taken to make such a determination could have given a decisive advantage to the other ship or aircraft: all unauthorised ships and aircraft in the zone were deemed to be threatening and so liable to attack in self defence. It should be noted that, contrary to a widely held misconception, the TEZ was stated to be:

... without prejudice to the right of the United Kingdom to take whatever additional measures may be needed in exercise of its right of self-defence, under Article 51 of the United Nations Charter

Thus, when the Argentinian cruiser *General Belgrano* presented, in the view of the United Kingdom, a threat to the task force, it was sunk notwithstanding that it was some way outside the zone. The TEZ was replaced, after the cessation of hostilities, by a 150-mile 'Falkland Islands Protection Zone', which Argentinian ships and aircraft were asked not to enter without the permission of the British Government. The 1958 and 1982 Law of the Sea Conventions make no provision for any such zones, but the Falklands zones have generally been respected. Similar zones have been established in the Gulf, in the context of the Iran–Iraq conflict.[3]

On this view, the Laws of War have no application as such, and no general rights of, say, visit and search or blockade would exist, although such action might be justified in specific cases on the basis of self-defence as a proportionate response to threats to the State. This seems to be the position adopted by the major naval States in relation to the Gulf conflict, where the right of the combatants to stop and search foreign merchant ships reasonably suspected of carrying war *matériel* to the enemy appears to have been accepted, but without conceding any more general right to the combatants to restict the freedom of navigation in the area.

A second view is that the Laws of War may apply as such in certain circumstances, perhaps on the basis that lawful use of force may in fact be of a scale and nature as to make it in law a war. The Swedish Government, in its declaration made on signature of the Law of the Sea Convention, stated that the Convention does not affect the rights and duties of a neutral State provided for in 1907 Hague Convention XIII, and the International Court in the *Nicaragua* case referred to the application of 1907 Hague Convention VIII (on automatic submarine contact mines) in time of war:[4] such statements may evidence a belief in the continued applicability of at least some of the Laws of War. Only when State practice has developed further will it be possible to say whether this, or the first, or some other view, is the correct one: but even if this second view should not be adopted in State practice, it is still possible that the principles underlying some of the traditional Laws of War will retain their importance as means of mediating the exercise of the right of self-defence.

Military uses of the sea in peacetime

Military activities in the seas relate to a variety of functions of naval vessels. First, there is the duty of routine law enforcement in national waters, usually in relation to fisheries, customs and immigration laws. Secondly, in preparation for their other roles, navies commonly engage in manoeuvres and weapons testing on the 'high seas', as they were under the 1958 rules. Third, the larger maritime States, following Lord Grey's dictum that 'Diplomacy without force is like an orchestra without instruments', use their navies for what we might call 'gunboat diplomacy'. This covers several types of action. It may involve no more than flying the flag in some part of the world to remind allies and enemies alike that the naval State has a military presence in the area. This is readily observable at times of particular tension in the Middle East, for instance, when both American and Russian fleets are to be found deployed in the Mediterranean or Indian Ocean. It may involve a more immediate display of force as, for example, when the Royal Navy asserted its right of passage through the Corfu Channel after Albanian shore batteries had fired on other passing British warships, or when the US Destroyer Division 31 sailed through the Lombok and Malacca straits to assert its right of passage after the Indonesian archipelagic waters claim of 1958. There may even be direct action against a hostile vessel such as occurred when the United States ship *Pueblo* was seized in 1968 by North Korean vessels for spying, allegedly, within Korean territorial waters.

Another example arose when, during the 'cod wars' of 1958–76, the Royal Navy sought to defend British trawlers from attempts by Icelandic naval vessels to enforce fishing regulations against them, the British view being that the laws constituted unwarrantable extensions, first to twelve, and then to fifty and 200 miles, of jurisdiction on to the high seas, and were inadmissible under international law. And navies may also be used to provide logistic support for land-based actions, as they were during the American landing in Lebanon in 1958 and, more recently, during the abortive American attempt in 1980 to free diplomatic hostages held in Teheran.

Some of the problems to which these give rise, such as the questions of rights of passage for warships and of the legality of high seas weapons tests, have been discussed in previous chapters (see chapters four, five and eleven). The important point is not that these legal questions are insoluble, but that the uncertainty which persists makes it possible for coastal or flag States intent for political reasons on, say, denying passage to foreign warships to do so under the colour of the enforcement of legal rights. That is equally true of the remaining issues, not treated elsewhere, which arise.

Of the many issues which could be chosen to illustrate the impact of the law of the sea on military activities, two will suffice. The first stems from the establishment of the EEZ. In the declarations which they made on signature of the 1982 Convention, Brazil, Cape Verde and Uruguay announced that they did not consider the Convention to authorise the carrying out of military exercises or manoeuvres, or the deployment of any installations whatsoever, in the EEZ without the permission of the coastal State. Since this position, if widely adopted, would close off enormous areas of the seas for such routine military activities, it is not surprising that the position has been rejected: Italy, for instance, expressly rejected it in its declaration made on signature of the Convention. The problem lies in the fact that although the freedoms of navigation and overflight and other internationally lawful uses of the seas related to them are preserved in the EEZ (LOSC arts. 58, 87), it is not clear whether such activities as exercises involving weapons testing are included within those freedoms. Nor is it clear how the question is to be resolved: on one view, exercises and so on are included within the permitted freedoms; on another, they are unattributed rights falling for decision under article 59 of the Convention (see chapter nine).[5]

The second problem concerns the deployment of monitoring devices such as the United States' Sonar Surveillance Systems which lie on the continental shelf off the coasts of the United States, in the North Sea, and in the Mediterranean. These devices may be regarded as 'structures', and therefore within the provisions of article 60 of the Convention, which gives the coastal State the exclusive right to authorise the construction and operation in the EEZ of installations and structures which may interfere with the exercise of its rights in that zone. Similar provisions would apply to their deployment on the continental shelf beneath the high seas (LOSC, art. 80). On the other hand it might be argued that a right to lay them in the EEZ or on the continental shelf arises by the application, or extension by analogy, of the freedom to lay submarine cables and pipelines (LOSC, arts. 58, 79, 87), subject only to the duties not to interfere with coastal State rights in the zone and to deploy them with due regard to the interests of other users of the seas: however, some jurists regard their deployment as different in nature from the immersion of cables and pipelines, and outside that freedom. The only thing that can be said with confidence is that it is most unlikely that the major naval powers will cease from the use of the seas for military exercises and the deployment of such systems, no matter what the Convention might say.

These are only examples of the many problems which arise. Some others are discussed elsewhere: for instance, the question of weapons testing on the high seas is discussed in chapter eleven.

Special treaties concerning military uses

Apart from treaties dealing with rules of naval warfare, which we cannot consider here for reasons of space, there are three main categories of international agreement concerning military uses of the seas.

First, there are treaties regulating the kind and quantity of naval power which the parties are allowed to possess. For example, the 1922 Washington Treaty for the Limitation of Naval Armament, the first of a series of such treaties made during the inter-war years, limited the number, size and armament of the navies of the signatories — Great Britain, the United States, France, Italy and Japan. The treaty lapsed at the end of 1936. Post-war naval policy has generally been to increase, rather than limit, naval forces. The most notable exception is the Strategic Arms Limitation Agreement (SALT) of 1972 between the United States and the Soviet Union, which *inter alia* limits the number and armament of submarines carrying nuclear missiles. A successor to SALT, agreed in 1979, has not been ratified by the American Senate. Such treaties as these are, though often simple in appearance, extraordinarily complex political agreements, often involving accommodations on other issues, such as territorial claims and economic relations.

A second set of treaties limits the right to test and deploy certain weapons. The Nuclear Test Ban Treaty of 1963 was the first significant agreement, prohibiting nuclear weapon test explosions in the atmosphere or under water, including territorial waters and high seas. Most States — with the exception of China and France — are parties to this treaty. It was supplemented in 1971 by the Treaty on the Prohibition of the Emplacement of Nuclear Weapons and other Weapons of Mass Destruction on the Sea Bed, which prohibits the emplacement of such weapons (which could include biological and chemical weapons of mass destruction) and of installations specially designed to store, test or use them, on the sea bed beyond twelve miles from the shore. Each party has the right to verify through observation the compliance of other parties.

Two regional treaties have similar aims, but apply only to areas under the jurisdiction of the parties and only to nuclear weapons. The treaty of Tlatelolco, 1967, the parties to which are Latin-American States, prohibits the testing, deployment and use of nuclear weapons both on the sea-bed and in the superjacent waters. At present, it is limited to the waters over which the parties have sovereignty, which is generally understood to mean the (twelve-mile) zone of sovereignty recognised in international law; but the treaty is capable of extension to a very much wider area of the Pacific and Atlantic at such time as all nuclear powers and all Latin-American States adhere to it. Further east, the Treaty of Raratonga, which was concluded in 1985 by States members of the South Pacific Forum, applies in an area south of the equator, including Australia on the west and extending to the meridian of 115° west. Parties are bound to prevent the stationing and testing of nuclear devices within their territory, including internal, archipelagic and territorial waters, and remain free to decide whether to allow visits of foreign ships and aircraft carrying nuclear weapons to visit their ports or to transit their waters in any manner not included in rights of innocent passage or transit or archipelagic sealanes passage, which rights are to be respected. New Zealand, in particular, has taken steps to secure a ban on such visits to its ports. While some nuclear powers are parties to Protocols of both treaties, which bind those powers to the main provisions of the treaties, it is not likely that this will inhibit deployment of nuclear missile submarines beyond territorial sea limits in the regions covered: indeed, the United Kingdom takes the view that the transportation of nuclear missiles through the Treaty area does not violate the Treaty of Tlatelolco.

The final category of agreements concerns the conduct of naval operations. Clearly there is some overlap with the other categories. The treaties of Tlatelolco and Raratonga could affect submarine operations, and the 1930 London Naval Treaty — one of the inter-war arms limitation agreements — contained in its 1936 Protocol important rules concerning submarine warfare, which were reaffirmed in the 1937 Nyon Agreement under which the Mediterranean powers organised patrols for the suppression of piratical submarine attacks during the Spanish Civil War. The 1930 treaty expired at the beginning of 1937, while the other treaties terminated with the outbreak of the Second World War. Some other agreements are solely concerned with the operational matters. The second Hague Convention of 1907, limiting the use of pacific blockade, is one example. And more recently the United States and the Soviet Union, seeking to reduce the chances of nuclear war breaking out by accident, concluded the Agreement on the Prevention of Incidents on and over the High Seas, 1972. This agreement and its 1973 Protocol include rules of conduct for naval surveillance and other operations on the high seas, and provide for the exchange of information concerning actual and potential incidents. A similar agreement was concluded between the Soviet Union and the United Kingdom in 1986.

Demilitarisation of the seas

Finally, mention must be made of efforts within the United Nations to demilitarise some sea areas. The General Assembly has adopted a series of resolutions endorsing the idea of the establishment of nuclear-free zones in Africa, the Middle East, south Asia, the South Pacific and Latin America; such zones are based upon the voluntary assumption by the States concerned of obligations not to deploy nuclear missiles within these zones (see GA Res. 3472B (xxx)). More ambitious is the solemn designation of the Indian Ocean by the General Assembly as a zone of peace (see GA Res. 2832 (xxvi)). It has so far proved impossible to implement this resolution, not least because of the vagueness of the concept. Some States regard it as involving total demilitarisation of the area; others, including the major powers, see the deployment of conventional and nuclear weapons as essential to the maintenance of peace, rather than a threat to it. At present it seems unlikely that the resolution will find concrete expression.

Finally, it may be noted that neither article 301 of the Law of the Sea Convention, headed 'Peaceful uses of the seas', which obliges all States to refrain from the threat or use of force in any manner inconsistent with the principles of international law embodied in the United Nations Charter when using the seas, nor article 88 of the Convention, which reserves the high seas for 'peaceful purposes', nor article 141, which reserves the International Seabed Area exclusively for peaceful purposes, is generally understood to forbid anything other than aggressive actions at sea. Certainly the major naval powers do not regard any of these articles as imposing restraints upon routine naval operations.

Notes

1   See e.g., A. Roberts and R. Guelff, *Documents on the Laws of War*, Oxford, 1982; H. Lauterpacht, *Oppenheim's International Law*, vol. ii, 7th ed., London, 1952; C. J. Colombos, International Law of the Sea, 6th ed., London, 1967, Part II.

2   See C. J. Greenwood, 'The concept of war in modern international law', 36 *ICLQ* 283–306 (1987).

3   For the texts of statements on the zones, see *Parliamentary Debates* (Hansard), House of Commons, 6th Series, vol. 21, col. 1045, 7 April 1982 (MEZ, in effect from 12 April 1982); *ibid.*, vol. 22, col. 296, 28 April 1982 (TEZ, in effect from 30 April 1982); *ibid.*, vol. 28, col. 235, 22 July 1982 (Falkland Islands Protection Zone, in effect from 22 July 1982). See further, R. P. Barston and P. W. Birnie, *op. cit.*, in 'Further reading'.

4   For the Swedish declaration see 5 *LOSB* 22 (1985). For the statement in the *Nicaragua* case see [1986] ICJ Rep. 12, at 112. See also US Department of State Special Report No. 166, *US Policy in the Persian Gulf*, Washington, 1987, which uses the terms 'neutrality' and 'belligerency' and other language from the vocabulary of the traditional laws of war.

5   See 5 *LOSB* 6–7, 8, 15–16, 24 (1985), for the statements by Brazil, Cape Verde, Italy and Uruguay. See further, A. V. Lowe, 'Some legal problems arising from the use of the seas for military purposes', 10 *Marine Policy* 171–84 (1986); B. Kwiatkowska, 'Military uses in the EEZ: a reply', *ibid.*, vol. 11, pp. 249–50, (1987), and A. V. Lowe, 'Rejoinder', *ibid.*, pp. 250–2.

Further reading

R. P. Barston and P. W. Birnie, 'The Falkland Islands/Islas Malvinas conflict. A question of zones', 7 *Marine Policy* 14–24 (1983).

K. Booth, *Law, Force and Diplomacy at Sea*, London, 1985.

B. Buzan, 'Naval power, the law of the sea, and the Indian Ocean as a zone of peace', 5 *Marine Policy* 194–204 (1981).

B. Buzan, *Sea of Troubles? Sources of Dispute in the New Ocean Regime*, Adelphi Paper No. 143, London, 1978.

Sir James Cable, *Gunboat Diplomacy*, London, 1981.

H. L. Cryer, 'Legal aspects of the *Joanna V* and *Manuela* incidents, April 1966', 2 *Australian Yearbook of International Law* 85–98 (1966).

W. J. Fenrick, 'Legal limits on the use of force by Canadian warships engaged in law enforcement', 18 *Canadian Yearbook of International Law* 113–45 (1980).

S. G. Gorshkov, *The Sea Power of the State*, London 1977.

T. Halkiopoulos, 'Interférence des règles du nouveau droit de la mer et celles du droit de la guerre', in R-J. Dupuy and D. Vignes (eds.), *Traité du Nouveau Droit de la Mer*, Paris, 1985, pp. 1095–104.

F. C. Leiner, 'Maritime security zones: prohibited yet perpetuated', 24 *VJIL* 785–807 (1984).

L. Lucchini, 'Les opérations militaires en mer en temps de paix', 88 *RGDIP* 9–45 (1984).

P. Merciai, 'La démilitarisation des fonds marins', 88 *RGDIP* 114–203 (1985).

R. W. G. de Muralt, 'The military aspects of the UN Law of the Sea Convention', 32 *Netherlands International Law Review* 78–99 (1985).

D. P. O'Connell, *The Influence of Law on Sea Power*, Manchester, 1975.

—, 'International law and contemporary naval operations', 44 *BYIL* 19–85 (1970).

B. H. Oxman, 'The regime of warships under the United Nations Convention on the Law of the Sea', 24 *VJIL* 809–63 (1984).

N. Ronzitti, 'Demilitarization and neutralization in the Mediterranean', 6 *Italian Yearbook of International Law* 33–54 (1985).

T. Treves, 'Military installations, structures and devices on the seabed', 74 *AJIL* 808–57 (1980); R. Zedalis, 'Military installations, structures and devices on the seabed: a response', *ibid.*, vol. 75, pp. 926–33 (1981), and T. Treves, 'Reply', *ibid.*, pp. 933–5.

—, 'La notion d'utilisation des espaces marins à des fins pacifiques dans le nouveau droit de la mer', 26 *AFDI* 687–99 (1980).

B. Vukas, 'L'utilisation pacifique de la mer, dénucléarisation et désarmement', in R-J. Dupuy and D.Vignes (eds.), *Traité du Nouveau Droit de la Mer*, Paris, 1985, pp. 1047–94.

CHAPTER EIGHTEEN
Landlocked and geographically disadvantaged States

Introduction

Of the world's approximately 170 States, thirty have no sea coast. Of these thirty States, fourteen are in Africa,[1] nine in Europe,[2] five in Asia[3] and two in Latin America.[4] Not only do these landlocked States suffer from the lack of direct access to the sea and its resources, but many of them are also deficient in natural land resources and thus are amongst the world's poorest States. In addition to landlocked States, there are quite a number of States which are said to be geographically disadvantaged as far as the sea is concerned — for example, because their coastline is very short in proportion to the size of their land territory, e.g. Iraq and Zaire; or because the presence of neighbouring States prevents the generation of maritime zones (especially a continental shelf and EEZ) commensurate with the length of their coastline or the size of their territory, e.g. East and West Germany, Singapore, Togo; or because their EEZ is poor in natural resources, e.g. Jamaica, Nauru, Tanzania. Obviously the degree of disadvantage varies enormously from one State to another. Later in this chapter we shall consider a more precise definition of geographically disadvantaged States.

As far as the law of the sea is concerned, landlocked and geographically disadvantaged States raise three main questions: (1) the right of landlocked States' ships to navigate on the sea; (2) the access of landlocked and geographically disadvantaged States to marine resources; and (3) the access of landlocked States to the sea. Nearly all the international law dealing with these questions has been developed since the end of the First World War in 1918. This development has taken place in a number of forums, principally the League of Nations (particularly its two Conferences on Communications and Transit, held in 1921 and 1923); UNCTAD; and UNCLOS I and III. At UNCLOS I the question of landlocked States was discussed by the Fifth Committee, which had before it a memorandum submitted by the Preliminary Conference of Landlocked States, held in February 1958[5] (the question of landlocked States not having been considered by the ILC). At UNCLOS III no separate committee to deal with questions relating to landlocked and geographically disadvantaged States was established: instead such questions were discussed in each of the conference's three main committees. In order to try and improve their negotiating position at the conference, the landlocked and some geographically disadvantaged States formed themselves into a group comprising fifty-three States (about a third of the total conference membership). Although the States which were members of this group were very diverse politically, economically and geographically (and included both developed and developing States, and States from both East and West), they agreed on trying to obtain at UNCLOS III confirmation of the existing navigational rights of landlocked States; transit rights through States lying between landlocked States and the sea; access to the resources of neighbouring coastal States' EEZs; and proper recognition of their interests in the international sea bed regime. As we shall see, these demands met with mixed success.

The navigational rights of landlocked States

Before 1914 there was doubt as to whether under customary international law ships of a landlocked State had the right to sail on the sea and fly the flag of that State. Those who denied such a right, principally France, Great Britain and Prussia, argued that, since landlocked States had neither maritime ports nor warships, they could not verify the nationality of merchant vessels nor exercise effective control over them. However, under the Treaty of Versailles, 1919 (art. 273) and the other peace treaties concluded at the end of the First World War the parties agreed to recognise the flag flown by the vessels of a landlocked party which were registered at a specified place in its territory, which was to serve as the port of registry of such vessels. The right thus accorded to some landlocked States was put on a more general footing in the Declaration recognising the Right to a Flag of States having no Sea Coast, adopted at the 1921 League of Nations Conference on Communications and Transit.[6] Since then the view that landlocked States have the same navigational rights as coastal States has become firmly established. Thus both the Geneva Conventions and the Law of the Sea Convention provide specifically that the ships of all States, whether coastal or landlocked, have the right of innocent passage in the territorial sea and freedom of navigation in the waters beyond (TSC, art. 14(1); HSC, arts. 2(1), 4; LOSC, arts. 17, 38(1), 52(1), 53(2), 58(1), 87, 90). These rights now also appear to be the same under customary international law. At present only seven landlocked States (Austria, Bolivia, Czechoslovakia, Hungary, Paraguay, Switzerland and Uganda) possess merchant fleets[7] and so exercise these rights in practice.

Access to ports. The right to navigate through the territorial sea and EEZ and on the high seas is of limited benefit to landlocked States unless they

also have the right to use the ports of a coastal State (particularly an adjoining coastal State), and a right of access to the sea across the territory of
States lying between landlocked States and the sea. The latter question
will be considered in the final section of this chapter. As regards the use of
ports, we saw in chapter three that under customary international law there
is no general right of access to ports (except for ships in distress). Rights of
access are, however, granted under bilateral treaties of friendship, commerce and navigation and, for the thirty-three States parties to it (which
include five landlocked States), under the 1923 Convention and Statute on
the International Regime of Maritime Ports. The Law of the Sea Convention provides that 'ships flying the flag of landlocked States shall enjoy treatment equal to that accorded to other foreign ships in maritime ports' (LOSC,
art. 131). The scope of this provision is not entirely clear. Does treatment
include — as it does specifically under the 1923 Convention — access to
ports? Or does article 131 simply deal with the treatment to be accorded to
a vessel of a landlocked State which already enjoys a right of access under
some other provision? If the latter is the case, the article would seem to be
of little practical application, for the obligation it contains already results
from the 1923 Convention and from most, if not all, bilateral treaties giving
access. In either case the treatment to be enjoyed is that 'accorded to other
foreign ships'. This need not be most-favoured-nation treatment: indeed,
there seems nothing to prevent the port States offering least-favoured-
nation treatment.

The access of landlocked and geographically disadvantaged States to marine resources

The question of the access of landlocked and geographically disadvantaged
States to marine resources has three main aspects: the access of such States
to the resources of the high seas; the role of such States in the international
sea-bed regime; and the access of such States to the resources of the EEZ.
Landlocked and geographically disadvantaged States have never sought
access to the resources of the territorial sea of other States, presumably
because this zone is part of a coastal State's territory, and thus other States
have never been accorded any general right of access to its resources.

Access to high-seas resources.   As far as access to high-seas resources is
concerned, article 2 of the High Seas Convention and article 87 of the Law
of the Sea Convention each provide that the freedoms of the high seas may
be exercised by all States, whether coastal or landlocked. This means that
landlocked (and geographically disadvantaged) States have access to and
may exploit the living resources of the high seas, as well as sea-bed nodules
(if such exploitation can be regarded as a freedom of the high seas — see

chapter twelve). It also means that landlocked and geographically disadvantaged States can engage in non-resource uses of the high seas, such as scientific research, overflight and the laying of submarine cables and pipelines, as well as navigation.

International sea-bed regime.   As far as the second aspect of access to marine resources is concerned, landlocked and geographically disadvantaged States have sought to ensure that they play a full part in the international sea-bed regime and do not suffer because of their geographical situation. The Law of the Sea Convention contains a number of provisions specifically aimed at promoting the interests of landlocked States and, to a lesser extent, geographically disadvantaged States. Thus, article 148 formulates as one of the guiding principles of the international sea-bed regime that:

The effective participation of developing States in activities in the Area shall be promoted as specifically provided for in this Part [i.e. Part XI], having due regard to their special interests and needs, and in particular to the special need of the land-locked and geographically disadvantaged among them to overcome obstacles arising from their disadvantaged location, including remoteness from the Area and difficulty of access to and from it.

In the same vein, article 152 provides that the International Sea Bed Authority is not to act discriminatively in exercising its powers, but may nevertheless give 'special consideration for developing States, including particular consideration for the land-locked and geographically disadvantaged among them', as provided for in Part XI of the Convention. Article 160(2)(k) requires the Assembly of the Authority to consider:

problems of a general nature in connection with activities in the Area arising in particular for developing States, as well as those problems for States in connection with activities in the Area that are due to their geographical location, particularly for land-locked and geographically disadvantaged States.

It should be noted that all these provisions apply only to *developing* landlocked and geographically disadvantaged States.

The Law of the Sea Convention also provides for the special representation of landlocked and geographically disadvantaged States on the thirty-six-member Council, the only organ of the Authority which has limited State membership. Six members of the Council are to be elected from among developing States representing special interests. Such interests include, *inter alia*, being landlocked and geographically disadvantaged (LOSC, art. 161(1)(d)). Furthermore, in electing members of the Council, the Assembly must ensure that landlocked and geographically disadvantaged States (the latter is not defined — except in relation to rights in the EEZ: see p. 321 — and neither group this time is limited to developing

States), 'are represented to a degree which is reasonably proportionate to their representation in the Assembly' (LOSC, art. 161(2)(a)).

However, the Law of the Sea Convention contains no special provisions for landlocked and geographically disadvantaged States as far as the effect of sea-bed mining on land-based producers or the distribution of the Authority's revenues are concerned. As to the former, it is developing States generally for which the Convention makes special provision (see LOSC, arts. 150(h), 151(10)). In the case of the latter, it is again developing States generally which are to receive preferential treatment (see LOSC, arts. 140, 160(2)(f)), although it should be noted that when distributing the revenues it receives from a coastal States's exploitation of the resources of its continental shelf beyond the 200 mile limit the Authority is to take into account 'the interests and needs of developing States, particularly the least developed and the land-locked among them' (LOSC, art. 82(4)).

Taken together, the above provisions offer landlocked and geographically disadvantaged States less guarantee of active participation in and benefit from the international sea-bed regime than they sought.

Access to EEZ resources. The extension of coastal State jurisdiction resulting from the Law of the Sea Convention's provisions on the EEZ and continental shelf means a considerable diminution in the area of the high seas and international sea bed, and therefore in the marine resources available to landlocked and geographically disadvantaged States. By way of compensation these States proposed at UNCLOS III that they should be given access to both the living and non-living resources of the EEZ and continental shelf of neighbouring States. As far as non-living resources were concerned, the aspirations of landlocked and geographically disadvantaged States were firmly rejected by coastal States because the proposals of the former would have deprived the latter of their vested continental shelf rights. On the other hand, landlocked and geographically disadvantaged States have been given limited access to the living resources of neighbouring EEZs.

In chapter fourteen we saw that under the Law of the Sea Convention a coastal State is to establish the total allowable catch for the fish stocks in its EEZ and that that part of the total allowable catch which the coastal State's vessels are not capable of harvesting (the surplus) is to be made available to other States. Articles 69(1) and 70(1) provide that landlocked States and geographically disadvantaged States have:

the right to participate, on an equitable basis, in the exploitation of an appropriate part of the surplus of the living resources of the exclusive economic zones of coastal States of the same subregion or region, taking into account the relevant economic and geographical circumstances of all the States concerned [LOSC, art. 69(1), 70(1)] and in conformity with articles 61 and 62. The terms and modalities of such participation are to be established by the States concerned through bilateral, sub-regional or regional agreements, taking into account various specified factors (LOSC, arts. 69(2), 70(3)). Where the harvesting capacity of a coastal State reaches the point which would enable it to harvest the whole of the total allowable catch in its EEZ, the coastal State and other States concerned 'shall co-operate in the establishment of equitable arrangements on a bilateral, sub-regional or rgional basis to allow for participation' by developing landlocked States and developing geographically disadvantaged States of the same sub-region or region in the exploitation of the living resources of the EEZs of coastal States of the sub-region or region, 'as may be appropriate in the circumstances and on terms satisfactory to all parties', and taking into account various specified factors (LOSC, arts. 69(3), 70(4)).

For the purpose of Part V of the Law of the Sea Convention, concerning the EEZ, 'geographically disadvantaged States' comprise coastal States (1) whose geographical situation makes them dependent upon the exploitation of the living resources of the EEZs of other States in the sub-region or region for adequate supplies of fish for the nutritional needs of their population or parts thereof, or (2) which can claim no EEZ of their own (LOSC, art. 70(2)). The right to equitable participation in the surplus, given by articles 69(1) and 70(1), applies in the case of developed landlocked States and developed geographically disadvantaged States only to the EEZs of other developed States; and here regard also has to be had to the extent to which the coastal State, in giving access to other States to the living resources of its EEZ, has taken into account the need to minimise detrimental effects on fishing communities and economic dislocation in States whose nationals have habitually fished in its zone (LOSC, arts. 69(4), 70(5)).

The rights given to landlocked and geographically disadvantaged States by articles 69 and 70 may not be transferred to third States or their nationals unless all the States concerned agree (LOSC, art. 72). It is always open to coastal States to grant to landlocked and geographically disadvantaged States rights greater than those laid down in the above provisions (LOSC, arts. 69(5), 70(6)). On the other hand, a coastal State 'whose economy is overwhelmingly dependent on the exploitation of the living resources of its exclusive economic zone' is under no obligation to allow access by other States to these resources (LOSC, art. 71).

The rights given to landlocked and geographically disadvantaged States by the above provisions are fairly tenuous, and largely depend on how much a coastal State is prepared to concede in negotiating an agreement. The language of the provisions is also vague and ill-defined. Perhaps the most serious failing in this regard is the lack of any definition of 'region' or 'sub-region', and the failure to explain the distinction between these two terms. The difficulties arising from this can be illustrated by the case of landlocked Chad. To which 'region' does it belong for the purposes of article 69? It borders four coastal States — Libya, Sudan, Cameroon and Nigeria. Is the 'region' to which it belongs therefore the Mediterranean, the Red Sea or the Gulf of Guinea? Or does it belong to all three?

Although, as we saw in chapter fourteen, many coastal States have already claimed 200 mile EEZs or fishing zones, there appear as yet to be no agreements providing for the access of landlocked States to such zones.[8] This is scarcely surprising, since no landlocked State yet possesses a marine fishing industry and very few landlocked States have an inland fishing industry. It may be wondered, in the light of the cost and formidable difficulties for landlocked States of starting a marine fishing industry, whether giving such States some access to the living resources of neighbouring States' EEZs is really the most effective way of providing an equitable share of marine fish resources for landlocked States. It would have been a more economic and effective division of labour to provide that, rather than landlocked States attempting to establish their own fishing industries, the more developed coastal States should be obliged to give landlocked States part of their catch or a cash equivalent. As regards geographically disadvantaged States, it is difficult to say whether any have been given access to neighbouring States' 200 mile economic or fishing zones in pursuance of article 70, both because of the difficulty of deciding which States are geographically disadvantaged within the meaning of article 70 and because access might be accorded for reasons other than that a State is geographically disadvantaged.

Related to the question of the access of landlocked and geographically disadvantaged States to the EEZs of neighbouring coastal States is the subject of marine scientific research. Part XIII of the Law of the Sea Convention, which deals with research, contains one provision specifically concerning landlocked and geographically disadvantaged States. Under article 254 third States and international organisations undertaking a pure research project in the EEZ of a coastal State must notify neighbouring landlocked and geographically disadvantaged States of that project: the latter States must also be given an opportunity to participate in the project 'whenever feasible', and in any case must be given an assessment of the results of the project. In so far as the rights of fisheries exploitation given to landlocked and geographically disadvantaged States are of practical benefit, the right given in article 254 may be a useful supplement, although somewhat limited: first, because it is confined to projects concerning pure research and does not apply where the project is directly concerned with fishery resources; and secondly, because there are no obligations on the coastal State when conducting research in its EEZ corresponding to those on third States and international organisations under article 254.

The access of landlocked States to the sea

The navigational rights of landlocked States (particularly their exercise for the purposes of engaging in seaborne trade) and the rights of access of landlocked States to marine resources would be of little practical benefit unless landlocked States also enjoy a right for their nationals and goods to cross the territory of States lying between them and the sea (which will be referred to as a right of transit). Whether and to what extent there is such a right of transit in international law is therefore an important question which we must now consider.

Customary law. It is controversial whether there is a general right of transit in customary international law. In the *Right of Passage* case (1960) the International Court of Justice found that Portugal enjoyed a right of transit across Indian territory between the various enclaves it at that time possessed in India. The Court found this right derived from a local custom and therefore it did not consider it necessary to decide whether a right of transit existed as a general rule of customary international law. The evidence for such a general rule is scant (the most recent State practice apparently being characterised by frequent denials of transit rights), and the considerable treaty practice on the subject which we shall consider in a moment suggests the absence of such a rule or at least casts considerable doubt on its existence; since if such a rule of customary international law was clearly to be found, treaty rules would not be necessary.[9] Of course, local customary rules may always exist, as in the *Right of Passage* case.

Quite separately the question has been asked whether under customary international law there exists a right of transit in relation to one specific mode of transit — navigation on international rivers. Opinion is divided, but the view of the majority of writers appears to be that under customary international law there is no right for vessels of one State — at least of a non-riparian State — to navigate a river passing through another State.[10] Again, as we shall see, this is a right that is sometimes conferred by treaty.

Treaty law. Although a general right of transit probably does not exist under customary international law, such a right has been granted in a number of treaties. The Convention and Statute on Freedom of Transit of 1921 obligates the parties 'to facilitate free transit' of goods and persons across their territory by rail or waterway on routes in use convenient for international transit without distinction as to nationality. Only dues to defray expenses and reasonable tariffs may be charged. The Convention is general in scope and is not limited to, nor does it deal specifically with, landlocked States or access to the sea. A further disadvantage of the Convention is the relatively low number of contracting parties — forty, of which ten are landlocked. Article V of the General Agreement on Tariffs and Trade (1947) provides for a general 'freedom of transit' along lines similar to those of the 1921 Convention. For this freedom to be exercised by a party to GATT, its nationals or their goods must not only pass through the territory of a party to GATT, but both the State of origin and the State of destination must also be parties to GATT. In spite of the high number of parties to GATT — eighty-eight, of which fifteen are landlocked — this triple requirement (which also applies in the case of the 1921 Convention) may in practice prove a considerable limitation on the freedom granted by article V.

The High Seas Convention, unlike the two earlier treaties, deals with transit specifically in relation to the access of landlocked States to the sea. Article 3 provides:

1. In order to enjoy the freedom of the seas on equal terms with coastal States, States having no sea-coast should have free access to the sea. To this end States situated between the sea and a State having no sea-coast shall by common agreement with the latter, and in conformity with existing international conventions, accord:
   (a) To the State having no sea-coast, on a basis of reciprocity, free transit through their territory; and
   (b) To ships flying the flag of that State treatment equal to that accorded to their own ships, or to the ships of any other States, as regards access to sea ports and the use of such ports.

2. States situated between the sea and a State having no sea-coast shall settle, by mutual agreement with the latter, and taking into account the rights of the coastal State or State of transit and the special conditions of the State having no sea-coast, all matters relating to freedom of transit and equal treatment in ports, in case such States are not already parties to existing international conventions.

This article in fact confers no direct rights on landlocked States. Rights of access and transit are to be agreed between landlocked and coastal States in separate treaties. It is thus a *pactum de contrahendo*, requiring parties to the High Seas Convention to enter into negotiations for such treaties in good faith. Although according to its preamble the High Seas Convention is generally declaratory of customary international law, this would not seem to be the case as far as article 3 is concerned, because, as has already been suggested, a right of transit does not exist under customary international law. Furthermore, unlike the rest of the Convention, article 3 is not the result of the ILC's largely codifying work, but was added at the 1958 Geneva Conference in response to the recommendations of the Preliminary Conference of Landlocked States.

Since the adoption of the High Seas Convention in 1958 a number of bilateral treaties have been signed,[11] as well as an important multilateral treaty — the Convention on Transit Trade of Landlocked Countries of 1965. Article 2 of this convention grants freedom of transit across a State lying between a landlocked State and the sea (the transit State) for goods travelling by road, rail or river between the landlocked State and the sea. No customs duties may be levied on goods in transit, and only dues to defray expenses and reasonable charges may be levied (arts. 3, 4). Transit must not be hindered by administrative or customs practices (art. 5). Exceptions to all these provisions may be made on grounds of public health and security, or in case of emergency and war (arts. 11–13). The great drawback with this convention is the low number of ratifications. Only thirty-one States are parties, of which sixteen are landlocked. However, of these sixteen, only seven (Byelorussia, Chad, Czechoslovakia, Hungary, Mali, Mongolia and Niger) adjoin transit States which are also parties to the 1965 Convention, and so can obtain any practical benefit from its provisions.

In addition to the above treaties which deal with transit by a number of different modes of transport, there are also treaties dealing with transit by only one mode of transport. The Convention and Statute on the International Regime of Railways of 1923, which has twenty-five parties (four of which are landlocked), contains a number of provisions designed to facilitate the international traffic of goods and persons by railway. The Convention and Statute concerning the Regime of Navigable Waterways of International Concern of 1921 gives its twenty-six parties (five of which are landlocked) a right of navigation on international rivers. In addition, there are a number of treaties dealing with individual rivers. The most important of these, so far as landlocked States are concerned, are the treaties relating to the Rhine,[12] Danube[13] and Niger,[14] which give freedom of navigation on these rivers to all States, including those riparian States that are landlocked, viz. Switzerland; Austria, Czechoslovakia and Hungary; and Burkina Faso, Chad, Mali and Niger respectively. As far as transit by air is concerned, a number of multilateral treaties dealing with civil aviation — the Convention on International Civil Aviation (1944), article 5, the International Air Services Transit Agreement (1944) and the International Air Transport Agreement (1944) — give aircraft varying rights of transit, but in practice bilateral agreements are at least, if not more, important. Finally, the facilitation of road transit is provided for by the widely ratified multilateral Convention on Road Traffic of 1968 (replacing the 1949 Convention on Road Traffic) and a host of bilateral agreements.

The Law of the Sea Convention. Although quite numerous, the existing multilateral treaties dealing with transit are each in one way or another not wholly satisfactory for landlocked States. At UNCLOS III these States therefore pressed for the Law of the Sea Convention to contain a guaranteed right of transit. At first sight their demands appear to have been satisfied. Article 125(1) provides that:

Land-locked States shall have the right of access to and from the sea for the purpose of exercising the rights provided for in this Convention including those relating to the freedom of the high seas and the common heritage of mankind. To this end, landlocked States shall enjoy freedom of transit through the territory of transit States by all means of transport.[15]

However, what appears to be an absolute right of transit becomes considerably qualified when one reads paragraphs 2 and 3 of article 125. They provide:

2. The terms and modalities for exercising freedom of transit shall be agreed between the land-locked States and transit States concerned through bilateral, subregional or regional agreements.
3. Transit States, in the exercise of their full sovereignty over their territory, shall have the right to take all measures necessary to ensure that the rights and facilities provided for in this Part [i.e. Part X] for land-locked States shall in no way infringe their legitimate interests.

The exercise of the right of transit will therefore in practice very much depend on the terms and modalities agreed between transit States and landlocked States and on the measures taken by transit States under article 125(3). It is clear that a transit State must in good faith seek to conclude a transit agreement (what happens where the States concerned cannot reach agreement is not entirely clear),[16] and that the terms and modalities of such an agreement, as well as unilateral measures taken by a transit State, cannot be such that they effectively negate the right of transit in principle. Furthermore, such terms and modalities and unilateral measures must comply with the provisions of articles 127 and 130, which deal with customs duties and other charges and measures to avoid delays in a way similar to that of the 1965 Convention on Transit Trade of Landlocked Countries.

In the case of some landlocked States, particularly those of Africa, the right of transit may not be exercisable in practice because of the lack of navigable rivers, railways or adequate roads. Article 129 of the Law of the Sea Convention recognises this problem and provides that in these situations the States concerned 'may co-operate' in taking remedial measures. While the details of how such measures are to be taken can of course only be agreed on by the States concerned at a bilateral or regional level, the Convention might nevertheless have contained a stronger exhortation to co-operate in this matter.

Nearly all the multilateral treaties on transit, particularly the High Seas Convention and the Law of the Sea Convention, contemplate the conclusion of bilateral treaties to regulate transit rights in detail. There are in fact quite a number of these treaties, particularly in relation to the landlocked States of Europe, Latin America and, to some extent, Asia (for examples, see the works of Delupis, Glassner, Govindaraj, Sarup and the UN Secretariat listed in 'Further reading' at the end of this chapter). In Africa an important regional transit agreement has recently been concluded — the Northern Corridor Transit Agreement,[17] which gives a right of transit to

Burundi, Rwanda and Uganda to the Kenyan port of Mombasa. The agreement is one of the most comprehensive and detailed transit agreements yet concluded. In spite of the existence of bilateral and regional transit treaties, multilateral treaties such as the 1965 Convention and the Law of the Sea Convention which confer a general right of transit remain of great importance. In negotiating with a transit State a landlocked State is in a weak bargaining position because it usually has little to offer the transit State in return for the favour it is seeking. It therefore strengthens the position of a landlocked State in negotiating a new bilateral treaty or renewing an existing treaty if it can point to a general right of transit laid down in a multilateral convention.

The special problems experienced by landlocked and geographically disadvantaged States in relation to the law of the sea appear now to have received general recognition. On the other hand, the rights that have been accorded to these States do not deal with those problems in a manner wholly to their satisfaction. Furthermore, the rights themselves, particularly those relating to access to the living resources of neighbouring EEZs and to transit, are subject to so many qualifications and limitations and are expressed in such imprecise language that it is doubtful how much practical benefit they will give (as a matter of law) to landlocked and geographically disadvantaged States.

Notes

1   Botswana, Burkina Faso, Burundi, Central African Republic, Chad, Lesotho, Malawi, Mali, Niger, Rwanda, Swaziland, Uganda, Zambia and Zimbabwe.
2   Austria, Byelorussian SSR, Czechoslovakia, Holy See, Hungary, Liechenstein, Luxembourg, San Marino and Switzerland. The status of the Byelorussian SSR, Holy See, Liechenstein and San Marino as States is somewhat controversial.
3   Afghanistan, Bhutan, Laos, Mongolia and Nepal.
4   Bolivia and Paraguay.
5   UNCLOS I, *Official Records*, Vol. VII, pp. 67–79.
6   7 *LNTS* 14.
7   *Lloyds Register of Shipping Statistical Tables*, 1986, pp. 4–5. It is not clear whether these tables cover only seagoing ships or whether they include ships used in inland navigation. In any case the tables refer only to ships over 100 tons gross.
8   Although there are no agreements providing for the access of landlocked States, two States provide for such access in their national legislation. See Morocco, Decree No. 1–81–179 of 8 April 1981, art. 13, and Togo, Ordinance No. 24 of 16 August 1977, art. 4. *Smith*, pp. 303 and 439.
9   Some writers have, however, claimed that a right of transit exists in customary law, e.g. E. Lauterpacht (see the reference in 'Further reading') and J. E. S. Fawcett, 'Trade and finance in international law', 123 *Recueil des Cours* 215 (1968), at 266–7. Against this view see, e.g., L. C. Caflisch (see the references in 'Further reading' at pp. 361–4 and 77–9 respectively).

10 See, e.g., R. R. Baxter, *op. cit.* in 'Further reading', pp. 149–59, and B. Vitanyi, *op. cit.* in 'Further reading', chapter four. See also the *Faber* case (1903), where the German Commissioner of the Germany — Venezuela Mixed Claims Commission thought there was a general right of navigation on rivers (*X RIAA* 438, at 444–5): the Venezuelan Commissioner (pp. 448–9) and the Umpire (pp. 464–7), however, disagreed. In any case, the question was essentially *obiter*.

11 For examples, see Delupis, *op. cit.* in 'Further reading', pp. 105–8, and UN Doc. A/AC 138/37.

12 Convention for Rhine Navigation, 1868, as amended.

13 Convention regarding the Regime of Navigation on the Danube, 1948.

14 Act regarding Navigation and Economic Co-operation between the States of the Niger Basin, 1963, and Agreement concerning the Niger River Commission and the Navigation and Transport on the River Niger, 1964. The 1964 Agreement has been superseded by the Convention creating the Niger Basin Authority, 1980.

15 But 'means of transport' is defined in art. 124 as excluding pipelines and air transport, unless the States concerned agree to the contrary.

16 Where one party has not shown good faith, there is presumably breach of an international obligation (and cf. art. 300 of the Law of the Sea Convention): in any case the Convention's provisions on settlement of disputes could be invoked by the dissatisfied party.

17 The agreement was signed on 19 February 1985 and came into force on 15 November 1986. We have been unable to locate the text of the agreement. A summary of its provisions is given in 11 *Commonwealth Law Bulletin* 1001–2 (1985) and 13 *ibid.* 641–3 (1987).

Further reading

L. M. Alexander, 'The "disadvantaged" States and the law of the sea', 5 *Marine Policy* 185–93 (1981).

L. M. Alexander and R. D. Hodgson, 'The role of geographically disadvantaged States in the law of the sea', 13 *San Diego Law Review* 558–82 (1976).

R. R. Baxter, *The Law of International Waterways*, Cambridge, Mass., 1964.

L. C. Caflisch, 'Land-locked and geographically disadvantaged States and the new law of the sea', in *The Law of the Sea*, Thesaurus Acroasium, Vol. VII, Thessaloniki, 1977, pp. 341–404.

L. C. Caflisch, 'Land-locked States and their access to and from the sea', 49 *BYIL* 71–100 (1978).

I. Delupis, 'Landlocked States and the law of the sea', 19 *Scandinavian Studies in Law* 101–20 (1975).

R-J. Dupuy and D. Vignes (eds.), *Traité du Nouveau Droit de la Mer*, Paris, 1985, chap. 9 and pp. 905–30 (*passim*).

J. H. E. Fried, 'The 1965 Convention on Transit Trade of Landlocked States', 6 *IJIL* 9–30 (1966).

M. I. Glassner, *Access to the Sea for Developing Land-locked States*, The Hague, 1970.

M. I. Glassner, *Bibliography on Land-locked States*, 2nd ed., The Hague, 1985.

I. Hussain, 'A study of Pakistan's attitude towards the question of free access to the sea of landlocked states', 24 *IJIL* 319–45 (1984).

E. Lauterpacht, 'Freedom of transit in international law', 44 *Transactions of the Grotius Society* 313–56 (1958–59).

R. Makil, 'Transit rights of land-locked countries', 4 *Journal of World Trade Law* 35–51 (1970).

Memorandum submitted by the Preliminary Conference of Landlocked States, UNCLOS I, *Official Records*, Vol. VII, pp. 67–79.

F. Mirvahabi, 'The rights of the landlocked and geographically disadvantaged States in exploitation of marine fisheries', 26 *Netherlands International Law Review* 130–62 (1979).

A. Sarup, 'Transit trade of land-locked Nepal', 21 *ICLQ* 287–306 (1972).

A. M. Sinjela, *Land-Locked States and the UNCLOS Regime*, New York, 1983.

UN Secretariat, 'The question of free access to the sea of land-locked countries', UNCLOS I, *Official Records*, Vol. I, pp. 306–35.

UN Secretary General, 'Study of the question of free access to the sea of land-locked countries and of the special problems of land-locked countries relating to the exploration and exploitation of the resources of the seabed and the ocean floor beyond the limits of national jurisdiction', UN Doc. A/AC. 138/37 (1971).

B. Vitanyi, *The International Regime of River Navigation*, Alphen aan den Rijn, 1979.

I. J. Wani, 'An evaluation of the Convention on the Law of the Sea from the perspective of landlocked States', 22 *VJIL* 627–65 (1982).

CHAPTER NINETEEN
Settlement of disputes

Settlement of disputes under the traditional law of the sea

The law of the sea presents many opportunities for disputes. Adjacent or opposite States may disagree over the boundaries separating their respective maritime zones; one State may claim the right to conduct naval manoeuvres in the EEZ of another State which denies that such a right exists; a fisherman may challenge the right of a foreign State to arrest him for fishing fifty miles from its coasts. These three examples (and many more may be found in previous chapters) illustrate different kinds of dispute which may arise. For the purposes of settlement, the important distinction is between the first two examples, which represent inter-State or international disputes, and the third, which represents disputes between a State and an individual. However, as we shall see, disputes of the latter kind may become translated into international disputes proper.

Municipal courts

When an individual has, to use our example, been arrested under foreign laws which in his view violate international law, he may attempt to raise the issue with the arresting officer or, if that is unsuccessful, with the municipal court before which he is brought for trial. The response of the court to arguments based upon international law will be determined largely by the standing of international law in the legal system concerned. For example, under English and Scottish law domestic statutes invariably prevail, in accordance with the doctrine of parliamentary sovereignty, over international customary law and treaties. Accordingly, when it was argued in the case of *Mortensen* v. *Peters* (1906) that the conviction of the Danish captain of a Norwegian ship for fishing in the Moray Firth was contrary to international law because it involved a claim to jurisdiction over a foreign ship more than three miles from shore, the conviction was nevertheless upheld. The Scottish Court of Justiciary held that even if the statute under which Mortensen was convicted was contrary to international law, the court was bound to give effect to the intention of Parliament and enforce it. The remedy is then diplomatic (see below). In this case the British government subsequently pardoned the fishermen and repaid their fines.

Other States have different rules. In States with civil law systems (based upon comprehensive legislative codes descended from Roman law rather than the mixture of judicial decisions and statute which characterises the English and other common law systems) treaties are commonly given precedence over domestic legislation — at least over prior, if not over later legislation; and some, such as the Federal Republic of Germany, also give customary international law this status. In such States it is possible in at least some cases (depending upon the precise rules of the legal system in question) for international law to be invoked so as to prevent the application of the local law. Thus, in the French case of the *Sally* and the *Newton* (1806), the jurisdiction of French courts to prosecute assaults committed on board American ships in French ports was held to be ousted by a rule of international law reserving matters of 'internal discipline' to the flag State (see chapter three). Each legal system has its own rules for determining the relationship between municipal and international law, but most adopt a position somewhere between the 'nationalism' of English and the 'internationalism' of German law. Thus in the United States, for example, the self-executing provisions of treaties have direct effect in American law and overrule prior (but not later) statutes, but statutes prevail over customary law. Whatever the doctrine espoused by their States, it is the usual practice of courts to construe statutes, wherever possible, so as not to conflict with the international obligations of their State. So, for instance, the English Court of Appeal in *Post Office* v. *Estuary Radio Ltd.* (1968) decided that any ambiguity in the Order defining British territorial waters should be resolved so as to accord with the provisions of the Territorial Sea Convention 'in so far as that is a plausible meaning of the express words of the Order'.[1]

Diplomatic protection

It may be that municipal courts insist upon enforcing the legislation which is alleged to conflict with international law. If so, if the dispute is to be pursued, it must be taken up on behalf of the aggrieved individual and continued as a dispute between States. A State could take up such a case by exercising the right of diplomatic protection, which extends to the State's nationals (including companies incorporated in the State) and ships and aircraft flying its flag. In the absence of some link of nationality of this kind, diplomatic protection may not be exercised. Furthermore, diplomatic protection is a right, and not a duty: the individual has no right to insist upon his State exercising diplomatic protection on his behalf; nor, indeed, to prevent his State from doing so. In taking up an individual case a

State is, in law, asserting its own rights, which have been challenged when they were exercised by the State through one of its nationals: it is not asserting the rights of the individual concerned as such. At this stage the dispute is between two States: the one exercising diplomatic protection and the one whose actions are challenged. For example, the United Kingdom has taken up the cases of British trawler owners denied access to or arrested in 'Icelandic' fishing grounds during the successive 'cod wars' of 1958–76 against Iceland.

Disputes which arise immediately between States, rather than between individuals and States, are on the international plane from the outset. Examples are boundary disputes, such as the Libyan-Tunisian continental shelf dispute; and cases involving the armed forces, which are considered to embody the sovereignty of the State, such as the Corfu Channel dispute between the United Kingdom and Albania. International disputes of this kind never go before municipal tribunals, it being a rule of international law that no State should be required to submit to the courts of another. However, States are under an obligation to settle disputes by peaceful means, such as negotiation, enquiry, mediation, conciliation, arbitration or judicial settlement (see article 33 of the UN Charter, and the 1982 Manila Declaration on Peaceful Settlement of Disputes between States, UN GA Res 37/10, (1982)).

Negotiations

Once the dispute arises on the international plane, it is normal to seek a settlement by negotiation. Indeed, in cases where a State is exercising its right of diplomatic protection, negotiations may have been started before the individual has been convicted, or even arrested. This is typically the case where the source of the dispute is a piece of legislation; it is not unusual for diplomatic representations, which may lead to negotiations, to be made while the legislation is still at its Bill stage, before final adoption by the legislature. During the disputes over the American liquor laws in the 1920s diplomatic negotiations proceeded in respect of the general issue, rather than specific cases, and produced in 1924 a series of bilateral treaties embodying the agreed settlement.

Fact-finding and conciliation commissions

If negotiations do not resolve the dispute, it may be necessary to involve a third party. This may involve no more than the provision of good offices or mediation, or the third party may play a more conclusive role, settling disputed questions of fact or law or both. For example, in the dispute following the seizure of the *Red Crusader* (1962) much turned upon the question whether the fishing vessel was within or without the Faroese fishing zone, and the United Kingdom (as flag State) and Denmark agreed to set up a commission of enquiry to settle the matter. Occasionally, a conciliation commission may be established to propose a settlement to the dispute. This occurred recently in relation to the continental shelf around Jan Mayen island, disputed between Norway and Iceland, who agreed to the establishment of a commission, and accepted its recommendations (see p. 127).

Arbitration

Where questions of law are concerned, third-party settlement may take one of several forms. The parties may agree to set up an *ad hoc* arbitral tribunal whose composition and terms of reference they jointly determine. This course was adopted in the *Anglo-French Continental Shelf* arbitration of 1977. The Permanent Court of Arbitration — which is really no more than a panel of arbitrators — may be used in this connection, each State nominating from the panel two arbitrators who together choose a fifth as umpire. Tribunals established under this system gave awards in the *Muscat Dhows* (1905) and *North Atlantic Coast Fisheries* (1910) cases, among others. Alternatively, there may be a standing tribunal with jurisdiction over disputes arising between the States in question, such as the US–Panamanian General Claims Commission, which decided the case of the *David* (1933). Also, treaties may provide for disputes to be settled by special arbitral procedures (e.g. the 1964 European Fisheries Convention, and the 1969 International Convention relating to Intervention on the High Seas in Cases of Oil Pollution Casualties.

In the case of all international tribunals, whether arbitral tribunals, or the International Court of Justice or other special tribunals, cases can be brought before them only when local remedies — that is to say, the system of appeals in municipal courts, and any other appeals which the municipal legal system might offer — have been exhausted, although, as we have noted, a dispute which arises between two States (rather than an individual and a State) does not have to be submitted to a municipal court and so there will in such cases be no question of exhausting local remedies.

The International Court of Justice

Sometimes States have preferred to take the matter to the Permanent Court of International Justice or (since 1945) its successor, the International Court of Justice. This has the disadvantage that the parties are not wholly free to determine the composition of the Court, the judges being elected for nine-year terms by the UN General Assembly and Security Council in accordance with the Court's statute. However, each party to a dispute has a right to appoint a judge of its choosing if there is no judge of its nationality on the bench; and, furthermore, the parties may agree to put the dispute before a chamber of the Court in which case, as was decided in the *Gulf of Maine* case where such a procedure was used, the parties may choose which of the judges shall constitute the chamber.

On the other hand, because a number of States (about forty-six, at present) have opted under article 36(2) of the Statute to accept the Court's jurisdiction in advance of any specific dispute arising, and because this acceptance cannot be withdrawn once proceedings have been instituted against that State, this system does have some advantages. Thus cases were brought against Norway, in the *Anglo-Norwegian Fisheries* case (1951), and France, in the *Nuclear Tests* cases (1974), despite the fact that in the latter cases France refused to co-operate — a refusal which would have prevented arbitration of the issue, because arbitration depends upon the willingness of both parties to agree to and participate in the arbitration. While the refusal of France to appear before the International Court detracted from the proceedings, there is no doubt that recourse to the Court put considerable pressure upon her to comply with the applicable rules of international law.

Article 36(2) is not the only way in which a dispute may be brought before the International Court. The States involved may decide by special agreement to submit the dispute to the Court (as the three States involved in the *North Sea Continental Shelf* cases did). In addition, many bilateral and multilateral treaties contain a provision that any dispute arising out of the application of the treaty is to be referred to the Court. An example of a treaty containing such a compromissory clause is the Iceland–United Kingdom Agreement of 1961, and it was on this treaty that the Court's jurisdiction was founded in the *Fisheries Jurisdiction* case (1974). Even where there are no declarations under article 36(2) of the Statute, special agreement, or treaty containing an applicable compromissory clause, a State may be prepared to accept the Court's jurisdiction when another State brings a case against it. This form of jurisdiction (known as *forum prorogatum*) is highly exceptional, one of the very few cases which the Court has decided on this basis being the *Corfu Channel* case (1949). It will be noted that all the ways in which a case may come before the Court (and, indeed, all forms of third party dispute settlement in international law), are based upon the consent of the States concerned.

There are many treaties containing compromissory clauses which relate to the law of the sea, and an attempt was made to adopt this system in respect of the four Geneva Conventions on the Law of the Sea. An optional protocol provided that all disputes arising from the interpretation or application of the Conventions should be referred to the International Court, unless the parties agreed within a reasonable time upon some other means of peaceful settlement. Just over thirty States have accepted this obligation: its unpopularity, like that of declarations under article 36(2) of the International Court's Statute, derives mainly from an unwillingness on the part of States to accept an open-ended obligation to submit disputes — whose nature it is almost impossible to predict — to a particular settlement procedure, and in fact no case has yet been referred to the Court under the optional protocol. Despite this inauspicious background, UNCLOS III has provided for an elaborate system of dispute settlement, which we will now examine.

Settlement of disputes under the Law of the Sea Convention

The Law of the Sea Convention lays down a basic scheme for the settlement of disputes arising from the interpretation and application of the Convention, and makes exceptions from this for certain categories of dispute. The exceptions are largely motivated by the fact that States are particularly unwilling to allow some kinds of dispute, which touch their vital interests more than others, to be determined by third-party procedures, and to a lesser extent by the need to provide specialist panels to adjudicate on some questions. We outline the general procedure first, and then the exceptions.

The basic framework (LOSC, Part XV)

Conciliation.   States must settle disputes by peaceful means (LOSC, art. 279), and are always free to agree to adopt some means other than that prescribed in the Convention (LOSC, art. 280). Some States have bound themselves to use other procedures — the EEC States, for example, must submit fisheries disputes arising between them to the European Court of Justice under the terms of the EEC Treaty — and these obligations supplant those in the Law of the Sea Convention (LOSC, art. 282). If the parties to a dispute fail to reach a settlement through agreed procedures, one of them may invite the other to submit to the conciliation procedure (LOSC, art. 284). If this invitation is accepted, each party chooses two conciliators of which one may be one of its nationals, from a list to which each State party to the Convention is entitled to nominate four people. The four conciliators chosen select a fifth, who acts as chairman. The panel has one year within which to hear the parties and report, making any recommendations which it sees fit. If the report is accepted and implemented, all is well. But if it is not, the conciliation procedure is deemed to be terminated (LOSC, Annex V).

Compulsory settlement.   Subject to the exceptional cases which we consider below, any dispute not resolved under the foregoing provisions is to be referred for compulsory settlement (LOSC, art. 286). States may, on signing the Convention or at some later date, choose one or more of the following forums to decide disputes: (1) the International Tribunal for the

Law of the Sea; (2) the International Court of Justice; (3) an arbitral tribunal constituted under Annex VII of the Convention; or, for specified kinds of disputes, (4) a special arbitral tribunal constituted under Annex VIII (LOSC, art. 287).

The International Tribunal for the Law of the Sea (hereafter, the Law of the Sea Tribunal), established under Annex VI of the Law of the Sea Convention, would have twenty-one members, elected by parties to the Convention so as to ensure the representation of the world's principal legal systems. Not all members would necessarily be present in every adjudication: the tribunal's quorum is eleven, and it is also empowered to operate through special chambers of three or five members (LOSC, Annex VI, art. 15), and also through the eleven-man Sea Bed Disputes Chamber, which may itself operate through three-man *ad hoc* chambers (LOSC, Annex VI, section 4). The tribunal selects its own president.

Arbitral tribunals under Annex VII of the Law of the Sea Convention are composed of five members, one chosen by each of the parties and the other three chosen jointly by the parties, from a panel to which each State party to the Convention may nominate four people. If the disputants cannot agree on the three jointly chosen arbitrators, these are to be appointed by the president of the Law of the Sea Tribunal. Arbitrators must have some experience in maritime affairs — a rather wider criterion than the 'recognized competence in matters relating to the law of the sea' required of members of the Sea Tribunal.

Special arbitral tribunals under Annex VIII of the Law of the Sea Convention can deal only with disputes concerning fisheries, environmental protection, scientific research or navigation. States may nominate two experts to each of four lists, each dealing with one of these categories, and maintained respectively by the FAO, UNEP, IOC and IMO. Each party to the dispute may choose two arbitrators (of whom only one may be its national) for each case, preferably from the appropriate list, and a president, who is to be a national of a third State, is chosen by agreement between the parties. These special tribunals may also be used by parties to a dispute, if they so agree, as fact-finding commissions.

These bodies, like the International Court of Justice, which is the fourth of the forums included in article 287, all apply the rules of the Convention and other rules of international law, although the disputants may agree to request a decision *ex aequo et bono* — that is, one based on general principles of fairness and equity (LOSC, art. 293). If it thinks it necessary, any of these bodies may appoint two or more non-voting scientific experts to sit with it while it is hearing a case (LOSC, art. 289). All decisions are taken by majority vote, all are reasoned, and all are final and binding on the parties.

If a State has not selected one of the available forums under article 287, it is deemed to have accepted 'Annex VII' arbitration. When a dispute arises which is not settled by the conciliation procedure (or where one party refuses to follow that procedure), it must be submitted to one of these forums at the request of any disputant (LOSC, art. 286). If both parties have chosen the same forum under article 287, it goes to that body; otherwise, the dispute its to be referred to an 'Annex VII' arbitral tribunal unless the parties otherwise agree (LOSC, art. 287).

States need not choose the same forum for every purpose: for example, the Soviet Union and three other Eastern European States have chosen 'Annex VII' arbitration as the 'basic' means for dispute settlement, but have chosen Annex VIII special arbitration for disputes concerning fisheries, environmental protection, scientific research and navigation, and the Law of the Sea Tribunal for disputes concerning the prompt release of detained vessels and their crews (see LOSC, art. 292).[2]

Provisional measures

It may be that one of the parties is proposing to take action which would prejudice the rights of the other even if the dispute were ultimately to be settled in the other's favour. For example, if one State is proposing to insist on a right of innocent passage for a cargo that the other regards as so inherently dangerous as to prejudice the safety of its coastal communities, there is little point in deciding in favour of the coastal State if the passage has taken place and an accident resulted. In such cases, or if it is necessary to prevent serious harm to the environment, the 'article 287' forum hearing the case may prescribe appropriate provisional measures — a power modelled on that under article 41 of the Statute of the International Court of Justice (which Greece tried to invoke in order to prevent Turkish vessels conducting seismic surveys — unsuccessfully, because the surveys carried no risk of irreparable prejudice — on the disputed shelf, in the *Aegean Sea Continental Shelf (Interim Measures)* case (1976)). If the case is to be heard by an arbitral tribunal which has not been constituted at the time, provisional measures may be indicated by the Law of the Sea Tribunal (LOSC, art. 290).

Application of dispute settlement procedures

The exercise of coastal States' sovereign rights or jurisdiction is subject to these procedures only in so far as it is alleged that it has interfered with freedoms of navigation, overflight or immersion, or other internationally lawful uses of the EEZ, or, where such jurisdiction can only be exercised consistently with international standards concerning pollution, has contravened those international standards (LOSC, art. 297(1)). Otherwise, all disputes arising from the application or interpretation of the Law of the Sea Convention are included, subject to the special procedures described below.

Marine scientific research.   States may, but are not obliged to, submit disputes arising from decisions to refuse permission to engage in scientific research in their EEZs or continental shelves to the procedures under article 287. If they do not, such disputes must be submitted to the 'compulsory conciliation procedure' under section 2 of Annex V (LOSC, art. 297(2)). This procedure is the same as the ordinary conciliation procedure described above, except that States cannot choose not to participate: the conciliation commission would proceed with its work (exactly how is not clear) without the co-operation of a defaulting State. The conciliation commission may not question a State's exercise of its discretion to refuse consent but could, presumably, find that the refusal was based upon patently impermissible grounds.

EEZ fisheries.   States are not obliged to accept article 287 procedures in relation to disputes concerning their sovereign rights over EEZ fisheries, including those arising from failures to determine total allowable catches and coastal harvesting capacities, the allocation of surpluses to other States, and the terms of conservation measures. But where it is alleged that the coastal State has manifestly failed to ensure that the maintenance of EEZ fish stocks is not seriously endangered, or that there has been an arbitrary refusal to determine total allowable catches or harvesting capacity or to allocate a surplus to other States, the 'compulsory conciliation procedure' is to operate (LOSC, art. 297(3)).

The international sea bed.   Special procedures are laid down for the settlement of disputes arising from the exploration and exploitation of the international sea bed area and its resources (LOSC, Part XI, section 6). These provisions are complicated, not least because not only States, but also the Authority and its organs, the Enterprise, and individual contractors (which may be State-owned industries or commercial operators), may all be parties to disputes, which may concern not only the Convention but also rules laid down by the Authority and the terms of contracts and licences. The provisions are unclearly drafted, but their general effect is that in the absence of agreement upon some other means of settlement, disputes are to be referred to the Sea Bed Disputes Chamber, or an *ad hoc* chamber thereof, apart from disputes concerning contracts which would be submitted to commercial arbitration under UNCITRAL rules. In cases where contractors appear, their sponsoring

States may, but are not obliged, to do so too: this gives the Chamber an unusual 'transnational' character, mixing features of international and municipal law, which is also evident in the provision that its decisions are to be enforceable in municipal courts (LOSC, Annex VI, section 4). (See, further, chapter twelve.)

Optional exceptions. Parties to the Law of the Sea Convention are entitled to declare, on or after signature, that they will not accept any or all of the article 287 procedures in respect of any or all of three specified categories of dispute (LOSC, art. 298). Two of these — disputes concerning military activities and disputes in respect of which the UN Security Council is exercising its functions — are rooted in the need for deference to States' sovereign rights and to international settlement procedures. These categories are subject only to the general obligation to reach a settlement by peaceful means agreed by the parties.

The third category is that of delimitation disputes, which are excepted from the general regime because of lack of agreement on delimitation criteria and procedures at UNCLOS III. If a State declares that it will not accept compulsory settlement of disputes over the boundaries of its territorial sea, EEZ or continental shelf, it must nonetheless accept 'compulsory conciliation' if no agreement is reached within a reasonable time. Furthermore, disputants are obliged to negotiate an agreement on the basis of the conciliation commission's report; if they do not do so, they must agree upon some other procedure for settling the dispute — a rather insubstantial obligation.

Several States have invoked the optional exceptions under article 298. Most, such as the Soviet Union and other Eastern European States and Tunisia, have excepted all three categories of dispute. Others have excepted only some: Iceland, for instance, has excepted only questions of continental shelf delimitation.[3]

General principles applicable in dispute settlement

Almost every dispute which arises has characteristics which mark it out from others, but there are nevertheless some general points of importance, which we should make in conclusion.

Locus standi

Not every State will have the right to institute proceedings in respect of any violation of the Law of the Sea Convention which might arise. Generally, a State must show that it has some particular legal right, such as the right of innocent passage, or the freedom of navigation on the high seas, which has been infringed. An international tribunal would not accept a complaint by a State that some other State's rights have been infringed: the State would not have *locus standi* to present such a case. Sensible as this rule is in cases where at least one State is in fact directly affected, it hampers the enforcement of the law when only a 'community interest' is at stake. For example, it is usually difficult to show that any State's legal rights are infringed by pollution of the high seas and so, although the world at large may suffer from such pollution, it may be that no State has *locus standi* to bring proceedings in respect of it. The question of defending community interests was raised, but not resolved, in the *Nuclear Tests* cases (1974), where Australia and New Zealand based their claims in part upon the right of the international community to be preserved from radioactive fall-out, apart from any direct infringement of their own rights. But this area of international law is still poorly developed, and the institution of community proceedings — the *actio popularis*, as it is known — may yet be recognised (note the role of the supervisory authorities under the Nordic Convention, which can bring actions in the courts of any State party: above, p. 281).

Deciding the case

Disputes arising under the Law of the Sea Convention or any other international treaty will usually be decided by the interpretation of the treaty in question. The rules for interpretation are conveniently summarised in the 1969 Vienna Convention on the Law of Treaties. The basic rule is that the treaty must be interpreted in good faith in accordance with the ordinary meaning to be given to its terms in their context and in the light of the treaty's object and purpose: 'context' here includes not only the treaty and its preamble and annexes, but also any other instruments, such as protocols, made in connection with the treaty. Any subsequent agreement between the parties concerning interpretation must be taken into account, as must any subsequent practice of parties in the application of the treaty which establishes their (perhaps tacit) agreement concerning its interpretation. Comparison of authentic texts in different languages may also clarify the meaning: the Law of the Sea Convention has six authentic texts, in Arabic, Chinese, English, French, Russian and Spanish (LOSC, art. 320). If the meaning remains ambiguous or obscure, recourse may be had to the preparatory works (*travaux préparatoires*) and circumstances of the treaty's conclusion, as supplementary means of interpretation. However, UNCLOS III, unlike its predecessors, lacks full *travaux préparatoires*, and some of the critical parts of the final text of the 1982 Convention were the product of unrecorded negotiations. This reduces the importance which can properly be given to the conference records as an aid to interpretation.

Disputes over matters not regulated by treaty would be determined by the application of customary international law, as established by the general practice of States. Customary law may be supplemented by general principles of law recognised by civilised nations (such as the rule that no one may profit from his own wrong).

Where neither treaty nor customary law contains rules determining the dispute, it is necessary to fall back upon certain presumptions. The most significant are those concerning maritime jurisdiction: in the absence of other rules, coastal States are presumed to have complete jurisdiction over ships of all flags in their territorial seas, and ships on the high seas are subject only to the jurisdiction of their flag State. Unfortunately, in the case of the EEZ, where many disputes are likely to arise, there is no presumption either way, disputes being resolved on the basis of the elusive criteria of article 59 of the Law of the Sea Convention (see chapter nine). Other general rules of international law, such as that requiring the use of minimum force when effecting an arrest, whether it be after hot pursuit, as in the case of the *I'm alone* (1935) or in any other circumstances, will also be applied.

Finally, we must emphasise a point made at the beginning of this book. The law of the sea is no more than a part of international law. Questions concerning nationality, international claims, State responsibility and so on are bound to be involved in any controversy concerning international law, and no one can properly claim a thorough understanding of the law of the sea without an understanding of the rest of international law. We have tried here to outline, in rather more detail than the general textbooks on international law, the major features of the contemporary law of the sea — but no more than that.

Notes

1 [1968] 2 Q.B. 740, at 757.
2 See 5 *LOSB* 7 (Byelorussian SSR), 12 (German Democratic Republic), 23 (Ukrainian SSR and USSR) (1985). As yet few States have made a choice of forum. Apart from those mentioned in the text, the others show support for the range of options, including the Law of the Sea Tribunal (Belgium, Tanzania, Uruguay), the ICJ (Belgium, Uruguay), Annex VII arbitration (Egypt) and Annex VIII special arbitration (Belgium). Other declarations on this matter are regularly reprinted in the UN *Law of the Sea Bulletin*.
3 For the Soviet and east European declarations see *loc. cit.*, n. 2. For the Tunisian and Icelandic declarations see *LOSB* Special Issue I, pp. 7 and 5 respectively (1987). Other relevant declarations are reprinted regularly in the UN *Law of the Sea Bulletin*.

Further reading

A. O. Adede, *The System for Settlement of Disputes under the United Nations Convention on the Law of the Sea*, Dordrecht, 1987.
P. W. Birnie, 'Dispute settlement procedures in the 1982 UNCLOS', in W. E.

Butler (ed.), *The Law of the Sea and International Shipping: Anglo-Soviet Post-UNCLOS Perspectives*, New York, 1985, pp. 39–68.

E. D. Brown, 'Dispute settlement', 5 *Marine Policy 282–6* (1981).

A. R. Carnegie, 'The Law of the Sea Tribunal', 28 *ICLQ* 669–84 (1981).

David Davies Memorial Institute of International Studies, *International Disputes: The Legal Aspects*, London, 1972.

M. P. Gaertner, 'The dispute settlement provisions of the Convention on the Law of the Sea: critique and alternatives to the International Tribunal for the Law of the Sea', 19 *San Diego Law Review* 577–97 (1982).

J. G. Merrills, *International Dispute Settlement*, London, 1984.

R. Ranjeva, 'Le règlement des différends', in R. J. Dupuy and D. Vignes (eds.), *Traité du Nouveau Droit de la Mer*, Paris, 1985, pp. 1105–67.

W. Riphagen, 'Dispute settlement in the 1982 United Nations Convention on the Law of the Sea', in C. L. Rozakis and C. A. Stephanou (eds.), *The New Law of the Sea*, Amsterdam, 1983, pp. 281–301.

L. B. Sohn, 'US policy toward the settlement of law of the sea disputes', 17 *VJIL* 9–22 (1976–77).

APPENDIX

1. Claims to maritime zones

This table sets out the current claims made by States to a territorial sea, exclusive fishing or exclusive economic zone, continental shelf and other maritime zones. Unless otherwise stated, the breadths of zones are given in nautical miles and are measured from the baseline. Dates in brackets refer to the year when the claim was first made. Where the claim is embodied in legislation, the date is the year in which the legislation was enacted: this is not always the same as the year in which the legislation entered into force. Where an entry in the EEZ, EFZ or other zones columns is blank, it means that no claim has been made to such a zone: in the case of the continental shelf column it means that no claim to a precise area of continental shelf has been made. 'CZ for LOSC purposes' means a contiguous zone for the purposes set out in the Law of the Sea Convention, viz. the control to prevent and punish infringement of customs, fiscal, immigration or sanitary regulations. States are arranged in alphabetical order and a summary of claims is given at the end. The information has been taken from *Limits in the Seas*, No. 36, fifth revision (1985) and R. W. Smith, *Exclusive Economic Zone Claims* (1986), with some additions and updating by the authors. As far as possible the information is correct as at 1 June 1987.

State	Territorial sea	EEZ or EFZ	Continental shelf	Other maritime zones
Albania	15 (1976)			
Algeria	12 (1963)			
Angola	20 (1975)	200 EFZ (1975)		
Antigua and Barbuda	12 (1982)	200 EEZ (1982)	200 or outer edge of continental margin (1986)	24 CZ for LOSC purposes (1982)
Argentina	200 (1966)		CSC definition (1966)	
Australia	3 (1878)	200 EFZ (1978)	CSC definition (1967)	

State	Territorial sea	EEZ or EFZ	Continental shelf	Other maritime zones
Bahamas	3 (1878)	200 EFZ (1977)	CSC definition (1970)	
Bahrain	3			
Bangladesh	12 (1971)	200 EEZ (1974)	Outer limit of continental margin (1974)	18 CZ for LOSC purposes plus security (1974)
Barbados	12 (1977)	200 EEZ (1978)		
Belgium	3 (1929)	EFZ up to median line with neighbouring States (1978)	Up to the median line with opposite and adjacent States (1969)	10 km customs zone (1832)
Belize	3			
Benin	200 (1976)			
Brazil	200 (1970)			
Brunei	12 (1982)	200 EFZ (1982)		
Bulgaria	12 (1951)			
Burma	12 (1968)	200 EEZ (1977)	200 or outer limit of continental margin (1977)	24 CZ for LOSC purposes plus security (1977)
Cameroon	50 (1974)			
Canada	12 (1970)	200 EFZ (1977)	200 or outer edge of continental margin (1981)	100 anti-pollution zone in Arctic waters (1970). Anti-pollution zone coterminous with EFZ (1971)
Cape Verde	12 (1977)	200 EEZ (1977)		
Chile	12	200 EEZ	350 around Easter and Sala y Gomez Islands (1985)	24 CZ for LOSC purposes
China	12 (1958)			

Country	Territorial sea	EEZ/EFZ	Continental shelf	Contiguous zone
Colombia	12 (1970)	200 EEZ (1978)		
Comoros	12 (1976)	200 EEZ (1976)		
Congo	200 (1977)			
Costa Rica	12 (1972)	200 EEZ (1975)	CSC definition (1967)	
Cuba	12 (1977)	200 EEZ (1977)	200 metres (1954)	
Cyprus	12 (1964)		To depth of exploitation (1974)	
Denmark	3 (1966)	200 EFZ (1976)	CSC definition (1963)	4 customs zone (1928). 12 anti-liquor smuggling zone (1926)
Djibouti	12 (1979)	200 EEZ (1979)		24 contiguous zone for fiscal, health and immigration matters (1979)
Dominica	12 (1981)	200 EEZ (1981)		24 CZ for LOSC purposes (1981)
Dominican Republic	6 (1967)	200 EEZ (1977)	200 or outer edge of continental margin (1977)	24 CZ for LOSC purposes (1977)
Ecuador	200 (1966)		100 miles beyond 2500 metre isobath (1985)	
Egypt	12 (1958)	200 EEZ (1983)	CSC definition (1958)	24 contiguous zone for security, navigation, fiscal and sanitary matters (1983)
El Salvador	200 (1950)			
Equatorial Guinea	12 (1970)	200 EEZ (1984)	CSC definition (1970)	
Ethiopia	12 (1953)			
Fiji	12 (1976)	200 EEZ (1977)		
Finland	4 (1956)	EFZ to equidistance line with neighbouring States (1981)	Defined as in arts 1 and 6 of CSC (1965)	6 customs zone (1939). 12 anti-liquor smuggling zone (1932)
France	12 (1971)	200 EEZ (1976)		
Gabon	12 ?	200 EEZ (1984)		24 CZ for LOSC purposes (1984)

State	Territorial sea	EEZ or EFZ	Continental shelf	Other maritime zones
Gambia	12 (1969)	200 EFZ (1977)		18 contiguous zone to prevent and punish infringement of any law (1969)
German Democratic Republic	12 (1984)	EFZ to equidistance line with neighbouring States (1977)	CSC definition (1964)	
Germany, Federal Republic of	3 — up to 16 in Heligoland Bight (1984)	200 EFZ (1976)	CSC definition (1964)	
Ghana	12 (1986)	200 EEZ (1986)	200 (1986)	24 CZ for LOSC purposes (1986)
Greece	6 (1936)		CSC definition (1969)	10 security zone (1913)
Grenada	12 (1975)	200 EEZ (1978)		
Guatemala	12 (1939)	200 EEZ (1976)		
Guinea	12 (1980)	200 EEZ (1980)		
Guinea Bissau	12 (1978)	200 EEZ (1978)		
Guyana	12 (1977)	200 EEZ (1977)	200 or outer edge of continental margin (1977)	
Haiti	12 (1972)	200 EEZ (1977)	To depth of exploitation (1977)	24 contiguous zone for customs, fiscal and security matters (1977)
Honduras	12 (1965)	200 EEZ (1980)	200 or outer edge of continental margin (1982)	24 contiguous zone (1982)
Iceland	12 (1979)	200 EEZ (1979)	200 or outer edge of continental margin (1979)	

Country	Territorial sea	Continental shelf	EEZ / EFZ	Other zone
India	12 (1967)	200 or edge of continental margin (1976)	200 EEZ (1976)	24 CZ for LOSC purposes plus security (1976)
Indonesia	12 (1957)	To depth of exploitation (1969)	200 EEZ (1980)	
Iran	12 (1959)		50 EFZ (1973)	
Iraq	12 (1958)			
Ireland	3 (1959)		200 EFZ (1976)	
Israel	6 (1956)	To depth of exploitation (1953)		
Italy	12 (1974)	CSC definition (1967)	200 EEZ (1977)	
Ivory Coast	12 (1977)	200 metres (1967)	200 EEZ (1977)	
Jamaica	12 (1971)			
Japan	12 — 3 in some straits (1977)		200 EFZ (1977)	
Jordan	3 (1943)			
Kampuchea	12 (1969)	200 (1982)	200 EEZ (1978)	24 CZ for LOSC purposes plus security (1982)
Kenya	12 (1969)		200 EEZ (1979)	
Kiribati	12 (1983)		200 EEZ (1983)	
Korea, North	12		200 EEZ (1977)	50 security zone (1977)
Korea, South	12 — 3 in Korea Strait (1978)			
Kuwait	12 (1967)			
Lebanon	12 (1983)			
Liberia	200 (1976)	CSC definition (1969)		
Libya	12 (1959)			

State	Territorial sea	EEZ or EFZ	Continental shelf	Other maritime zones
Madagascar	12 (1985)	200 EEZ (1985)	200 or to limit determined with adjacent States, or 100 miles from 2,500 metre isobath (1985)	24 CZ for LOSC purposes (1985)
Malaysia	12 (1969)	200 EEZ (1980)	CSC definition (1966)	
Maldives	No precise claim (1975)	Polygonal EEZ, from 37 to 310 (1976)		
Malta	12 (1978)	25 EFZ (1978)	CSC definition (1966)	24 CZ for LOSC purposes (1978)
Mauritania	70 (1978)	200 EEZ (1978)	200 or outer limit of continental margin (1978)	
Mauritius	12 (1970)	200 EEZ (1977)	200 or outer edge of continental margin (1977)	
Mexico	12 (1969)	200 EEZ (1976)	200 or outer edge of continental margin (1986)	24 CZ for LOSC purposes (1986)
Monaco	12 (1973)			
Morocco	12 (1973)	200 EEZ (1980)	CSC definition (1958)	24 CZ for LOSC purposes (1980)
Mozambique	12 (1976)	200 EEZ (1976)		
Nauru	12 (1971)	200 EFZ (1978)		
Netherlands	12 (1985)	200 EFZ (1977)		
New Zealand	12 (1977)	200 EEZ (1977)	200 or outer edge of continental margin (1977)	

Country	Territorial sea	Fishing/EEZ zone	Continental shelf	Other zones
Nicaragua	200 (1979)			
Nigeria	30 (1971)	200 EEZ (1978)	200 metres (1948)	
Norway	4 (1812)	200 EEZ (1976)	CSC definition (1969) 200 or outer edge of continental margin (1985)	10 customs zone (1921)
Oman	12 (1972)	200 EEZ (1981)	CSC definition (1972)	50 pollution control zone (1974) 24 contiguous zone for security, customs, fiscal, immigration and sanitary matters (1976)
Pakistan	12 (1966)	200 EEZ (1976)	200 or outer edge of continental margin (1976)	
Panama	200 (1967)			
Papua New Guinea	12 (1977)	200 EEZ (1977)	CSC definition (1977)	
Peru	No territorial sea claim as such but exclusive sovereignty claimed over air-space within 200 (1965)	200 EFZ (1947)	200 (1947)	
Philippines	No precise claim	200 EEZ (1978)	To where depth admits of exploitation (1968)	
Poland	12 (1978)	EFZ up to line to be determined by international agreement (1977)		
Portugal	12 (1977)	200 EEZ (1977)	CSC definition (1969)	
Qatar	3	EFZ corresponds to limits of continental shelf (1974)		
Roumania	12 (1951)	200 EEZ (1986)	CSC definition (1961)	

State	Territorial sea	EEZ or EFZ	Continental shelf	Other maritime zones
St Christopher and Nevis	12 (1984)	200 EEZ (1984)		24 contiguous zone (1984)
St Lucia	12 (1984)	200 EEZ (1984)	200 or edge of continental margin (1984)	24 CZ for LOSC purposes (1984)
St Vincent	12 (1983)	200 EEZ (1983)	200 (1983)	24 CZ for LOSC purposes (1983)
Samoa	12 (1971)	200 EEZ (1977)		
São Tomé e Príncipe	12 (1978)	200 EEZ (1978)		
Saudi Arabia	12 (1958)	EFZ of unspecified area (1974)		18 contiguous zone for security, navigation, fiscal and health matters (1958)
Senegal	12 (1985)	200 EEZ (1985)	200 or edge of continental margin (1976)	24 CZ for LOSC purposes (1985)
Seychelles	12 (1977)	200 EEZ (1977)	200 or edge of continental margin (1977)	
Sierra Leone	200 (1971)			
Singapore	3 (1878)			
Solomon Islands	12 (1978)	200 EEZ (1978)		
Somalia	200 (1972)			
South Africa	12 (1977)	200 EFZ (1977)	CSC definition (1963)	200 CZ for LOSC purposes (1977)
Spain	12 (1977)	200 EEZ (1978)	To depth of exploitation (1969)	

Sri Lanka	12 (1971)	200 EEZ (1976)	200 or outer edge of continental margin (1976)	24 CZ for LOSC purposes plus security (1976), 200 pollution prevention zone (1976)
Sudan	12 (1960)	12 (1960)	CSC definition (1970)	18 CZ for LOSC purposes plus security (1970)
Suriname	12 (1978)	200 EEZ (1978)	CSC definition (1966)	
Sweden	12 (1979)	EFZ up to equidistance line with neighbouring States (1977)		
Syria	35 (1981)			
Tanzania	50 (1973)		CSC definition (1963)	
Thailand	12 (1966)	200 EEZ (1981)		
Togo	30 (1977)	200 EEZ (1977)		
Tonga	12 (1978)	200 EEZ (1978)		
Trinidad and Tobago	12 (1969)	200 EEZ (1986)	CSC definition (1969)	24 contiguous zone
Tunisia	12 (1973)			
Turkey	6 — 12 outside Aegean (1964)	12 EFZ (1964)		
Tuvalu	12 (1983)	200 EEZ (1983)		
USSR	12 (1909)	200 EEZ (1984)	CSC definition (1968)	24 CZ for LOSC purposes (1983)
United Arab Emirates	3 — 12 for Sharjah	EEZ up to boundary with neighbouring States, or when no boundary agreed, median line (1980)		
United Kingdom	12 (1987)	200 EFZ (1976)		
USA	3 (1793)	200 EEZ (1983)		12 customs zone (1930). 12 pollution zone (1970)

State	Territorial sea	EEZ or EFZ	Continental shelf	Other maritime zones
Uruguay	200 (1969)			
Vanuatu	12 (1978)	200 EEZ (1978)	200 or outer edge of continental margin (1981)	24 CZ for LOSC purposes (1981)
Venezuela	12 (1956)	200 EEZ (1978)	CSC definition (1956)	15 zone for purposes of maritime control and vigilance (1956)
Vietnam	12 (1964)	200 EEZ (1977)	200 or outer edge of continental margin (1977)	24 CZ for LOSC purposes plus security (1977)
Yemen, North	12 (1967)		CSC definition (1967)	18 security, navigation, fiscal and sanitary zone (1967)
Yemen, South	12 (1970)	200 EEZ (1977)	200 or outer edge of continental margin (1977)	24 contiguous zone for security, customs, sanitary and fiscal matters (1977)
Yugoslavia	12 (1979)		CSC definition (1965)	
Zaire	12 (1974)			

Summary of claims

1. *Territorial sea*

Three miles: thirteen
(including FR Germany)
Four miles: two
Six miles: four
Twelve miles: ninety-seven
(including Gabon but not Turkey
and United Arab Emirates)
Fifteen miles: one

Twenty miles: one
Thirty miles: two
Thirty-five miles: one
Fifty miles: two
Seventy miles: one
200 miles: twelve
No precise claim: three

2. *EFZ or EEZ*

Twelve-mile EFZ: one
Twenty-five-mile EFZ: one
Fifty-mile EFZ: one
200 mile EFZ: fifteen

EFZ up to median line with
neighbouring States: four
EFZ of unspecified area: three
200 mile EEZ: seventy-two
Other EEZ: two

3. *Continental shelf*

CSC definition: thirty-one
200 metres: three
200 miles:* thirty-nine
200 miles or edge of continental margin:
twenty-two (including Madagascar)
Up to median line with neighbouring
States: one

To depth of exploitation: six
Edge of continental margin: one
350 miles: one
100 miles beyond 2,500 metre isobath:
one
No precise claim: thirty-four (not
including Chile)

4. *Other zones*

Fifteen-mile contiguous zone: one
Eighteen-mile contiguous zone (including security): five (including Gambia)
Twenty-four-mile contiguous zone (excluding security): sixteen
Twenty-four-mile contiguous zone (including security): nine
Twenty-four-mile contiguous zone for unspecified/unknown purposes: three
200 mile contiguous zone: one
Four-mile customs zone: one
Six-mile customs zone: one
10 km customs zone: one
Ten-mile customs zone: one
Twelve-mile customs zone: one
Twelve-mile anti-liquor smuggling zone: two
Ten-mile security zone: one
Fifty-mile security zone: one
Twelve-mile pollution control zone: one
Fifty-mile pollution control zone: one
200 mile pollution control zone: two

* This includes claims to a 200 mile continental shelf as such, and claims to a 200 mile EEZ or territorial sea where no precise claim is made to a continental shelf.

2. Ratifications of the Geneva and Law of the Sea Conventions

This table shows which States have ratified the four Geneva Conventions — the Convention on the Territorial Sea and the Contiguous Zone (TSC), the Convention on the High Seas (HSC), the Convention on Fishing and Conservation of the Living Resources of the High Seas (FC) and the Convention on the Continental Shelf (CSC) — and the United Nations Convention on the Law of the Sea (LOSC). The date in each case refers to that on which the State concerned deposited its instrument of ratification, accession etc. An '×' in the LOSC column indicates signature of the Convention. The position is shown as at 31 December 1986.

	TSC	HSC	FC	CSC	LOSC
Afghanistan		28.4.1959			×
Albania		7.12.1964		7.12.1964	
Algeria					×
Angola					×
Antigua and Barbuda					×
Argentina					×
Australia	14.5.1963	14.5.1963	14.5.1963	14.5.1963	×
Austria		10.1.1974			×
Bahamas					29.7.1983
Bahrain					30.5.1985
Bangladesh					×
Barbados					×
Belgium	6.1.1972	6.1.1972	6.1.1972		×
Belize					13.8.1983
Benin					×
Bhutan					×
Bolivia					×
Botswana					×
Brazil					×
Brunei					×
Bulgaria	31.8.1962	31.8.1962		31.8.1962	×
Burkina Faso		4.10.1965	4.10.1965		×
Burma					×

	TSC	HSC	FC	CSC	LOSC
Burundi					×
Byelorussian SSSR	27.2.1961	27.2.1961		27.2.1961	×
Cameroon					19.11.1985
Canada				6.2.1970	×
Cape Verde					×
Central African Republic		15.10.1962			×
Chad					×
Chile					×
China					×
Colombia			3.1.1963	8.1.1962	×
Comoros					×
Congo					×
Costa Rica		16.2.1972		16.2.1972	×
Cuba					15.8.1984
Cyprus				11.4.1974	×
Czechoslovakia	31.8.1961	31.8.1961		31.8.1961	×
Denmark	26.9.1968	26.9.1968	26.9.1968	12.6.1963	×
Djibouti					×
Dominica					×
Dominican Republic	11.8.1964	11.8.1964	11.8.1964	11.8.1964	×
Ecuador					
Egypt					26.8.1983
El Salvador					×
Equatorial Guinea					×
Ethiopia					×
Fiji	25.3.1971	25.3.1971	25.3.1971	25.3.1971	10.12.1982
Finland	16.2.1965	16.2.1965	16.2.1965	16.2.1965	×
France			18.9.1970	14.6.1965	×
Gabon					×
Gambia					22.5.1984
German Democratic Republic	27.12.1973	27.12.1973		27.12.1973	×
Germany, Federal Republic of		26.7.1973			
Ghana					7.6.1983

	TSC	HSC	FC	CSC	LOSC
Greece				6.11.1972	×
Grenada					×
Guatemala		27.11.1961		27.11.1961	×
Guinea					6.9.1985
Guinea Bissau					25.8.1986
Guyana					×
Haiti	29.3.1960	29.3.1960	29.3.1960	29.3.1960	×
Holy See					
Honduras					×
Hungary	6.12.1961	6.12.1961			×
Iceland					21.6.1985
India					×
Indonesia		10.8.1961			3.2.1986
Iran					×
Iraq					30.7.1985
Ireland					×
Israel	6.9.1961	6.9.1961		6.9.1961	
Italy	17.12.1964	17.12.1964			×
Ivory Coast					26.3.1984
Jamaica	8.10.1965	8.10.1965	16.4.1964	8.10.1965	21.3.1983
Japan	10.6.1968	10.6.1968			×
Jordan					
Kampuchea	18.3.1960	18.3.1960	18.3.1960	18.3.1960	×
Kenya	20.6.1969	20.6.1969	20.6.1969	20.6.1969	×
Kiribati					
Korea, North					×
Korea, South					×
Kuwait					2.5.1986
Laos					×
Lebanon					×
Lesotho	23.10.1973	23.10.1973	23.10.1973	23.10.1973	×
Liberia					×
Libya					×
Liechenstein					×
Luxembourg					×
Madagascar	31.7.1962	31.7.1962	31.7.1962	31.7.1962	×
Malawi	3.11.1965	3.11.1965	3.11.1965	3.11.1965	×
Malaysia	21.12.1960	21.12.1960	21.12.1960	21.12.1960	×
Maldives					×
Mali					16.7.1985

	TSC	HSC	FC	CSC	LOSC
Malta	19.5.1966			19.5.1966	×
Mauritania					×
Mauritius	5.10.1970	5.10.1970	5.10.1970	5.10.1970	×
Mexico	2.8.1966	2.8.1966	2.8.1966	2.8.1966	18.3.1983
Monaco					×
Mongolia		15.10.1976			×
Morocco					×
Mozambique					×
Nauru					×
Nepal		28.12.1962			×
Netherlands	18.2.1966	18.2.1966	18.2.1966	18.2.1966	×
New Zealand				18.1.1965	×
Nicaragua					×
Niger					×
Nigeria	26.6.1961	26.6.1961	26.6.1961	28.4.1971	14.8.1986
Norway				9.9.1971	×
Oman					×
Pakistan					×
Panama					×
Papua New Guinea					×
Paraguay					26.9.1986
Peru					
Philippines					8.5.1984
Poland		29.6.1962		29.6.1962	×
Portugal	8.1.1963	8.1.1963	8.1.1963	8.1.1963	×
Qatar					×
Roumania	12.12.1961	12.12.1961		12.12.1961	×
Rwanda					×
St Christopher and Nevis					×
St Lucia					27.3.1985
St Vincent					×
Samoa					×
San Marino					
São Tomé e Príncipe					×
Saudi Arabia					×
Senegal	25.4.1961 [1]	25.4.1961	25.4.1961 [1]	25.4.1961 [1]	25.10.1984
Seychelles					×

	TSC	HSC	FC	CSC	LOSC
Sierra Leone	13.3.1962	13.3.1962	13.3.1962	25.11.1966	×
Singapore					×
Solomon Islands	3.9.1981	3.9.1981	3.9.1981	3.9.1981	×
Somalia					×
South Africa	9.4.1963	9.4.1963	9.4.1963	9.4.1963	×
Spain	25.2.1971	25.2.1971	25.2.1971	25.2.1971	×
Sri Lanka					×
Sudan					23.1.1985
Suriname					×
Swaziland	16.10.1970	16.10.1970		16.10.1970	×
Sweden				1.6.1966	×
Switzerland	18.5.1966	18.5.1966	18.5.1966	18.5.1966	×
Syria					
Tanzania					30.9.1985
Thailand	2.7.1968	2.7.1968	2.7.1968	2.7.1968	×
Togo					16.4.1985
Tonga	29.6.1971	29.6.1971	29.6.1971	29.6.1971	
Trinidad and Tobago	11.4.1966	11.4.1966	11.4.1966	11.7.1968	25.4.1986
Tunisia					24.4.1985
Turkey					
Tuvalu					×
Uganda	14.9.1964	14.9.1964	14.9.1964	14.9.1964	×
Ukrainian SSR	12.1.1961	12.1.1961		12.1.1961	×
USSR	22.11.1960	22.11.1960		22.11.1960	×
United Arab Emirates					×
United Kingdom	14.3.1960	14.3.1960	14.3.1960	11.5.1964	
UN Council for Namibia					18.4.1983
USA	12.4.1961	12.4.1961	12.4.1961	12.4.1961	
Uruguay					×
Vanuatu					×
Venezuela	15.8.1961	15.8.1961	10.7.1963	15.8.1961	
Vietnam					×
Yemen, North					×
Yemen, South					×
Yugoslavia	28.1.1966	28.1.1966	28.1.1966	28.1.1966	5.5.1986
Zaire					×

	TSC	HSC	FC	CSC	LOSC
Zambia					7.3.1983
Zimbabwe					×
Total number of ratifications	46	57	36	54	32[2]

Notes
1. Senegal purported to denounce the TSC and FC in 1971, and the CSC in 1976.
2. The Convention has been signed by 159 States and entities, which include, apart from the States shown above as having signed or ratified, the Cook Islands, the EEC and Niue.

INDEX

(see also Table of Cases and Table of Conventions)

Straits; Territorial sea. *For claims, see Appendix*
Martens, G. F. von 4
Mauritania, EEZ legislation 145
Mauritius, archipelagic legislation 107; EEZ legislation 145
Mediterranean, marine pollution 246–8,250–1, 263, 271, 273, 279–81
Memorandum of Understanding on Port State Control 217–9, 284
Merchant ships *see* Ships
Mexico, islands 135
Miles, are nautical miles 31
Military activities, generally 307–15; in EEZ 141, 310–11; *see also* Naval manoeuvres; Navies; Weapons testing
Monaco, territorial sea 30
Montevideo Declaration on the Law of the Sea 149
Moratorium Resolution (G A RES. 2574 (XXIV)) 180
Morocco, EEZ legislation 146, 295, 327; straight baselines 32
Mozambique, EEZ legislation 146

National liberation movements 20
Nationality of ships 205–9; stateless ships 172; ships of uncertain nationality 172
Nauru, baselines legislation 44, 46
Naval manoeuvres, 88, 141, 168, 311
Navies, generally 307–15; limitations on size, etc. 95, 311–12
Navigation, generally 209–10; archipelagic waters 105–6; EEZ 141, 337; freedom of navigation on high seas 129, 165–8, 210; through straits 70, 87–97, 209, 310; through territorial sea 68–76, 209; *see also* Archipelagic sea-lanes passage; Freedom of the high seas; Innocent passage; Ships; Transit passage
Necessity, as ground for intervention on high seas 173–4
Negotiating texts, at UNCLOS III 15
Netherlands, continental shelf delimitation 155–6
Neutrality zones 65, 114, 307
New International Economic Order 197, 301–2

New Zealand, baselines legislation 45; Cook Islands, maritime zones legislation 108; non-nuclear policy 313; Tokelau Islands maritime zones legislation 44, 46, 108, 136
Nigeria, EEZ legislation 146
Non-independent territories, participation in UNCLOS III 20; maritime zones of 130, 136
Nordic States, marine pollution 246, 264, 281
North Atlantic Salmon Conservation Organisation 236–7
North-east Atlantic, marine pollution 246, 271, 273–5, 278–9, 301
North East Atlantic Fisheries Commission 236
North Pacific Fur Seal Commission 301
North Sea, marine pollution 246, 263–4, 273–5, 278–9, 301; continental shelf delimitation 155–6
North-west Atlantic Fisheries Organisation 235, 236, 301
Norway, fisheries arrangements with EEC 234–5, with USSR 235; straight baselines 7, 28–33, 98; *see also* Nordic States
Nuclear-powered ships, and innocent passage 76; liability for damage 267–8; *see also Savannah*
Nuclear waste *see* Radioactive waste
Nuclear weapons, deployment of 90, 312–3; testing of 141, 168, 311; Treaty of Tlatelolco 312–13

Ocean Data Acquisition Systems 297–9; see also Installations; Marine scientific research
Oil and gas offshore 121, 128–30; cross-boundary deposits 161; *see also* Continental shelf
Open registry 206–8, 254; *see also* Ships, nationality of
OPOL 275
Opposability of rules of customary international law 6–8, 66, 108, 158, 295
Organisation for Economic Co-operation and Development 18, 271
Oslo Commission, 18, 264, 276, 279
Overflight, generally 311, 337; of